Filipinx American Studies

Filipinx American Studies

Reckoning, Reclamation, Transformation

Rick Bonus and Antonio T. Tiongson Jr., Editors

FORDHAM UNIVERSITY PRESS

NEW YORK 2022

Fordham University Press has no responsibility for the persistence or accuracy of URLs for external or third-party Internet
websites referred to in this publication and does not guarantee
that any content on such websites is, or will remain, accurate or
appropriate.

Fordham University Press also publishes its books in a variety of
electronic formats. Some content that appears in print may not
be available in electronic books.

Visit us online at www.fordhampress.com.

Library of Congress Cataloging-in-Publication Data available
online at https://catalog.loc.gov.

Printed in the United States of America

24 23 22   5 4 3 2 1

First edition

Cover art by Kimberley Acebo Arteche

Bodyless 4899 (2017)

Digital Archival Print, 44″×66″

This book is dedicated to Dawn Bohulano Mabalon, for her tireless work on historic, cultural, and community preservation; to Amado Khaya Canham Rodriguez, for his deep commitment to social justice that defied national borders; and to Filipinx American studies scholars who came before us and paved the way for this project.

CONTENTS

Section A: Reckoning

Part I: Empire as Endless War

Filipinx American Studies

Rick Bonus and Antonio T. Tiongson Jr.

I suggest that the Filipino experience of American subjugation, beginning in 1899, confounds the question of representation for Filipinos in
the United States and Filipino Americans. They need to reckon with
their incorporation into the American body politic not only in terms of
the history of immigration, acculturation, and community formation,
but also in terms of the "trauma" by which the Philippines was both
annexed and disowned by the United States as an experiment in
imperialism.

> —OSCAR V. CAMPOMANES, "The Institutional Invisibility of American
> Imperialism, the Philippines, and Filipino Americans"

Search, discover, and reclaim.

> —STEVEN DE CASTRO, "Identity in Action: A Filipino American's
> Perspective"

If language acts as a tool of colonialism, then it also acts as the tool of
transformation, a means of departure, if you will.

> —MARIE-THERESE C. SULIT, "Through Our Pinay Writings: Narrating
> Trauma, Embodying Recovery"

*What is Filipinx American studies? What does it mean to think, write, speak
about, and act upon it? How is it configured? What are its critical interventions?
What does it engage and interrogate, for what reasons, and with what disciplinary
lens? Fundamentally, what does it aim to transform?* The thirty-four essays in
this volume collectively engage these questions from the purviews of each
of our contributors' particular disciplines, subjects of interest, and relevant
experiences to perform a kind of accounting or a mode of chronicling a field
of inquiry—an *interdiscipline*—that they participate in. We consider each

essay to be an individual sketch of Filipinx American studies, an analytic interpretation of a piece of thought that the field is in a relationship with, even a rumination of an issue or an angle through which the field operates. But taken as a whole, this anthology is an aggregate expression of what we conceive Filipinx American studies is about, a kind of intellectual tapestry that defines the field's collective engagement with its histories, contemporary realities, and futures—a reckoning, a reclamation, and a transformation, as emphasized by our opening quotes. So, through such a set of engagements, we collectively propose that while Filipinx American studies is indeed a product of a historical struggle to mark as well as circumscribe its subjects' relationships to their colonial and imperial past, it is also a continuing project to align its intellectual knowledge production—its *interrogation* of US empire and its *reckoning* with and *reclamation* of their histories of labor, migration, community formation, and resistance—with the pursuit of social *transformation* within and beyond its boundaries. These, we attempt to accomplish from and through the multiplicity of our ideas, methods, and actions that altogether animate Filipinx American studies as a site of our communal and interdisciplinary *critique*.

Through this particular endeavor, *Filipinx American Studies: Reckoning, Reclamation, Transformation* brings together into one volume a robust collection of essays that perform both distinct and interrelated analyses of specific matters that are understood through the prisms of Filipinx American studies. We compiled essays that engage with particular phenomena not only as they are connected with or relevant to our field but, more importantly, how such phenomena are engaged with from the perspectives of select scholars who locate themselves within the field, bringing to the fore the ways in which Filipinx American studies dialogically and dialectically produces and reproduces knowledge as much as it is a product of intersecting knowledges and experiences. It is quite apparent among all the authors here that *empire* looms large and deep in their studies of Filipinx communities in northern America and, at times, elsewhere, both as that which has subjected them to imperial incorporation, but also that which continues to be an index of their traumatic disownership from the state, as stipulated in Oscar V. Campomanes's analytic. Such a contradictory logic, long given form by a history of racialized labor extraction and the varied acts of resistance to it, persists irresolvably as a foundational ontology, a starting point, if you will, in our work. So, the essays in this book not only perform an act of reckoning with this ontological logic, they also chart the multiple ways in which this logic is manifested, modified, or even contested in several or specific knowledge locations.

This project of mapping out the contours of Filipinx American studies is also a spatial and temporal undertaking. We gathered scholars to ruminate on an issue, an angle, or a node of engagement—identified in terms of a specific knowledge space and set within particular historical contexts—to arrive at an aggregate expression of what Filipinx American studies is about and to express our investment in laying bare the field's connective histories, contemporary preoccupations, and future aspirations. But in doing so, we were not aiming for uniformity and tight coherence among our contributors. Rather, we tried to maintain a capacious but fluid interdisciplinary disposition among the contributors, highlighting the field's presences in otherwise scattered nodes of inquiry but also its collective inclination to always reorient, recalibrate, and evolve, most ostensibly because or in spite of its non- or semi-institutionalized status in North American academia. To this date, there is no Department of Filipinx American Studies that we know of, perhaps a reflection of the field's simultaneous devaluing, resource limitation, and reluctance to become institutionalized. But as a corollary, there are manifold sites and modalities of Filipinx American presences in scattered geographical, academic, and intellectual locations, portions of which we identify in this volume.

To wit, *Filipinx American Studies* follows what may already be a tradition in the field to historicize, interrogate, and amplify critical subjects of analyses from the unique perspectives of its contributors who are the leading and emerging scholars in the field, insofar as they jointly resonate with or provide multiple and alternative views to the specific and broader areas of inquiry within which Filipinx American studies is located. This scholarly practice of performing a collective field critique—already started by the work of politically motivated student organizations such as the Philippine American Collegiate Endeavor (or PACE) at San Francisco State College and the Filipino Students Association (later, the Pilipino American Alliance) at the University of California, Berkeley in the 1960s and the 1970s,[1] the establishment of various chapters of the Filipino American National Historical Society by Fred and Dorothy Cordova beginning in the 1970s, the formation of the Critical Filipino and Filipina Studies Collective in 2003, all the way to the holding of the 2008 and 2016 Philippine Palimpsests conferences in Illinois and California respectively, the publication of *Positively No Filipinos Allowed: Building Communities and Discourse* in 2006, the release of the anthology *Filipino Studies: Palimpsests of Nation and Diaspora* in 2016, and more recently, the founding of the e-journal *ALON: Journal for Filipinx American and Diasporic Studies*—is one that we continue to represent and amplify here.[2] In our case, we present in this collection an illumination and a distillation of what a Filipinx American set of critiques looks like at the current moment and what it is able to offer to its readers from primarily our North American locations: not merely a set of descriptive entries but, for sure, an analytical and reflective reading of the field's contemporary engagement with the conditions of its production and practice, its impact on worldviews locally and globally, and in the overall, the productive possibilities of its alternative deployment. Accordingly, this volume is intended to be of paramount utility to those whose scholarship and activism are directly linked to Filipinx American studies as well as to those whose work and practice are conversant with or potentially resonant with Filipinx American studies. It is a resource for scholars, students, and community practitioners/advocates of Filipinx American studies, as it is also an intellectual companion for scholars engaged in interdisciplinary work, given the broader relevance, significance, and oftentimes irreducibility of phenomena explored in this volume.

Tracing the Genealogy of Filipinx American Studies

How do we intend to understand the contours and contents of Filipinx American studies? We wish to offer our readers a deep genealogy and continuing tradition of Filipinx American *critique*—signposted here through the use of a nonbinary "x" within the naming of its two social identifications—that was borne out of a vexed relationship to the historical formation of the US as a global empire at the turn of the twentieth century. For Filipinxs, this violent encounter with the US, forged in the aftermath of centuries of Spanish colonization and defined constitutively in terms of labor extraction and racialization, will haunt their lives forever, as evident from the earliest chronicles of anti-Filipinx racism during the earliest periods of modern Filipinx migration in the works of Emory Bogardus (1930), Carey Mc-Williams (1939), Bruno Lasker (1969), Howard de Witt (1976), H. Brett Melendy (1981), and their student scholars. Bogardus and his group of Filipinx students, mostly recruited from a Christian missionary organization into graduate schoolwork at the University of Southern California where Bogardus taught, would respond to anti-Filipinx violence through research work that would align with the tenets of the Chicago School of Sociology in which they were trained. In such a framework, racism against a minority group was but a phase in a cycle of impending assimilation, especially experienced by members of a colonized group who were understood to be the beneficiaries of American benevolence and Christian salvation. Their collective and individual works, most notably represented by the studies conducted by Marcos Berbano, Benicio Catapusan, Severino Corpus, and Honorante Mariano, would thereby explain racial antagonism as a result of "misunderstandings" or expressions of ignorance, and that were it not for a few Filipinx men who were "maladjusted," these immigrants were demonstrably quite capable of being integrated properly into US society through careful state molding and moral intervention.

But despite their persistent characterization as an unassimilable racial problem or as ill-disposed troublemakers, and notwithstanding their status as colonial subjects who were not ineligible for citizenship, Filipinxs proactively and creatively devised ways to resist, recover, and remember. Here, Carlos Bulosan's *America Is in the Heart* (1946, 1973, 2014) stands out as a primary historical text that was pivotal in the development of Filipinx American studies as a subfield of Asian American studies when it was newly institutionalized. Particularly interesting is the way several contributors in this volume engage with *America Is in the Heart* from multiple disciplinary vantage points, an indication of the continued relevance of this text among practitioners in the field. For in quite significant ways, *America Is in the Heart* persistently remains as a chronicle of transnational subject and community formation for Filipinxs in the US that first linked colonization with tutelage and labor extraction, local antiracist struggle with Third World liberation, and the limits of national subject incorporation with the contradictions of "citizenship" upon which American mythologies of democracy and freedom have been based.[3] It also led the way in charting an *exilic* proclivity among Filipinx American writers to persist in imagining the US as a non-terminal point or, at least, a mere point among many others within a wide transnational field, for being and becoming Filipinx American.[4]

Emerging out of the race-based identity initiatives in the latter part of the Civil Rights Movement of the 1960s and 1970s, activists for and on behalf of Filipinx American studies embraced but also questioned the terms of their inclusion within the panethnic Asian American rubric. On one hand, the invocation to be part of a larger group was especially appealing politically and institutionally; it was, indeed, in line with what has been an alliance-building tradition for Filipinxs ever since their cross-racial labor mobilization movements especially from the 1920s to the 1930s and beyond.[5] But on the other hand, the marginalized status within which US Filipinxs found themselves positioned within the larger race-based grouping animated claims about their *invisibility* and *powerlessness* (or experiences of *forgetfulness* and *exile*) within Asian America and the US society in general. At least two generations of scholarly production emanated from this critique: the earlier cohort of trailblazing figures such as Fred and Dorothy Cordova (1983), Jesse Quinsaat et al. (1976), Antonio J. A. Pido (1986), Royal Morales (1974), Roberto V. Vallangca (1977), Adelaida Castillo-Tsuchida (1979), Benjamin V. Cariño (1981), Edwin B. Almirol (1985), Caridad Concepcion Vallangca (1987), Marina E. Espina (1988), and E. San Juan Jr. (1996 and 1998), and the later and continuing generation of scholars whose works elaborated a more robust rendition of Filipinx American historical specificity, differential treatment, and modes of alterity and resistance. In hindsight, these works would serve as seedbeds for a critique of Filipinx American studies' location within conventional ethnic and Asian American studies, marking its rejection of the deployment of an immigrant frame within these fields to erroneously narrate the modern migration of Filipinxs into the US simply as a "search for milk and honey," a prominent but problematic way of integrating their histories into the master narratives of American nationhood and belonging.[6] Instead, these scholars, most particularly San Juan, argued for a racial global capitalist frame, one that critically narrates such a history of migration not as a history of immigration and settlement, but fundamentally a history of racialized and gendered labor extraction in the service of US empire expansion.[7]

In this later generation of scholarly production, one that comprised and simultaneously arose out of the influential work of E. San Juan Jr. and

Oscar V. Campomanes (1997), the terms *invisibility* and *forgetfulness* took on a more aggressive turn as they began to be understood as causes and products of hegemonic imperialism, racial capitalism, and structural inequality, rather than as essentialist attributes of Filipinx culture and being.[8] Maria Root's edited volume *Filipino Americans: Transformation and Identity* (1997) was the first one to collect and cohere this new generation of scholars whose subjects of study defined Filipinx Americanness as distinct from other groups, given their histories of colonization, their statuses as disadvantaged minorities, and their uneasiness about being categorized under such a larger rubric of Asian Americans. Moreover, many of the essays in this book addressed the transnational, emergent, or *liminal* nature of US Filipinx lives, severely putting into question the appropriateness of applying the straightforward logics of departure, arrival, and permanent settlement to conventionally describe ethnic, American, or Asian American generational flows. Soon, many other authors, within and following the book's lead as well springing from a tradition exemplified by Bulosan, took on a more global reach in their analyses of Filipinx American lives, moving beyond the US as the principal or only locus of identity and community formation, and thereby collectively resisting the US as the terminal point for Filipinx American identities and communities. The movement of Filipinx labor on a worldwide scale that was begun at least a century and a half ago, which was quite fundamentally a central component of the US global imperial project and is still increasing rapidly and qualitatively transforming in this century, is a condition that has since then preoccupied scholars in Filipinx American studies. Within these contexts, the work of studying Filipinxs in North America has oftentimes necessitated a serious consideration of their global, regional, and transnational vectors from the purviews of scholars trained in literary studies, the social sciences, as well as historical and area studies.[9]

Ironically, many of these scholars were institutionally housed in or affiliated with larger academic units such as Asian American studies and American or ethnic studies, locations that nevertheless enabled them to address internal critiques of knowledge production at the same time as dominant pockets within these locations were and continue to be antithetical to or, at the least, very different from, an anti-assimilative project of Filipinx American critique. Such an irony would, in 1994, manifest its troubling side by way of a protest and walkout by several Filipinx American scholars, alongside their allies, against the Association for Asian American Studies for awarding a book prize to an author who allegedly perpetuates stereotypical Filipinx representations in their work.[10] Afterwards, in 1998, also in the annual conference of the association, yet another best book prize was awarded to the same author.[11] Many would consider this event, one that took place in Hawai'i (itself a quintessential site of labor recruitment for many Filipinx *sakadas*[12]), a most defining and climactic moment, for the protests this time caused the organization to be temporarily dismantled as it marked a most unbearable condition of disassociation between Filipinx American scholars and the larger academic field that they had been uneasily a part of. Even though many of the discussions that occurred during and in the aftermath of these events focused on the worthiness of the particular books that were being recognized, including ruminations on the overarching contexts of artistic merit and literary freedom, these events raised important and disturbing questions about the presence or, for some, the absence of Filipinx voices in the association and in Asian American studies in particular, persisting on through many years and into the present, despite the continued active membership and even presidencies of at least two Filipinx American scholars.[13]

The centrality of US empire within national and global frames by which to analyze later and newer phenomena of migration, national (dis)identification, movement, diaspora, queer and multiracial identifications, including pandemic outbreaks and environmental change, and their intersections with Filipinx lives has continued to become both the key theoretical apparatus and optic for almost every scholar engaged with Filipinx Americans as objects and subjects of study. That centrality has been most particularly evident in the pioneering individual research projects of scholars such as Pauline Agbayani-Siewert (1994), Yến Lê Espiritu (1995 and 2003), Steffi San Buenaventura (1996), Jonathan Y. Okamura (1998), and Barbara Posadas (1999)[14] as well as in the edited collections that have been led by scholars such as Vicente L. Rafael (*Discrepant Histories: Translocal Essays on Filipino Cultures*, 1993); Nick Carbo (*Returning a Borrowed Tongue: An Anthology of Filipino and Filipino American Poetry*, 1995); Anatalio Ubalde (*Filipino American Architecture, Design, and Planning Issues*, 1996); Enrique de la Cruz ("Essays into American Empire in the Philippines," Parts I and II, *Amerasia*, 1998, as guest editor); Luis H. Francia and Eric Gamalinda (*Flippin': Filipinos on America*, 1996); Nick Carbo and Eileen Tabios (*Babaylan: An Anthol-*

ogy of Filipina and Filipina American Writers, 2000); Angel Velasco Shaw and Luis H. Francia (*Vestiges of War: The Philippine-American War and the Aftermath of an Imperial Dream, 1899–1999*, 2002); Oscar V. Campomanes (*American Studies Asia* 1, Number 1, June 2002); Rocio G. Davis (Special Issue on Filipino American Literature, *MELUS*, 2004); Melinda L. de Jesús (*Pinay Power: Peminist Critical Theory—Theorizing the Filipina/American Experience*, 2005); Antonio T. Tiongson Jr. (*Positively No Filipinos Allowed: Building Communities and Discourse*, coedited with Edgardo V. Gutierrez and Ricardo V. Gutierrez, 2006); Kevin L. Nadal (*Filipino American Psychology: A Collection of Personal Narratives*, 2010); Dina C. Maramba and Rick Bonus (*The "Other" Students: Filipino Americans, Education, and Power*, 2013); Abe Ignacio, Enrique de la Cruz, Jorge Emmanuel, and Helen Toribio (*The Forbidden Book: The Philippine-American War in Political Cartoons*, 2014); Mark Villegas (*Empire of Funk: Hip Hop and Representation in Filipina/o America*, coedited with Kuttin' Kandi, Roderick N. Labrador, and Jeff Chang, 2014); Martin F. Manalansan IV and Augusto F. Espiritu (*Filipino Studies: Palimpsests of Nation and Diaspora*, 2016); Rene Ciria Cruz, Cindy Domingo, and Bruce Occena (*A Time to Rise: Collective Memoirs of the Union of Democratic Filipinos [KDP]*, 2017); and most recently, Robyn Magalit Rodriguez (*Filipino American Transnational Activism: Diasporic Politics among the Second Generation*, 2019).

In all of these expressions of analytical engagement with race, empire, identity, and community, an interrogative or critical stance persists, making the interdiscipline of Filipinx American studies oftentimes in conflict with US-centric and, therefore, narrow and limiting modes of analysis usually found in conventional American studies, Asian American studies, ethnic studies, and globalization studies. At the same time, alliances with other groups, communities, and fields—with those led by Southeast Asian Americans, South Asian Americans, Pacific Islanders, Blacks, Indigenous, and Latinx communities, as prominent examples—continue to be attempted and forged to engage with historical and current strands of convergences. Moreover, the COVID-19 pandemic, the ongoing efforts to argue that Black Lives Matter, as well as the advocacies pursued on behalf of queers of color, those who are undocumented, and those who are disadvantaged because of disability, stand out as sites of political work where Filipinx Americanists are involved. The interdiscipline of Filipinx American critique has been victorious in many of its battles, signaled by its fast-growing cadre of emerging, tenured, and full professors, its robust scholarly production, and its active presence in professional academic venues. But it has also experienced, and continues to experience, disempowerment in the form of limited career opportunities, publication and teaching challenges, and career fatigue for its scholars. Within its ranks, just like any field or interdiscipline, there are hierarchies, conflicts, exclusions, and disagreements. But despite all of these challenges, and largely because of its hesitation to become institutionalized in academia, Filipinx American studies continues to depart, emerge, and evolve.

Project Claims

Now, for ***Filipinx American Studies: Reckoning, Reclamation, Transformation***, we wish to take stock with and move this scholarly tradition forward as we collectively make three major claims:

> that our analytic rendition of Filipinx Americanness is an ongoing project of reorientation and recalibration from one that is strongly based on narratives of immigration, settlement, and assimilation to another that connects Filipinx presence in the US and beyond with the larger histories and current manifestations of imperialism, colonization, global capitalism, racialization, and gendered/sexualized labor;
>
> that our geographic, ideological, and socio-political frames for understanding Filipinx Americanness are neither solely situated nor firmly placed within the borders of what is understood as the United States, so much so that the US is not the only exceptional and terminal point of being and becoming Filipinx American, and that Filipinx American lives are intricately connected with the interlocking histories and contemporary trajectories of global capitalism, racism, sexism, and heteronormativity;
>
> and that our political project continues the quest for pushing for the distinctiveness of Filipinx Americanness as a category of group identification by way of its unique experiences of US empire domina-

tion that have animated their collective formation and resistance, as well as by way of its differentiation from the histories of other groups. And that simultaneous with such a push, the project for Filipinx American studies remains proactively conscious about and alert to the possibilities of solidarity with other groups—possibilities that have already been realized in historical and current collaborations and identifications of Filipinxs with others, as well as productive relationships that have yet to be imagined across various boundaries.

Project Genesis and Rationale

We believe that this is a fortuitous time to put out a project that revolves around an interrogation of the cohering assumptions and anchoring analytics of Filipinx American studies, and this is one of the first volumes of its kind to offer a rigorous and sustained engagement with Filipinx American studies as a site for critical analysis. In our view, the launching of this project is long overdue given how Filipinx American studies has become an established field of study and given what Martin F. Manalansan IV references as the "Filipino turn" in Asian American studies. As Manalansan puts it, there is "a renaissance of sorts in terms of the dramatic emergence and increase in the numbers of scholars and publications that come under the aegis of 'Filipino American.'"[15] Articulated in another way, there seems to be a critical mass of scholars as well as activists and artists that share a strong commitment to and investment in the project of Filipinx American studies. At the same time, Manalansan is quick to point out that this is not necessarily a cause for celebration but more an occasion to grapple with existing intellectual fissures and structural hierarchies that have animated and continue to animate the field. To illustrate, Manalansan directs our attention to the material conditions that underwrite the so-called Filipino turn, casting light on the asymmetrical circulation and exchange of intellectual productions between Philippine-based and US-based scholars.

It is also an opportune moment, given critical currents reverberating across disciplines, currents that have come to be increasingly seen as indispensable to the projects of multiple disciplines rather than confined to a particular discipline. We have in mind, for example, the turn toward the theorization of settler colonialism and the afterlives of slavery; the recognition of disability as a critical site of inquiry that is entangled with other vectors of power; and the reliance on comparative analytics to account for the imbrication of structuring logics (such as empire and settler colonialism), to name a few. We are particularly interested in how these currents have been taken up within Filipinx American studies, animated the field's critical edge, and pushed its scholars to new or unexpected directions. Even more pressingly, we believe that in moments of *ongoing* crisis and devastation, it is paramount to ruminate about what a Filipinx American criticism might offer to the urgencies of the current period while not losing sight of the limits of institutionalization, including how Filipinx American studies is embedded in the structuring logic of the neoliberal university.

The idea for this volume came about from ongoing conversations between the two coeditors about the timeliness of undertaking a critical appraisal of Filipinx American studies given the increasing legibility of Filipinx American studies within the confines of the academe and beyond. These conversations crystallized in a series of roundtable discussions organized by the coeditors at the annual meetings of the Association for Asian American Studies (AAAS) beginning in 2017. From 2017 to 2019, we organized roundtable discussions revolving around a consideration of Filipinx American studies as a site of critique, what it means to do work in Filipinx American studies, and how that work is being done. In these discussions, we centered Filipinx American studies in our consideration of the conference theme: For example, the 2017 theme was "At the Crossroads of Care and Giving" and our roundtable focused on the ways Filipinx American studies serves as a site of "care and giving" and the different forms that "care and giving" take within the confines of the neoliberal university.

Initially, we conceived of the volume as a "keywords" project that aimed to interrogate what we considered foundational and emergent terms that have profoundly shaped and continue to shape the terrain of Filipinx American studies. In addition to filling a gap (i.e., putting together the first keywords book for Filipinx American studies), in our view, an engagement with terms such as "empire," "labor," and "performance" might offer useful entry points to illuminate the contours and trajectories of Filipinx American studies. At the same time, we became well aware that keywords projects have now become an established genre of knowledge production and a common form of field validation that has resulted in a glut of these kinds of projects. For this reason, we took our cue from a 2014 American Studies Association (ASA) session titled "Kill That Keyword" that took a self-reflexive approach to keywords projects. Organized to be both playful and serious, the session scrutinized American studies' reliance on a set of terms (that is somehow perceived as stable and self-evident) and how the overuse of select terms can compromise their critical edge and evacuate them of meaning and specificity.[16] In response, we drew an alternative inspiration from a volume titled *Native Studies Keywords* (edited by Stephanie Nohelani Teves, Andrea Smith, and Michelle Raheja) because of its marked departure from conventional keywords projects in the way the editors employ multiple scholars to comment on a particular term. This kind of format, we believed, was more conducive to drawing out the multivalent and contested nature of analytical terms, how these terms do not operate in a vacuum but are situated in a shifting disciplinary terrain. But, as one of the anonymous readers who evaluated our initial manuscripts pointed out, the keywords framework may have outlived its utility, ceasing "to engage fields and engender progressive pedagogies" and inadvertently contributing "to an essentializing didacticism that contradicts the activist aims" of interdisciplines such as Filipinx American studies.

In taking heed of the anonymous reader's suggestion as well as our desire to move beyond the strictures of keywords projects, we opted to reframe the scope of the project so that it aligned tighter with our initial vision for the volume. In putting together this collective project, therefore, we strived to do more than a keywords volume or a "state of the field" volume that will ostensibly mark the "arrival" of Filipinx American studies. In our view, the aforementioned projects (while useful in terms of providing a mapping of a particular field) tend to reify and obscure, glossing over flash points, dissonances, and fault lines that mark field formations like Filipinx American studies. Accordingly, we started to view our collective project in more expansive ways, as something that began to provide a reflective and critical space for thinking through the ways Filipinx American studies is uniquely and especially suited to the interrogation of formations such as US imperialism, labor, or migration.

Upon further reflection on how to name our collective project, the word that comes to mind is *invitation*, or, even more pointedly, *provocation*. Conventionally understood, *provocation* suggests some form of movement or signals some sort of flux, being moved to do something as in to incite, instigate, or elicit a particular response or reaction. It suggests being aroused or stirred to action in order to bring about a particular result. What we find useful is to think about provocation in disciplinary terms that compel us to take a self-reflexive appraisal of Filipinx American scholarship, to take stock of our analytic priorities and how these priorities both open up and fore-close lines of inquiry. As Erica Browne puts it, "Provocations are critical to scholarship because they assert, challenge, and move us beyond what is convenient, conventional, and comfortable towards new ways of thinking."[17] Provocations, therefore, have been crucial to the work of field formation, as they potentially open up a space for practitioners to transgress disciplinary boundaries and normative protocols and mitigate against stasis and calcification. We might also view provocation as a form of reckoning or a coming-to-terms with not only the potentials but also the disavowals, silences, and omissions that mark Filipinx American studies. Accordingly, we hope then that this volume will *defamiliarize* Filipinx American studies— that is, to render it *unfamiliar* in order to cast a critical light on the modes of critique we rely on rather than take them for granted and not be able to discern unforeseen relations and entanglements.

To therefore suggest that our collective project is a provocation means to conceive of it as an incitement to move beyond familiar iterations of Filipinx American studies scholarship, to reexamine our distinct disciplinary attachments and investments in analytic categories that heretofore have proven to be tremendously useful and generative and continue to be so. We have in mind, for example, the term "empire" that has historically served as a field-defining analytic and generated much of the field imaginary of Filipinx American studies.[18] To a large extent, Filipinx American studies has accrued legibility and legitimacy in the US university vis-à-vis its engagement with the disavowed history of US empire. It is precisely for this reason that we encouraged the contributors tasked with interrogating this analytic to reflect not just on its indispensability to the project of Filipinx American studies but also on its attendant limits and complications. What would it mean, for example, to enact a mode of critique that places empire-building and settler colonialism in the same analytic frame without collapsing differences between them? It is in this spirit we offer our collective project and our hope is that in compelling us to do things differently, it will render apparent new modes of critique and call forth the unexpected and the yet-to-be-realized.

Section Summaries

Taken as a whole, *Filipinx American Studies: Reckoning, Reclamation, Transformation* showcases a compendium of foundational and emergent phenomena—not singularly, but multidimensionally defined as nodes of engagement—that have originated both from the specificities of Filipinx American conditions outlined above as well as circumstances that have profoundly shaped and continue to shape the terrain of Filipinx American studies.

First and foremost, *Filipinx American Studies* constitutes a *reckoning* with the project of Filipinx American studies, a critical appraisal of the work that is being done and the work *that needs to be done*. In our view, reckoning constitutes a messy and complicated process that does not aim for reconciliation or closure. Instead, it simultaneously demands thinking through the possibilities but also the blind spots and tensions that animate the field. Such a reckoning compels a rethinking of the project of Filipinx American studies given the exigencies of the current moment. Filipinx American studies' reckoning with empire has compelled other interdisciplinary formations to take up empire as a core analytic and reckon with the history, legacies, and ongoing violences of empire. Such reckoning has proven to be necessarily unsettling in terms of the cohering assumptions and analytical engagements of interdisciplines such as Asian American studies.

At the same time, *Filipinx American Studies* involves a *reclamation*, a term we invoke to spotlight Filipinx American studies' engagement with other interdisciplinary formations while signaling the historical and, to a certain extent, continuing active forgetting, devaluation, and marginalization of the subjects and logics of our studies. In these senses, reclamation for us entails not a reinsertion of what was previously erased, set aside, or ignored, but a reconstitution of analytical frames, argumentative claims, and methodological approaches so that qualitatively different insights are drawn from such new calculations. To wit, our goal in this instance is to avoid the assimilative tendencies of inclusionary projects while sidestepping the repetition or reinforcement of boundary-making. Hence, our desire to re-claim is synonymous with our attempts to proactively engage, reorganize, and reconstitute.

In invoking the notion of *transformation*, our aim is to put into sharp fo-cus the disruptive or transformative possibilities of Filipinx American studies. It signals the ways Filipinx American studies is taking up and cul-tivating analytical frameworks that have rendered the field's analytical pur-view more capacious. At the same time, "transformation" is meant to render discernible and signal the field's continued growth via its engagement with currents animating interdisciplinary formations such as critical ethnic stud-ies and American studies.

Reckoning

Part I—"Empire as Endless War"—encompasses essays that speak to the foundational status of empire in Filipinx American studies, how it has an-chored much of critical inquiry in the field and why it is indispensable to the project of Filipinx American studies. At the same time, the essays stretch the limits of empire as an analytic, expanding the grounds from which to engage empire in their consideration of other historical processes. In the essay that opens this section, **Vernadette Vicuña Gonzalez** delineates the indispensability of empire as an analytic in Filipinx American studies, how the field's engagement with empire has been influenced by developments in fields like postcolonial studies and American studies. Gonzalez scrutinizes both the utility and limits of empire as a foundational lens or thematic or-der, taking into account critiques raised by fields like Indigenous studies and settler colonial studies, and including within such critiques a (re)consider-ation of the continued deployment of "American" in Filipinx American studies. Along similar lines, **Nerissa S. Balce** examines how empire has been taken up in Filipinx American studies, specifying how scholars in the field have approached empire as a political idea and as culture that registers its ongoing legacies—what Balce describes as the afterlives of empire. Balce also reflects on the current manifestations of empire in the form of fascism and the rule of war, epitomized by the US global war on terror and the Duterte regime in the Philippines. Heeding settler colonial critiques mentioned by Gonzalez in her essay, **Dean Itsuji** Saranillio situates his analysis of empire as emerging out of processes of settler colonialism, advancing the notion that empire is a function of the "failures" or unsustainability of settler colonialism and capitalism. For Saranillio, a consideration of the rise of the US as the largest militarized empire in world history cannot be disentangled from the establishment of white settler colonies. **Cynthia Marasigan** casts a critical light on the afterlives of empire, focusing on the constitutive role of war in Filipinx movement and migration across the US empire. Specifically, Marasigan delineates what she terms as "the profound persistence of the Philippine-American War," a war that continues to reverberate, giving rise to both intra-imperial dynamics and dynamics between colonized subjects. Following a similar thread, **JoAnna Poblete** investigates how Filipinxs have been situated in the interstices of US political, economic, social, and cultural systems, or what she describes as the "third spaces of being within the United States." For Poblete, this compels Filipinx American studies to view Filipinx American liminality as a basis for advancing comparative, even cross-racial, analyses of Filipinx American history. In the last essay within this section, **Dylan Rodríguez** situates Filipinx American Studies as an emergent critical project that profoundly unsettles the logics, grammar, and fictions of what he terms "Filipino Americanism." Rodríguez is particularly interested in poetic appropriations and rearticulations of genocide that can underwrite the project of Filipinx American studies in its critical engagement against empire and its various iterations.

Part II—"Labor and Knowledge/Power"—presents a collective rumination on the prospects for reconfiguring modes and contents of social analysis, utilizing select iterations of Filipinx American critique, to illuminate otherwise richer and more provocative forms and consequences of knowledge production beyond oversimplified and oftentimes erroneous accounts of successive migration flows and social group formations. Beginning, for example, with key points taken from Carlos Bulosan's *America Is in the Heart*, **Josen Masangkay Diaz** argues that even though it has already been claimed that the study of labor within Filipinx American studies cannot be fully accounted for without its complex linkages with empire, it has been equally imperative in the field to study labor from the particular lenses of intertwined geopolitical economies, overlapping boundaries of national space, and alternative forms of social belonging. Diaz is particularly interested in how labor and empire may not always be expected to take on a linear and, therefore, predictable flow, a parallel claim explicated by **Victor Bascara** through his discussion of the uneven vectors utilized in the work of historicizing. In his essay, Bascara probes into the uses and misuses of arcs of "development" and "progress" in plotting courses of history while simultaneously undoing unquestioned unilinear forms in such an emplotment. Taking cues from eminent historian Reynaldo Clemeña Ileto and cultural theorist Raymond Williams, and mining the critical work of scholars positioned within Filipinx American studies, Bascara tackles the possibilities of reformulating Filipinx American history as dynamically and simultaneously emergent, dominant, and residual. Applied to the case of chronicling Filipinx migration to and beyond the US, **Roy B. Taggueg Jr.** and **Robyn Magalit Rodriguez** thus focus their attention on the importance of centering empire in the narration of labor mobilities as opposed to depicting such histories through conventional accounts of unidirectional immigration flows and patterns. By doing so, Taggueg Jr. and Rodriguez throw into sharp relief the limits of linear immigration models as organizing frameworks of labor analysis because of the ways in which they valorize the US as a nation of immigrants while obscuring its histories of imperialism. Offering then a much more specific case of nonlinear labor migration analysis, **Richard T. Chu** transports the spatial breadth and depth of Filipinx American history into new directions by considering the histories of migration of Chinese into the Philippines and the consequences of anti-Chinese exclusions in the US, broadening and complicating what could be a narrow account of Filipinx migration to the United States. For Chu, a focus on ethnic or racial groups within and outside of the US, and more broadly, on the intersections of "migration" and "race," puts into comparative clarity the differential racializations of Chinese and Filipinx labor. Applied to a more contemporary vein, **Anna Romina Guevarra** argues that this business of undoing linear histories of labor extraction can be most suitably employed by centering the ways in which Filipina careworkers occupy key nodes in the social reproduction of the global neoliberal economic order at the same time as they recalibrate the ways in which carework is performed across time and space. In so doing, Filipina labor is not simplistically and erroneously understood as embodiments of workplace progress in an inevitable chain of economic productivity. Rather, it stands at the intersections of transnational and virtual mobilities, occupying, yet troubling, new vocabularies, technologies, family arrangements, and practices of work exploitation. Such a re-calculative strategy of complicating what is transacted as "history" is equally pronounced in **Jody Blanco**'s take on the saga of Filipinx labor in the US and elsewhere. Inspired by Bulosan's desire to envision a place "where the past . . . would not determine the future all the way to the end," Blanco proposes situating Filipinx American history not in the usual temporal-spatial narrative of Filipinxs coming to America but, rather, in the struggles to reckon with the contradictions of historical legacies of labor extraction and global expansion across generations and locations.

Reclamation

The next five essays in Part III—"Across Language, Sex-Gender, and Space-Time Geographies"—constitute the field's efforts to construct or recalibrate ideas and practices of meaning-making with respect to language use, sex-gender constructs, and to matters of time and space that altogether propose situating Filipinx American history and subjectivity in terms that are less narrow in scope, inadequately limiting in depth, and not overly constricting in circulation. In the essay by **Joi Barrios**, herself a scholar and teacher of Filipinx language and literature, socially and politically meaningful work for most Filipinx Americans—whether in reference to their multiple forms of activism or their collective quest to rediscover roots—is equivalent to, even impossible without, language learning, language use, and most significantly, language teaching. Barrios is invested in underscoring the import of language as a site of politics, so she deploys an arsenal of narratives that depict the powers of code-switching, critical pedagogy, and poetry in engaging with struggles for self-determination and sovereignty. For **Kale Bantigue Fajardo**, a rigorous consideration of sex-genders as an indispensable analytic within Filipinx American studies necessitates intersectional analysis, given how sex-genders have served as a vehicle for racialization and anti-Filipinx racism. Fajardo relies on a queer-of-color critique lens in his reading of a foundational text and survey of relevant literature, aiming for a decolonized understanding of sex-genders. **Allan Punzalan Isaac** looks to *dating* (pronounced as "dah-teeng" and translated from Tagalog into English as a kind of force or impression) as a type of affect that constitutes a potentially generative site to explore the workings and circulation of affect on a global scale. Building on scholarship on the affective dimensions of Filipinx labor migration and, specifically, on care and carework, Isaac poses the question of what it would mean to shift our focus from "return" to "arrival"—in his words, to bend the time and space of the present—as a means to recover what might have been lost during movement or to find pleasure in fantasizing about alternative possibilities. **Denise Cruz** takes a self-reflexive and time/space expansive approach to gender, interrogating how it has been foundational to the project of Filipinx American studies. Providing a critical survey of scholarship and how various interlocutors in the field have engaged with gender at different historical moments, Cruz utilizes a transpacific analytical lens to further nuance our understanding of gender across different geographical sites and circulatory configurations. Finally, **Robert Diaz** provides a diasporic optic to examine the ways gender/sexuality and other markers of social identities have been configured and "rescripted" in the Filipinx diaspora. Looking specifically at mass media representations and key works of several Filipinx American studies scholars, Diaz offers a more generative and always contingent process of reading and recognizing gender/sexuality among Filipinx communities within shifting time/space contexts.

Part IV—"Critical Schooling and Justice in Other Words"—exemplifies scholarship that aims to consider education as a site of trenchant advocacy that is attentive to the specificities of Filipinx American schooling experiences along with works that attempt to broaden the contours of Filipinx American political activism via a consideration of the ways in which race, class, gender, and sexuality have shaped and are shaped by activism on the ground. We offer in this part the myriad ways in which ideas and practices of justice work are formulated through the double references of justice as self-evident by its very definition (as in, "in other words, justice") and as one that is in excess of its conventional permutations (as in, "justice, in other words"). First, **Dina C. Maramba** draws on her experiences as a student affairs practitioner and an education scholar and professor to reflect on the vocabularies used by educational institutions—themselves critical sites of knowledge production within schools—to categorize social identities and benchmarks of success for their students and faculty. But, to underscore and simultaneously unsettle claims regarding Filipinx American invisibility and nonrecognition, otherwise equally productive of misperception and ignorance, Maramba offers "counternarratives" of group social identification that may effectively prove disruptive to educational institutions' hegemonic powers. In a similar vein of articulating yet another form of justice work in schools, **Reuben B. Deleon**'s essay contribution pursues the imperative of calculating identity as a dynamic and liminal formation. Peering into the lives of Filipinx American college students to counterargue the distorted imagination of identities as subjectivities that are simplistically developed through stages, to instead regard identities as processes that are much more fluid and collectively experienced, we imagine Deleon's intervention in education, akin to Maramba's, as fundamentally attuned with the pursuit of self-determination, broadly and justly defined. Next, a US-based Filipinx radical tradition that utilizes the "living archives" of intergenerational cultures of opposition based on *manong* knowledge (partly translated as the "wisdom of elders") is how **Michael Schulze-Oechtering** postulates what the pursuit of justice means in and for Filipinx American studies. Theorizing the manners by which grassroots activism and social critique are indelibly mapped onto the sustained histories of labor and antigentrification movements organized by Filipinx and their allies, Schulze-Oechtering's essay, much like Cruz's in Part III, is an eloquent testimony of the transpacific orientations of the field's subjects of study. Following this, **Jeffrey Santa Ana** scrutinizes activist works by Filipinx writers and artists to reveal how the histories as well as ongoing realities of the US empire are tightly intertwined with environmental violence and devastation, making appeals for justice especially in recent times much more palpably urgent as themselves appeals for the preservation of life. For Santa Ana, such intertwined calls for justice in the pursuit of life are not new, but have already been de rigueur all throughout the activist labors of Filipinxs across nations and generations. In the next instance, **Karín Aguilar-San Juan** focuses on specific examples, including union activism and Manny Pacquiao's charity work, to trouble taken-for-granted notions of activisms that do not address questions about homophobic masculinities, state-sponsored violence, and global labor exploitation. And finally, continuing our critique of the universality of the meanings of justice in activist work, **Kim Compoc** looks into the interstices of

Filipinx experience in Hawaiʻi to calculate how struggles against US imperial domination in the Pacific and Asia expose the limits of civil rights discourses of multicultural democracy that have usually guided mainland justice movements. Compoc clarifies how such differences matter critically in articulating visions of justice that affirm rather than extinguish struggles for Indigenous self-determination.

Transformation

Part V—"Relationalities, Intimacies, and Entanglements"—includes essays that gesture toward the indispensability of relational thinking in Filipinx American studies. In their deployment of comparative frameworks, the five essays here cast light on hitherto obscured linkages among purportedly disparate formations and historical processes, opening up multiple pathways that serve to broaden the terrain of Filipinx American studies. In this section's initial entry, **Anthony Bayani Rodriguez** provides a genealogy of "Filipino" that links back to the period of Spanish colonialism, through the period of US colonial rule, and up to the early twenty-first century. Advancing a decolonial/epochal conceptualization of Filipinxness, Rodriguez directs our attention to the various permutations of "Filipino," including liberal multiculturalist formulations that conform with Western liberal notions of humanity and alternative formations that unmoor it from notions of ethnic belonging. The next essay covers similar ground temporally as **Sony Coráñez Bolton** focuses his attention on how the "x" in Filipinx and Latinx indexes the intersections of Spanish colonialism and US imperialism in Filipinx and Latinx America. Drawing on critical ethnic studies, queer-of-color critique, and Filipinx American studies, Bolton is interested in the ways that a critical consideration of what he terms the double "x" of Filipinx and Latinx open up conversations informed by relational thinking that are otherwise foreclosed. The next two essays, by **Angelica J. Allen** and **J. A. Ruanto-Ramirez**, speak to the indispensability of relational thinking and the way Filipinxness is inextricably tied with other purportedly disparate formations. Based on her ethnographic research among Black Amerasians, Allen examines how the experiences of Black Amerasians are obscured in normative accounts of Filipinx American history and culture. She contrasts the invisibility of Black Amerasians in discourses pertaining to the Filipinx American experience with their hypervisibility in the Philippines, which speaks to the vexed status of Blackness in Filipinx American studies and the need for sustained and critical dialogues between Filipinx American studies and Black studies. Similarly, Ruanto-Ramirez problematizes the notion of Filipinxness, this time through a consideration of indigeneity and Indigenous communities. To counteract the violence that inheres in the category "Filipino," Ruanto-Ramirez advances the notion of *katutubo* as a critical lens that serves to denaturalize and dehomogenize "Filipino." **Theodore S. Gonzalves**'s essay concludes this section and, in it, he calls for a more expansive understanding of repertoire, one that is not confined to the realm of the performing arts. Gonzalves extends our understanding of repertoire to encompass scholarship, what he terms "scholarly repertoires," that gestures toward relational thinking and comparative analyses.

Part VI—"Recalcitrant Bodies, Unruly Vernaculars"—comprises essays that cohere loosely around the disruptive possibilities of Filipinx American formations, directing our attention to the ways Filipinx American bodies, vernaculars, and idioms exceed normative metrics and logics. In so doing, the essays lay bare the unruliness of Filipinx American bodies and make apparent the contingent and contested nature of meanings and the generative possibilities of vernaculars. Approaching performance as a mode of being in the world, **Lucy MSP Burns**'s essay contribution discusses how scholars in the field have taken up performance in relation to histories of empire, migration, and diaspora that are all encoded within the Filipinx performing body. Burns scrutinizes the deployment of a 1970s Filipinx folk song in a dance production based on an Indian epic, exploring how the movement and migration of performance traditions serve to resignify these practices. Likewise, **Alana J. Bock** centers her investigation on Filipinx bodies, advancing the notion of illegibility to account for Filipinx bodies and performances rendered unknowable within frameworks of (in)visibility and recognition. Bock closely examines the performance of a punk band fronted by a Filipinx, Black, and trans artist in order to demonstrate the ways that Filipinx performativity exceeds Filipinx American studies and registers with other fields such as Black studies. In his essay contribution, **Edward Nadurata** focuses on a particular body—the figure of the elderly Filipinx migrant—in order to expose the valorization of able-bodied subjects in Filipinx American studies. Nadurata makes a compelling case for the need to crip Filipinx American studies, troubling considerations of labor that do not engage with (dis)ability and age because of the way these considerations leave in place ableist and normative assumptions that have historically structured the field. **Evelyn Ibatan Rodriguez** traces the evolving status of gender within Filipinx American studies, putting into focus the identities and experiences of those who exceed the male-centered narratives that initially undergirded the historiography of the field. In so doing, Rodriguez tracks how the field has opened to encompass other identities and experiences including Filipinx American youth and nonbinary Pinxys. The next two essays, by **Martin F. Manalansan IV** and **Sarita Echavez See**, look to the vernacular and idioms as sites for the reconfiguration of meanings. Manalansan critically interrogates scholarly and popular imaginings of *hiya* or "shame" as an index of Filipinx "values" and "character." Placing its multiple iterations under critical scrutiny, Manalansan calls for a recasting of *hiya* by treating it as an affective and discursive idiom, thus circumventing certain problems associated with its deployment. In the last essay of this section, See scrutinizes what is at stake in theorizing the relationship between language, power, and knowledge through an investigation of the history of "amok." See makes a compelling case for letting Filipinx American studies run amok as a way to disrupt meaning and engage in nonpropertied or decolonial modes of knowledge production.

Finally, we offer an afterword, by way of a reflection piece written by famed novelist **Gina Apostol**, herself a scholar of and a provocative contributor to the multiple incarnations of Filipinx American studies. We are honored by her incisive reading and profound engagement with all the work we have collectively invested in this project as well as the ways she amplifies the stakes expressed in this anthology.

At the end of the main sections, we offer two appendixes. The first is an annotated list of resources by **Gerardo A. Colmenar**, Asian American studies librarian at the University of California, Santa Barbara. It aims to serve as a useful compendium of selected books and other media materials, as well as resource sites, both physical and online, that are pertinent to our fields of study. The second resource is a selected list of scholarly works relevant to Filipinx American studies that we compiled with the research assistance of **Edward Nadurata**.

The vision upon which we conceptualized *Filipinx American Studies: Reckoning, Reclamation, Transformation* rested on expressing a particular kind of cartographic engagement with the state and the stakes of the field in order to assess, calculate, and assist in expanding the interdiscipline's intellectual labors. This labor, we feel, is crucial to the field's raison d'être as it is one that has underscored our pursuit to be accountable to our provenances and all the communities that we study. Historically, our formation as an interdiscipline was born out of a set of critiques against the very disciplinary foundations of the academy we were trying to enter or were already a part of. We appeared in the horizons of the university and its professional academic communities, already critical of the conditions that we were subjected to, the disciplinary models and logics that we were trained under, and the unitary analytical emplotments of our subjects' ontologies. It is, therefore, unimaginable for many of us to speak of Filipinx American studies without reference to a Filipinx American *critique*, a way of hailing the conditions of possibility within which we mark the historical interrogation of our erasure and exclusion, as well as our current engagement with multiple field formations and formulations in spite of our exclusions. In this tradition of critical practice, we assert the unique suitability and situatedness of Filipinx American studies both as a site for starting and continuing the work of historicizing US empire in all of its entanglements, as well as a location for keeping alive the cultivation of transformative ventures along its wake. As such, many scholars in Filipinx American studies, especially all those who are included in this volume, are oriented toward currency rather than stability, underscoring the field's propensities for pursuing ongoing conversations instead of fixed conclusions.

While usually placed at the junctures of American studies, Asian American studies, area studies, and ethnic studies, the essays in this volume speak to both an indirect reckoning with the uneasiness within which our scholarship in these fields is historically positioned as much as they are direct provocations of the varieties of alternative epistemologies and ontologies that this interdiscipline seeks to recognize, reclaim, and transform. They are, on many levels, all products and productive of the juxtaposition of the categories Filipinx and American, inclusive of both their unities and fissures, as well as agreements and fault lines, as exemplified by several essays here that contest not only how we name ourselves, but in the ways we may also exclude others because of such a naming. Taken as a whole, our collection of essays articulates our multiple nodes of critical engagement, each showcasing points in an ongoing intellectual map that holds the field together in ways that are intersecting, uneven, and open to possibilities, while seeking to defy conventions and remaining as flexible and as imaginative as we can in our moments of despair and hope.

NOTES

1. Theodore S. Gonzalves, *The Day the Dancers Stayed: Performing in the Filipino/American Diaspora* (Philadelphia: Temple University Press, 2010), 114.

2. Fred Cordova, Dorothy Laigo Cordova, and Albert A. Acena, *Filipinos, Forgotten Asian Americans: A Pictorial Essay, 1763–Circa 1963* (Dubuque, Iowa: Kendall/Hunt, 1983); Antonio T. Tiongson Jr., Edgardo V. Gutierrez, and Ricardo V. Gutierrez, eds., *Positively No Filipinos Allowed: Building Community and Discourse* (Philadelphia: Temple University Press, 2006); Martin F. Manalansan IV and Augusto F. Espiritu, eds., *Filipino Studies: Palimpsests of Nation and Diaspora* (New York: New York University Press, 2016).

3. Susan P. Evangelista, "Carlos Bulosan and Third World Consciousness," *Philippine Studies* 30, no. 1 (First Quarter 1982): 44–58.

4. See Oscar V. Campomanes, "Filipinos in the United States and Their Literature of Exile," in *Discrepant Histories: Translocal Essays on Filipino Cultures*, ed. Vicente L. Rafael (Philadelphia: Temple University Press, 1995), 159–92. Also see Manuel Buaken, *I Have Lived with the American People* (Caldwell, Idaho: Caxton Printers, 1948); Augusto F. Espiritu, *Five Faces of Exile: The Nation and Filipino American Intellectuals* (Stanford, Calif.: Stanford University Press, 2005); Royal F. Morales, *Makibaka: The Pilipino American Struggle* (Los Angeles: Mountainview Publishers, 1974); Noel V. Teodoro, "Pensionados and Workers: The Filipinos in the United States, 1903–1956," *Asian and Pacific Migration Journal* 8, no. 1–2 (1999): 157–78.

5. Rick Baldoz, *The Third Asiatic Invasion: Empire and Migration in Filipino America, 1898–1946* (New York: New York University Press, 2011); Yến Lê Espiritu, *Asian American Panethnicity: Building Institutions and Identities* (Philadelphia: Temple University Press, 1992); Dorothy Fujita-Rony, *American Workers, Colonial Power: Philippine Seattle and the Transpacific West, 1919–1941* (Berkeley: University of California Press, 2003); Jonathan Y. Okamura, *Imagining the Filipino American Diaspora: Transnational Relations, Identities, and Communities* (New York: Garland Publishing, 1998).

6. A pertinent example is Dawn Bohulano Mabalon's invocation in her work to "rewrite the dominant narrative of Asian American history, which has downplayed Filipina/o American community building to favor a male-centered,

sojourner narrative," in *Little Manila Is in the Heart: The Making of the Filipina/o Community in Stockton, California* (Durham, N.C.: Duke University Press, 2013), 11.

7. E. San Juan Jr., "Filipino Writing in the United States: Reclaiming Whose America?," *Philippine Studies* 41 (1993): 141–66.

8. By "racial capitalism," we mean the development of a socioeconomic system constitutively predicated on capital accumulation through racial differentiation. See Cedric Robinson's acute formulation and analysis of this term in *Black Marxism: The Making of the Black Radical Tradition* (Chapel Hill: University of North Carolina Press, 2000).

9. See for example, Burns (2013), Cruz (2012), and Vergara (2009).

10. The author and book are Lois-Ann Yamanaka, *Saturday Night at the Pahala Theatre* (Honolulu: Bamboo Ridge Press, 1993).

11. Lois-Ann Yamanaka, *Blu's Hanging* (New York: Farrar, Straus and Giroux, 1997).

12. Ilocano term for agricultural worker.

13. Martin F. Manalansan IV, "Tension, Engagements, Aspirations: The Politics of Knowledge Production in Filipino American Studies," in *Flashpoints for Asian American Studies*, ed. Cathy J. Schlund-Vials (New York: Fordham University Press, 2018), 191–204.

14. The list of scholars engaged in Filipinx American studies is much more extensive than this short enumeration. See, for example, the works listed in Appendix B of this volume.

15. Manalansan, "Tensions, Engagements, Aspiration," 190.

16. In the introduction to *Keywords for African American Studies*, the coeditors make the point that the "Kill that Keyword" session is symptomatic of how the keyword (and by extension keyword projects) have become ubiquitous to such an extent that the keyword has been drained or emptied of its novelty. Erica R. Edwards, Roderick A. Ferguson, and Jeffrey O. G. Ogbar, eds., *Keywords for African American Studies* (New York: New York University Press, 2018). See also J. Jack Halberstam, Fred Moten, and Sandra K. Soto, "The Fun and the Fury: New Dialectics of Pleasure and Pain in the Post-American Century," American Studies Association; *https://convention2.allacademic.com/one/theasa/theasa14/.*

17. Erica Browne, "Karen Nakamura on Disability Studies and Race," Othering & Belonging Institute; *https://haasinstitute.berkeley.edu/karen-nakamura-disability-studies-and-race.*

18. For an elaboration of the notion of "field imaginary," see Donald E. Pease, "'New Americanists': Revisionist Interventions into the Canon," *boundary 2* 17, no. 1 (Spring 1990): 1–37. See also Robyn Wiegman, *Object Lessons* (Durham, N.C.: Duke University Press, 2012).

Reckoning

Empire as Endless War

ONE

Empire: Turns and Returns

Vernadette Vicuña Gonzalez

Empire as a framework and an analytic is a gift of postcolonial studies, which itself was born from a global anticolonial movement that gained traction after World War II. Scholars of the Filipinx diaspora are embedded in the enduring and transnational sweep of this struggle as well as in the intellectual constellation that emerged to grapple with the workings of power under its conditions. Figures such as Franz Fanon and Aimé Césaire articulated trenchant critiques of European colonialism grounded in the militant postwar resistance from Algeria to Vietnam. Pushing back against the sedimented formations of knowledge and legal structures that underpinned territorial theft and extraction, postcolonial studies as a field was a response to and an undoing of European imperialism's profoundly violent and racist worldview. Its particular gift was the unabashed recognition of the struggles of colonized peoples and their critical roles in the formation of the modern world. Europe was the main fixation of postcolonial studies, dominated by a focus on its colonial ambitions in Africa, Asia, and the Americas.

Analyses of the United States as imperial power came late to the field, deferred by dearly held understandings of its exceptionalism. Amy Kaplan's pathbreaking work on the blind spots and omissions that exempted the United States from the early gaze of postcolonial studies looks to American exceptionalism's denial of American empire as well as the il/legal acrobatics it used to reterritorialize its colonial holdings into something far more innocent.[1]

"Empire" as a critical descriptor of the United States emerged in full force with the "imperial turn" in the field of American studies, which marked the centennial of the 1898 overseas military and political interventions of the United States as the originary moment of American imperialism. Of course, empire—where one state desires and exerts control over territories and peoples that are not its own—was not introduced to the Philippines by the United States, nor was 1898 the United States' first imperial foray. Spain had colonized the Philippines for well over three centuries, and scholars of the Philippines had readily understood the archipelago through the framework of Spanish empire.[2] For Filipinxs who subsequently resisted American encroachments on their sovereignty, "empire" was a concept that encapsulated the contradictions of a young republic flexing its military muscle around the world. As in its own hemisphere, where Latin America felt the imperial sting of US "interventions," the United States' pivot to Asia and the Pacific in the late nineteenth century made manifest its vision of global supremacy. Despite its profound pattern of imperial behavior— military assistance in the overthrow of the Hawaiian Kingdom; a violent pacification campaign in the Philippines that laid the foundation for decades of colonial rule; the conversion of Cuba into a protectorate and Puerto Rico into a commonwealth, to name a few—the United States maintained a sense of innocence about its place in the world. Few things would genuinely trouble the image that Americans had of themselves—the Vietnam War later on in the twentieth century was one of them. The social, political, and intellectual paradigm shifts stemming from a global decolonial movement that reached its apex in the 1960s and 1970s recognized the United States as among the world's modern imperial powers.

Yet it was not until the 1990s, with the hundredth anniversary of the Spanish-American War and the Philippine-American War, that the United States as empire came into focus for postcolonial studies and American studies scholars alike.[3] The imperial turn in American studies as a field recast the US-Philippines "special relationship" through a history of imperial power, rather than the innocent myth of "benevolent assimilation."[4] This approach spawned an interdisciplinary subfield with empire as an analytic and the Philippines, along with Guåhan (Guam), Hawai'i, Puerto Rico, and Cuba as the units of analysis. Aside from examining the military and political forms of occupation that had come to define empire, the imperial turn in large part focused on the myriad cultural forms that undergirded the machinery of war, the diplomatic maneuvers, and the international posturing of global powers.[5]

Scholars coming out of the US context's imperial turn looked to the Philippines to understand the norms, beliefs, and practices of "uplifting our little brown brothers." The archipelago served as a case study for how the United States' racial politics served and shaped its imperial project, and how empire-building, in turn, affected US national racial imaginaries and policy.[6] The wars in the Philippines were also an international political theater where ideas about nation and gender were defined.[7] And as colonial rule was established, it became clear that the mission of empire was not only about public administration, but also the imposition of American civilization in domestic spaces.[8] Scholars of the imperial turn looking to the Philippines demonstrated how notions of progress and civilization were sedimented through institutions like law, education, and public health, stretching both the meaning and periodization of empire beyond warfare or formal political rule.[9]

Turning to empire's cultures animated studies of its racialized, gendered, and sexualized logics, particularly when the focus of inquiry shifted to Filipinx life under empire rather than American colonial institutions. These logics informed and reinforced military violence and occupation and the theft of sovereignty from people deemed "unfit for self-governance"—as evidenced by Nerissa Balce's account of the visual archive of Filipinx racial abjection during the Philippine-American War and Sarita Echavez See's study of imperial ways of knowing—rationalized the acquisition of land and labor.[10] Much of the critical heft of this work was steeped in the ethnic studies movement, an intellectual project grounded in anti-imperialist, antiracist praxis, which might be seen both as a response to an American studies oriented toward exceptionalism and myth, and as a homegrown offshoot of postcolonial studies. Wielded from this intellectual genealogy, "empire" helped to explain how "we are here because you were there," moving narratives of Asian (and Filipinx) migration beyond and deeper than theories of push and pull and more squarely within the racial gendered matrix of settler desire and violence.

For the field of Filipinx American studies, the reframing of US-Philippine political and cultural history through the lens of empire was profoundly formative. It positioned the field as a critical intervention in Asian American studies, which had been defined by an immigrant paradigm and a largely economic explanation for why migrants of Asian ancestry came to the United States. Empire better described the terms of the Filipinx people's relationship with the United States. Recruited as part of a racialized labor force, Filipinx laborers bypassed Asian exclusion laws due to their ambiguous legal status and operated as a reserve and flexible labor force precisely through this ambiguity. Within Asian American studies, reframing Filipinxs as subjects of US empire helped explain the "unrecognizability" and "unassimilability" of the Filipinx experience within both the US nation-state and the field of Asian American studies, as pointed out by Oscar V. Campomanes.[11] As "wards" of the new American tropics, the liminal status of Filipinxs highlighted the racial legal contradictions at the heart of alien exclusion and white citizenship.[12] In other words, Filipinx mobilities to (and from) the metropole, their patterns of community formation, their sociocultural experiences, and their legal identities were shaped by the evolving relations of US empire in the Philippines.[13]

For the Philippines and Filipinx in the diaspora today, empire continues to explain the material realities and conditions of life in the archipelago and beyond. As postcolonial scholars have argued, postcoloniality is a condition, not a periodization (or to extend Patrick Wolfe, it is a structure, and not an event[14]). Empire also illuminates how this structure was and is held together through race and sex, violence and benevolence. Historically, US empire's outright brutality worked hand in velvet glove with the promises and coercions of intimacy and belonging as part of the overall management of the islands. This particular mix of carrot and stick methods was overlaid with the United States' special brand of exceptionalism, which saw its overseas territories as laboratories for the white man's burden. Yet despite claims to moral and racial superiority, it was apparent that white colonial men, in particular, had few qualms when it came to sexual arrangements with the people over whom they ruled.[15] This was a great cause for colonial anxiety.[16] White American tolerance for interracial relations in the colonies, however, did not extend so easily to Filipinxs who migrated to the metropole. Filipinx migrant laborers on the continent, in particular, were framed as hypersexual predators of white women, stoking anti-Filipinx sentiments and violence down the West Coast.

What empire as an analytic allows in these instances is a broader transnational framework through which Filipinx migrant labor and Philippine life can be apprehended. As Neferti Xina M. Tadiar puts it, the sexual economies of empire march on in the sociocultural and political forms of the global world order of late capitalism championed by the Washington consensus. Under this neo-imperial formation, the libidinal relations of empire trade in the currency of Filipinas.[17] The exportation of certain kinds of labor for the world economy—particularly different kinds of gendered carework—is built on the foundation of US-Philippine colonial history.[18] These interventions illuminate how empire is useful for thinking through how power is operationalized in similar or different ways in sites of historical or present-day occupation and control, and what shapes empire might take beyond that of brute military domination.[19]

With the Filipinx diaspora stretching beyond the United States, the concept of empire has allowed for mappings beyond a US-centric cartography, and for articulations with other colonized spaces and other colonized subjects. This affiliative remapping pulls together sites like Puerto Rico and Hawai'i through an intercolonial lens to parse out the routes and experiences of migrant laborers in imperial spaces.[20] It also opens up questions about how colonized peoples might themselves be mobilized to be part of imperial maneuvers elsewhere, even as they also remain some of its most vulnerable subjects. The clearest articulation of this critique has come from the framework of Asian settler colonialism, which provocatively points out how diasporic Asians—including Filipinx, whose geographic and sociocultural mobilities are enabled particularly in and through imperial circuits—may also be agents of empire in places where they settle.[21] In Hawai'i, for instance, where Native Hawaiians are outnumbered by Asian and Filipinx settlers, the economic and political "success" of ethnic settler groups needs to be examined with an eye to how it might contribute to the dispossession of Indigenous peoples.[22] In this critique, informed by Indigenous studies and theorizations of anti-Blackness, the citizenship ideal of Filipinx American-ness is revealed to be a manifestation and apparatus of empire.

In tandem and in tension with the ways in which Filipinx should under-stand how they might be laying claim to settler innocence, the analytic of empire also sheds light on how power is unsettled precisely through the con-nectivities and networks that empire's far-flung geographies activate. Em-pire plants the seeds of its own undoing: It generates unruly, ungovernable subjects who work within and against its aims. The demilitarization move-ment that continues to thrive in the Pacific, for instance, maps its connec-tions and actions across the sites that the United States has militarized over the last century, connecting the Philippines to Okinawa, Guåhan, Hawai'i, and other places in the region whose peoples and lands have felt the impact of American security.[23] Understanding how empire's logics work to position Filipinx in the Philippines and in the diaspora links the experience of vul-nerable overseas contract workers around the world to people whose liveli-hoods and in/securities rely on militarized economies and their often-violent collateral consequences.

In some ways, these movements, organized around political issues as op-posed to Filipinx identity, operate as critiques with regard to the field of Fili-pinx *American* studies. They decenter "American" as an identifier and as a project, which signals several interrelated reframings. Moving away from American is a refusal to uphold ideas of American exceptionalism through inclusion. As the still-implied end point of Filipinx settlerhood in the United States, attachments to "American" bind us to the imaginative poverty of stat-ist political definitions of citizenship rather than more capacious and revo-lutionary models of sovereignty. It also binds us to an imaginative and theoretical cartography that centers the United States, and the limited ways in which empire allows us to dream and see beyond its contours.

The field defined by Filipinx people and diaspora might do well to dis-card these investments as part of the work that needs to happen alongside and after empire. With whom do we ally ourselves as a field and group of scholars? What paths do our political and intellectual loyalties take? We have models to follow: The critical interventions of Indigenous feminisms, the continuing work of transnational demilitarization and decolonization movements, and the field of Asian settler colonial studies grapple with and move beyond empire and its national obsessions. This is not to say "empire" has outlived its utility, only that its critique might be turned toward the Philippines and Filipinx at home and elsewhere, and especially to how Indigenous lands, rights, and peoples might be better accounted for as the enabling presences in its analyses.

NOTES

1. Amy Kaplan, "'Left Alone with America': The Absence of Empire in the Study of American Culture," in *Cultures of United States Imperialism*, ed. Kaplan and Donald Pease (Durham, N.C.: Duke University Press, 1992), 3–21. See also Allan Punzalan Isaac on the insular cases that legally transformed categories of sovereignty according to the needs of US empire in the American tropics: *Articulating Filipino America* (Minneapolis: University of Minnesota Press, 2006).

2. Vicente L. Rafael, *Contracting Colonialism: Translation and Christian Conversion in Tagalog Society under Early Spanish Rule* (Durham, N.C.: Duke University Press, 1992); John D. Blanco, *Frontier Constitutions: Christianity and Colonial Empire in the Nineteenth Century Philippines* (Berkeley: University of California Press, 2009); Augusto F. Espiritu, "American Empire, Hispanicism, and the Nationalist Visions of Albizu, Recto, and Grau," in *Formations of United States Colonialism*, ed. Alyosha Goldstein (Durham, N.C.: Duke University Press, 2014), 157–79.

3. Others periodize the US imperial moment earlier, looking to Latin America as the first imperial territory upon which the US exerted both military and political intervention.

4. Stuart Creighton Miller, *Benevolent Assimilation: The American Conquest of the Philippines, 1899–1903* (New Haven: Yale University Press, 1982).

5. Amy Kaplan and Donald E. Pease, *Cultures of U.S. Imperialism* (Durham, N.C.: Duke University Press, 1994).

6. Paul A. Kramer, *The Blood of Government: Race, Empire, the United States, and the Philippines* (Chapel Hill: University of North Carolina Press, 2006); Michael Salman, *The Embarrassment of Slavery: Controversies over Bondage and Nationalism in the American Colonial Philippines* (Berkeley: University of California Press, 2001).

7. Kristin L. Hoganson, *Fighting for American Manhood: How Gender Politics Provoked the Spanish-American and Philippine-American Wars* (New Haven: Yale University Press, 2000).

8. Amy Kaplan, "Manifest Domesticity," in *The Anarchy of Empire in the Making of U.S. Culture* (Cambridge, Mass.: Harvard University Press, 2002).

9. Julian Go, "Chains of Empire, Projects of State: Political Education and U.S. Colonial Rule in Puerto Rico and the Philippines," *Comparative Studies*

in Society and History 42, no. 2 (2000): 333–62; Catherine Ceniza Choy, *Empire of Care: Nursing and Migration in Filipino American History* (Durham, N.C.: Duke University Press, 2003); Warwick Anderson, *Colonial Pathologies: American Tropical Medicine, Race, and Hygiene in the Philippines* (Durham, N.C.: Duke University Press, 2006).

10. Nerissa S. Balce, *Body Parts of Empire: Visual Abjection, Filipino Images, and the American Archive* (Ann Arbor: University of Michigan Press, 2016); Sarita Echavez See, *The Filipino Primitive: Accumulation and Resistance in the American Museum* (New York: New York University Press, 2017).

11. Oscar Campomanes, "The New Empire's Forgetful and Forgotten Citizens: Unrepresentability and Unassimilability in Filipino-American Postcolonialities," *Critical Mass* 2, no. 2 (1995).

12. Allan Punzalan Isaac, *American Tropics: Articulating Filipino America* (Minneapolis: University of Minnesota Press, 2006); Rick Baldoz, *The Third Asiatic Invasion: Empire and Migration in Filipino America, 1898–1946* (New York: New York University Press, 2010).

13. Rick Bonus, *Locating Filipino Americans: Ethnicity and the Cultural Politics of Space* (Philadelphia: Temple University Press, 2000); Denise Cruz, *Transpacific Femininities: The Making of the Modern Filipina* (Durham, N.C.: Duke University Press, 2012); Rudy Guevarra, *Becoming Mexipino: Multiethnic Identities and Communities in San Diego* (New Brunswick, N.J.: Rutgers University Press, 2012); Dawn Bohulano Mabalon, *Little Manila Is in the Heart: The Making of the Filipina/o Community in Stockton, California* (Durham, N.C.: Duke University Press, 2013).

14. Patrick Wolfe, "Settler Colonialism and the Elimination of the Native," *Journal of Genocide Research* 8, no. 4 (2006): 387–409.

15. Tessa Marie Winkelmann, "Dangerous Intercourse: Race, Gender and Interracial Relations in the American Colonial Philippines, 1898–1946" (PhD diss., University of Illinois at Urbana-Champaign, 2014).

16. Victor Román Mendoza. *Metroimperial Intimacies: Fantasy, Racial-Sexual Governance, and the Philippines in US Imperialism, 1899–1913* (Durham, N.C.: Duke University Press, 2016).

17. Neferti Xina M. Tadiar, *Fantasy-Production: Sexual Economies and Other Philippine Consequences for the New World Order* (Hong Kong: Hong Kong University Press, 2004).

18. See Choy, *Empire of Care*; also, Robyn Magalit Rodriguez, *Migrants for Export: How the Philippine State Brokers Labor to the World* (Minneapolis: University of Minnesota Press, 2010).

19. Vernadette Vicuña Gonzalez, *Securing Paradise: Tourism and Militarism in Hawai'i and the Philippines* (Durham, N.C.: Duke University Press, 2013); Camilla Fojas, *Islands of Empire: Pop Culture and U.S. Power* (Austin: University of Texas Press, 2014).

20. Joanna Poblete-Cross, *Islanders in the Empire: Filipino and Puerto Rican Laborers in Hawai'i* (Chicago: University of Illinois Press, 2014). See also Julian Go, *American Empire and the Politics of Meaning: Elite Political Cultures in the Philippines and Puerto Rico during U.S. Colonialism* (Durham, N.C.: Duke University Press, 2008); Faye Caronan, *Legitimizing Empire: Filipino American and U.S. Puerto Rican Cultural Critique* (Chicago: University of Illinois Press, 2015).

21. Candace Fujikane, "Introduction: Asian Settler Colonialism in the U.S. Colony of Hawai'i," in *Asian Settler Colonialism: From Local Governance to the Habits of Everyday Life in Hawai'i*, ed. Candace Fujikane and Jonathan Y. Okamura (Honolulu: University of Hawai'i Press, 2008): 1–42.

22. Dean Itsuji Saranillio, "Colonial Amnesia: Rethinking Filipino 'American' Settler Empowerment in the U.S. Colony of Hawai'i," in *Positively No Filipinos Allowed: Building Communities and Discourse*, ed. Antonio T. Tiongson Jr., Ricardo Gutierrez, and Edgardo Gutierrez (Philadelphia: Temple University Press, 2006), 124–41.

23. Christine Taitano DeLisle, "Destination Chamorro Culture: Notes on Realignment, Rebranding, and Post 9/11 Militourism in Guam," *American Quarterly* 68, no. 3 (2016): 563–72; Kim Compoc, "Emergent Allies: Decolonizing Hawai'i from a Filipinx Perspective" (PhD diss., University of Hawai'i at Mānoa, 2017); Kim Compoc, Joy Lehuanani Enomoto, and Kasha Ho, "From Hawai'i to Okinawa: Confronting Militarization, Healing Trauma, Strengthening Solidarity," in *Frontiers: A Journal of Women Studies* (forthcoming).

Empire as the Rule of War and Fascism

Nerissa S. Balce

"Empire" is a critical concept that describes the realities of people from the Global South, in this case Filipinos in the Philippines, Filipino immigrants, and their descendants in North America. Empire is the originary trauma of Filipinos and Filipino immigrant life. If seeing or witnessing the violence of slavery is the "original generative act" in the creation of Black subjectivity and identity (Hartman 1997), then seeing and witnessing the violence of empire—through literary, visual, or artistic forms—is the moment of the creation of the Filipinx subject.[1] Empire is a historical experience that binds us to Latinx communities given our shared histories forged by American wars of conquest (Campomanes 1992, 1999, 2008; San Juan 2008), the destruction of Indigenous land and cultures (Rodríguez 2010; Gonzalez 2013), the violent suppression of Independence movements (Ileto 2017), the modern US-sponsored wars against communist insurgencies in our homelands (Tadiar 2016), our common experience of farmwork and labor organizing (Baldoz 2011; Mabalon 2013), surviving the violence of anti-miscegenation laws (Volpp 2000), and the reality of our shared status as undocumented immigrants (Francisco and Rodriguez 2014; Guevarra 2016).[2]

As an academic construct, it refers to the conquest and occupation of a territory by a foreign power, often through military violence and war. It is also a shorthand for the historical legacies, traumas, and the cultural forms of people affected by an imperial culture. In Filipino diasporic studies or Filipinx studies, "empire" often refers to the US empire or the violent American colonization of the Philippines after the Philippine-American War (1899–1902), a historical moment that, according to cultural studies critic Dylan Rodríguez, was a "reflection of a genocidal white nationalist-imperialist common sense" and a reflection of "white civilization-making and native social liquidation across the Pacific."[3] The Philippine-American War of 1899 ushered the dawn of the American empire into the Asia-Pacific and was a historical moment of "white supremacist statecraft" defined by genocide as an American "nation-building project."[4] The "Filipino condition," as Rodríguez refers to Filipino American or Filipinx immigrant life in the US, must be understood as a "social existence" entangled with "the generative legacy of genocidal contact with the United States" that began with a war of conquest that remains unrecognized and forgotten.[5] While the Philippines was also colonized by Spain (1521–1898) and by the Japanese imperial army during World War II (1942–46), the status of the Philippines as the first and only formal colony of the United States highlights the significance of empire as the foundational historical narrative of Filipinx America. Just as "war and militarization" are the experience of Korean Americans, Vietnamese Americans, Cambodian Americans, Laotians, Hmong, and Okinawans, "empire" refers to different approaches in the study of Filipinx immigrant life.

Our historical entanglement with the American empire explains our visibility *and* invisibility in American culture, an invisibility so deeply felt by some Filipino American writers that they used the term "forgotten Asian Americans" to refer to their forebears (Cordova, Cordova, and Acena 1983).[6] And yet as the cultural archive from the late nineteenth century and the early twentieth century will show, Filipinos were in fact "hypervisible" due to an American war for empire. The body of the Filipino Native, similar to the Oriental as a Western or European idea, could be seen in the new print and visual technologies that promoted the importance of winning a war against Filipino *insurrectos* or insurgents: They appeared on printed newspapers, illustrated magazines, literary and academic journals, stereocards, postcards, travel and adventure books, romances, theater performances, and political pamphlets.[7] As such, as descendants of colonial subjects of America's only formal colony in Asia, the story of Filipinxs in America cannot be limited to the experience of assimilation and settlement. The story must include the grisly stereocards of Filipino cadavers in battle trenches in Manila as well as newspaper accounts of Igorot tribe members forced to perform their dog-eating practice for the delight and the horror of early twentieth-century Americans in the world's fairs. The American empire in Asia was inaugurated by war and by fairs that promoted the logic of nineteenth-century "Anglo-Saxon supremacy," with pavilions that showcased racial ideas about "white civilizations" and the "darker races." After 1898, the Philippine colony became part of the "American tropics," as literary critic Allan Punzalan Isaac puts it, making the Philippine Islands part of America's racial imaginary that promoted the nation's destiny as an empire and its romance with white supremacy.[8]

Reviewing the work of scholars who study the Philippines and the Filipino diaspora, there are two approaches to the study of empire. First, there is the notion of *empire as a political idea*. Second, there is the notion of *empire as culture* or the afterlives of empire that we trace in the cultural forms authored by or created by the "subjects of imperial rule."[9] In the case of Filipinx studies, empire refers to the history of the Philippines as an American colony (or "imperial rule") *and* the cultures of the Filipinx diaspora (or the expressive forms and cultural practices of the "subjects of imperial rule"). Both approaches to the study of empire—as idea/ history and as culture— are different but interconnected since Filipinx studies is an interdisciplinary field.

Empire as an *idea* can be traced to the late nineteenth-century American writings on the frontier as a romantic space of white settlement enabled by Native dispossession, land grab, and Native death. Empire as an idea refers to American national identity, in particular the nineteenth-century discourse of Anglo-Saxonism, a language that rested on the racial supremacy of the Anglo-Saxon or white race. Anglo-Saxonism is the world view based on the notion that Anglo-Saxons were gifted with "the blood of government" and whose manifest destiny required the dispossession and death of the darker, "inferior races."[10] By the early twentieth century, Anglo-Saxon supremacy would transform to white supremacy. And so the origin of white supremacy is tied to the language of American imperialism. In current Filipinx studies, empire is an idea about foreign policy or the expansion of the US nation's borders articulated in the ideologies of Manifest Destiny (late nineteenth century) and Pax Americana (mid-twentieth century). Rodríguez adds that these imperial articulations are in fact "elaborations" of genocide as the "central modality of U.S. nation-building and white supremacist globality."[11]

A second Filipinx studies approach to studying empire is *culture* or the notion of peoples and cultures affected by empire. In this instance, empire refers to the lived or historical experiences of those subjected to US rule after 1898. In the Filipinx migrant experience, this includes both the history of US colonial rule in the Philippine Islands and the global migration of Filipinos to North America as migrant workers in the early twentieth century and after. Empire as culture also refers to the legacies of empire or what empire left behind such as governance, social structures, and the arts (the visual, literary, and expressive arts). The related notions of Orientalism and militarism as racial and gendered concepts are important analytical tools for the study of the cultural archives of the American empire and the formation of Filipinx America.

In the early scholarship produced by the field known as Filipino American studies, the scholars centered on the great Filipino immigrant saga that started in the 1920s with the arrival of mostly male farmworkers who worked in the fields of California and the Pacific Northwest. Like many scholars in the early days of Asian American studies, the experience of immigration to the US was the paradigm for understanding a community's history and culture. But by the 1990s, the writings of E. San Juan Jr. and Oscar V. Campomanes, followed by the 2006 anthology *Positively No Filipinos Allowed* edited by Tiongson Jr. et al., shifted the way Filipino America was studied and understood.[12] As performance studies scholar Theodore S. Gonzalves put it, the narrative coordinates of Filipino America were no longer limited to the fields of the US West Coast, but shifted to the battlefields of Manila when seventy thousand US troops started a war against the newly constituted Philippine Republic in 1898.[13] In Filipinx studies then, the story of the American empire in the Asia-Pacific is the origin of Filipinx immigrant life. After all, before Filipinxs landed on the shores of California as migrant farmworkers, American soldiers landed in the Philippines to enforce US rule against the will of the Filipino people. The expansion of the American empire into Southeast Asia, in particular the history of the violent conquest of the Philippines by the United States at the turn of the twentieth century, marks the beginning of Filipinx America. In other words, before Filipinxs were immigrants, they were colonial subjects of the United States for forty years, until the end of World War II in 1946.

A historian of Philippine studies, Reynaldo Clemeña Ileto, argues that the history known by most Filipinos and Americans about the US colonization of the Philippines is in fact a legacy and a product of empire. He writes that the "collective memory" regarding US rule of the Philippines was shaped by what American colonial officials wanted Filipinos to "remember": that the US Army came as liberators and not as new colonial rulers.[14] For example, the textbook *A History of the Philippines* was written by the colonial official David Barrows, who served as director of education of the Philippine Islands from 1903 to 1906. This textbook was used for "at least two decades" and was the text that shaped the first generation of Filipinos who were to be "future professionals and politicians of the country."[15] Barrows's book taught Filipinos to accept class discrimination and Anglo-Saxon supremacy, the earlier instantiation of white supremacy. He wrote that the Katipunan was a "secret association composed largely of the uneducated classes,"[16] that Europe was the center of progress and "all histories," and "The white, or European, race above all others, the great historical race."[17] Further, Barrows was one of the early American writers to describe the Philippines as a backward, feudal "Oriental culture," stunted from modernity by conservative Spain. Western enlightenment or modernity could only be introduced by America. As Barrows put it, "The modern ideas of liberty, equality, fraternity, and democracy . . . having done their work in America and Europe, are here at work in the Philippines today. It remains to be seen whether a society can be rebuilt here on these principles, and whether Asia too will be reformed under their influence."[18] Barrows's foundational text thus created "knowledge" about the Philippine-American War of 1899 as a "great misunderstanding" between Americans and Filipinos by presenting the Filipino desire for independence as "immaturity," a lack of "political experience and social self-control."[19] Barrows's history book successfully erased the memories of the violence of empire, in particular the history of American suppression of Filipino revolutionary and nationalist dreams of independence. Through the legacy of a colonial education, succeeding generations of Filipinos viewed the Philippine revolution against the United States as "misguided," "stupid," and proof of our backwardness since we rejected American tutelage.[20] Despite these acts of colonial erasure and forgetting, Filipinx studies scholars attempt to address this historical amnesia in their work.

In the early twenty-first century, Filipinx studies scholars define empire by its afterlives: the legacies, the hauntings, and the continuities of US imperial rule. As media scholar Sarita Echavez See put it, the cultural forms created by Filipino American visual artists and writers illustrate how "a culture survives the violence particular to the American empire."[21] According to See, "Filipino America owes its existence to the monumentally violent and monumentally forgotten inclusion of the Philippines into the United States more than a century ago when the Philippine-American War broke out in 1899."[22] Studying the visual art and the performances of Filipino American artists, See's "decolonized eye" traces the "disavowal of imperialism." If the violence of the American empire resulted in the destruction of vernacular languages, history, and literature, See focuses on the expressive cultures of Filipino American artists who invoke "depictions of bodily injury and degradation, acts of aggressive joking and teasing, sophisticated forms of camp, and cross cultural and translingual punning."[23] Filipino American visual art and performances center on the bodily humiliation, pain, and humor responding to an imperial "matrix of historical, psychic, and cultural dispossession by producing a visual and rhetorical grammar of violence that in turn 'disarticulates' empire."[24] These cultural acts of "disarticulation" are in fact the Filipino American artist's attempt to "break up" or take apart empire as an idea. See argues that Filipino American texts respond to "the relegation of Filipino America to invisibility and absence" in visual art and performance.[25] Through a decolonized lens, Filipino American cultural forms are defined by "excessive embodiment," in particular the study of the Filipino body, as an aesthetic response to imperial forgetting.[26] Whether it be Manuel Ocampo's painting series, entitled *Heridas de la Lengua* (translated as "Wounds of the Tongue") depicting the *pasyón* or Christ figures portrayed as images of decapitation and amputation, or the video art of Angel Velasco

Shaw, entitled *Nailed*, that records the Lenten practice of a Filipina named Lucy Reyes who reenacts the crucifixion of Christ, the Filipino body in Filipino American art is "part of a combative engagement" with "the violence of Spanish and American colonization and the violence of American amnesia."[27] A decolonized eye views empire through the traumas, violence, wounding, or bodily injury of a Filipino figure.

Another cultural studies critic, Neferti Xina M. Tadiar, updates empire with the phrase "the rule of global war" and describes the rise of fascism as the current form of the American empire.[28] She notes that in the current era, "the economic globalization of capital is being rehearsed to the ends of [American] political-military domination by means of war." Tadiar upends the popular narrative of the twilight of the American empire and argues that after the US bombing of Afghanistan in 2001 and the launching of the "war on terror," the new form of the American empire is "global fascism."[29] She writes: "Some progressive scholars in the United States are in fact calling for a new analysis and at least recognition of the emergent conditions of fascism that confront not only the people in the United States, but also all the peoples in the paths of the global-U.S. 'war on terror.' . . . The war on terror, the war on drugs, the war against crime, the war against poverty—these are all instantiations of the rule of war. War has become a bureaucratic matter, with the military turned into police. . . . The rule of war is not only the rule of might, but also the rule of absolute and arbitrary [US] power as the normal and legitimate state of affairs."[30] These different wars according to Tadiar—the war on terror, drugs, crime, and poverty— underscore how the US military defines and promotes the "absolute and arbitrary" rule of the American empire. If in the nineteenth century the American empire waged war with American soldiers and Gatling guns, in the current era war is waged through economic sanctions, domestic and foreign policies to maintain and to preserve the American imperium. The US-led war on terror is a twenty-first-century example of the rule of war. The roots of this US rule of war can be traced to America's imperial past: the colonization of "the Philippines, Puerto Rico, Cuba, Hawai'i, Samoa and Guam . . . the onset of the Cold War . . . and the bloody track record of U.S. foreign interventions in the last hundred years."[31] After the Civil Rights Movement of the 1960s and the rise of decolonizing nationalist movements around the world, what followed in the Global South were counterinsurgency campaigns funded by the US military-industrial complex and financial restructuring programs to squash the revolts led by labor and minoritized populations.[32] The rise of the US security state, enabled by the war on terror and the current repressive policies of US government institutions such as the Department of Homeland Security and the Immigration and Customs Enforcement (ICE) illustrate what many consider as the emergence of American fascism under President Donald Trump's administration.

The current national debate regarding the use of the term "concentration camps" for the migrant jails at the US-Mexico border highlights the anxiety of some to recognize American fascism. Journalist and writer Masha Gessen, for example, writes that when Representative Alexandra Ocasio-Cortez of New York likened the migrant camps to concentration camps, the controversy wasn't about language or the semantics of concentration camps (Gessen 2019).[33] Gessen says that what is actually at stake is the horror of seeing what used to be unimaginable for some Americans—the violence of America's global power: "It is the choice between thinking that whatever is happening in reality is, by definition, acceptable, and thinking that some actual events in our current reality are fundamentally incompatible with our concept of ourselves—not just as Americans but as human beings—and therefore unimaginable." Gessen stops short of naming "the unimaginable" as American fascism. And so while some American scholars and international writers might name the migrant camps as concentration camps, the words "American empire" and "fascism" are muted or never mentioned.[34] Philippine and Filipinx artists, writers, and scholars however, are clear-eyed about the connections between America's imperial past and its fascist present.

Empire as the rule of war offers a lens for understanding the "war on drugs" under the regime of Rodrigo Roa Duterte, the sixteenth president of the Philippine Republic. As Tadiar put it, since the Philippines is a "coalitional state" in America's war on terror, the drug war is in fact a form of global fascism with the Philippine police as part of the American global war apparatus. By conducting a "drug war," the Philippine state "secures consent for the rule of war" led by the US security state and secures consent for a culture where the enemies of the Philippine state must be executed.[35] Duterte's fascism is a logic of violence and terror: Death is necessary to rid the republic of the existential threat posed by drug addicts. This purging of the drug scourge, however, is an alibi for the repression of other enemies of the government: critics of the administration, human rights activists, journalists, students, *lumad* or Indigenous folk, and the urban poor. And since the rise of Duterte to power in May 2016, many forms of state-sanctioned violence have been met by thousands of Filipino disappearances, torture, and extrajudicial punishments committed by the Philippine police or paramilitaries.[36] More than thirty thousand Filipinos, mostly from the slums of the country, have been killed by Duterte's so-called drug war.[37] The drug killings are considered by some scholars as a genocide of the poor but also as an extension of the "brutal U.S.-led counterinsurgency military and paramilitary campaigns" conducted to secure American imperial power since the Cold War.[38] And in December 2018, Duterte made these connections clear by ordering the Philippine military to "destroy and kill" the Philippine Left.[39] The rise of Duterte fascism is also the moment of a local and transnational opposition. To record the horror of the state, hundreds of photographs of the dead have appeared in print and social media through the efforts of a new generation of Filipino photojournalists. The Instagram account #EverydayImpunity features photographs of the drug war killings by different Filipino photographers who are part of the Night Shift, a cohort of young men and women who cover the murders that happen late at night.[40] The photographs of the drug killings have appeared in the US and international press, and in Philippine and international documentaries.[41] The photographs have also appeared in diverse exhibitions, in Manila and around the world, from the church grounds of Baclaran Church in Manila, at an art fair in a tony suburb of Makati City, to a photo exhibition in the Tower Bridge in London. Cultural studies critic Josen Masangkay Diaz argues for a "transpacific feminist historiography" for studying Duterte's authoritarianism by linking the photographs of the drug war to the violence of US and European colonialism and empire.[42]

A literary text that explores *all* the early twenty-first-century meanings of empire—from the trauma of military occupation to the rule of global war and fascism—is the novel *Insurrecto* by Filipina American novelist Gina Apostol.[43] The novel's title refers to the figure of the Filipino as an insurgent, the unruly and unassimilable colonial subject of the American imaginary first introduced to American readers during the Philippine-American War. It is also a reference to the various insurrections or interruptions in the novel's attempt at narrating the history of a war that launched the American empire in Asia. Apostol is part of a generation of Filipinx American fiction writers who mine and map the traumas of Philippine history, from colonialism to authoritarianism. These fiction writers include Carlos Bulosan, Ninotchka Rosca, Linda Ty Casper, Jessica Hagedorn, Lara Stapleton, Sabina Murray, Eric Gamalinda, R. Zamora Linmark, Eileen Tabios, Cecilia Manguerra Brainard, Brian Ascalon Roley, M. Evelina Galang, Mia Alvar, Elaine Castillo, Lysley Tenorio, Randy Ribay, Laurel Flores Fantauzzo, Ricco Villanueva Siasoco, and others.

In Apostol's novel, the author's decolonized eye sees the colonial past and the fascist present under the Duterte regime as interconnected, mapping the traumas of empire on different bodies, places, objects, and time periods. The imagined Philippines is a country that "has become an icon of extrajudicial horror, a dystopia of brazen extermination even in broad daylight, an international emblem of criminal slaughter by fascist police."[44] The histories of violence committed by the American colonial state and later the Philippine state are linked, like images in a triptych, since "everything in the world is doubled."[45] *Insurrecto* narrates the travels of an American filmmaker named Chiara who goes to the Philippines to make a movie about the Philippine-American War, following the footsteps of her famously eccentric but loving filmmaker father who was obsessed with the history of the war to the point of some madness.[46] Chiara travels to Samar, the site of the infamous Balangiga Massacre, with a Filipina immigrant scholar from New York named Magsalin, whose name literally means "to translate." When the women travel to Duterte's Philippines, they clash and compete to tell the story of empire through two different scripts: Chiara's story of a white female photographer and Magsalin's story of a Filipina schoolteacher.

Through the language of a mystery (What happened to Ludo, Chiara's father? What happened in the Balangiga Massacre in Samar?), two "movie scripts," various puns, irony, dark humor, multiple doppelgängers, and references to Philippine and American history, the novel narrates the traumas and the legacies of the Philippine-American War through a postmodern structure. Apostol disarticulates the linear narrative of empire and modernity through the novel's intentionally dizzying "triptych impressions" or triptych-like structure.[47] Divided into three eras, the narratives of the women protagonists connect in a kaleidoscopic way in three historical moments:

1898 (the era of empire and war), the 1970s or the Marcos regime, and 2016 or the Duterte regime (the eras of fascism). Before their trip, Chiara gives Magsalin an envelope of stereocards from the Philippine-American War and Magsalin is both intrigued and shocked. She concludes: "The pictures of the dead Filipino bodies and the burned Filipino towns are remarkably precise. But they are hard to see."[48] Similar to the project of Filipinx studies scholars, *Insurrecto* is a novel about what is "hard to see"—that is, to translate Philippine and American histories by making historic connections to empire, war, and fascism. Ironic and satirical, with many moments that ask the reader to question history and ways of seeing, *Insurrecto* is a novel about the legacies of empire as told through the intersecting lives of women in different periods. As the filmmaker Chiara asks: "The question, it seems to me, is how to keep the past from recurring. I mean, what the fuck is the point of knowing history's goddamned repetitive spirals if we remain its bloody victims?"[49] The novel *Insurrecto* is thus a literary text that narrates the traumas of empire in different forms, on different bodies, and in different eras. As a Filipinx studies text, it is a novel about the ideas of empire, the horror and humor of empire, and its legacies for its living bloody victims—both Filipinos in the Philippines and Filipinxs in the global diaspora.

Apostol's historical and postmodern novel is an example of the literary afterlives of empire. Returning to See's decolonized eye as the act of seeing empire through traumas and violence, the novel, like the project of Filipinx studies, questions the veracity of a neat and easy story for understanding Filipinx lives. In one scene in Chiara's film script on the Philippine-American War, an American doctor explains the "ordinary miracle of stereopsis" or binocular vision.[50] The emergence of the "Holmes viewer" or the stereoscope in the late nineteenth century became an important moment in the creation of empire. As Chiara writes in her script, Americans "manufactured how to see the world."[51] So rather than accepting the imperialist "propaganda" one sees in a stereocard, the work of Filipinx studies is to push against the sanitized, easily digestible stories of US-Philippine relations, or happy celebratory narratives of Filipinx immigrant communities in the United States.[52] Filipinx studies scholars, recalling the meaning of Magsalin's name, are tasked with translating the past and our present. Scholars and artists of Filipinx studies must make sense of our colonial inheritance, our status as descendants of colonial subjects that fought an "unfinished" revolution against empire, a "story of war and loss so repressed and so untold."[53] But, as Magsalin notes, our inheritance includes "stories within stories within stories that begin too abruptly, in media res."[54] Filipinx life in the early twenty-first century is as complicated and semiotically rich as a Manila mall named the Ali Mall, what Magsalin describes as a "motif" of the Filipino postmodern life.[55] Like the modest but aesthetically interesting mall, Filipinx studies are narratives on the beauty, absurdity, horror, and humor of life after empire.

NOTES

1. Saidiya V Hartman, *Scenes of Subjection: Terror, Slavery, and Self-Making in Nineteenth Century America* (New York: Oxford University Press, 1997).

2. Oscar V. Campomanes, "Filipinos in the United States and Their Literature of Exile," in *Reading the Literatures of Asian America*, ed. Shirley Geok-lin Lim and Amy Ling (Philadelphia: Temple University Press, 1992), 49–78; Oscar V. Campomanes, "1898 and the Nature of the New Empire," *Radical History Review* 73 (1999): 130–46; Oscar V. Campomanes, "Images of Filipino Racialization in the Anthropological Laboratories of the American Empire: The Case of Daniel Folkmar," *PMLA: Publications of the Modern Language Association* 123, no. 5 (2008): 1692–99; E. San Juan Jr., "Carlos Bulosan, Filipino Writer-Activist: Between a Time of Terror and the Time of Revolution," *CR: The New Centennial Review* 8, no. 1 (2008): 103–34; Dylan Rodríguez, *Suspended Apocalypse: White Supremacy, Genocide, and the Filipino Condition* (Minneapolis: University of Minnesota Press, 2010); Vernadette Vicuña Gonzalez, *Securing Paradise: Tourism and Militarism in Hawai'i and the Philippines* (Durham, N.C.: Duke University Press, 2013); Reynaldo Clemeña Ileto, *Knowledge and Pacification: On the U.S. Conquest and the Writing of Philippine History* (Quezon City, Philippines: Ateneo de Manila University, 2017); Neferti Xina M. Tadiar, "Challenges for Cultural Studies under the Rule of Global War," in *Filipino Studies: Palimpsests of Nation and Diaspora*, ed. Martin F. Manalansan IV and Augusto F. Espiritu (New York: New York University Press, 2016), 15–32; Rick Baldoz, *The Third Asiatic Invasion: Empire and Migration in Filipino America, 1898–1946* (New York: New York University Press, 2011); Dawn Bohulano Mabalon, *Little Manila Is in the Heart: The Making of the Filipina/o American Community in Stockton, California* (Durham, N.C.: Duke University Press, 2013); Leti Volpp, "American Mestizo: Filipinos and Antimiscegenation Laws in California," *UC Davis Law Review* 33, no. 795 (2000); Valerie Francisco and Robyn Magalit Rodriguez, "Globalization and Undocumented Migration: Examining the Politics of Emigration," in *Hidden*

Lives and Human Rights in the United States: Understanding the Controversies and Tragedies of Undocumented Immigration, ed. Lois Ann Lorentzen (Santa Barbara, Calif.: Praeger, 2014), 107–22; Anna Romina Guevarra, "The Legacy of Undesirability: Filipino TNTs, 'Irregular Migrants,' and 'Outlaws' in the US Cultural Imaginary," in *Filipino Studies: Palimpsests of Nation and Diaspora*, ed. Martin F. Manalansan IV and Augusto F. Espiritu (New York: New York University Press, 2016), 355–74.

3. Rodríguez, *Suspended Apocalypse*.

4. Rodríguez, *Suspended Apocalypse*, 100.

5. Rodríguez, *Suspended Apocalypse*, 140.

6. Fred Cordova, Dorothy Laigo Cordova, and Albert A. Acena, *Filipinos, Forgotten Asian Americans: A Pictorial Essay 1763–Circa 1963* (Dubuque, Iowa: Kendall/Hunt, 1983).

7. Nerissa S. Balce, *Body Parts of Empire, visual Abjection, Filipino Images and the American Archive* (Ann Arbor: University of Michigan Press, 2016).

8. Allan Punzalan Isaac, *American Tropics: Articulating Filipino America* (Minneapolis: University of Minnesota Press, 2006).

9. Moon-Ho Jung, "Empire," in *Keywords for Asian American Studies*, ed. Cathy J. Schlund-Vials, Linda Trinh Võ, and K. Scott Wong (New York: New York University Press, 2015).

10. Paul A. Kramer, "Empires, Exceptions, and Anglo-Saxons: Race and Rule between the British and United States Empires, 1880–1910," *The Journal of American History* (2002): 1315–53, and *The Blood of Government: Race, Empire, the United States, and the Philippines* (Chapel Hill: University of North Carolina Press, 2006).

11. Rodríguez, *Suspended Apocalypse*, 99.

12. Antonio T. Tiongson Jr., Edgardo V. Gutierrez, and Ricardo V. Gutierrez, eds., *Positively No Filipinos Allowed: Building Communities and Discourse* (Philadelphia: Temple University Press, 2006).

13. Theodore S. Gonzalves, *The Day the Dancers Stayed: Performing in the Filipino/American Diaspora* (Philadelphia: Temple University Press, 2010).

14. Ileto, *Knowledge and Pacification*.

15. Ileto, *Knowledge and Pacification*, 253.

16. Ileto, *Knowledge and Pacification*, 254.

17. Ileto, *Knowledge and Pacification*, 255.

18. Ileto, *Knowledge and Pacification*.

19. Ileto, *Knowledge and Pacification*, 257.

20. Ileto, *Knowledge and Pacification*.

21. Sarita Echavez See, *The Decolonized Eye: Filipino American Art and Performance* (Minneapolis: University of Minnesota Press, 2009).

22. See, *The Decolonized Eye*, xii.

23. See, *The Decolonized Eye*, xviii.

24. See, *The Decolonized Eye*, xviii.

25. See, *The Decolonized Eye*, 34.

26. See, *The Decolonized Eye*, 34.

27. See, *The Decolonized Eye*, 15–20, 24–32, 35.

28. Tadiar, "Challenges for Cultural Studies."

29. Jeremy Scahill, "Donald Trump and the Coming Fall of the American Empire," *The Intercept*, July 22, 2017, https://theintercept.com/2017/07/22/donald-trump-and-the-coming-fall-of-american-empire/; Tadiar, "Challenges for Cultural Studies," 18.

30. Tadiar, "Challenges for Cultural Studies," 18–19.

31. Tadiar, "Challenges for Cultural Studies," 15.

32. Tadiar, "Challenges for Cultural Studies," 16–17.

33. Masha Gessen, "The Unimaginable Reality of American Concentration Camps," *The New Yorker*, June 21, 2019, https://www.newyorker.com/news/our-columnists/the-unimaginable-reality-of-american-concentration-camps.

34. Omer Bartov, Doris Bergen, Andrea Orzoff, Timothy Snyder, and Anika Walke, "An Open Letter to the Director of the US Holocaust Memorial Museum," *The New York Review of Books* (2019), https://www.nybooks.com/daily/2019/07/01/an-open-letter-to-the-director-of-the-holocaust-memorial-museum/; Christopher R. Browning, "The Suffocation of Democracy," *The New York Review of Books* (2018), https://www.nybooks.com/articles/2018/10/25/suffocation-of-democracy/; Alberto Manguel, Maaza Mengiste, Valeria Luiselli, Margaret Atwood, and Colm Tóibin, "Our Concentration Camps: An Open Letter," *The New York Review of Books* (2018).

35. Tadiar, "Challenges for Cultural Studies," 17, 20.

36. Nick Cumming-Bruce, "U.N. Rights Council to Investigate Killings in Philippine Drug War," *The New York Times*, July 11, 2019, https://www.nytimes.com/2019/07/11/world/asia/philippines-duterte-killings-un.html?searchResultPosition=1.

37. Sheila S. Coronel, Clarissa David, Lorna Kalaw-Tirol, and Benjamin Pimentel, *The Drug Archive* (2018), https://drugarchive.ph/.

38. After Globalism Writing Group, "State Violence is Redundant," *Social Text* 36, no. 1 (2018): 65–71; Dahlia Simangan, "Is the Philippine 'War on Drugs' an Act of Genocide?" *Journal of Genocide Research* 20, no. 1 (2018): 68–89.

39. Dahlia Simangan and Jess Melvin, "'Destroy and Kill the Left': Duterte on Communist Insurgency in the Philippines with a Reflection on the Case of Suharto's Indonesia," *Journal of Genocide Research* 21, no. 2 (2019): 214–26.

40. James Fenton, "Murderous Manila: On the Night Shift," *The New York Review of Books* (2017), https://www.nybooks.com/articles/2017/02/09/murderous-manila-on-the-night-shift/.

41. *Duterte's Hell. Field of Vision*, directed by Aaron Goodman and Luis Liwanag (2017), *https://fieldofvision.org/duterte-s-hell*; *On the President's Orders*, directed by James Jones and Olivier Sarbil, Frontline PBS (2019); *The Night-crawlers*, directed by Alexander Mora, National Geographic Documentary Films (2019); *Aswang*, directed by Alyx Ayn Arumpac, Philippines (2020).

42. Josen Masangkay Diaz, "Following La Pieta: Toward a Transpacific Feminist Historiography of Philippine Authoritarianism," *Signs: Journal of Women in Culture and Society* 44, no. 3 (2019): 693–716.

43. Gina Apostol, *Insurrecto* (New York: Soho Press, 2018).

44. Apostol, *Insurrecto*, 69.

45. Apostol, *Insurrecto*, 13.

46. Apostol, *Insurrecto*, 18.

47. Apostol, *Insurrecto*, 79.

48. Apostol, *Insurrecto*, 81.

49. Apostol, *Insurrecto*, 50.

50. Apostol, *Insurrecto*, 159.

51. Apostol, *Insurrecto*, 160.

52. Apostol, *Insurrecto*, 161.

53. Apostol, *Insurrecto*, 292.

54. Apostol, *Insurrecto*, 91.

55. Apostol, *Insurrecto*, 67–68.

THREE

Empire: US States at the Intersection of Diaspora and Indigeneity

Dean Itsuji Saranillio

The United States is often perceived as existing within the neat and tidy spatial geographies of fifty US states. Yet, this perception constrains imaginative space, normalizing a web of colonial and imperial formations that make absent the over 574 federally recognized tribal nations as of 2020. This number is still not an accurate index of the different Native nations navigating settler governments.[1] The discourse of fifty states further obscures US territories in Guåhan (Guam), American Sāmoa, Puerto Rico, the US Virgin Islands, and the Commonwealth of the Northern Mariana Islands, and, importantly, the diverse movements for self-determination across these sites. It similarly obscures the estimated eight hundred military bases as of 2015, outside of the United States, that make it the largest militarized empire in world history.[2] Still, this is only a glimpse into how far-reaching the United States is outside of the territorial borders of fifty states, given its use of black sites, drone warfare, and the imperial legacies of overt and covert wars that have led to the overthrow of numerous countries.[3]

As we reach a critical point in this planet's history, global systems of US empire, militarism, and capitalism reveal themselves as accountable to abstract notions of profit and power, yet increasingly materialize in their capacity to destroy the resources and relations sustaining various forms of life. Given the massive scale and different ways of examining such a complex analytic, I wish to make three simple points about "empire." The first is to tie the "fail-forward" nature of capitalism to both US settler colonialism and empire formation. Secondly, I show how settler colonialism is self-erasing—in other words, that the US empire is a knowledge-making project that relied on propaganda campaigns that, for instance, during the Cold War made use of multiculturalism to make empire seem like the spreading of democracy as opposed to imperialism. And lastly, I wish to show that such formations are unsustainable as an economic system and a major cause of climate crisis. Many Native American and Pacific Islander scholars have traced the intricate relations of power necessary for US expansion to the devastating environmental degradation on their lands. This might serve as an impetus for Filipinx American studies, with its commitment to anti-imperial critique and migration onto such lands occupied by the United States, to place our fields and communities in relation to Indigenous movements, many of whom aim to create alternative futures from the settler state.

US empire emerges out of processes of settler colonialism and the violent work of replacing one landscape with another, various modes of life with another, various peoples with another, all of which necessitates a discursive regime—underpinned by self-referential juridical and military force—that normalizes occupation and makes sense of the genocide that this kind of replacement requires. Thus, while the Northwest Ordinance of 1787—a blueprint for expansion and the formation of US territories and states—is popularly imagined as foundational US national policy, Philip J. Deloria (Dakota) argues that it should instead be understood as US Indian policy.[4] The ordinance states that after achieving a large enough settler population (five thousand "free male inhabitants of age"), white settlers could proceed to organize and incorporate themselves as new territories. After proving capable of reaching a population of sixty thousand and drafting a state constitution, these territories could petition Congress to recognize them as newly formed states on equal footing with previous US states.

It is through the fictive creation of US states and property that such settlers are able to seize Native wealth. What is not mentioned in this seemingly smooth formation of US territories and states is the genocidal state violence used in the removal or containment of Native nations—frequently, with assistance from the military and territorial militias led by former generals turned territorial governors who were promised land in exchange for governance. The settlement of what would be called the state of Colorado led to the 1864 Sand Creek massacre committed by the Colorado US Volunteer Cavalry against two hundred unarmed Cheyenne and Arapaho. In California, Governor Peter Burnett, the first civilian governor replacing a military bureaucracy, argued to sustain an official policy of genocide in his 1851 message to the California legislature, arguing that the ongoing wars against California Indians "must continue to be waged between the races until the Indian becomes extinct."[5] US statehood operates as a knowledge-making spectacle that abates US occupation and settler colonialism by giving the illusion of settler-state permanence, yet requires constant recalibration to shore up ongoing processes of dispossession.

US imperialist ventures were often not the result of a strong nation swallowing weak and feeble island nations, but rather a result of a weakening US nation whose mode of production—capitalism—was increasingly unsustainable without enacting a more aggressive policy of imperialism. I have argued elsewhere that if we think of forms of white supremacy, such as settler colonialism and capitalism, as emerging from positions of weakness, not strength, we can gain a more accurate understanding of the nature of US empire.[6] As such, settler colonialism "fails forward" into its various imperial formations.[7] This framing highlights how the present failures of capitalism have long been imagined to be resolved through settler futures. Political thinkers in Europe imagined that the establishment of white settler colonies, particularly in North America, would resolve the poverty that capitalism produced in Europe.[8] Thus, European civil society was understood to be neither stable nor sustainable without relying on the external establishment of settler colonies.

In this way, the failures of capitalism are most apparent from the colonies rather than the imperial metropoles. Such crises, caused by underconsumption and overproduction, reoccurred long after the initial colonization schemes of Europe. In 1893, the same time that Frederick Jackson Turner argued that the US frontier was settled, an economic depression led to mass-scale labor unrest throughout the United States. Thus, US president Benjamin Harrison's administration initiated a foreign policy that Walter

LaFeber calls "depression diplomacy," targeting colonies for access to markets to alleviate a glut of industrial goods.[9] It was this policy that enabled the US military-backed coup of the Hawaiian nation in 1893. Such imperial ventures were accompanied by shifting ideas of race propagated by Smithsonian anthropologists who argued that there remained three "modern types of savagery" in the world: Americans (Native Americans), Negroids, and the Malayo-Polynesians.[10] The collapsing of Malay and Polynesians in 1893 clears the way for future US imperial projects. Again, more land and markets were sought after by the US government, which led to the violent occupation of different island nations in the late 1890s—the Philippines, Hawai'i, Guåhan, American Sāmoa, Puerto Rico, Cuba, the US Virgin Islands—and their incorporation into the United States as stepping-stones to larger markets as a means to alleviate such economic and political crises. E. San Juan Jr. argues that for these reasons: "The colonized 'ward' from 'las islas Filipinas' occupies a space between the indigenous Indian and the 'inscrutable Oriental.'"[11]

While the fail-forward pattern of capitalism often relies on colonial and imperial dispossession to resolve economic crises, such acts of state violence have a theatrical and discursive component to them. These forms are important elements in the affective work of settler statecraft.[12] Using tactics of theatricality and futurity, the settler state both imagines and propagandizes itself as a more deserving power, which seemingly absolves the settler state and its citizens from present accountability. Advertising strategies utilize "abstraction" to produce a place or state of being that escapes from the present toward an imagined future where consumers are promised things that they will have, or lifestyles they can take part in.[13] Thus, non-Native subjectivities, though widely diverse, are often both in a state of incompletion and in transition to their future selves, escaping to a future place seemingly devoid of imperial violence and difficulties.

As a result of the presidency of Donald Trump, white supremacy has become more pronounced, illuminating why, more than ever, we need a politics other than liberalism. Liberal multiculturalism has often worked in tandem with white supremacy, allowing for forms of racism, settler colonialism, and militarism to be insulated from large movements seeking their end. Indeed, the seemingly smooth transition from white supremacy to liberal multiculturalism functions to disavow how white supremacists used liberal multiculturalism as a means to achieve global hegemony, facilitating the structural necessity for violent extractive projects to continue at a time when internationalist movements were pursuing labor rights and decolonization.

To make this clearer, we might look to the specific way that racial diversity was used to the benefit of US global hegemony during the Cold War. For the majority of the first half of the twentieth century, Congress deemed Hawai'i unqualified for US statehood because it was considered a largely nonwhite territory. In order to make Hawai'i statehood more attractive in the eyes of Congress, proponents of statehood began to use Hawai'i's racial diversity in the service of Cold War politics. In the post–World War II moment, when decolonization was transforming an international order, Cold Warrior ideologues realized that Hawai'i's multiracial population had ideological value in winning the "hearts and minds" of newly decolonized nations—an opinion campaign developed by the "father of public relations" Edward L. Bernays.[14] This US liberal multicultural discourse—articulated through a multicultural "nation of immigrants" narration—helped achieve seemingly permanent control of Hawai'i through statehood while creating a multicultural image of the United States that facilitated the establishment and maintenance of US military bases throughout much of Asia and the Pacific.[15]

Not only is capitalism unsustainable as an economic system but we are currently in a critical moment where the planet itself can no longer sustain such human-centered ways of living. Extreme weather patterns, rising sea levels, the warming of the planet, nonhuman extinctions, and even zoonotic pandemics caused by viruses jumping from one species to another (as may have happened with COVID-19), all tell us that the fail-forward pattern of settler colonialism and capitalism has hit a limit, even as arguments for the colonization of other planets proliferate.[16] This calls for a critical engagement with the past and present as a means to produce alternative futures to the settler state.

Edward W. Said writes that the colonial project of settlers seeks to "cancel and transcend an actual reality . . . by means of a future wish—that the land be empty for development by a more deserving power."[17] Such temporal and spatial tactics set the ideological conditions for capitalism and its accompanying environmental degradation via ongoing forms of primitive accumulation—divorcing Native peoples from the means of production and the "material conditions of resistance"—and its seemingly permanent structure, a kind of settler accumulation by Native dispossession. As Noenoe K. Silva and Jonathan Goldberg-Hiller point out, a key difference between Western and Indigenous notions of sovereignty is that Indigenous epistemologies describe the human and nonhuman divide not as a binary, but as interdependent familial relations.[18] As such, the United States has often sought to make Native peoples vulnerable by disrupting those familial relations through the elimination of one or more sets of human-to-nonhuman relations. This is a tactic of Native dispossession, whether it is targeting *kalo* (taro) in Hawai'i through water expropriation; the US Army's elimination of the buffalo; the genetic modification of corn, wild rice, taro, and salmon in the Pacific Northwest; or military tactics that target the elimination of food sources and ecosystems, as was done in the Philippine-American War, the Korean War, and the Vietnam War—the latter two using herbicides such as Agent Orange.

Our present moment *is* the afterlife of this "future wish" that has targeted nonhumans for elimination to make the "material conditions of resistance" impossible, to literally produce so-called "domestic dependent nations" or "underdeveloped nations." In the death of these nonhuman relations is the continual birth and rebirth of capitalism, the particular mode of production that has evolved to set the current environmental conditions of climate crisis. Given this, the renewal and protection of Native relationality to nonhumans and land can move us toward a more sustainable, healthy, and equitable system for all currently vulnerable than can ever be imagined in this current system.

When we recognize that empire relies on imperialist expansion to respond to the failures of capitalism, we can also identify such *problems* as *possibilities* for replacement. In different colonial situations, historical examples of groups liberating themselves from being used as agents in a system of colonial violence help illustrate alternative ways of being under conditions of occupation.[19] During the Philippine-American War, for instance, many Black soldiers of the Twenty-Fourth Infantry Colored Regiment who had been deployed to the Philippines defected from the US military to fight alongside Filipinx "insurgents."[20] Critical Filipinx scholar Nerissa S. Balce traces the work of Apolinario Mabini, who lost the use of both legs to polio at the start of the war and was a critical intellectual during the Philippine Revolution against both Spain and the United States. Mabini wrote letters addressed specifically "To the American Colored Soldier" that were dropped in villages that US soldiers were passing through. Mabini, who was eventually captured and exiled to Guåhan, asked Black soldiers to consider fighting on the side of Filipinxs: "You must consider your situation and your history, and take charge that the blood of Sam Hose proclaims vengeance." At the time that the Twenty-Fourth Infantry were deployed to the Philippines, Sam Hose had been violently lynched in Georgia in April of 1899. What's more, prior to arriving in the Philippines, members of the Twenty-Fourth Infantry Regiment caused a race riot in Tampa, Florida, after they saved the life of a young Black boy who had been forced to hold a can atop his head as target practice for white soldiers.[21] Critical ethnic studies scholar Dylan Rodríguez argues that through complex political and creative acts, those whose every day is constituted by the genealogies of genocide are able to reckon and create within this genealogy by embracing the impasse between themselves and a "racially genocidal state."[22] This is to say that under conditions of genocide, liberation is not to reform the state from corruption but, rather, to urgently liberate oneself from the state.

Refusal to participate in such colonial violence is a form of affinity-based politics that creatively orchestrates interdependency. Black soldiers turned themselves into "fugitives" and identified their life chances as better served in affinity with those who were also the targets of a genocidal state. In this way, learning how one is being used and then refusing to be used as such in a system of violence is a form of radical affinity and mutuality. This tactic could inform Filipinx migration onto Native lands currently occupied by the United States, living in the assemblage of multiple genocides and a continued historical moment when Native people in struggle call on others to defect and support their movement to build alternatives to US empire.

Michi Saagiig Nishnaabeg storyteller, scholar, and activist Leanne Simpson argues that "Indigenous resurgence, in its most radical form, is nation building, not nation-state building, but nation building, again, in the context of grounded normativity by centering, amplifying, animating, and actualizing the processes of grounded normativity as flight paths or fugitive escapes from the violences of settler colonialism."[23] Indigenous resurgence within diverse contexts for grounded normativity shows how the routes and roots of diaspora and indigeneity can be thought through in "reciprocal relationship." Indeed, Pohnpeian and Filipinx scholar Vicente M. Diaz argues that Native and non-Native relationships should be theorized in a manner similar to the fluid and relational dynamics of the ocean. Such possible forms of kinship can be articulated not in opposition, but in mutual interdependence. Indeed, Indigenous resurgence may serve as "flight paths or fugitive escapes" from the fail-forward violence of settler colonialism, as the search for alternatives to the current unsustainable system may bring us closer together as kin.

NOTES

1. Vine Deloria Jr. and Clifford M. Lytle, *The Nations Within: The Past and Future of American Indian Sovereignty* (New York: Pantheon Books, 1984).

2. Chalmers Johnson, *The Sorrows of Empire: Militarism, Secrecy, and the End of the Republic* (New York: Metropolitan Books, 2005), 4; David Vine, "The United States Probably Has More Foreign Military Bases Than Any Other People, Nation, or Empire in History," *The Nation*, September 14, 2015.

3. Stephen Kinzer, *Overthrow: America's Century of Regime Change from Hawaii to Iraq* (New York: Henry Holt and Company, 2006).

4. Suzan Shown Harjo, "American Indian Land and American Empire: An Interview with Philip J. Deloria," in *Nation to Nation: Treaties between the United States and American Indian Nations*, ed. Suzan Shown Harjo (New York: National Museum of the American Indian, 2014), 12–13.

5. Haunani-Kay Trask, "The Color of Violence," in *Color of Violence: The INCITE! Anthology* (Cambridge, Mass.: South End Press, 2006), 82; see also Brendan C. Lindsay, *Murder State: California's Native American Genocide, 1846–1873* (Lincoln: University of Nebraska Press, 2012); David E. Stannard, *American Holocaust: Columbus and the Conquest of the New World* (New York: Oxford University Press, 1992), 144.

6. Dean Itsuji Saranillio, *Unsustainable Empire: Alternative Histories of Hawai'i Statehood* (Durham, N.C.: Duke University Press, 2018).

7. See Rosa Luxemburg, *The Accumulation of Capital*, trans. Agnes Schwarzschild (New York: Routledge, 2003), xxxv, 328–65; Jamie Peck, *Constructions of Neoliberal Reason* (Oxford: Oxford University Press, 2010).

8. Gabriel Paquette, "Colonies and Empire in the Political Thought of Hegel and Marx," in *Empire and Modern Political Thought*, ed. Sankar Muthu, 292–323 (New York: Cambridge University Press, 2014); Georg Wilhelm Friedrich Hegel, *Elements of the Philosophy of Right*, ed. Allen W. Wood (Cambridge: Cambridge University Press, 1991); Edward Gibbon Wakefield,

England and America: A Comparison of the Social and Political State of Both Nations (London: W. Nicol, 1833); Wakefield, *A Letter from Sydney: The Principal Town of Australasia, Together with the Outline of a System of Colonization* (London: Joseph Cross, 1829); Wakefield, *A View of the Art of Colonization: In Letters between a Statesman and a Colonist* (Oxford: Clarendon Press, 1849).

9. Walter LaFeber, *The New Empire: An Interpretation of American Expansion, 1860–1898*, 35th anniversary ed. (Ithaca, N.Y.: Cornell University Press, [1963] 1993), 19.

10. Robert W. Rydell, *All the World's a Fair: Visions of Empire at American International Expositions, 1876–1916* (Chicago: University of Chicago Press, 1984), 59–60.

11. E. San Juan Jr., *After Postcolonialism: Remapping Philippines-United States Confrontations* (Boston: Rowman & Littlefield Publishers, Inc., 2000), 3.

12. Ann Laura Stoler, "Affective States," in *A Companion to Anthropology of Politics*, ed. David Nugent and Joan Vincent (Malden: Blackwell, 2004), 4–20.

13. Marita Sturken and Lisa Cartwright, *Practices of Looking: An Introduction to Visual Culture* (Oxford: Oxford University Press, 2003), 189.

14. Edward L. Bernays, "Hawaii—The Almost Perfect State?," *New Leader*, November 20, 1950; "Bernays Gives Analysis of Hawaii Community," *Hawaii Chinese Journal*, August 17, 1950; Dean Itsuji Saranillio, "Colliding Histories: Hawai'i Statehood at the Intersection of Asians 'Ineligible to Citizenship' and Hawaiians 'Unfit for Self-Government,'" *Journal of Asian American Studies* 13, no. 3 (October 2010): 283–309.

15. Christina Klein, *Cold War Orientalism: Asia in the Middlebrow Imagination, 1944–1961* (Berkeley: University of California Press, 2003), 250–51.

16. See Walden Bello, Herbert Docena, Marissa de Guzman, and Marylou Malig, *The Anti-Development State: The Political-Economy of Permanent Crisis in the Philippines* (London: Zed Books, 2006).

17. Edward W. Said, *The Question of Palestine* (New York: Vintage, 1972), 9.

18. Tasha Hubbard, "Buffalo Genocide in Nineteenth-Century North America: 'Kill, Skin, and Sell,'" in *Colonial Genocide in Indigenous North America*, ed. Alexander Laban Hinton, Andrew Woolford, and Jeff Benvenuto, 292–305 (Durham, N.C.: Duke University Press, 2014).

19. Candace Fujikane, "Asian American Critique and Moana Nui 2011," *Inter-Asia Cultural Studies* (2012), 4.

20. Patricio N. Abinales, *Making Mindanao: Cotabato and Davao in the Formation of the Philippine Nation-State* (Quezon City, Philippines: Ateneo de Manila University Press, 2000); Rene G. Ontal, "Fagen and Other Ghosts: African-Americans and the Philippine-American War," in *Vestiges of War: The Philippine-American War and the Aftermath of an Imperial Dream, 1899–1999* (New York: New York University Press, 2002), 118–33.

21. Nerissa S. Balce, "Filipino Bodies, Lynching and the Language of Empire," in *Positively No Filipinos Allowed: Building Communities and Discourse*, ed. Antonio T. Tiongson Jr., Ed Gutierrez, and Rick Gutierrez (Philadelphia: Temple University Press, 2006), 43–60.

22. Dylan Rodríguez, "Inhabiting the Impasse: Racial / Racial-Colonial Power, Genocide Poetics, and the Logic of Evisceration," *Social Text* 33, no. 3 (124) (2015): 33.

23. Leanne Betasamosake Simpson, "Indigenous Resurgence and Co-resistance," *Critical Ethnic Studies* 2, no. 2 (Fall 2016): 22.

FOUR

The Persistence of War through Migration

Cynthia Marasigan

Key historical trajectories unveiled in Filipinx American studies demonstrate that the violence of war reverberates through migrations. In particular, the movement of Filipinx bodies, fraught philosophies, and tangible materials has regenerated the ideological, militarized, and economic work of war, amid entanglements of variously colonized and noncolonized people of color navigating the US empire. In using the construct "migration," or the movement from one location to another, and migration's derivatives ("migrant," "migratory"), scholars of Filipinx American studies have problematized nation-state borders, broadened purviews of racialized geographies, and demonstrated why and how Filipinx and Filipinx Americans have circulated through a diaspora webbed in a US empire operated by ideologies and practices of white supremacy. With migration as a focal point of inquiry, scholars have accentuated the particularity of and diversity among moving Filipinx bodies across space and time, and have distinguished between and relationally situated the migration of Filipinxs, Asians, and other people of color, including those historically impacted by transitions from Spanish to American empires. When viewing "migration" through the prism of "war," the focus of "migration" redirects toward the origins and catalysts of migration; the prolonging of war through migration; and, especially for Filipinx American studies, migration and war as two intertwined mechanisms offering moments of contingency, when actors can rupture, negotiate, or strengthen the US empire's apparatus. Here, meanings of war are dynamic, given varied contestations over people, labor, land, and resources, and can overlap or fluctuate between wars of direct military clashes and aggressions (e.g., the Philippine-American War, World Wars I and II, the Cold War, the War on Terror) and wars with more than or less direct military hostilities or non-military forms of political, economic, or social violence (e.g., race wars, trade wars, war on drugs).

This essay explores the profound persistence of the Philippine-American War via multiple, overlapping Filipinx and other relevant migrations in the early twentieth century, considering the US empire's intra-imperial dynamics and the historical intersections among colonized and noncolonized people of color.[1] This war, resulting in over one million Filipinx deaths and 4,200 American deaths, carried on after President Roosevelt disputably declared the official "end" of the "insurrection" in July 1902.[2] The war endured not only through military warfare and Filipinx resistance, but also through evolving racial violence via the perpetual deferment of political sovereignty, the psychological warfare of colonial education, and as I emphasize here, Filipinx migrations. These Filipinx migrations converged with other moving bodies impacted by war, capitalism, colonization, and slavery. This essay examines how intra-imperial dynamics, including multiple sites within an empire (e.g., the Philippines, Puerto Rico, Guåhan [Guam], Hawai'i), facilitated "circuits of exchange and movement, constituted by the flow of goods, people, and ideas," as Julian Go has stressed;[3] it also takes into account both colonized (Filipinxs, Chamorros, Puerto Ricans, etc.) and noncolonized peoples of color (African Americans, Chinese, etc.). Moon-Kie Jung reminds us, "In an empire-state, racial domination of colonized peoples does not happen in isolation from that of noncolonized peoples, and vice versa. Though qualitatively different, they are intimately and intricately linked."[4]

The first section of this essay shows how migrations during the Philippine-American War widened and utilized broad circuits of US empire, including

US soldiers carrying ideologies and prior experiences of American expansion and Jim Crow America, as well as Filipinx "nationals" permitted to traverse the empire per the US Supreme Court's Insular Cases. The second section examines how the work of Filipinx collaborators and the psychological warfare of colonial education established during the Philippine-American War persisted through the migration of pensionados studying in American universities and Filipinxs displayed as human exhibits at the 1904 St. Louis World's Fair. The third section illustrates how American economic and military motivations driving the Philippine-American War continued via the migration of Filipinx laborers to the territory of Hawai'i, Filipinx US Navy men to military sites of an increasingly global US empire, and Filipinx seasonal laborers moving through California, the Pacific Northwest, and Alaska.

Circuits of US Empire during the Philippine-American War

During the Philippine-American War, one hundred twenty-five thousand American soldiers deployed to the Philippines and expanded the US empire's circuits, which geographically and figuratively connected multiple sites of American racial violence. White military officers and men, backed by a whopping $400 million wartime investment by the US government as well as the guise of state-endorsed "Benevolent Assimilation,"[5] brought with them ideologies of Social Darwinism and the "White Man's burden" to civilize Filipinxs. Many carried to the Philippines their baggage from fighting against Native Americans and alongside Cubans, both deemed racially inferior and politically incapable. Such attitudes and experiences informed soldiers serving in an archipelago unfamiliar to Americans even at the highest government and military positions. As I demonstrate elsewhere, six thousand African American soldiers served in the war, and fresh memories of Jim Crow and lynching in America tainted and motivated their desire for full citizenship rights through military service, which came at the expense of fighting against Filipinxs who sought independence and were regularly deemed "niggers" by white soldiers.[6] Meanwhile, political cartoons in *Harper's Weekly*, *Puck*, and other publications widely distributed in the United States comparatively portrayed colonized and noncolonized peoples of color in varying levels of incompetency, savagery, and infantilism.[7] Photographs and stereo-cards, as Nerissa S. Balce shows, also disseminated visual representations of "white American imperial masculinity," of death, which minimized Filipinx suffering and celebrated American victory, and of "docility," which erased American atrocities and attested to Filipinxs in need of uplift.[8]

During the war, the US Supreme Court monitored circuits of US empire by setting the terms of migration for Filipinxs, and in its deliberations over Puerto Rico after the Spanish-American War, directly tied Filipinx migration to the Philippines' "unincorporated" territory status, to American capitalist expansion, and to Filipinxs' exclusion from the American body politic. In *Downes v. Bidwell* (1901), the first of a series of Insular Cases, the US Supreme Court declared that Puerto Rico, and by extension the Philippines and Guåhan, constituted "unincorporated" territories that "belonged to but were not part of the United States," and were "foreign in a domestic sense." Allan Punzalan Isaac argues that the US government legalized "a dual mandate of containment and expansion," where "the islands' exclusion was based on cultural difference," and that "their ambiguous tethering to the U.S. polity was based on economic demand."[9] This "unincorporated" designation allowed the US to treat Puerto Rico as domestic for revenue purposes and to pursue economic aspirations that propelled the Philippine-American War—namely, trade access to China, natural resources such as sugar and abaca, and overseas markets given American overproduction and industrialization. The Court classified Filipinxs, Puerto Ricans, and Chamorros of "unincorporated" territories as "non-citizen nationals" who could migrate in unlimited numbers to the metropole and to other parts of the US empire. Such migration proved the United States was not exceptional but rather resembled other empires that permitted such movement—for example, the British allowing Indian migration to Canada. Importantly, Isaac recognizes the "problematic" concept of "immigration," as Filipinxs "did not necessarily move through borders, but rather, borders continually enfolded them."[10] Further mapping racialized geographies, the Insular Cases codified inequality by ruling "the Constitution did not follow the flag," and Filipinxs, Puerto Ricans, and Chamorros were granted only "fundamental" rights rather than full Constitutional rights.

The US Supreme Court's legal interpretations of incorporation and separation that set the parameters of Filipinx migration were likely influenced by prior legislation and judicial decisions that unjustly impacted Native Hawaiians, Native Americans, and African Americans. For example, Hawaiʻi proved a "deviant case" as it was an "incorporated" territory mandated for eventual statehood per the 1787 Northwest Ordinance. According to Jung, "because U.S. white supremacy was already and sufficiently guaranteed" by white settlers who dominated Hawaiʻi's economy and politics, "Hawaiʻi was incorporated while other overseas territories were not."[11] *Cherokee Nation v. Georgia* (1831)—decided soon after the 1830 Indian Removal Act that displaced Native Americans and forced them into resettlement—resolved that the Cherokee did not constitute a "foreign state" but rather a "domestic dependent nation," rendering the people not citizens nor aliens but as unrepresentable "wards." Furthermore, as Isaac notes, the US Supreme Court that justified racial segregation as "separate but equal" in the 1896 *Plessy v. Ferguson* case was the same court that ruled in the first Insular Case of *Downes v. Bidwell*, which determined "how to legalize and constitute separate (but certainly not equal) *national* entities in relation to the American polity."[12]

Wartime Collaboration, Colonial Education, and Migration

During the Philippine-American War, the US military's "pacification" campaigns partly depended upon the cooperation of Filipinx collaborators as well as the psychological warfare of American colonial education, and both were sustained after the war's "official" end via early Filipinx migrations to the United States. While at war, not only did the US military use Filipinxs as guides, spies, laborers, and office holders in an attempt to confront revolutionary guerrilla warfare, but also American administrators welcomed alliances with former *ilustrados* who launched the Federalista Party in late 1900 and who found attractive American promises of socio-economic security and colonial government positions. Beginning in 1903, pensionados studying in the United States extended such collusion. The pensionado program allowed government-sponsored Filipinx students from elite backgrounds to enroll in American universities for the purpose of holding colonial leadership positions upon graduation and return to the Philippines. This program sought to advance the work of wartime collaborators; despite the US military inflicting atrocities resulting in over one million Filipinx deaths, Americans still needed the assistance of Filipinx elites to quell the ongoing resistance and to establish more firmly colonial rule.

Pensionados embodied extensions of colonial education in the Philippines that furthered the US military's "pacification" objectives and that drew from educational curricula aimed at maintaining the subordination of other students of color—namely, African Americans, Native Americans, and Native Hawaiians. In 1901, the Philippine Commission established the Bureau of Education to stress primary education and English as the language of instruction, with Major General Arthur MacArthur regarding school appropriations "exclusively as an adjunct to military operations, calculated to pacify the people."[13] With American soldiers and later American civilians such as the Thomasites teaching in primary schools, Filipinx schoolchildren would learn to become "self-regulating subjects that would mark the new American world order as a constellation of autonomous, liberal democracies," according to Kimberly Alidio.[14] Educational administrators modeled the industrial education curriculum in the Philippines after the Hampton Normal and Agricultural Institute, Tuskegee Normal and Industrial Institute, and Carlisle Indian Industrial School that educated African American and Native American students and that, in turn, drew from public schools established by missionaries in Hawai'i. As Funie Hsu and Gary Y. Okihiro have shown, such "miseducation" advanced "schooling for subservience" for both colonized and noncolonized peoples of color in America's empire, steering boys toward manual labor and girls toward domestic work.[15] While Filipinx students in the Philippines learned to fulfill such subordinate roles, Filipinx pensionados studied at American institutions such as the University of Michigan, Cornell University, and Harvard University. Although pensionados, upon return to the Philippines, held leadership positions in politics, education, and business, they still occupied subservient roles under American colonial administrators and agents. Additionally, pensionados attested to the symbol of America as a land of opportunity by the time self-supporting students arrived in the United States in the 1920s.[16] Pensionados thereby sustained the wartime goals of maintaining elite collaborators and educating future generations of Filipinx colonial subjects who would accept American sovereignty.

In an extension of wartime collaboration and colonial education, 1,100 Filipinxs migrated to St. Louis, Missouri, to serve as human exhibits in the 1904 St. Louis World's Fair, simultaneously justifying and erasing the violence of the Philippine-American War to audiences curious about America's newest colonial subjects. Some Filipinxs migrated under duress or deception, and others willingly traveled to gain prestige or money. Forced or not forced to collaborate, all were sent by the Philippine Commission to legitimize America's civilizing mission in the Philippines. Whereas US Secretary of War William Howard Taft claimed he wanted the Filipinxs in St. Louis to learn about America firsthand, fair visitors did not have to travel to the Philippines to learn about Filipinxs, nor to other places problematically represented at the exposition. The fair acted as the world's university and "brought the world to Americans."[17] Lucy Mae San Pablo Burns argues that in this US-Philippine "'contact zone,' a complex terrain of interaction between American patrons and Filipino/a performers," Filipinxs acted as living displays in "brownface performances."[18] They purportedly exhibited a linear evolutionary scale from "savage" to "civilized," and were classified by scientists who implemented theories of racial progress as well as categories constructed in the 1903 American-administered census in the Philippines. To fairgoers, "Non-Christian tribes" such as Igorots, Moros, and Negritos portrayed "savage" Natives, with dog-eating and G-string-clad Igorots as the most popular and sensationalized fair spectacle. Fair advertisements described the Visayans as Christians "representing the higher type of lower class civilization,"[19] while the Philippine Constabulary and Philippine Scouts, or Filipinx policemen and soldiers, respectively, symbolized the disciplined products of American rule. Interestingly, Walter Loving, the conductor of the Philippine Constabulary Band and an African American veteran of the Philippine-American War, disrupted colonial scripts that claimed only whites could uplift Filipinxs. Loving, as I discuss elsewhere, also sought to prove Black racial uplift during this Jim Crow era, but at the cost of promoting the Philippine exhibit's imperialist vision and its display portraying Filipinxs from their "savage" to "civilized" states.[20] Of this spectrum, Benito M. Vergara Jr. argues that the "deliberate juxtaposition of extremes made visible . . . the seemingly contradictory conditions of representation of the civilizing process: inferiority and improvement."[21] Such conditions of inferiority and improvement reprised racial ideologies that identified Filipinxs as disunified savages incapable of self-government and in need of American uplift during and since the Philippine-American War.

The enormous Philippine Reservation at the St. Louis World's Fair exhibited America's massive investment to legitimize the civilizing mission begun during the Philippine-American War; it compared with other fair exhibits that demeaned and displayed other people of color, and it contrasted with American exhibits affirming the United States at the forefront of technology, science, and culture. The Philippine Reservation spanned forty-seven acres, included nearly one hundred structures, housed seventy-five thousand catalogued exhibits, and cost the Philippine government over $1.2 million and the World's Fair $200,000.[22] As fair organizers displayed brown colonial subjects from the Philippines, the United States boasted its modernity through grandiose buildings dedicated to machinery, manufactures, transportation, and other indicators of progress, juxtaposing yet surpassing the advancements displayed by nations such as Britain, Germany, and Japan. American exhibits further claimed white dominance over Native Americans, "Pygmies" from Africa, "Patagonian giants" from Argentina, and other nonwhites portrayed as racially inferior spectacles in ethnological exhibits. Like other colonizers that had hosted world's fairs, such as the 1900 World's Fair in Paris that exhibited French colonies in Africa, Americans in St. Louis showed off the expanding US empire with displays of the Philippines, Cuba, Alaska and "Indian Territory." Therefore, the Filipinxs at the fair, including at least some forced into collaboration, served as the subjects of colonial education for audiences beyond the Philippines and for fairgoers who would learn to rationalize the Philippine-American War and support American colonial projects.

Labor, Militarism, and Migrations

While wartime collaboration and colonial education endured via Filipinx migrations, the economic and military motivations that drove the Philippine-American War and the US empire at large also persisted via Filipinx migrations. In Hawai'i, another contested site of US empire, American planters sought exploitable laborers to work on sugar and other cash-crop plantations, whereas in the Philippines, Filipinx small farmers bore the brunt of American investments in the archipelago's unindustrialized export economy since the Philippine-American War. In both Hawai'i and the Philippines,

American businessmen sought overseas markets and stopovers to Asian trade networks. Roderick N. Labrador has shown that the history of Filipinxs in Hawai'i must be understood "within the context of capitalist expansion in the United States and the development of U.S. agribusiness interests in the Philippines that effectively stifled the growth of Philippine agricultural production and industrialization."[23] While many Filipinxs in the Philippines economically suffered from landlessness, tenancy, and poverty, about seventy thousand *sakadas* (Filipinx contract laborers) migrated to Hawai'i from 1906 to the late 1920s, and topped one hundred thousand by the mid-1940s. Their plantation work in Hawai'i was propelled by the aforementioned economic dislocations during and after the Philippine-American War and was enabled by American economic and political interests in Hawai'i. Following the Native Hawaiians' massive population collapse due to contact with diseased Westerners, Filipinx migrants joined other Asians who served as the major source of plantation laborers in Hawai'i. In 1893, haole businessmen, descendants of missionaries, and the US minister, in collusion with the US Navy, overthrew Queen Lili'uokalani despite her protests to what US president Grover Cleveland acknowledged as an "Act of War." Cleveland's withdrawal of an annexation treaty proved inconsequential when, under US president William McKinley, the United States annexed Hawai'i in 1898 under the nonbinding Newlands Resolution and declared Hawai'i an incorporated territory with the Organic Act of 1900. Filipinx labor migration to Hawai'i was facilitated by such US interventions, and was bolstered by the growing labor activism of Japanese laborers there.

Filipinxs, along with Chinese, Japanese, Korean, and Puerto Ricans also historically impacted by war and military aggression, partook in settler colonialism in Hawai'i. According to Dean Saranillio, settler colonialism "disrupts notions that minorities who are racially oppressed are incapable of simultaneously participating in the colonial oppression of Native Hawaiians." Filipinxs were effectively settlers "in a colonized nation where the Indigenous peoples do not possess their human right to self-determination."[24] Filipinx migration to Hawai'i intersected with those of Chinese migrants to Hawai'i following the first Opium Wars with the British in 1839–42, Japanese migrants affected by US gunboat diplomacy in Japan especially after 1853, and Korean migrants torn from the 1895 Sino-Japanese War in Korea and subsequent Japanese colonization in 1910. Filipinx migrations to Hawai'i also coincided with those from Puerto Rico. The US Supreme Court declared Puerto Rico an "unincorporated" territory following the Spanish-American War, thereby sanctioning the militarization of the island and Puerto Ricans' movement to Hawai'i as "non-citizen nationals." JoAnna Poblete demonstrates that, without government representatives, Puerto Ricans and Filipinxs in Hawai'i relied on community leaders to navigate labor issues and grievances, given their position as "intra-colonial laborers" and as "colonized people in a second colonized place," Hawai'i.[25] Indeed, Filipinx, other Asian, and Puerto Rican plantation laborers in Hawai'i faced grueling work, abusive lunas, low wages, and poor working conditions. Candace Fujikane and Jonathan Y. Okamura have shown that even with such systemic racism on the plantations, and even with such histories of war and colonization, Filipinx, Asian, and Puerto Rican laborers and their descendants lived and still live as settlers in the US settler state of Hawai'i, and must be distinguished from Native Hawaiians whose population collapse, land dispossession, and fight for sovereignty continues to this day.[26]

As the US empire kept building its economic foundations at the turn of the nineteenth century, it also incorporated Filipinxs into its military apparatus, whether as soldiers and policemen during the Philippine-American War, or afterward as US Navy men migrating to other sites spanning the US empire's reach. In 1901, following the lead of other colonizers who enlisted colonial subjects of color, the Philippine Commission established the Philippine Constabulary as the Native police force, and the US Army incorporated Philippine Scouts into this military branch by establishing ethnically and linguistically segregated companies (e.g., companies of Macabebes, Tagalogs, Ilocanos). White officers led both institutions of Filipinx policemen and soldiers, who helped quell the prolonged resistance to US rule in the Philippines while American soldiers returned home. Filipinxs recruited from American military bases in the Philippines established during and after the war served in the US Navy, with Filipinx enlistments peaking at six thousand during World War I. As did Filipinx constables and scouts, these Filipinx US Navy men aided American wars and military occupations, broadened the roles of Filipinxs in the US military apparatus after the Philippine-American War, and moved within a widening US empire that increasingly intervened politically and militarily in numerous nations across the globe.

Filipinx US Navy men's status as "nationals," derived from the Philippine-American War, coincided with the second-class, forced, or denied citizenship for other people of color, who were also segregated or subordinated to low positions in the US military. While the US Army segregated both African American regiments and Philippine Scouts from white soldiers, the US Navy was formally racially integrated yet relegated both Filipinxs and African Americans to steward and mess attendant ranks.[27] Filipinx navy men's enlistment during World War I coincided with the 1917 Jones Act that granted citizenship to Puerto Ricans and thereby imposed draft eligibility on Puerto Ricans. Comparatively, the Naturalization Act of May 9, 1918, offered naturalized citizenship to "any alien" who served in the US armed forces during World War I, yet judges inconsistently and arbitrarily bestowed citizenship to Chinese, Japanese, and Indian soldiers. However, the Act "explicitly granted the privilege of naturalization to Filipinos who served in the U.S. Navy or Marine Corps."[28] The 1925 *Toyota v. United States* case clarified that Asian veterans of World War I did not meet the racial prerequisites for naturalized citizenship, but specified that "native-born Filipino servicemen" could indeed naturalize as American citizens.[29] Ten years later, the 1935 Nye-Lea Act offered naturalized citizenship to other Asian veterans of World War I, despite the preservation of official racial prerequisites for nonveteran Asians.[30]

Filipinx laborers, enabled by their "national" status derived from the Philippine-American War, also migrated to multiple parts of the United States in the 1920s and 1930s, especially after the immigration restriction or exclusion of other Asians, and alongside the possible shortage of Mexican laborers likewise impacted by colonial violence and US wars. Predominantly young Filipinx males worked in migratory, seasonal labor circuits. They found employment in agricultural labor in California, in the salmon canneries of Alaska, in other fish-processing industries in the Pacific Northwest, and in domestic and service work in urban areas such as Seattle, San Francisco, and Los Angeles. As "nationals," Filipinxs were exempt from legal restrictions on Asian immigration, including the 1917 Immigration Act's Asiatic Barred Zone and the 1924 Immigration Act's denial of entry to those ineligible for citizenship. In addition, growers, concerned about the availability of Mexican labor given visa fees, taxes, literacy tests, and the 1924-mandated Border Patrol, turned to Filipinxs for agricultural labor.[31] Like Filipinxs, Mexicans experienced enfolding borders, having gained independence from

Spain in 1821 only to cede their northern lands to the United States at the end of the Mexican-American War in 1848. Like Mexicans, Filipinos in the United States faced dire working and living conditions and forged their own identities, cultures, and families. In Stockton, California, Filipinxs created communities through labor unions, churches, and community organizations, as illustrated by Dawn Bohulano Mabalon.[32] Linda España-Maram analyzes how Filipinxs in Los Angeles's Little Manila created "an ethnic, predominantly male, working-class culture" where "mass-produced newspapers, gambling dens, commercialized boxing matches, and taxi dance halls were as important as fraternal associations, mutual-aid societies, and labor unions for the construction, affirmation, or rejection of identities."[33] Filipinxs also branched out to other parts of the country. For example in Chicago, Filipinxs studied as self-supporting students and also worked at the Pullman Car Company with African American porters.[34]

The Philippine-American War as a "race war" resurfaced in the United States in the 1920s and 1930s, as white politicians and working-class men targeted Filipinx laborers and other migrants as racial, economic, and health threats via numerous forms of violence or "race wars." This "third Asiatic invasion" of Filipinx migrants, referencing previous "invasions" by Chinese and Japanese immigrants, drove American government officials to sanction segregation, antimiscegenation laws, and physical violence that included a deadly 1930 riot in Watsonville, California. White working-class men expressed fears of Filipinxs mixing with white women in taxi dance halls, stealing jobs from whites, and carrying diseases like meningitis—fears that correlated with racist attitudes from the Philippine-American War. During the war, both imperialists and anti-imperialists rejected the prospect of brown Filipinx hordes entering the United States and racially infecting the nation. Many Americans characterized Filipinx resisters as ladrones (thieves), and colonial health policies judged "the Filipino . . . as a dangerous and promiscuously contaminated racial type and the major threat to white health."[35] Nativists endorsed the 1934 Tydings-McDuffie Act not because they believed Filipinxs worthy of self-government, but because it changed Filipinxs' status from "nationals" to "aliens" for immigration purposes and restricted their entry into the United States to fifty persons per year. With anti-Mexican sentiment raging in California and the deportation of thousands of Mexicans and Mexican Americans in the early 1930s under President Herbert

Hoover's repatriation program, the US Congress passed the 1935 Repatriation Act that offered, albeit unsuccessfully, Filipinxs free passage back to the Philippines. While their new status as "aliens" facilitated their exclusion from the United States, Filipinxs already in the country overwhelmingly refused to take up this purportedly benevolent offer of government-funded repatriation that essentially amounted to deportation.[36] Therefore, Filipinxs in the US actively protested systemic violence in this "race war" rooted in imperialist ideologies of the Philippine-American War.

The Philippine-American War's reverberations through migrations shows how military, political, economic, and psychological warfare persisted through racialized circuits of migration, and signifies how Filipinx migrants, colonized, and noncolonized peoples of color have traversed and navigated the US empire's messy, webbed apparatus. In implementing this relational framework in my own research, I have focused on triangulated amigo warfare during the Philippine-American War, shedding light on how African American soldiers, Filipinx revolutionaries, and white military men negotiated unstable allegiances and racialized power arrangements at the intersection of Jim Crow, anticolonial resistance, and US empire. The wide-ranging interactions between Black soldiers and diverse Filipinxs not only exposed varied forms of amigo warfare, but also impelled the long-term or even permanent settlement of about 1,200 African Americans in the Philippines at the expiration of their military service in 1901 and 1902. Here, Black emigration schemes uneasily merged with the colonial project, with African American veterans seeking socio-economic mobility yet benefiting from American colonization in the Philippines.[37] Filipinx American studies proves an intellectually vibrant space to analyze such intense overlap between war and migration amid a volatile, multilayered US empire. Space limitations prevent me from discussing how scholars have compellingly linked Filipinx migration to World War II, the Cold War, the War on Terror, and other wars.[38] Further comparative and relational work can only enhance Filipinx American studies as a site of critical inquiry. Possibilities for further research include but are not limited to work on the experiences of Filipinx cannery workers in relation to the Indigenous peoples of Alaska, an incorporated territory that entered statehood the same year as Hawai'i in 1959, and studies that address Keith Camacho's statement that "no comparative history exists on the Carolines, Hawai'i, the Marianas, the Marshalls, the Philippines, and

Sāmoa, areas variously and sometimes simultaneously colonized by the United States since the late nineteenth century."[39] Filipinx American studies can continue to flourish by interrogating such intra-imperial dynamics, by critically analyzing the experiences and agency of both colonized and noncolonized people of color in a single frame, and by taking seriously the connections between war and migration that expose the vulnerabilities and contradictions of American racial projects and that challenge, sustain, and transform the operations and foundations of the US empire.

NOTES

1. Paul Kramer, in his seminal work on the Philippines and the United States before World War II, recognizes this "profound historical persistence of the Philippine-American War." See Paul Kramer, *The Blood of Government: Race, Empire, the United States, and the Philippines* (Chapel Hill: University of North Carolina Press, 2006), 32.

2. See Angel Velasco Shaw and Luis H. Francia, eds., *Vestiges of War: The Philippine-American War and the Aftermath of an Imperial Dream, 1899–1999* (New York: New York University Press, 2002); Kramer, *Blood of Government*; Luzviminda Francisco, "The First Vietnam: The U.S.-Philippine War of 1899," *Bulletin of Concerned Asian Scholars* 5, no. 4 (1973): 2–16.

3. Julian Go and Anne L. Foster, eds., *The American Colonial State in the Philippines: Global Perspectives* (Durham, N.C.: Duke University Press, 2003), 20.

4. Moon-Kie Jung, *State of White Supremacy: Racism, Governance, and the United States* (Stanford, Calif.: Stanford University Press, 2011), 10.

5. US President William McKinley, Benevolent Assimilation Proclamation, Washington, DC, December 21, 1898.

6. Cynthia Marasigan, *Empire's Color Lines: How African American Soldiers and Filipino Revolutionaries Transformed Amigo Warfare* (forthcoming, Duke University Press).

7. Abe Ignacio et al., *The Forbidden Book: The Philippine-American War in Political Cartoons* (San Francisco: T'Boli, 2004).

8. Nerissa S. Balce, *Body Parts of Empire: Visual Abjection, Filipino Images, and the American Archive* (Ann Arbor: University of Michigan Press, 2016).

9. Allan Punzalan Isaac, *American Tropics: Articulating Filipino America* (Minneapolis: University of Minnesota Press, 2006), 32.

10. Isaac, *American Tropics*, 38.

11. Jung, *State of White Supremacy*, 7.

12. Isaac, *American Tropics*, 25.

13. Arthur MacArthur to Office of the US Military Governor in the Philippines, November 20, 1900, in *Annual Reports of the War Department for*

the Fiscal Year Ended June 30, 1901 (Washington, DC: Government Printing Office, 1901), I:4:257–58.

14. Kimberly Alidio, "A Wondrous World of Small Places: Childhood Education, US Colonial Biopolitics, and the Global Filipino," in *Filipino Studies: Palimpsests of Nation and Diaspora*, ed. Martin F. Manalansan IV and Augusto F. Espiritu (New York: New York University Press, 2016), 114.

15. Funie Hsu, "Colonial Lessons: Racial Politics of Comparison and the Development of American Education Policy in the Philippines," in *The "Other" Students: Filipino Americans, Education, and Power*, ed. Dina C. Maramba and Rick Bonus (Charlotte, N.C.: Information Age Publishing Inc., 2012), 39–62; Gary Y. Okihiro, *Island World: A History of Hawaiʻi and the United States* (Berkeley: University of California Press, 2008), 98–134.

16. Barbara M. Posadas and Roland L. Guyotte, "Unintentional Immigrants: Chicago's Filipino Foreign Students Become Settlers, 1900–1941," *Journal of American Ethnic History* 9, no. 2 (Spring 1990): 26–48.

17. Lucy Mae San Pablo Burns, *Puro Arte: Filipinos on the Stages of Empire* (New York: New York University Press, 2013), 30.

18. Burns, *Puro Arte*, 22–23.

19. Scrapbooks, X:89, Special Collections, St. Louis Public Library.

20. Cynthia Marasigan, "Race, Performance, and Colonial Governance: The Philippine Constabulary Band Plays the St. Louis World's Fair," *Journal of Asian American Studies* 22, no. 3 (Oct. 2019): 349–85.

21. Benito M. Vergara Jr., *Displaying Filipinos: Photography and Colonialism in Early 20th Century Philippines* (Quezon City: University of the Philippines Press, 1995), 121.

22. See Robert W. Rydell, *All the World's a Fair: Visions of Empire at American International Expositions, 1876–1916* (Chicago: University of Chicago Press, 1984), 154–83; Nancy J. Parezo and Don D. Fowler, *Anthropology Goes to the Fair: The 1904 Louisiana Purchase Exposition* (Lincoln: University of Nebraska Press, 2007); Kramer, 232–51.

23. Roderick N. Labrador, *Building Filipino Hawaiʻi* (Urbana: University of Illinois Press, 2015), 37.

24. Dean Saranillio, "Colonial Amnesia: Rethinking Filipino 'American' Settler Empowerment in the U.S. Colony of Hawaiʻi," in *Positively No Filipinos Allowed: Building Communities and Discourse*, ed. Antonio T. Tiongson Jr., Edgardo V. Gutierrez, and Ricardo V. Gutierrez (Philadelphia: Temple University Press, 2006), 126.

25. JoAnna Poblete, *Island in the Empire: Filipino and Puerto Rican Laborers in Hawaiʻi* (Urbana: University of Illinois Press, 2014).

26. Candace Fujikane and Jonathan Y. Okamura, eds., *Asian Settler Colonialism: From Local Governance to the Habits of Everyday Life in Hawaiʻi* (Honolulu: University of Hawaiʻi Press, 2008).

27. Yến Lê Espiritu, *Home Bound: Filipino American Lives across Cultures, Communities, and Countries* (Berkeley: University of California Press, 2003), 28–29.

28. Lucy E. Salyer, "Baptism by Fire: Race, Military Service, and U.S. Citizenship Policy, 1918–1935," *Journal of American History* 91, no. 3 (Dec. 2004): 858.

29. *Toyota v. United States*, 268 U.S. 402 (1925).

30. Salyer, "Baptism by Fire," 847–76.

31. Rick Baldoz, *The Third Asiatic Invasion: Empire and Migration in Filipino America, 1898–1946*, Nation of Newcomers: Immigrant History as American History (New York: New York University Press, 2011), 65.

32. Dawn Bohulano Mabalon, *Little Manila Is in the Heart: The Making of the Filipino/a American Community in Stockton, California* (Durham, N.C.: Duke University Press, 2013).

33. Linda España-Maram, *Creating Masculinity in Los Angeles's Little Manila: Working-Class Filipinos and Popular Culture, 1920s–1950s* (New York: Columbia University Press, 2006), 12.

34. Posadas and Guyotte, "Unintentional Immigrants"; Barbara Posadas, "The Hierarchy of Color and Psychological Adjustment in an Industrial Environment: Filipinos, the Pullman Company, and the Brotherhood of Sleeping Car Porters," *Labor History* 23, no. 3 (June 1982): 349–79.

35. Warwick Anderson, *Colonial Pathologies: American Tropical Medicine, Race, and Hygiene in the Philippines* (Durham, N.C.: Duke University Press, 2006), 8.

36. Maria Paz G. Esguerra, "Interracial Romances of American Empire: Migration, Marriage, and Law in Twentieth Century California" (PhD diss., University of Michigan, 2013), 144.

37. Marasigan, *Empire's Color Lines*.

38. See Robyn Magalit Rodriguez, "Toward a Critical Filipino Studies Approach to Philippine Migration," in *Filipino Studies: Palimpsests of Nation and Diaspora*, 33–55.

39. Keith L. Camacho, "Filipinos, Pacific Islanders, and the American Empire," in *The Oxford Handbook of Asian American History*, ed. David Yoo and Eiichiro Azuma (New York: Oxford University Press, 2016), 13.

FIVE

Liminal Services: Third Spaces of Being within the United States

JoAnna Poblete

Colonial categories, such as citizen or foreigner and assimilable or forever alien, present false binaries for identity and action based on imagined imperial dualisms. Contrary to these seemingly stark divides, since the war of 1898 and the 1901 Insular Cases, Filipinxs have occupied third spaces of being within the United States. Federal policies, legal decisions, government actions, and nongovernmental political actors, as well as community and individual efforts, result in contested definitions and experiences for Filipinx Americans.

Scholarship on Filipinx American history has a long tradition of discussing how US empire encouraged and enabled migration and ideological connections to the United States. These studies have also highlighted how ground-level racial discrimination in America contradicted federal government rhetoric about Filipinxs' special relationship to the United States. Facing such ambiguous circumstances, Filipinx immigrants, including intellectuals, workers of many types, and artists, developed creative ways to survive, resist, and even thrive within this liminality.

Such research includes Linda España-Maram's *Creating Masculinity* about Los Angeles, Dorothy B. Fujita-Rony's *American Workers, Colonial Power* about intellectuals and workers in the Pacific Northwest, Augusto F. Espiritu's *Five Faces of Exile* about intellectuals, Catherine Ceniza Choy's *Empire of Care* about nurses, Rick Baldoz's *Third Asiatic Invasion* about US rhetoric and policies toward Filipinxs and their actions within such contexts, and Dawn Bohulano Mabalon's *Little Manila Is in the Heart* about Stockton, California. Martin F. Manalansan IV in *Global Divas*, Sarita Echavez See in *The Decolonized Eye*, Lucy MSP Burns in *Puro Arte*, and Christine Bacareza Balance in *Tropical Renditions* examine how performers and artists have created alternative ways of relating to and belonging within the US empire. Dylan Rodríguez's *Suspended Apocalypse*, Allan Punzalan Isaac's *American Tropics*, and Nerissa S. Balce's *Body Parts of Empire* examine how American popular culture masks US domination and oppression over the Philippines and its people. My own work, *Islanders in the Empire*, and Faye Caronan's *Legitimizing Empire* also focus on liminality as both a consequence of colonization as well as a condition of possibility or resistance for both Filipinxs and Puerto Ricans. These multiple moments of construction and dispute compose the foundation of US-Filipinx American colonial relationships.

Historic oppressions experienced by Filipinx Americans in the United States, the ways Filipinx American rights have been pursued within US systems, American racial and cultural dynamics, as well as US legal history all highlight the in-between or liminal statuses of Filipinx Americans in the United States. Blacks and American Indians have also had similar experiences in areas such as US military service. This essay hopes to further the conversation on how Filipinx American histories and experiences can link with other subjected peoples in the United States to develop interconnections and bases for contemporary coalition building. In fact, Filipinx American studies can serve as an indispensable and unique site for critical analysis by providing such comparative insight to systemic racism through multiple subjects, disciplines, locations, and time periods including but not limited to US and Spanish colonialism, diaspora and migration studies, race, identity, and the experiences of people of color in the US and abroad, as well as

Indigenous, gender, borderlands, religious, military, environmental, labor, resistance, and futurity studies.

The colonial relationship between Filipinxs and the United States began on December 10, 1898, through the Treaty of Paris with Spain after the War of 1898. Even though Filipinxs declared independence from Spain on July 12 and proclaimed their own constitution on November 29, the US government ignored such national status and took control of the region that same year. During the US-Philippine War, which began on February 4, 1899, Filipinxs were stereotyped as niggers and insurgents, codifying them with dangerous racial and politically radical characteristics historically associated with blacks and American Indians by Euro-American society since settlement.

By default, the 1901 Supreme Court decision in the Insular Cases about Puerto Ricans also categorized Filipinxs as belonging to but not part of the United States: foreign in a domestic sense. This ruling grounded Filipinxs' political-legal status in the economic needs and goals of the continental United States, such as sugar, labor, and access to Asian markets. This liminal status as people under the direct authority of the US federal government, or US colonials, fluctuated with the shifting demands and desires of US mass agriculture industries, consumerism, politics, and military.

The case of Filipinx soldiers who served in the US armed forces during World War II exemplifies multiple aspects of federal policies where Filipinxs start off as insiders with special connections to the United States, at least belonging enough to serve and die for the country, then transition into positions of outsiders in later years. After the Tydings-McDuffie Act of 1934, the US government started transitioning the Philippines toward independence. However, the United States still had unrestricted power over the archipelago. Consequently, President Franklin Roosevelt called upon Filipinx US colonials to serve in World War II on behalf of the US on July 26, 1941. This obligatory executive military order involved more than two hundred fifty thousand Filipinxs, including the Old Philippine Scouts (enlisted Filipinxs under US Army officers), the Philippine Army, recognized guerillas, the New Philippines Scouts (who served in postwar Japan and related Asian territories), and Filipinxs in the US who volunteered to serve.

Despite loyal service throughout the war, President Harry Truman signed two Rescission Acts in 1946 that deemed Filipinx service outside the Old

Philippine Scouts ineligible for the full rights, privileges, or benefits of active military, naval, or air service. Filipinx veterans could qualify for service-related disability or death benefits, but only at half the rate of US citizens. The massive amount of bureaucracy and funds needed to implement non–service related benefits, like disability or death pensions, vocational rehabilitation and education, as well as Veterans Affairs medical care, were all provided as reasons to curtail assistance. However, President Truman also stated that Filipinx US colonials "fought with gallantry and courage under most difficult conditions. . . . I consider it a moral obligation of the United States to look after the welfare of Philippine Army veterans."[1] While the executive branch spoke freely about the great service supplied by Filipinxs, the federal government was not willing to provide equitable financial or social service support to these veterans after the war.

Filipinx US colonials never were and never would be viewed and treated as equal members of America. Such discriminatory in-between status had been built into the historical treatment of US colonials. Throughout the twentieth century, the Supreme Court continuously ruled that Congress could use "'rational bases' for differential treatment" of territories based on the Territorial Clause that gives Congress plenary power, or "the power to dispose of and make all needful rules and regulations."[2] For example, in *Quiban v. Veterans Administration*, the court used rational logic to rule that since the Philippines never put money into the US federal system, its people had no claim to receive funds back.[3] The political-legal liminality of this group, as neither full members nor complete foreigners, enabled Filipinxs to contribute their lives and labor for the protection of the United States and its empire without any reciprocal obligation by the US government to fair and just treatment, especially in the long term.

For fifty years, Filipinx veterans and their supporters fought for equitable benefits. Since 1989, different versions of a benefits equity bill were introduced but never passed. After the formation of an official lobby group in 1995, the US Congress and executive branch finally acknowledged and honored Filipinxs for their wartime service through a Concurrent Resolution and Presidential Proclamation, both passed in 1996. The rhetoric of this resolution and proclamation clearly identified the key role Filipinx veterans played in the war for the United States. However, such statements were still a far cry from tangible assistance.

While another equity bill was introduced in 1998, no real action for compensation occurred until 2009 when President Barack Obama authorized a one-time lump-sum payment for each Filipinx veteran. Eligible veterans who were US citizens qualified for $15,000 and noncitizens could receive $9,000. Almost sixty-five years after their tours of duty, these amounts were small compared to the scope of military service and decades of denied benefits. Most of the veterans had already passed away with no opportunity to apply for this compensation. Others had difficulty obtaining the payment. As of January 2019, two cases were still pending with 18,983 claims granted and 23,772 denied.

In October 2017 the US Congress gave Filipinx veterans of World War II the Congressional Gold Medal. Seventy years after the war, the federal government still expressed glorious patriotic rhetoric about Filipinx US colonial service. However, such consistent praise over the years is tarnished by the legacy of an extremely delayed lump-sum payment that has been difficult to obtain for some and will never be used by the many deceased veterans.

Such Filipinx liminality can be connected with the mistreatment of other people of color in the US armed forces, such as blacks and American Indians. In the twentieth century, all three groups were expected to fight heroically abroad but were not treated as full-fledged members of the United States. Despite the abolition of slavery in 1865, Jim Crow laws and practices continued to separate blacks from whites in public and private settings throughout the country. However, in the War of 1898 and both World Wars, blacks were recruited to serve in segregated battalions to defend their white supremacist nation. Racial division of the US armed forces remained official government policy until 1948. Full integration of the Army did not occur until the Korean War. Despite such segregation, being assigned mostly manual labor positions in the armed forces, and harsh discrimination at home, over three hundred fifty thousand blacks served in World War I and about one million served in World War II.[4]

Black veterans could and did become heroes in foreign lands but remained vilified as threatening enemies at home. After both World Wars, black veterans experienced increases in racial violence due to white fears over black empowerment from serving in the military. In fact, after World War II some black veterans were attacked during their travel home from service abroad.[5]

In addition to heightened racial aggression, returning black service members were often denied military benefits. For example, black veterans could not use some G.I. Bill programs like low mortgages because they were unable to get bank loans for homes in black communities and were prohibited from buying in white communities.[6] Black service people occupied similar liminal spaces as Filipinx veterans, recruited to fight for the country but denied full access to their earned benefits.

Like the belated acknowledgment of Filipinx veterans over fifty years after their service, seven black World War II veterans were issued the Medal of Honor by President William Clinton on January 13, 1997. Despite these overdue individual honors, there has been no government effort to acknowledge or compensate black veterans for lost benefits as there were for Filipinxs.

Since the seventeenth century, settler colonialists have pushed American Indians off their lands. Skilled Native individuals were often used as informants for Euro-Americans to effectively navigate within and extract from Indigenous lands and waters. This trend continued during the World Wars when American Indians (who could not be US citizens until 1924) were recruited to use their Native languages for secret war communications. During World War I, "Code Talkers sent messages encrypted in their Native languages over radio, telephone, and telegraph lines which were never broken by Germany."[7] During World War II, the US military formally used Indigenous languages for communications. More than twelve thousand American Indians served in the US Army during World War I and forty-four thousand of the total population of three hundred fifty thousand American Indians served in World War II.

Despite such key roles in defending the United States, just like black veterans, American Indian service people returned to high racial discrimination. Native veterans also experienced severe unemployment and poverty. Compounding these circumstances, the US federal government started to reduce support for reservations in 1944. By 1953, Congress passed a termination policy that disbanded some tribes and sold their lands. Such a push to assimilate American Indians into mainstream society decimated several Indigenous groups, with the effects of such liminality still felt today.

Over forty years after service, like the lengthy wait by black and Filipinx veterans, government acknowledgment of Code Talkers occurred in 1982.

On July 28, President Ronald Reagan provided a presidential proclamation, as requested by a House Joint Resolution, to designate August 14 as National Navajo Code Talkers Day. In 2001, Congress honored Navajo Code Talkers with Congressional Gold and Silver medals. Twelve years later, other Native groups were also acknowledged. On November 20, 2013, "33 tribes were recognized for the dedication and valor of Native American code talkers to the U.S. Armed Services during World Wars I and II. Of the tribes recognized, 25 were presented with their Congressional Gold Medals."[8] While scholars have written about reconciliation and reparations for Indigenous veterans, no government action has developed.[9]

Can American Indian and Filipinx veteran efforts to obtain just recognition for their valiant service in the face of racial discrimination inspire black veterans and their families to seek additional action by the US government? While most World War II veterans have passed, could the campaign for Filipinx veterans' compensation be a guide for other people of color in liminal military positionalities to work for more equal treatment (like American Sāmoan US colonials who live in an unincorporated territory but serve in larger proportions than populations from states of the union)?

In these contemporary and historical contexts, what kind of collaborative work can develop among Filipinx US colonials and other subjugated peoples? As Cynthia Marasigan has shown, black soldiers joined Filipinxs resisting the US during the Philippine-American War.[10] What lessons can be learned from past moments of coalition, as well as each groups' particular experiences fighting against the legacy of US discrimination and aggression toward people of color in the armed forces? Can uniting for specific military jurisdiction and restitution cases provide more effectiveness in contemporary national and global campaigns for demilitarization and decolonization?

Filipinx American studies should continue to investigate the historical intricacies and nuances of Filipinx American in-between statuses in the US, claim this liminality, and use such malleable positionalities to pursue comparative analyses of Filipinx American history. Such work can uncover past and inspire future creative actions and partnerships within the community and with other subjected and liminal groups throughout the United States and the globe for pursuits of social justice in the twenty-first century.

NOTES

1. Harry Truman, "Statement by the President Concerning Provisions in Bill Affecting Philippine Army Veterans," February 20, 1946, Public Papers Harry S. Truman 1945–1953.

2. See David Indiano and Harry Cook, "Harris v. Rosario," *Case Western Reserve Journal of International Law* 12, no. 3 (1980): 650–51.

3. Michael Cabotaje, "Equity Denied," *Asian American Law Journal* 6, no. 67 (January 1999): 87.

4. Henry Louis Gates Jr., "What Was Black America's Double War?," PBS, 1; *https://www.pbs.org/wnet/african-americans-many-rivers-to-cross/history/what-was-black-americas-double-war/*.

5. Peter Baker, "The Tragic, Forgotten History of Black Military Veterans," *The New Yorker*, November 27, 2016.

6. "After the War: Blacks and the G.I. Bill," Smithsonian American Art Museum, 1; *https://americanexperience.si.edu/wp-content/uploads/2015/02/After-the-War-Blacks-and-the-GI-Bill.pdf*.

7. Cynthia Smith, "Native Americans in the First World War," World Revealed: Geography and Maps at the Library of Congress.

8. "Code Talkers Recognition Congressional Medals Program," United States Mint; *https://www.usmint.gov/learn/coin-and-medal-programs/medals/native-american-code-talkers*.

9. Rebecca Tsosie, "Acknowledging the Past to Heal the Future," in *Reparations*, ed. Jon Miller and Rahul Kumar (Oxford: Oxford University Press, 2007), 43–68.

10. See Cynthia Marasigan, "'Between the Devil and the Deep Sea,'" (PhD diss., University of Michigan, 2010).

"Genocide" and the Poetics of Alter-Being
in the Obsolescence of the "Filipino American"

Dylan Rodríguez

Introduction: Affinities and Productive Violence

Filipinx American studies, as a critically disruptive and rejuvenating project, invites constant radical reflection on the "Filipino American" formulation as a disavowal of racial-colonial genocide. The emergent critical project
inscribed by this collection is, in part, a welcome and productive disarticulation of what was once called "Filipino American studies." Filipinx American can be interpreted as an ambivalent, queer, nonbinary adjoining that may
be structured in a coercive blurring of border and geography (nation/hemi-
sphere/transpacific) as well as historicity and colonial subjection (Filipinx
as antagonist and subordinate to the coloniality of "America"). The productive violence of this adjoining/blurring enacts a decisive demystification of
the Cordovan (et al.) school of Filipino American studies[1] as a curricular
construction that inhabits a mundanely aspirational—if utterly fraudulent—
archival and epistemological frame: The orthodoxy of this stubbornly

persistent field of scholarship consistently presumes the legitimacy and coherence of the United States on its own terms while enacting a historical fiction of Filipino American presence that reproduces liberal humanist conceptualizations of subjectivity, agency, mobility, and access to racial capitalist notions of liberty and self-determination. The originating iterations and institutionalizations of Filipino American studies—as well as what I have elsewhere called the discursive and cultural infrastructures of "Filipino Americanism"—constitute a minor contribution to a late-twentieth-century United States nation-building project that pivots on the reproduction and expansion of the settler colonial, antiblack logics within a capacious, if not solicitous, multiculturalist narrative regime.[2]

The emergence of Filipinx American studies, on the other hand, resituates the conjoining of the field's key terms—the tethering of Filipinx to American and vice versa—as a problem for pedagogy, archive, episteme, and even narrativity as such. In this sense, the critical project convened by this book offers an opportunity to *rescript* the fictions of origin—the narrative genesis of the "Filipino American" relation—through a radical, anticolonial genealogy of genocide. To engage this analytic of modernity is to revisit the context of its formulation as a response to *European* catastrophes of racialization and physical extermination, as well as to reconsider the term's incomplete signification of a world-deforming, epochal violence that exceeds the compartmentalized racial-temporal, archival, and legal schemas of its institutionalization by the United Nations, academic discourse, and a historical common sense that effaces the US conquest of the Philippines at the turn of the twentieth century.

The anticolonial, queer, feminist, diasporic, transnational, and abolitionist affinities catalyzed by the epistemic and pedagogical openings created by Filipinx American studies constantly refract the untenability of Filipino Americanism's formal grammar of articulation as well as its foundational fictions of political coherence. To engage the capacious terms of Filipinx American studies is to address the United States as a regime of evisceration that subsumes the figure of the Filipinx historical being (in their gendered, sexual, racial indeterminacy) to an atrocity that cannot be narrated through the terms of liberal humanism nor reconciled through the gestures of self-correcting postconquest governance. Put another way, Filipinx being refracts and reflects as it inhabits a regime of colonial genocide that is structured in transpacific antiblackness and the aspirational structures of the ongoing white supremacist civilizational ambition. In this sense, Filipinx American studies allows for a situated conceptualization of genocide as a modality of dominance that cannot be temporally compartmentalized, in part because its production of terror, subjection, demoralization, and epistemic disruption is perpetual.

Genocide is a formative, productive relation of violence/power that toxifies the stuff of historicity, including notions of identity, nationality, citizenship, and kinship. The work of Filipinx American studies facilitates this reckoning, which is really to embrace the instability of the "x," its signification of vulnerability as well as its incessant encouragement to insurgency. In what follows, i will attempt to contribute to this collective critical labor by providing a schematic reformulation of genocide as a primary technology of empire that confounds geographic provincialization as well as temporal containment. My modest ambition in the following pages is to instigate the use of a critical analytical and theoretical schema that works within— and in friction with—a conceptualization of genocide that centers the Philippine instance as a significant one among non-European others.

Genocide as Logic

There are few instances in which racial-colonial modernity's logic of epistemological bureaucratization has graver consequences than in the conceptualization and theorization of "genocide"—and thus the calibration of its meanings, consequences, and inhabitations. There are two hegemonic structures through which genocide tends to be understood. First, there is a *legal regime on genocide* structured by the United Nations Human Rights apparatus. This legal regime moves from the compulsory assumption that the 1948 UN Convention on the Prevention and Punishment of the Crime of Genocide serves as the intractable center of gravity for any viable discourse on genocide, law, and rights. Second, there is an *academic regime on genocide* that has generally come to identify itself with the field of "genocide studies." This professional scholarly discourse has cohered since the 1980s and has convened an identifiable field of academic journals, high-profile anthologies, and circuits of scholarly debate.

Across the broad field of hegemonic genocide discourses, there is widespread consensus on two matters: the importance of Polish legal scholar and Nazi Holocaust survivor Rafael Lemkin as the foundational innovator of the term, and the weakness of the UN Convention on Genocide as either a legal or conceptual framework. Beyond these points, there is little to no broad agreement on what genocide is, whether and how it might be prevented, how to define its perpetrators and victims, or which historical experiences ought to be included within the definitional-historical terms of genocide. There is radical and creative opportunity in departing from this messiness, particularly in the possibility of reading and thinking the concept of "genocide" in friction with the human rights moral and juridical apparatus as well as the academic fields it has spawned. This chapter attempts to exemplify a critical practice that situates genocide as an incomplete signification of the conditions of empire, implicating the necessarily ongoing violence of its self-securing (and extramilitary) structures of dominance, within which the inheritors and descendants of the apocalyptic US occupation(s) of the Philippine archipelago are inescapably entangled.

"Genocide," as a modern conceptual and jurisprudential formulation, is the impasse of the racial: To invoke its terms already suggests exceptionality and absolute abnormality, yet the making of racial power—in all its iterations—rests on *logics of the genocidal* that collapse into regimes of normalcy/normativity, universality/humanism, and sociality/civil society. Racialization—that is, the characterization and discursive marking of human bodies and groups within hierarchical valuations of life and being—structures and permeates virtually every form of social differentiation, external identification, military-police mobilization, jurisprudence, national development, and environmental intervention (from the destructive to the allegedly protective) in modern globality and its precedents in the conquest period. The logic of genocide, shaped in the material-historical domains of the formation of global racialization, thus paradoxically precedes the inauguration of the "genocide" nomenclature—that is, of the term itself—during the postwar period.

This genocidal logic surfaces in the dispersal of human beings within what Sylvia Wynter identifies as the construction of modernity's fatal racial continuum—the devastating distinction and schematic binary of existence between the "selected" and the "dysselected" (the latter, for Wynter, "the category of 'natives' and 'niggers'"):

By placing human origins *totally* in evolution and natural selection . . . [the bourgeois/white thinkers of the modern West] map the structuring principle of their now bourgeois social structure, that of the *selected* versus *dysselected*, the *evolved* versus *non-evolved*, on the only still extra-humanly determined order of difference which was left available in the wake of the rise of the physical and, after Darwin, of the biological, sciences. This is the difference that was provided by the human hereditary variations which we classify as *races*. This is where Du Bois's colour line comes in.[3] [emphasis in the original]

Wynter's (and Du Bois's) conception of racial modernity focuses on the emergence of the overlapping Western scientific and humanistic epistemes as knowledge forms that symbiotically intertwine the (rationalist) production of racial difference (via the biological, social, and natural sciences) with the discursive-ideological, and thus broadly *cultural* installation of global white ascendancy. Western science and humanism signify (and violently *realize*) this ascendancy through fluctuating notions of historical *telos*, aesthetic-cultural supremacy, and the white human's "transparency"[4] as a metasymbiosis of power/dominance that aspires to apprehend, shape, and anticipate human destinies—generally, globally, and permanently. *This ascendancy is the condition of possibility for empire, as well as its consistent and primary physiological and socio-discursive expression.*

Contrary to dominant historical caricatures of antiblack and racial-colonial genocide—as in the manner of hegemonic (and increasingly multi-culturalist) national narratives of nation-states like Australia, the Philippines, Brazil, Canada, and the United States—genocide does not simply unfold as a self-contained tragic chapter in the modern nation-building project, with a discrete "beginning" and "end." Conceptualized as a *determination of the "social"* and not simply as its antithesis or obliteration (an argument i will further elaborate in what follows), genocide's logic of evisceration encompasses a form of power/dominance that is entirely (if tacitly) central to normative discursive and institutional operations of peace, democracy, and law and order. The vulnerabilities and marks of racial and racial-colonial genocide outlast the incidence of their most acutely militarized demonstrations—genocides thus produce a historical-geographic continuum of violence, rather than a compartmentalized (and eventually ignorable) periodization within an otherwise progressive humanist *telos*.

In resonance with Wynter and DuBois, Edward Said examines how the modern disciplinary and cultural institutionalizations of empire draw a clear and durable distinction between *those who know* (empire and the West as "Knowledge") and *that which is to be known* (Egypt, the Orient, the colony, et al., as "the object[s] of such knowledge"): "To have such knowledge of such a thing is to dominate it, to have authority over it."[5] In confrontation with racial and racial-colonial power, Said's analytic confronts a racial-colonial modernity that has always linked the *epistemic supremacy of empire* (routed through White Being)[6] to the physiological destruction, denigration, and/or compartmentalization of its racial antagonists (objects of external study/knowledge/classification, dispersed along spectra of nonrationality to nonbeing). To rephrase Said, there are those who *know and must live*, and those who *are to be known in their proximity to death/obsolescence.*

Limits/Poetics of "Genocide"

Yet, the *political* legibility (and ethical traction) of the term "genocide" and its accompanying legal regime sometimes serve as useful leverage points for movements and collectivities struggling to win ground in struggles against various forms of antiblack violence and racial-colonial oppression (e.g., Chicago-based collective We Charge Genocide, Palestinians organizing against Israeli occupation/apartheid, prison and carceral abolitionists). It is necessary, in these instances, to consider whether and how such struggles are deploying the genocide concept in order to burst the discursive seams of other, prevailing languages that avert acute reference to conditions of normalized, racially formed suffering and degradation. Genocide, when repurposed as a *tactical* description of antiblack terror and racial-colonial power, has a way of tearing apart the edifices of liberal-progressive pretension that tend to suggest the possibility of rigorous state and societal reform as the difficult, though achievable solution to a social order that is structured in fatal dominance.[7]

By way of concrete example, Chicago's intergenerational grassroots organization We Charge Genocide (which thrived from 2014 to 2016) linked its organizational purpose to a tradition of Black radicalism highlighted by the eponymous 1951 petition addressed to the recently formed United Nations.[8] Its 2014 report to the UN Committee Against Torture, *Police Violence against Chicago's Youth of Color*, mobilizes the conceptual frame of genocide as an organizing narrative foundation for its compilation of empirical and testimonial evidence of the conditions of normalized police terror surrounding the lives of Black and Latinx youth in Chicago. The report's citations encompass police killings of unarmed Black and Brown children and young adults, sexual violence committed by law enforcement, mass-based racial profiling/arrest, and rigorous illustration of an apparent culture of state-sanctioned impunity for Chicago Police Department officers.[9] The organization thus constructs a living archive around the condition of police terror *as genocide*, radically reframing targeted peoples' vulnerability to everyday, normally functioning, nonscandalous state violence.

We Charge Genocide's narrative, legal, and analytical praxis are a poetic appropriation of the formal juridical and institutional infrastructures of genocide. Challenging the UN Genocide Convention's pretentious aspiration to "liberate mankind from such an odious scourge," We Charge Genocide refutes the overtures of liberal humanist universalisms and mobilizes a militant (self-)defense of Black and Brown body, flesh, and being. Against the hegemonic legal and academic institutionalizations of genocide discourse, such poetic *appropriations and rearticulations* of "genocide" form a creative, irruptive, counterhumanist archive that can both inform and shape Filipinx American studies as a collective critical project against empire in its various iterations.

Of course, there are multiple genealogies of genocidal violence and racialized dominance. A vast body of scholarship shows how these genealogies resist equilibration and easy comparison: each particular formation of genocide requires specific, situated analysis and critical/archival delineation, even and especially as scholarly activist practices continually work to narrate and mobilize around the possible relationalities between these singular genealogies. In abrogation of this careful work, the institutionalized canons of genocide—from the United Nations to the academic field of genocide studies—suggest a discrete, but identifiably *common* historical modality of modern suffering within which an otherwise discrepant totality of human experiences can be rationalized, remediated, and potentially repaired—or at least universally acknowledged. Yet, to part ways with the arrogant pretensions of hegemonic genocide discourses—which is to allow for the possibility that racial power's constitutive dehumanizations are both the precursor and conceptual disarticulation of genocide's allegations of coherence—is to incite an appropriation and creative refashioning of genocide's vernacular and conceptual legibilities to furnish a critical apprehension of the bottom line, lowest common denominators of racial and racial-colonial power.

The mind-numbing, inexhaustible devastation that "genocide" attempts to access seems to already escape its parameters of discursive engagement precisely because such devastation is, finally, *not* exceptional, abnormal, or historically episodic when accounting for the historical continuums of racial and racial-colonial dominance.

A certain rejoinder is made both possible and necessary by this line of inquiry, particularly to the extent that much theoretical and empiricist thinking around the historical processes of racialization is structured in the assumption of a relatively (that is, empirically) identifiable spectrum of violence and exclusion, within which can be identified variations in the contingency, paradigmatic permanence, and relationality within and between different modalities of race-making. Different schemas of racialization permeate the critical scholarly and activist fields, suggesting both a fungibility and persistence to racial power that roughly flows from assimilation and multiculturalist inclusion to chattel deracination and colonialist extermination/occupation. Certainly, the flourishing debates within and between Black studies, settler colonial studies, Indigenous and Native American studies, and critical ethnic studies are contributing a protracted rethinking of theoretical and pedagogical conceptions of antiblackness, race, coloniality, political ontology, and social movement.

Of interest here is whether and how Filipinx American studies can offer a theoretical, archival, curricular, and pedagogical apparatus through which to address the possibilities and pitfalls of "genocide" as another term in the unfolding critical discourses of antiblackness and racial-colonial power. That is, if we concede, for now, that the genocide concept cannot be fully disinterred from its foundations in modern human rights jurisprudence and the epistemic regime of Western liberal (academic) humanism, the urgent critical task may have little to do with whether hegemonic genocide discourses can be effectively (much less definitively) appropriated and refashioned for radical praxis. Rather, the primary challenge may entail rigorous, creative, speculative engagement with the concept's creative mobilizations as a signification of terror and violence in excess of genocide's established definitional and legal formalities. What *work* does an insurgent poetics of "genocide" do for liberation-oriented insurrections against the modern sociojuridical order? On the other hand, how do certain forms of counter- and antisystemic, anticolonial, Black liberationist, antiracist rebellion explicate logics of violence that resonate with—while ultimately rupturing—the historical and conceptual limits of modern genocide discourses?

The modern (post–WWII) institutionalization of "genocide" is stalked and disrupted by the world-making, civilization-building, socially productive technologies of empire that have made possible the consolidation of the very units of sociality—humanity, the civilized world, mankind, nation-state, and the international—on which the UN Convention on the Prevention and Punishment of the Crime of Genocide (and hegemonic genocide discourses more generally) depends for its epistemic and juridical cogency. Perhaps, then, it is less necessary to consider whether "genocide" provides an *adequate* rubric within which to categorize particular forms of racial-colonial power and violence to render them legible to "mankind and the civilized world" (in the words of the UN Genocide Convention[10]), than it is to rigorously examine how the distended field of genocide discourse creates a largely unintended opportunity for a radical critique of the very same civilized humanity it intends to righteously defend.

As signaled by the recent praxis of We Charge Genocide, a poetics of genocide lives and moves on the underside and disavowed edges of the dominant juridical and academic regimes. What would it mean for Filipinx American studies to sustain a critical archival and epistemic engagement with a genocide poetics that infiltrates and surrounds the long temporality and distended spatiality of U.S. coloniality and conquest? How can an activated Filipinx American studies poetics of colonial genocide catalyze and contribute to creative and scholarly revolt against the modern civilizational order?

The confrontation of Filipinx/American revisits the colonial archipelago as the originating site of "pacification," a form of genocidal counterinsurgency that instituted extinction for the alter-being of the native who refused, rebelled, disobeyed, or simply wandered.[11] There is no narrative reconciliation or closure in this zone of death, only an implosion of the "Filipino American" figure as an ambition founded in a delusional flight from atrocity and terror. Dwelling in the impasse of genocide and alter-being, Filipinx American studies can participate in a praxis of world-making that further demonstrates the necessity of obsoleting the overlapping totalities of colonial power, the United States, and civilization.

NOTES

1. Fred Cordova, Dorothy Laigo Cordova, and Albert A. Acena, *Filipinos, Forgotten Asian Americans: A Pictorial Essay, 1763–Circa 1963* (Dubuque, Iowa: Kendall/Hunt, 1983).

2. Parts of this chapter are drawn from specific arguments originally formulated in Chapter 3, "'Its Very Familiarity Disguises Its Horror': White Supremacy, Genocide, and the Statecraft of Pacifica Americana," in *Suspended Apocalypse: White Supremacy, Genocide, and the Filipino Condition* (Minneapolis: University of Minnesota Press, 2010), 98–149; and Chapter 4, "'Civilization in Its Reddened Waters': Anti-Black, Racial-Colonial Genocide and the Logic of Evisceration," in *White Reconstruction: Domestic Warfare and the Logics of Genocide* (New York: Fordham University Press, 2020), 135–75.

3. David Scott, "Interview: The Re-Enchantment of Humanism: An Interview with Sylvia Wynter," *Small Axe: A Caribbean Journal of Criticism* 4, no. 2 (2000): 119–207; here, 177.

4. Denise Ferreira da Silva, *Toward a Global Idea of Race* (Minneapolis: University of Minnesota Press, 2007).

5. Edward W. Said, *Orientalism* (New York: Vintage Books, 1979).

6. Casey Goonan, "Policing and the Violence of White Being: An Interview with Dylan Rodríguez," *Propter Nos* 1, no. 1 (Fall 2016): 8–18.

7. Stuart Hall, "Race, Articulation, and Societies Structured in Dominance" [1980], in *Black British Cultural Studies: A Reader*, ed. Houston A. Baker Jr., Manthia Diawara, and Ruth H. Lindeborg (Chicago: University of Chicago Press, 1996), 16–60.

8. William L. Patterson, *We Charge Genocide* (New York: International Publishers, 1970).

9. "We Charge Genocide: Police Violence against Chicago's Youth of Color," conference proceeding (Chicago: We Charge Genocide, 2014).

10. United Nations General Assembly, Convention on the Prevention and Punishment of the Crime of Genocide (United Nations, 1948); *https://www.un .org/en/genocideprevention/documents/atrocity-crimes/Doc.1_Convention%20on%20 the%20Prevention%20and%20Punishment%20of%20the%20Crime%20of%20 Genocide.pdf*.

11. Reynaldo Clemeña Ileto, *Knowledge and Pacification: On the U.S. Conquest and the Writing of Philippine History* (Quezon City, Philippines: Ateneo de Manila University Press, 2017).

PART TWO

Labor and Knowledge/Power

SEVEN

Filipinx Labor and the Contradictions of US Empire

Josen Masangkay Diaz

In Carlos Bulosan's 1943 novel, *America Is in the Heart*, Allos leaves the Philippines to search for work in the United States. Throughout his narrative, Allos toils on agricultural fields, in canneries, and in restaurants and homes along the western coast of the United States. The novel, regarded by many as the most popular—if not the first—Filipinx American novel, is, above all, a story of Filipinx American labor.[1] The text traces the experiences of Filipinx laborers in the United States in the early decades of the US colonization of the Philippines to reveal the ways that Allos's labor produces value for US industries while it makes Allos's life increasingly precarious. He recalls, "I stayed on in Santa Barbara, hoping the farmers in Goleta, a town ten miles to the north, would need hands for the carrot season. . . . Later, I found work in Solvang, farther north, picking flowers and seeds for a big company that supplied these to the nation. But the pay was only ten cents an hour, and what I earned in a week's time was scarcely enough to pay for the gloves I used to keep my hands from the cold."[2] As an autobiographical novel, the text's first-person narrative follows Allos's transformation from a colonial national into a Filipinx American subject while tracking Bulosan's own conceptualization of Filipinx America as an emergent US social formation. Yet, it is clearly Allos's labor that threads the Filipinx to the American: His description of his work and the subjectivity that his work forces him to inhabit articulates his coming-into-being as a US racial subject, what he names as "the beginning of [his] conscious life."[3] Where Bulosan's novel has come to signal a kind of Filipinx American literary origin, it is labor that structures this very conceptualization of Filipinx America.

For Filipinx American studies, labor often defines the Filipinx relationship to the United States. The US war against Filipinxs at the turn of the twentieth century and the US colonization of the Philippines in the half century after the war facilitated the migration of thousands of Filipinx workers to the plantations of Hawaiʻi, the fields of California, and the canneries of Washington. Bulosan's novel describes Filipinx laborers as workers in carrot and lettuce fields and fish canneries and as servers and busboys. The project of "benevolent assimilation," more than an insidious misnomer for the violence of the US conquest of the Philippines, enveloped Filipinxs into the folds of the US capitalist economy by transforming Filipinxs into a new, cheap, and temporary workforce. Filipinxs buttressed the rise of US agribusiness and helped strengthen US industrialization. As US nationals, Filipinx laborers responded to a high demand for labor in the United States and bypassed immigration policies.[4] The classification of Filipinxs as nationals and not citizens—what Filipinx American studies scholars have described as the conundrum of simultaneous inclusion and exclusion (or "foreign in a domestic sense")—positioned Filipinxs as both imperative for the economic and political development of the United States yet excluded from the protections afforded by citizenship and other forms of social belonging within the US nation, including the efforts and gains of organized labor movements.[5] This kind of contradiction has illuminated the central paradox of "free" labor. In this way, Filipinx American studies joins ethnic studies and American studies to interrogate the ways that Indigenous, Black, Latinx, and Asian workers have always been fundamental to US expressions of modernity. Where pronouncements of liberty and egalitarianism rendered the United States an exceptional model of democratic nationhood, the solidity of the US citizen-subject has always been intimately intertwined with the labor of racialized peoples.[6]

The stable migration of Filipinx workers to the United States in the first decades of the twentieth century intensified racial tensions between migrant workers and white citizens. Anti-Filipinx violence was a regular occurrence in agricultural towns that employed Filipinx laborers. In January of 1930, at the heels of a judge's condemnation of the "Filipino menace," a white mob in Watsonville, California, terrorized the Filipinx community for days and murdered Fermin Tovera.[7] The riot signaled the logic that has character-ized much anti-immigrant sentiment in the United States: While low-wage migrant labor is imperative for the survival of the US political economy and its system of aggressive accumulation, migrant workers bear violent racist attacks from white workers who are often also precariously positioned within the US political economy.

With the passage of the US Tydings-McDuffie Act in 1934, the status of Filipinxs changed from colonial nationals to foreign aliens. US immigra-tion law set a national quota system that allowed fifty immigrants into the United States from the Philippines each year, which decisively curtailed Fili-pinx labor migration. At the same time that immigration restrictions dras-tically lowered the numbers of Filipinxs who entered the country, Filipinxs continued to provide labor power for the United States in different ways. World War II saw the enlistment of Filipinx service personnel to the US military, many of whom settled in the United States after the war's end. The US bestowal of independence to the Philippines in 1946 continued to alter the trajectory of Filipinx labor migration by enlisting the newly sovereign Philippine government to operate as a junior partner in the expansion of US imperialism around the world. During the Cold War period, the Phil-ippines, along with Hawai'i and Guåhan (Guam), remained a crucial part of the United States' sphere of influence, a critical military post in its struggle with the Soviet Union over control of Asia and the Pacific islands. The US guest worker program, established in the 1950s and distinct from the earlier Bracero Program, lured Filipinx healthcare professionals, largely nurses, to migrate to the United States from the Philippines with temporary work visas. Encouraged by US and Philippine agencies' promises of higher pay and adventure, Filipinx nurses worked more difficult jobs with lower pay compared to their white counterparts.[8] In 1965, US president Lyndon B. Johnson signed the Hart-Celler Act (also known as the Immigration and Nationality Act) and removed earlier national origins quotas from US im-migration policy. The act saw a new influx of Filipinx migrants to the United

States who, unlike earlier migrants, were part of a high-skilled workforce of doctors, engineers, and scholars. The act, while unintentionally increasing emigration from Latin America and Asia to the country, deliberately sought skilled labor from elsewhere to mitigate US Cold War anxieties around technological development.

The final decades of the US Cold War saw the beginnings of deindustrialization in certain parts of the country and the materialization of global restructuring systems through the rise of multinational industries and the neoliberalization of labor. Throughout the 1980s and 1990s, Filipinx migrants continued to fill low-wage jobs in the metropolitan centers of the United States.[9] In the Philippines, this restructuring progressed through the feminization of the country's political economy.[10] Filipinas, in particular, functioned as an ideal workforce for multinational corporations, sex and entertainment work in and around US military bases and other imperial sites, and domestic and service work all over the world. The ubiquity of Filipinx labor, once an arm of the US colonial system in the early 1900s, has become a global fact. Overseas Filipinx Workers, a politically recognized group in the Philippines, are nannies in Hong Kong, seamen on the Pacific, maids in Saudi Arabia, and care workers in Italy.[11] Millions of Filipinx citizens work outside the Philippines.[12] And even many Filipinxs who stay in the Philippines perform outsourced affective and other immaterial labor for multinational corporations based elsewhere.[13] Filipinx American studies scholars work at various historical intersections and from different disciplinary positions; yet, they often coalesce in their incisive analyses of the myriad ways that industries and technologies continue to capitalize upon the materiality of the Filipinx laboring body to advance capital's movement.

For Filipinx American studies, labor is always mediated by the modalities of race, gender, and sexuality. When considering the Filipinx in relation to the Chinese "coolie" at the end of the nineteenth century, for example, it is the former's perceived capacity to assimilate into the nation and the latter's inability to do so that both defines the Filipinx's laboring position within a racial hierarchy (inside yet marginal) and legitimizes the extraction of his labor. The signification of Filipinxs as assimilable and compliant is never only an articulation of racial difference but always a promise of the Filipinx's capacity to and for work. Put differently, race is a condition of the Filipinx's labor. Further, the Filipinx worker as a racial subject is also understood through and against heteronormative conceptions of subjectivity. US antimiscegenation laws barred Filipinx migrant workers in the early decades of the twentieth century from marrying white people. Such mandates relied upon notions of Filipinx men's perverse sexualities as threatening to the enforced homogeneity and purity of white raciality. Notions of Filipina hospitality and docility, moreover, have been fundamental to the shape of their work within multinational industries that identify such characteristics as fundamental to efficiency and profit. These constructions of Filipinx race, gender, and sexuality, of course, have not been constant. One need only recall that the US Philippine Commission's early depictions of Filipinxs as primitive, bellicose, and inassimilable were imperative for its justification of war and conquest or that anti-Filipinx violence has always characterized the Filipinx historical experience in the United States. The interrogation of Filipinx labor thus helps interrogate and anticipate the shifting terrain of Filipinx subjectivity.

The study of Filipinx labor in the United States has also carved space for Filipinx American studies to illustrate the ways that Filipinxs construct other forms of social belonging that resistively organize other subjectivities. Filipinx agricultural workers in the United States have been at the forefront of organizing labor unions to mitigate the unobstructed extraction of their labor.[14] The story of the United Farm Workers begins with the organizing efforts of Filipinx laborers, and the history of Filipinx American labor is always outlined by traditions of strikes and stoppages.[15] Moreover, Filipinx workers developed public cultures that cultivated desire, play, and joy amidst and against the dehumanizing conditions of their work and the exclusion that structured their lives in the United States. Taxi dance halls, sporting clubs, and beauty pageants showcase the cultural formations that emerged from these experiences. Filipinx American studies has contributed to scholarship in cultural studies and performance studies that attend to the vibrancy and significance of these cultural expressions.[16]

The interrogation of Filipinx American labor is a necessarily complex task. At the same time that the coherency of Filipinx America assumes a distinct diasporic formation in the United States, the trajectory of Filipinx labor in the United States always challenges the boundaries of national space and the progressiveness of historicism. That is, Filipinx labor is characterized by the meandering and expansive circuits of migration and work that often follow no direct path and do not always begin and end in the United States. While empirical studies of migration often relegate Filipinx American immigration to three waves that begin at the turn of the twentieth century and end with the passage of the Hart-Celler Act, Filipinx labor often challenges such linearity to reveal the intricacies and continuities of Filipinx movement. While historical and sociological studies might point to post-1965 Filipinx American diasporic formations as the arrival of a new middle-class population, Filipinx American studies interrogates the politics of the period to reveal the uninterruptedness of Filipinx labor extraction by other means. Further, while Filipinx sex work around US military bases, entertainment work in Japan, and care work in Israel might not be considered Filipinx American labor in a national or spatial sense, such labor is always intertwined with US geopolitics, militarization, and a global political economy led, in part, by US investments. In this way, Filipinx American studies and its attention to labor help thread connections across divides to elucidate the interconnectedness of these political regimes.

As a composite of critical inquiries into colonialism, imperialism, empire, migration, and labor, Filipinx American studies presents an epistemology for contesting the familiarity of forms that emerge from these processes. It consistently interrogates the lines that demarcate history, nation, diaspora, race, gender, sexuality, and subjectivity. Even still, the study of Filipinx American labor, in particular, uncovers the possibilities and limitations of Filipinx American studies. On the one hand, Filipinx American studies directs necessary attention to the complexities of labor migration, especially the multifarious ways that Filipinxs have worked on behalf of empire's expansion, the means by which Filipinx labor export has become imperative for the economic development of the Philippines, and the ways that Filipinx labor has become saturated within the global economy. Such studies point to labor to unravel the defining contradictions of US empire and its claims to modernity. In order to attend to the multifariousness of these processes, Filipinx American studies has become a necessarily and undeniably transnational and interdisciplinary field of inquiry. At the same time, the circuits and histories of Filipinx labor make visible other points of entrance that push Filipinx American studies, in line with the conditions of its formations, to move beyond singular conceptions of nation, diaspora, and history. For instance, how might Filipinx American studies interrogate labor to contend with the continuity of settler colonialism in the Pacific?[17] How might the turn to the archipelagic trace intimacies between colonial laborers in the United States, the Philippines, and elsewhere? Such questions, I hope, gesture toward other affinities and relationalities and imagine new futures for Filipinx American studies.

NOTES

1. See Melinda L. De Jesus's "Rereading History, Rewriting Desire: Reclaiming Queerness in Carlos Bulosan's *America Is in the Heart* and Bienvenido Santos's *Scent of Apples*," *Journal of Asian American Studies* 5, no. 2 (2002): 91–111; and S. J. Gabriel Jose Gonzalez's "*America Is in the Heart* as a Colonial-Immigrant Novel Engaging the Bildungsroman," *Kritika Kultura* 8 (2007): 99–110.

2. Carlos Bulosan, *America Is in the Heart: A Personal History* (Seattle: University of Washington Press, 1991 [1946]).

3. Bulosan, *America Is in the Heart*, 29.

4. Joanna Poblete, *Islanders in the Empire: Filipino and Puerto Rican Laborers in Hawai'i* (Chicago: University of Illinois Press, 2017).

5. Sarita Echavez See, *The Decolonized Eye: Filipino American Art and Performance* (Minneapolis: University of Minnesota Press, 2009).

6. Lisa Lowe has written, "As the state legally transforms the Asian *alien* into the Asian American *citizen*, it institutionalizes the disavowal of the history of racialized labor exploitation and disenfranchisement through the promise of freedom in the political sphere." *Immigrant Acts: On Asian American Cultural Politics* (Durham, N.C.: Duke University Press, 1996), 10.

7. Estella Habal, "Radical Violence in the Fields: Anti-Filipino Riot in Watsonville," *Journal of History* 2 (1991): 1–6.

8. Catherine Ceniza Choy, *Empire of Care: Nursing and Migration in Filipino American History* (Durham, N.C.: Duke University Press, 2003).

9. See Lisa Lowe's *Immigrant Acts* and Grace Hong's *The Ruptures of American Capital: Women of Color Feminism and the Culture of Immigrant Labor* (Minneapolis: University of Minnesota Press, 2006).

10. Rolando Tolentino, "Macho Dancing, the Feminization of Labor, and Neoliberalism in the Philippines," *The Drama Review* 53, no. 2 (2009): 77–89.

11. See Kale Bantigue Fajardo's *Filipino Crosscurrents: Oceanographies of Seafaring, Masculinities, and Globalization* (Minneapolis: University of Minnesota Press, 2011); and Rhacel Parreñas's *Servants of Globalization: Migration and Domestic Work* (Stanford, Calif.: Stanford University Press, 2015).

12. See Vicente L. Rafael's "'Your Grief Is Our Gossip': Overseas Filipinos and Other Spectral Presences," in *White Love and Other Events in Filipino*

History (Durham, N.C.: Duke University Press, 1997); Robyn Magalit Rodriguez's *Migrants for Export: How the Philippine State Brokers Labor to the World* (Minneapolis: University of Minnesota Press, 2010); and Valerie Francisco's *The Labor of Care: Filipina Migrants and Transnational Families in the Digital Age* (Chicago: University of Illinois Press, 2018).

13. See Martin F. Manalansan IV's "Queering the Chain of Care Paradigm," *The Scholar & Feminist Online* 6, no. 3 (2008); and Jan M. Padios's *A Nation on the Line* (Durham, N.C.: Duke University Press, 2018).

14. Howard DeWitt, "The Filipino Labor Union," *Amerasia* 5, no. 2 (1978): 1–21.

15. See Marissa Aroy's film *Delano Manongs: Forgotten Heroes of the United Farm Workers* (Kanopy, 2014).

16. See Lucy MSP Burns's *Puro Arte: Filipinos on the Ages of Empire* (New York: New York University Press, 2012); Celine Parreñas Shimizu's "Can the Subaltern Sing, and in a Power Ballad?," *Concentric: Literary and Cultural Studies* 39, no. 1 (2013): 53–75; and Christine Bacareza Balance's *Tropical Renditions: Making Musical Scenes in Filipino America* (Durham, N.C.: Duke University Press, 2016).

17. See Haunani-Kay Trask's "Settlers of Color and 'Immigrant' Hegemony," *Amerasia* 26, no. 2 (2000): 1–24; and Dean Itsuji Saranillio's "Why Asian Settler Colonialism Matters," *Settler Colonial Studies* 3, no. 4 (2013): 280–94.

EIGHT

On History, Development, and Filipinx American Studies: Emergent, Dominant, *and* Residual

Victor Bascara

> From the moment typical Filipino students begin to learn about themselves, their society, history, and culture through books, the mass media, and the classroom, they become immersed in ideas of development, emergence, linear time, scientific reason, human pragmatism, governmental ordering, and nation building. They become so caught up in these that they take them to be part of the natural ordering of things. Little do they know that such categories are historical, that they were devised at a certain time in the past by men and women bound by their unique interests and environments.
>
> —REYNALDO CLEMEÑA ILETO, "Outlines of a Nonlinear Emplotment of Philippine History"

Ever since Reynaldo Clemeña Ileto critically reconsidered the meaning of "development" in his landmark 1988 essay, "Outlines of a Nonlinear Emplotment of Philippine History," an appreciation for the dialectical relationship of "history" and "development" has been crucial for a truly decolonial understanding of the Philippines and therefore of Filipinx America.[1] In Ileto's articulation, it may seem that the "typical Filipino student" may come across as a straw man Ileto sets up to knock down, an inheritor of the miseducation that Renato Constantino famously warned of back in 1959, and in numerous reprints and republications ever since. Now, more than three decades after Ileto's own reprinted essay, with the ascent of both neoliberal globalization and a resurgence in post–Cold War authoritarian nation-state rule, it may be that that straw man has gotten up again, or maybe never really got toppled in the first place. A critical appreciation of development and the challenges that that appreciation presents to the work of the historian are then necessary for understanding the interventions of critical Filipinx American studies. Toward making such interventions, Filipinx American studies can serve as a unique and generative site for critical analysis by drawing into visibility experienced convergences of hegemony and resistance that manifest as simultaneous engagement with formal and informal empire, modernization, capitalist expansion, and militarization on one hand, and with migrations and diaspora, local and translocal community formations, transnational decolonial movements and epistemologies, labor organizing, and antiracist mobilizations in and beyond the academy, on the other. In having Filipinx American studies serve as a site for this sort of critical analysis, "history" and "development" emerge dialectically as key concepts that have shaped both hegemony and resistance, illuminating how conceptions of the past, present, and future interact to make, or to break, our times.

Both "history" and "development" can be defined broadly as change over time. But "development," with its relationship to economic, social, and ideological frameworks, is the more technical of the two concepts of this essay, and is therefore more straightforward to define. And here we can again turn to Ileto, as he opens his essay with the following definition of development: "Most sensitive thinkers today regard the concept of 'development' not as universal but as historically conditioned, arising from social, economic, and ideological trends in eighteenth-century Europe. The idea of Progress—the belief that the growth of knowledge, capabilities, and material production makes human existence better—placed science at the summit of knowledge."[2] So then a key task of the historian, as performed by "sensitive thinkers," is to identify where and when the idea and practice of development emerges. And there one can map a genealogy of development through the capitalism, Enlightenment, and imperialism of eighteenth-century Europe, contexts out of which Development/Progress are routinely taken with the putative onset of secular and scientific modernity. In other words, one can historicize the tendency not only to dehistoricize but to interestedly mishistoricize. More to the point on those interests, Ileto makes the following important connection: "[Development/Progress] gave birth to high imperialism, as the West identified Progress with civilization and set out to dominate the rest of the world. Today, the idea of Progress and the development ideology it engendered are under attack."[3] For a time, especially the early part of the Cold War, the sun did not set on Progress despite decolo-

nization efforts. But such attacks on Progress and development and globalization have only proliferated and even mainstreamed. This has become
particularly notable in critical recognition of a geologically inflected epoch
that is coming to be called the Anthropocene, highlighting such things as
global warming and plastic bag vortices to rising waters and superbugs. So
between high imperial conquest and potentially irreversible environmental
ruin, development is turning out to be exactly the opposite of Progress, when
its history is told.

Ileto is asking sensitive and not-yet sensitive thinkers to truly reckon with
what it means to unlearn development and to reject unreconstructed Progress. History then is what enables that unlearning and how a recovery of
newly usable pasts can then be possible and meaningful. And he calls that
reconstructed history "nonlinear emplotment." In resisting the educa-
tionally ingrained impulse to make history meaningful through an arc of
development and Progress, nonlinear emplotment allows for recovery of
not only the forgotten but also the structurally repudiated, that which
was deemed alterity and backwardness to the forward progress of what
Walter Benjamin has called, in his 1940 essay "Theses on the Philosophy of
History," the "Angel of History."

> His face is turned toward the past. Where we perceive a chain of events, he
> sees one single catastrophe which keeps piling wreckage and hurls it in front of
> his feet. The angel would like to stay, awaken the dead, and make whole what
> has been smashed. But a storm is blowing in from Paradise; it has got him
> caught in its wings with such a violence that the angel can no longer close
> them. The storm irresistibly propels him into the future to which his back is
> turned, while the pile of debris before him grows skyward. This storm is what
> we call progress.[4]

In rejecting the dictates of a unified narrative arc of progress, Filipinx America can and perhaps must be understood as simultaneously emergent, dominant, *and* residual, to borrow the terms from Raymond Williams.

One key intervention of "nonlinear emplotment" is that history can strategically begin in places that were seen as middles or ends or tragic deviations.
Filipinx America can be just such a location. Near the end of a speculative
2002 essay on the impact of the Philippine revolution a century on, Vicente L. Rafael turns, perhaps unexpectedly and approvingly, to Filipinx

America, especially youth culture, as he catalogs a litany of the "bewildering variety" of contemporary Filipinx American formations:

> They identify themselves to an unknown and anonymous public as "queer," "transgendered," or "bisexual," who work in writers' collectives and practice using the *balisong*, teach design and poetry, direct videos, perform as DJs in raves, and stage one-woman performances as well as elaborate variety shows called "PCNs" (or Pilipino Cultural Nights), live in large metropolitan cities like New York, Los Angeles, and San Francisco, and fashion intricate Web sites that accommodate a bewildering variety of voices.[5]

Rafael is aware that such formations have been seen, from both the standpoints of the USA and the Philippines, as hybrid, diasporic, deracinated, and therefore distant from a celebrated and lamented point of revolutionary origin, and he seeks to push back against this tendency. Rafael continues:

> They would seem to be far removed from the "first" Filipinos, the generation of [Jose] Rizal, [Andres] Bonifacio, and [Emilio] Aguinaldo. And yet I would argue that such Filipino-American artists, writers, and activists much like their compatriots in the Philippines, are as much "heirs" to the revolution as, for example, the followers of José Ma. Sison's Communist Party holed up in the Netherlands and directing an armed struggle from a distance.[6]

History then is understood through connection and affect, rather than linear inheritance. On this Rafael then writes,

> Here, to "inherit" a revolution need not mean owning it, as if "revolution" were something that could be fixed into a tradition and bundled into a stable thing, then deeded like property to succeeding generations. Rather, it means coming to be traversed by the force of certain unsettled questions and unknowable futures that disrupt existing social arrangements. As such, overseas Filipinos in general and Filipino-Americans in particular come to share in the predicaments of Filipino-ness with which all of us who claim to be Filipinos of some sort are infected. They are, like Rizal, Bonifacio, and their generation, possessed by the ghosts of colonialism even as they seek to come to terms with its effects.[7]

These are formations of historicity that scholars in critical Filipinx American studies, such as (in no particular order and by no means complete) Oscar V. Campomanes, Martin F. Manalansan IV, Christine Bacareza Balance,

J. Lorenzo Perillo, Theo Gonsalves, Sarita Echavez See, Faye Caronan, Allyson Tintiangco-Cubales, Dylan Rodríguez, Antonio T. Tiongson Jr., Rick Bonus, Allan Punzalan Isaac, Linda España-Maram, Jeffrey Santa Ana, Genevieve Clutario, Victor Román Mendoza, Nerissa S. Balce, Rick Baldoz, Lucy MSP Burns, Denise Cruz, Mark Villegas, Martin Joseph Ponce, Eric Reyes, Robyn Magalit Rodriguez, José B. Capino, Ed Curammeng, Eric J. Pido, John D. Blanco, Augusto F. Espiritu, Rhacel Salazar Parreñas, and many others, have illuminated in their diverse studies that have emerged from the late twentieth century to the present, that have all directly and indirectly grappled with the meaning of something that Neferti Xina M. Tadiar has generatively called "Philippine historical experience."[8] Central to the accessing of that experience is a critical approach to development and Progress, even including that which historically fueled revolutions. Tadiar writes:

> What I find is that in order to construct proper political subjects capable of transforming history, social movement literatures draw on supplementary modes of experience that serve as vital supports for the material conditions of social life and struggle. However, to the extent that they exceed the valorized forms of political subjectivity defined by feminism, urban activism, and the revolutionary movement, these vital modes of experience are necessarily eschewed by the very political subjects they help to constitute.[9]

This eschewing is then precisely where to locate what Tadiar, in a reading of Doña Consolación in Rizal's *Noli Me Tangere*, refers to as "other politics" that revolutionary movements ignored or even actively disavowed in the making of a Progress-driven argument for the overthrow of the current empire. In a related context, specifically that of the British empire in South Asia, this figure of alterity has generatively been referred to as the subaltern, notably in the pioneering historical work of Ranajit Guha and conceptual elaborations of Gayatri Chakravorty Spivak. Tadiar observes,

> In rechanneling this experiential labor for the constitution of a proper historical subject, progressive and radical literary works tend to subsume the alterity of those experiential practices into universal forms of subjectivity and agency, which are meaningful within the dominant field of politics. The clearest example of this can be found in literary articulations in the period after the Second World War of a unitary sovereign nationalist subject as the

proper historical agent of an anti-imperialist movement. Much work has been accomplished by historians in subaltern studies in deconstructing this unitary nationalist subject constructed by the elite classes of newly independent former colonies and, further, in uncovering the cultural strategies of resistance of "the people" whom such a nationalist subject purportedly represents.[10]

Where then does this place Filipinx America in relation to development, history, and the work of transformative "sensitive thinkers"? It would be melodramatic and possibly repugnant to too easily align First World Filipinx Americans with the subaltern, especially given the material conditions of the metropole. Nor would it be appropriate to dismiss Filipinx America as exceptional to a national or anti-imperial or even diasporic paradigm. Indeed there is a compelling case to be made for ways in which Filipinx American history has fascinating and underexplored parallels with colonized populations who also lived lives and built communities in their imperial centers over the past century, such as Indians in England, Vietnamese in France, Indonesians in Holland, or Koreans in Japan. And all of these examples share a shift to migrations to the new imperial center: the USA, where they become Asian America.

It is also important not to exceptionalize Filipinx America because of those very material conditions, which are always uneven, to borrow a concept from development studies. Resistance to the presumption of developmental evenness may be precisely where a new historicity emerges. How do we recognize that resistance and its newly and nonlinearly emplotted histories? As various Filipinx studies scholars have shown, we can strategically turn to affect as a mode and embodied object for unlearning development and reconstructing history. One strong and recent example of an approach to "Philippine historical experience" and Filipinx American historical experience can be found in Christine Bacareza Balance's research on music and Filipinx America. From DJing and karaoke to YouTube celebrity and Pinoy indie rock, Balance's paired concepts of "disobedient listening" and "flip[ping] the beat" provide an approach to appreciating these formations as nonlinear emplotments of Filipinx American historical experience. She at once acknowledges the hybridized conditions of diaspora as bases of community without recourse to assertions of their being either exceptional or paradigmatic. And yet these formations are nevertheless challenging, expressive, and meaningful. Near the end of her book, as she reflects on the potentials and perils of achieving representation, Balance notes that,

> Throughout this book, voice has taken on various meanings and purposes—authenticating, prescribing, and often limiting identities. But equally important have been the practices of listening, against and beyond, in order to hear even the silences and gaps as forms of expression. When something isn't there, what do we allow to persist in its place? Perhaps it was always there, we just didn't know how to listen? If no longer apprehended as lost or missing, then, how do we make it resound (or sound again) but with a difference?[11]

In this approach, difference registers *as* difference in its capacities to be "against and beyond." What these musical scenes are against and beyond is, I suggest, the development ideology and conception of Progress that, as Ileto would put it, naturally orders history. At that resounding difference, we hear, see, taste, know, feel, and, yes, study Filipinx American historical experience.

NOTES

1. Reynaldo Clemeña Ileto, "Outlines of a Nonlinear Emplotment of Philippine History," in *The Politics of Culture in the Shadow of Capital*, ed. Lisa Lowe and David Lloyd (Durham, N.C.: Duke University Press, 1997), 98–131.

2. Ileto, "Outlines of a Nonlinear Emplotment," 98.

3. Ileto, "Outlines of a Nonlinear Emplotment," 98.

4. Walter Benjamin, "Theses on the Philosophy of History" [1938], in *Illuminations: Essays and Reflections* (New York: Schocken Books, 1969).

5. Vicente L. Rafael, "Parricides, Bastards, and Counterrevolution: Reflection on the Philippine Centennial," in *Vestiges of War*, ed. Angel Velasco Shaw and Luis H. Francia (New York: New York University Press, 2002), 361–75.

6. Rafael, "Parricides, Bastards, and Counterrevolution," 370.

7. Rafael, "Parricides, Bastards, and Counterrevolution," 370.

8. This growing and generative generation of engaged scholars and scholarship merits its own bibliographic essay in the near future.

9. Neferti Xina M. Tadiar, *Things Fall Away: Philippine Historical Experience and the Makings of Globalization* (Durham, N.C.: Duke University Press, 2009), 5.

10. Tadiar, *Things Fall Away*, 5–6.

11. Christine Bacareza Balance, *Tropical Renditions: Making Musical Scenes in Filipino America* (Durham, N.C.: Duke University Press, 2016), 185–86.

NINE

The Limits of "Immigration" Frameworks: Centering Empire in Analyzing Migration and the Diaspora

Roy B. Taggueg Jr. and Robyn Magalit Rodriguez

Because the Filipinx experience is one that is deeply shaped by migratory processes, it is essential that migratory processes, in turn, are analyzed through the lens of the Filipinx experience. The case of the Philippines challenges the preconceived notions upon which scholars of migration base their analyses of how and why people upend their lives to move across borders, as established theories on push and pull factors fail to completely explain the state of Filipinx migrants as a global labor force. Analysis of the Philippines, and Filipinx migrants more broadly, lays bare the themes of empire and colonialism within the narratives of migrants worldwide. Consequently, Filipinx scholars are able to both de-center the United States as the locus of study, while simultaneously highlighting the United States' role as the global hegemon within the context of migration.

As such, immigration, migration, and diaspora have thus been the foci of much of Filipinx and Filipinx American studies. To understand the hows and whys of contemporary Filipinx presence in the United States, critical Filipinx studies scholars must recognize Filipinx emigration as it's related to the American imperialism and colonialism of the early twentieth century that produced the dynamics that we see today. At the very core lies the fact that for almost half a century, the Philippines was a US colony. However, unlike other American territorial acquisitions (Hawai'i, Puerto Rico, and Guåhan [Guam], among others), it became independent as a result of the Tydings-McDuffie Act of 1934. As Oscar V. Campomanes describes it: "Technically speaking, you cannot consider the movement of Carlos Bulosan's generation (Pinoys/Manongs) . . . as immigration! . . . [I]t was the borders that moved and not people alone!"[1] Accordingly, Filipinx studies scholars have been critical of the deployment of the term "immigration" to characterize this migratory process of people from the Philippines, particularly to the United States, because to do so is to "effectively [valorize] the United States as the supreme nation of immigrants."[2]

On the other hand, in centering empire within the Filipinx experience, Filipinx studies scholars are able to understand migration theoretically, analytically, and conceptually through different perspectives as compared to the conventional narratives of immigration in Asian American studies. For instance, Catherine Ceniza Choy makes the case that the post-1965 influx of Filipinxs to the United States is merely symptomatic of broader trends in Philippine migration as a whole, and that the increase in the movement of Filipina nurses, in particular, was only possible due to the social transformation of Philippine society over the course of its tenure under the colonial system of Benevolent Assimilation.[3] Specifically, that the ways in which Filipinx education was shaped, the development of American-style institutions, and the professionalization of the healthcare system created for the purpose of consolidating US colonial rule in the Philippines produced conditions that enabled the development and proliferation of an even larger-scale movement of the Philippine peoples initially to the United States in the early twentieth century to various corners of the globe today. In short, while the more dominant narratives in Asian American historiography might center US labor demand in driving migration, to center empire is to shift focus to the enduring legacies of US imperialism in the Philippines and the transformation of Philippine society as a consequence to the emigration of Filipinxs.

Indeed, centering empire in analyzing Philippine migration is not only relevant for migration flows that originated in the colonial period, it helps us understand contemporary patterns of migration. Anna Romina Guevarra and Robyn Magalit Rodriguez, for example, argue that among the vestiges of US colonialism is the Philippine state's labor brokerage apparatus, which helps to train Filipinx low-wage workers, market their labor abroad, and facilitate their global deployment.[4] Most critical Filipinx scholars also distinguish between those in the Filipinx diaspora who work as temporary migrants in various countries and the work of those who have access to citizenship as legal permanent residents, particularly in white settler colonial states like the United States, Canada, or Australia. However, the lines of distinction between these broad groups of migrants blur as many engage in what is called "step-wise international migration" in order to overcome the particularly high barriers to entry to these industrialized Western countries.[5] This multistage process involves migrating to—and working in—multiple intermediate countries as a strategy to develop sufficient capital (social, cultural, economic, and migratory, to name a few) to be eligible for entry to their intended destination.[6] From this perspective, what emerges is an understanding of migration not as a singular event with defined beginning and end points, but rather an ongoing process embedded in the lives of migrants across the globe.

Belonging, Citizenship, and Identity

Migratory processes, which have led to the expansion of the Philippine diaspora, have necessarily raised questions related to trans/national belonging and citizenship. The protection of racialized (white settler) US citizenship animated debates related to US colonialism in the Philippines at the turn of the twentieth century. American pro-imperialist lawmakers were quick to justify their land acquisition at the conclusion of the Spanish-American War, using narratives of racial paternalism to argue that as the epitome of civilized society, it was their responsibility to provide governance and training to the uncivilized peoples of the Philippines.[7] Anti-imperialist lawmakers, however, feared that the acquisition of the Philippines, the largest and most densely populated land that the US annexed from Spain, would disrupt and degrade American society, especially if the government were to extend US citizenship to the Natives who live there. In what became known as the Insular Cases, the US Supreme Court granted the US Congress the flexibility to address this issue by clarifying the difference between territorial annexation and territorial incorporation.[8] As a consequence, the Philippines *"belonged to*, but was certainly not *part of* the United States," and Filipinxs were rendered US nationals, able to move readily between the two countries for work but could not participate in political life as citizens.[9] In taking a critical Filipinx studies perspective on migration, scholars take seriously the need to engage with the deeply racialized understandings of citizenship, as both pro- and anti-imperialist sentiments in the US were driven by the question of how the American government was going to address the issue of subsuming the Filipinx peoples. Rick Baldoz argued that it is precisely these racialized debates surrounding the status of the Philippines vis-à-vis the United States that shaped the (im)possibilities for US citizenship for Filipinx migrants.[10]

With the Philippines' emergence as a "labor brokerage state," the cultural underpinnings have transformed Philippine citizenship to justify the wholesale export of Filipinx labor as a commodity.[11] Philippine migrants were labeled as the *bagong bayani*, or "new national heroes," for whom service to the state (or more directly, the remittances they send back) became the new norm for what Filipinx citizenship or patriotism is or should be. But in going through the process of migration (particularly those who work outside of the Philippines as temporary workers), Filipinxs take unto themselves a liminal legal status, becoming individuals whose perennial legal status of being "at sea" leaves them outside the purview and responsibility of both their origin and receiving countries, leading to greater vulnerability to being exploited as they have no state under which they can receive protection.[12] Adelle Blackett compares Filipina contemporary domestic carework with slavery, noting the racial, hierarchical, and gendered tensions that remain (and are perpetuated) in the employer/employee relationships these migrants establish in their destination countries.[13] In contrast, both Rodriguez and Valerie Francisco-Menchavez find that Filipinx migrants leverage their Philippine citizenship to get protection from the Philippine state.[14] The transnationality of Filipinx labor and carework engenders the rise of "migrant citizenship," a solidarity among Overseas Filipinx Workers (OFWs) that transcends national borders.[15]

For the Filipinxs who seemingly enjoy a pathway to citizenship in white settler colonial states like the United States, Canada, Australia, and elsewhere, the extent to which they actually feel a sense of loyalty and root-edness in those countries is uneven. Benito M. Vergara Jr. argues that Fili-pinxs engage in forms of political and social behaviors that are embedded in the notion of serving as cultural ambassadors to their host countries while simultaneously strengthening their ties to the Philippines.[16] In es-sence, they engage in what is expected of them to be citizens, but do so in a distinctively Filipinx way. Eric J. Pido on the other hand, suggests that the performativity that Filipinx migrants engage in to feel a sense of belong-ingness is instead a response to their perception that they are "unassimila-ble and perpetually foreign."[17] As a consequence of their ongoing struggle to find their place in American society, Filipinx immigrants often also ex-perience a form of racial and ethnic liminality. In *Global Divas*, Martin F. Manalansan IV demonstrates how gay Filipinx men understand their sexu-ality through the framework of their diasporas, balancing and negotiating their cultural identities from the perspective of both their home and host countries.[18] In *The Latinos of Asia*, Anthony Christian Ocampo discusses how Filipinxs, particularly the children of Filipinx immigrants in the United States (what is referred to as the "second generation," as well as sub-sequent generations) must navigate their own liminal racial identities, as being perceived as Latinx in the US could have different educational, health, and work-related outcomes versus when they are perceived as being Asian.[19]

A Filipinx studies perspective takes into account these experiences unique to the Filipinx history of subjugation under white settler colonialism, rec-onciling how these themes operate within and throughout the process of migration. Oftentimes the violent impacts and legacies of American colo-nialism in the Philippines are intentionally and surreptitiously erased from mainstream academic and popular discourses surrounding the Filipinx migrant experience in the United States. It is precisely this struggle against the broader social forces of racism, white supremacy, power, and hierarchy inherent within the US colonial and imperial endeavor that defines the Filipinx and Filipinx American experience.[20] This sense of belonging and nonbelonging, engendered by the need for Filipinx labor but tempered by the capitalistic conditions that induce exploitation, is distinctive of the Filipinx experience in many ways because of Filipinxs' status as colonial subjects.[21]

Gender, Family Formations, and Migration

For decades under American governance, thousands of Filipinx men (particularly those from the Ilocos Region) left the Philippines in order to find work in the United States, settling mostly in the west in places such as Hawaiʻi, Seattle, Portland, and cities along the coast of California.[22] They were seen as a cheap, readily available workforce for the agricultural industry, as importing Filipinx workers required fewer bureaucratic hurdles than workers from other nations given their status as American nationals under colonial rule.[23] Moreover, their characterization as a docile people made Filipinxs the perfect counter to other migrant groups already in the United States, particularly the Japanese laborers in Hawaiʻi who were on the verge of becoming problematic as they learned and developed ways to organize and advocate for workers' rights.[24] Later streams of migration, in contrast, were characterized by the massive out-migration of Filipina nurses, facilitated by the rise of labor brokerage agencies under the development of the Philippines' labor export policies.[25] In more contemporary forms of migration, we see the proliferation of domestic caregivers all across the globe.[26]

From these works, Filipinx studies scholars explore the emergence of streams of gendered immigration. For example, across these patterns is the underlying theme of servility and servitude. Filipinxs were coming to the United States overall to fill the lower-end jobs and positions within their respective industries.[27] What results, however, is the racialization of these positions in American society and the perception of Filipinxs as a second class (or even a third, fourth, or fifth class) as Filipinxs were often also marginalized and othered by other migrant groups in the US.[28] Despite their long history and presence in significant numbers in the United States, the Filipinx immigrant experience continues to remain invisible.[29]

The creation of community and the formation of Filipinx identity can, in response, be contextualized as the ways in which Filipinxs in the United States are historically and institutionally rendered invisible, exploited, and racialized.[30] This can be seen in the emergence of Little Manilas in places like Daly City and Stockton as a form of cultural expression and community building.[31] This can also be observed in the rise of Filipinx activism and in the struggle for basic rights.[32] Diaspora has been increasingly deployed by Filipinx studies scholars against immigration as a framework for understanding

Filipinx migration. Harrod Suarez, for example, contends that diasporic maternal subjectivity can serve to delineate how *Inang Bayan*, or "mother country," and the themes of heroism and motherhood imposed on the labor of Filipinx migrant workers can work in tandem with the sexual objectification of the Philippines to drive forms of gendered migration.[33] "Whore or mother?" Suarez asks.[34] Through analysis of cultural schemas both in the Philippines and within the diaspora, a distinction need not be made as both work together to produce a narrative that rationalizes Filipinx labor abroad. Indeed, a diasporic framework brings into view—in a way that even a more expansive "migration" framework (and further yet, an "immigration" framework) does not—the role of forced emigration from the Philippines in producing these trends. Roland Sintos Coloma et al. in *Filipinos in Canada: Disturbing Invisibility* point out that the hypervisibility of gendered labor in the Filipinx diasporas in Canada—particularly the presence of domestic care workers and nurses—serves to further racialize Filipinx migration, and obscure the experience and erase the issues concerning other Filipinxs within their diasporic communities.[35] By focusing on diaspora, Filipinx studies scholars open up the possibility for comparative and relational analysis of Filipinx settlements and the second and subsequent generations beyond the United States.

Equally as important are the ways in which we centralize back into these discussions the role of imperialism, colonialism, and diaspora. In a short critique of fieldwork, ethnographies, and quantitative methods, Ocampo asks, "How do you ask your research subjects about themes of colonialism and imperialism?," noting that these concepts are often so abstract that their consequences are not readily apparent in an individual's daily life.[36] The Filipinx presence in the United States is a consequence of United States imperialism and colonialism, a dynamic that makes it somewhat distinctive from other Asian groups. Today, the Filipinx population in the United States is among the oldest and largest of all Asian/Pacific Islander groups. Filipinxs are one of the largest ethnic immigrant groups in the nation. In 2017 alone, Filipinxs constituted the fourth-largest immigrant population in the United States, with recent estimates numbering them at over 1.8 million.[37] Based on the 2010 census, approximately 3.4 million people in the United States identify as Filipinx, or Filipinx American; they constitute nearly 20 percent of the Asian population. The stories of their journey, the forces at work that gave them reason to leave their home country, and their presence in communities across the globe enable critical Filipinx studies scholars to develop the tools with which to challenge the ways in which we understand contemporary migration. In discussing migration from the perspective of Filipinx studies, what we come to realize is that the ways in which US immigration is framed is that it is a voluntary issue. The Philippine case challenges this conceptualization, because it occurs largely within the context of empire and subjugation. By putting into the foreground a more (to use Oscar Campomanes's term) worldly analysis of migration, a Filipinx studies perspective enables scholars to critique the power asymmetry between the US and the rest of the world.

NOTES

1. Oscar V. Campomanes, "On Filipinos, Filipino Americans, and U.S. Imperialism: An Interview with Oscar V. Campomanes," in *Positively No Filipinos Allowed: Building Communities and Discourse*, ed. Antonio T. Tiongson Jr., Edgardo V. Gutierrez, and Ricardo V. Gutierrez (Pasig City, Manila: Anvil, 2006), 41–42.

2. Oscar V. Campomanes, "New Formations of Asian American Studies and the Question of U.S. Imperialism," *Positions: East Asia Cultures Critique* 5, no. 2 (1997): 523–50.

3. Catherine Ceniza Choy, *Empire of Care: Nursing and Migration in Filipino American History* (Durham, N.C.: Duke University Press, 2003).

4. Anna Romina Guevarra, *Marketing Dreams, Manufacturing Heroes: The Transnational Labor Brokering of Filipino Workers* (New Brunswick, N.J.: Rutgers University Press, 2010); Robyn Magalit Rodriguez, *Migrants for Export: How the Philippine State Brokers Labor to the World* (Minneapolis: University of Minnesota Press, 2010).

5. Anju Mary Paul, "Stepwise International Migration: A Multistage Migration Pattern for the Aspiring Migrant," *American Journal of Sociology* 116, no. 6 (2011): 1842–86.

6. Paul, "Stepwise International Migration."

7. Julian Go, *American Empire and the Politics of Meaning: Elite Political Cultures in the Philippines and Puerto Rico during U.S. Colonialism* (Durham, N.C.: Duke University Press, 2008).

8. Rick Baldoz, *The Third Asiatic Invasion: Empire and Migration in Filipino America, 1898–1946* (New York: New York University Press, 2011).

9. Allan Punzalan Isaac, *American Tropics: Articulating Filipino America* (Minneapolis: University of Minnesota Press, 2006), 29.

10. Baldoz, *The Third Asiatic Invasion*.

11. Guevarra, *Marketing Dreams*; Rodriguez, *Migrants for Export*.

12. Rhacel Salazar Parreñas, "The Indenture of Migrant Domestic Workers," *Women's Studies Quarterly* 45, nos. 1–2 (2017): 113–27.

13. Adelle Blackett, "Introduction: Regulating Decent Work for Domestic Workers," *Canadian Journal of Women and the Law* 23, no. 1 (2011): 1–46.

14. Robyn Magalit Rodriguez, "Beyond Citizenship: Emergent Forms of Political Subjectivity amongst Migrants," *Identities* 20, no. 6 (2013): 738–54; Valerie Francisco-Menchavez, *The Labor of Care: Filipina Migrants and Transnational Families in the Digital Age* (Urbana: University of Illinois Press, 2018).

15. Rodriguez, "Beyond Citizenship"; Francisco-Menchavez, *The Labor of Care*.

16. Benito M. Vergara Jr., *Pinoy Capital: The Filipino Nation in Daly City* (Philadelphia: Temple University Press, 2009).

17. Eric J. Pido, "The Performance of Property: Suburban Homeownership as a Claim to Citizenship for Filipinos in Daly City," *Journal of Asian American Studies* 15, no. 1 (2012): 69–104.

18. Martin F. Manalansan IV, *Global Divas: Filipino Gay Men in the Diaspora* (Durham, N.C.: Duke University Press, 2003).

19. Anthony Christian Ocampo, *The Latinos of Asia: How Filipino Americans Break the Rules of Race* (Stanford, Calif.: Stanford University Press, 2016).

20. Rodriguez, *Migrants for Export*.

21. Isaac, *American Tropics*.

22. Roderick N. Labrador, "Performing Identity: The Public Presentation of Culture and Ethnicity among Filipinos in Hawaii," *Cultural Values* 6, no. 3 (2002): 287–307; Dorothy B. Fujita-Rony, *American Workers, Colonial Power: Philippine Seattle and the Transpacific West, 1919–1941* (Berkeley: University of California Press, 2003); Dawn Bohulano Mabalon, *Life in Little Manila: Filipinas/os in Stockton, California, 1917–1972* (Durham, N.C.: Duke University Press, 2003); Vergara, *Pinoy Capital*.

23. Fujita-Rony, *American Workers, Colonial Power*; Vergara, *Pinoy Capital*.

24. Labrador, "Performing Identity"; Baldoz, *The Third Asiatic Invasion*.

25. Guevarra, *Marketing Dreams*; Rodriguez, *Migrants for Export*.

26. Francisco-Menchavez, *The Labor of Care*; Parreñas, "The Indenture of Migrant Domestic Workers."

27. Choy, *Empire of Care*; Baldoz, *The Third Asiatic Invasion*; Parreñas, "The Indenture of Migrant Domestic Workers."

28. Baldoz, *The Third Asiatic Invasion*.

29. Fred Cordova, Dorothy Laigo Cordova, and Albert A. Acena, *Filipinos, Forgotten Asian Americans: A Pictorial Essay, 1763–Circa 1963* (Dubuque, Iowa: Kendall/Hunt, 1983); Campomanes, "New Formations of Asian American Studies."

30. Rick Bonus, *Locating Filipino Americans: Ethnicity and the Cultural Politics of Space* (Philadelphia: Temple University Press, 2000).

31. Vergara, *Pinoy Capital*; Mabalon, *Life in Little Manila*.

32. Estella Habal, *San Francisco's International Hotel: Mobilizing the Filipino American Community in the Anti-Eviction Movement* (Philadelphia: Temple University Press, 2007).

33. Harrod J. Suarez, *The Work of Mothering: Globalization and the Filipino Diaspora* (Urbana: University of Illinois Press, 2017).

34. Suarez, *The Work of Mothering*.

35. Roland Sintos Coloma, Bonnie S. McElhinny, and Lisa M. Davidson, eds., *Filipinos in Canada: Disturbing Invisibility* (Toronto: University of Toronto Press, 2012).

36. Ocampo, *The Latinos of Asia*.

37. United Nations, Department of Economic and Social Affairs, Population Division, 2017, International Migration Report 2017: Highlights; Keith McNamara and Jeanne Batalova, "Filipino Immigrants in the United States," Migration Policy Institute (2015).

Including the Excluded: The "Chinese" in the Philippines and the Study of "Migration" in Filipinx American Studies

Richard T. Chu

The theme of "migration" is very central in Filipinx American studies. Works on labor migrants such as the *manongs* of Hawai'i and their struggles to find a place in the heartland of "America" allow Filipinx American migration history to fit squarely within the metanarrative of nativist history celebrating the struggles and contributions of various groups making up "America."[1] Other works trace the migration of Filipinxs to specific locales and how they carve out a space for themselves in the making of "America," even as they negotiate its meaning.[2] Seeking to veer away from a US-centric approach to the study of the Filipinx American experience, other scholars take a transnational approach to demonstrate how Filipinx migration is also shaped by forces in the Philippines, or how it relates to the broader Filipinx diaspora.[3] Furthermore, scholars have compared their migration experiences with those of other ethnic groups affected by US imperialism such as the Puerto Ricans, Hawaiians, Mexicans, and Cubans.[4] Used as an analytic, "migration" has helped demonstrate the deeper workings of the US empire, Philippine nation-state, or globalization as these intersect with class, gender, sexuality, and race.[5]

In these aforementioned studies, the forms of Filipinx migration privileged are the ones made by "Filipinxs" as defined by the nation-state—i.e., by the various ethnolinguistic groups making up the "Filipinx" nation such as the Igorots of the Cordilleras, the *manongs* of the Ilocos Region, and the Tagalogs of Manila. However, the history of one group of "non-Filipino," the Chinese in the Philippines, deserves attention in our study of "migration" within Filipinx American studies. In particular, a discussion of the history of their exclusion in both the Philippines and the United States—and the creation of transnational linkages—constitutes a significant intervention given that it has not generally been within the purview of studies of Filipinx migration. Furthermore, by including the excluded—i.e., the Chinese from the Philippines—as part of the broader history of the Filipinx diaspora, Filipinx American studies provides a unique and indispensable site for critical analysis by pointing to ways in which US policing of people migration started not only within its "domestic" space, or through the control of bordering nation-states such as Mexico and Canada, but also in or through its territorial acquisitions overseas. The study of Filipinx American studies behooves us not to leave untouched the "imperialist moorings" related to "questions of U.S. nationality and nation building."[6]

The "Chinaman" in the Philippines: To Exclude or Not to Exclude

The Chinese living in the southern coastal regions of China have long been migrating to the Philippines, especially since Spain colonized the Philippines in 1565 and established a colonial economy that relied heavily on the Manila-Acapulco galleon trade. Chinese traders came to bring goods from China that were then shipped to Acapulco twice a year. Apart from traders, people from different occupational backgrounds came, such as carpenters, artisans, bakers, mason brick layers, unskilled laborers, dye makers, etc. In time, the Chinese established themselves as an indispensable part the Spanish colonial economy, and by the time the United States annexed the Philippines, their population had risen to nearly a hundred thousand.

In September 1898, not long after the Battle of Manila was waged, which effectively ended Spanish control over the Philippines, Commanding General of the US Army Elwell Otis extended the Chinese exclusion laws of the United States to the Philippines. It was a contingent measure put in place until the US Congress could come up with an official policy. Like its counterpart in the United States, this law prohibited Chinese laborers, skilled and unskilled, from entering the Philippines. Under Section 6 of the law, only those who could establish residency could stay, leave for China, and return.

In January 1899, President William McKinley created the Schurman Commission to collect information regarding the Philippines. One of its tasks was to examine the "Chinaman question" and to provide recommendations to the US government on how to deal with this issue. In their report made after their investigations, the commission stated that the Chinese in the Philippines had a long history of trade with "natives" of the islands, and that they exerted great influence on the Philippine economy, especially in the realm of "commerce, industry, wealth, and production."[7] In concluding their report, the commission recommended to the president of the United States the need for a careful consideration of the "question as to how, where, and for what purpose the Chinese should be allowed to enter the Archipelago."[8]

On the road toward the implementation of an official policy vis-à-vis the Chinese in the Philippines, different arguments for or against the application of the Chinese exclusion act in the colony surfaced in newspaper articles, editorials, and letters or were debated in the chambers of the US Congress. On the one side were those who argued for the continued immigration of the Chinese to the Philippines not only because of the latter's long history of migration to the Philippines but also for their usefulness in carrying out the colonialist aims of developing the newly US acquired territory for capitalist gains. American and foreign businessmen, as detailed later in this essay, pointed to the Chinese ability to work hard—a trait that was supposedly absent in Filipinxs—and for less money. On the other side were those who argued that allowing the Chinese to enter the country would send the wrong signal to the Filipinxs that the United States was more concerned about economic considerations than fulfilling its promise of developing the Philippines for the Filipinxs. They also argued that, given time, Filipinxs under American tutelage would learn how to value work.[9]

However, one of the main reasons for excluding the Chinese in the Philippines was American fear of the Chinese coming to the United States. As Erika Lee demonstrated in her work, the United States stemmed the migration of the Chinese by not only closing off its borders but also controlling those territories through which the latter could enter, such as Mexico and Canada.[10] By implementing the Chinese Exclusion Act in the Philippines, the United States hoped to deny the Chinese another way of migrating to the country. As O. F. Williams, appointed acting American consul to the Philippines, declared in his testimony before the Schurman Commission, "America is looked upon as a heaven by (the Chinese), and there is not anything that the Chinese would not do to get into America."[11] Furthermore, by nationalizing citizenship in the Philippines and categorizing the Chinese as "aliens," the United States effectively barred the Chinese from migrating as US nationals, a status accorded to Filipinxs.[12]

Racialized Discourse on the Chinese and "Filipinx" as Laborers

Including the Chinese in the study of the "migration" of Filipinxs to the United States is relevant because it was through the racial juxtaposition of Filipinxs not only to Indians or Blacks, as Steffi San Buenaventura points out, but also to the Chinese that the history of Filipinx migration to the United States can be more broadly understood.[13] Specifically, it was partly and initially through the racialized discourse on the qualities of the "Chinese" and the "Filipinxs" that the latter were later deemed either qualified or not to migrate to the United States as hired laborers.

Comparisons made between the "Filipinxs" and the "Chinese" started as early as the Spanish colonial period. Spanish writers such as Rafael Comenge y Dalmau pointed out that the Chinese were hardworking and thrifty.[14] On the other hand, Filipinxs were characterized as "indolent." Much of this discourse was carried over to the American colonial period.

An example of this can be seen in a newspaper article that was published in the *London Times* on August 23, 1902, and reprinted in the *New York Times* the following day.[15] In it, the author argued that the United States was making a mistake in applying the exclusion act in the Philippines. Citing the experiences of the British and Dutch empires, the author pointed out that in Malaya, the British had wisely allowed Chinese laborers to enter its colony and this had led to economic prosperity, both for the colony and for the Chinese. On the other hand, the economy of the Dutch colony in the "Malayan archipelago" suffered because Chinese immigration was "restricted." The Dutch relied on the "Malays" to do the work, and as a consequence, the colony had not prospered as much as the British colony had. Hence, in the case of the Philippines, the United States was making a mistake in thinking that it could "educate" the Filipinxs to work hard like the Europeans.[16] The author wrote:

> The hope that education will work miracles, transforming the Filipino into an American, is based upon a radical misunderstanding of the Oriental, and especially the Malayan character. The color of the Filipino's skin is not more unlike that of his white brother than is the whole cast in which nature had molded him. It is not a difference in degree, which might prove susceptible to amelioration, but a difference in kind, which is beyond the reach of any human agency. Those who are acquainted with the Malayan race, with its character, genius, limitations, and good and bad qualities, those who find most to love and most to admire in this people, are still compelled to admit that the Malay has not in him any of the elements which make his transformation into a European, no matter in what length of time or by the aid of what system of training, anything but the veriest [sic] dream of the armchair philanthropist.

This writer was pessimistic about the "trainability" of the Filipinxs to work, and urged the United States not to "(embark) upon a hopeless enterprise . . . to revolutionize the nature of its inhabitants" but instead permit the "immigration of the industrious and thrifty Chinese." But in the end, on April 29, 1902, the US Congress extended the act in the United States and approved its application to Hawai'i and the Philippines.

The racial discourse surrounding the Chinese exclusion policy in the Philippines had helped create the impression that the Filipinxs would not make good laborers not only in their own country but also in the United States. With the Chinese Exclusion Act being extended indefinitely from 1902 on, the United States had to find alternative sources of cheap labor, which the Japanese and Koreans had provided.[17] Even though by 1902 Filipinxs were already allowed to enter the US without any visa restrictions, it was not until a few years later that the first group of laborers migrated.[18]

Under the American colonial regime, preparations were first made to educate the Filipinxs and turn them into "little brown Americans." This was done by establishing a public educational system in the Philippines in 1901 where English became the medium of instruction and Filipinxs were schooled in US history, civics, and other subjects. In 1903, the US government sent a group of young Filipinxs from elite families to come to the United States as *pensionados*—i.e., as US government scholars studying in select American universities, who were expected to bring their knowledge back to the Philippines and help run the country. The Philippine Village exhibit mounted at the St. Louis World's Fair of 1904, where the different "tribes" of the Philippines from the "lowly" Aetas and Negritos who were deemed uncivilizable to the Visayans who could be were put on display, helped, for better or for worse, change the perception of the American public of the trainability of the Filipinxs.[19] Hence, it was not until 1906 that Filipinx migrant labor was first utilized in Hawai'i.[20] The influx of Filipinx migrant labor to the continental US did not begin until the 1920s, after the Immigration Act of 1924 excluded other Asians, especially the Japanese and Koreans, from entering the country.[21] By then, the United States felt that Filipinxs were ready to perform the manual labor needed—particularly "stoop" labor in the agricultural farms of the West Coast and other menial jobs such as cooking, domestic help, restaurant and hotel work—that other Asian migrant labor groups had performed before them.[22]

Conclusion

Our knowledge about the history of Filipinx migration can be broadened by relating it to the anti-Chinese sentiment in the United States that resulted in creating exclusionary laws to bar the migration of Chinese laborers to both the metropole and the peripheries. More specifically, Filipinx labor migration in the early twentieth century to the United States was made possible as well as limited by the racialization of the "Filipinxs" vis-à-vis other ethnic groups, and in particular, the "Chinese" from the Philippines. Being compared to the Chinese (as well as other racial groups) in their capacity to work had forestalled the immediate labor migration of the Filipinxs to the United States.[23] The irony is that, as soon as the Americans felt assured in the capacity of the Filipinxs to work and brought them in big numbers in the 1920s, it did not take long before anti-Filipinx sentiments began to percolate to also exclude them.[24] Just like the Chinese and other Asians before them, for many Americans the Filipinxs also had become a race whose migration to the United States had become a threat to white labor and the purity of "white" America.

NOTES

1. See, for example, Ronald Takaki, "Dollar a Day, Dime a Dance: The Forgotten Filipinos," in *Strangers from a Different Shore: A History of Asian Americans*, rev. ed. (Boston: Little, Brown and Company, 1998), 315–54.

2. See, for example, Dawn Bohulano Mabalon, *Little Manila Is in the Heart: The Making of the Filipina/o American Community in Stockton, California* (Durham, N.C.: Duke University Press, 2013); and Benito M. Vergara Jr., *Pinoy Capital: The Filipino Nation in Daly City* (Philadelphia: Temple University Press, 2008).

3. See, for example, Rick Bonus, *Locating Filipino Americans: Ethnicity and the Cultural Politics of Space* (Philadelphia: Temple University Press, 2000); Rhacel Salazar Parreñas, *Servants of Globalization: Migration and Domestic Work* (Stanford, Calif.: Stanford University Press, 2001); Robyn Magalit Rodriguez, *Migrants for Export: How the Philippine State Brokers Labor to the World* (Minneapolis: University of Minnesota Press, 2010); Catherine Ceniza Choy, *Empire of Care: Nursing and Migration in Filipino American History* (Durham, N.C.: Duke University Press, 2013).

4. See, for example, Rudy P. Guevarra Jr., "Mabuhay Compañero: Filipinos, Mexicans, and Interethnic Labor Organizing in Hawai'i and California, 1920s–1940s," in *Transnational Crossroads: Remapping the Americas and the Pacific*, ed. Camilla Fojas and Rudy P. Guevarra Jr. (Lincoln: University of Nebraska Press, 2012), 171–98; and Joanna Poblete, *Islanders in the Empire: Filipino and Puerto Rican Laborers in Hawai'i* (Champaign: University of Illinois Press, 2014).

5. Aside from some of the works previously mentioned, see Rick Baldoz, *The Third Asiatic Invasion: Migration and Empire in Filipino America, 1898–1946* (New York: New York University Press, 2013); and Martin F. Manalansan IV, *Global Divas: Filipino Gay Men in the Diaspora* (Durham, N.C.: Duke University Press, 2003).

6. Oscar V. Campomanes, "New Formations of Asian American Studies and the Question of U.S. Imperialism," *Positions* 5, no. 2 (1997): 530.

7. US Philippine Commission, *Report of the Philippine Commission to the President* (Washington, DC: Government Printing Office, 1899), 1: 152.

8. US Philippine Commission, *Report* (1899), 1: 159.

9. Richard T. Chu, "Transnationalizing the History of the Chinese in the Philippines during the American Colonial Period: The Case of the Chinese Exclusion Act," in *Filipino Studies: Palimpsests of Nation and Diaspora*, ed. Martin F. Manalansan IV and Augusto F. Espiritu (New York: New York University Press, 2016), 189. See also Tomas S. Fonacier, "The Chinese Exclusion Policy in the Philippines," *Social Sciences and Humanities Review* 14, no. 1 (1949): 3–28.

10. Erika Lee, "Enforcing the Borders: Chinese Exclusion along the U.S. Borders with Canada and Mexico, 1882–1924," *The Journal of American History* 89, no. 1 (June 2002): 72–84.

11. US Philippine Commission, *Report* (1900), 2: 254.

12. For more information, see Richard T. Chu, *Chinese and Chinese Mestizos of Manila: Family, Identity, and Culture 1860s–1930s* (Leiden: Brill, 2010), 289–91; Richard T. Chu, "The 'Chinaman' Question: A Conundrum in U.S. Imperial Policy in the Pacific," *Kritika Kultura* 7 (2006): 13.

13. Steffi San Buenaventura, "The Colors of Manifest Destiny: Filipinos and the American Other(s)," *Amerasia Journal* 24, no. 3 (1998): 6–22.

14. Rafael Comenge y Dalmau, *Cuestiones Filipinas*, Estudio Social y Político. 1a. parte. Los Chinos (Manila: Tipolitografía de Chofré y compa, 1894), 46–47.

15. "The Chinese in the Philippines: Question of Their Admission Considered in a New Light—Writer in London Times Contends that the Filipino Is Not Now Capable of Steady Work," *New York Times*, August 24, 1902.

16. See also Christopher A. Vaughan, "The 'Discovery' of the Philippines by the U.S. Press, 1898–1902," *The Historian* (1995): 303–14.

17. Though the Treaty of Paris signed by the Spanish and US governments effectively rendered the natives of the Philippines US nationals, in the beginning there was confusion on how to treat those wishing to come to the United States. Initially, they were also deemed as "aliens," and the Chinese exclusion laws were used as a basis to bar them (along with the Puerto Ricans) from entering the United States. See "No. 76—Publishing decision of the Secretary of the Treasury of the United States that citizens of the Philippines will be examined as aliens upon their arrival in the United States," *Official Gazette* 1, no. 14 (December 10, 1902): 12–13. It was only in 1902, after the Philippine Bill became law, that the US Congress allowed the issuance of passports to Filipinxs who, despite not being citizens of the United States, nevertheless owed allegiance to it. See Dudley O. McGovney, "Our Non-Citizen Nationals, Who Are They?," *California Law Review* 22, no. 6 (September 1934): 599, 603; and Filomeno Aguilar Jr., "The Riddle of the Alien-Citizen: Filipino Migrants as US Nationals and the Anomalies of

Citizenship, 1900s–1930s," *Asian and Pacific Migration Journal* 19, no. 2 (2010): 203–36.

18. Even before 1898, the idea of bringing Filipinxs to work in Hawai'i already had been considered. See "Marsden May Go to the Philippines," *Evening Bulletin*, March 21, 1906. However, that idea was scrapped as it was feared that some Chinese might be able to mix in and enter Hawai'i, thus violating Hawai'i's Chinese exclusionary laws. See Rubén Alcántara, *Filipino History in Hawaii before 1946: The Sakada Years of Filipinos in Hawaii* (Lorton, Vir.: n.p., 1988), chap. 1, 12, *https://scholarspace.manoa.hawaii.edu/handle/10125 /17651*. Furthermore, as early as 1901, the Hawaiian Sugar Planters Association (HSPA) floated the idea of recruiting Filipinx laborers, but the idea was also scrapped because the US secretary of war and the commanding general of the American army in the Philippines opposed it on the grounds that Filipinxs did not want to emigrate to Hawai'i (Alcántara, *Filipino History*, 12, 18). Also, the HSPA already had laborers coming in from Japan, Korea, and Puerto Rico. Lastly, reports from the Philippine Commission indicated that Filipinxs were not reliable workers and expensive compared to workers from Hong Kong (Alcántara, *Filipino History*, 12, 18).

Another time that this issue of recruiting Filipinx laborers to Hawai'i was raised was in 1902, when a certain "Mr. Samson" brought up the idea of sending Filipinx farmers. See "Filipinos al Hawaii," *El Renacimiento*, January 18, 1902. For the account of the recruitment of the first Filipinxs to Hawai'i, when Albert Judd was commissioned by the HSPA to leave for the Philippines in 1906, and succeeded in bringing back fifteen Filipinxs from the Ilocos region, see Alcántara, *Filipino History* (chap. 1, 11–33). See also "Commercial News," *Sunday Advertiser*, December 2, 1906. From 1907 on, Filipinx labor came in greater numbers. See John E. Reinecke, *Feigned Necessity: Hawaii's Attempt to Obtain Chinese Contract Labor* (San Francisco: Chinese Materials Center, Inc., 1979), 28.

19. See Baldoz, *The Third Asiatic Invasion*, 37–38. See also Paul Kramer, *The Blood of Government: Race, Empire, the United States, and the Philippines* (Chapel Hill: University of North Carolina Press, 2006), 271. Kramer writes that the St. Louis exhibition might even had produced a different (negative) effect on the "trainability" of the Filipinxs. Furthermore, he points out that American officials lamented the lack of technical expertise of Filipinxs, including that for labor/manual work. The image of the Filipino as indolent was propelled or initiated during the Spanish times, and the question of "Filipino labor had long been one of the regime's central preoccupations, given limited insular revenues and the desire to attract U.S. and other foreign capital to the islands." See Kramer, *Blood of Government*, 313.

20. Miriam Sharma, "Pinoy in Paradise: Environment and Adaptation of Pilipinos in Hawaii, 1906–1946," *Amerasia* 7, no. 2 (1980): 91.

21. Brett H. Melendy, "Filipinos in the United States," *Pacific Historical Review* 43, no. 4 (Nov. 1974): 523–29. In the 1853 Hawai'i census, there is a record of five Filipinxs. In the 1880s, there were some Filipinx musicians working for the San Francisco–based Chiarini's Royal Italian Circus who made their way to Hawai'i. See Alcántara, *Filipino History* (chap. 1, 30).

22. The absence of a reliable supply of Mexican workers also led, especially among farm owners in the West Coast, to the import of Filipinx labor. See Baldoz, *Third Asiatic*, 65.

23. Note however that Kramer points out that it was also a racial problem— i.e., the annexation of the Philippines brought also fears of the invasion of "Filipino" people, who were considered as semi-savage. Rebecca Taylor, writing in 1903, compared US colonization of the Philippines to ingesting food that became part of one's physical makeup, a process Kramer calls "digestive imperialism." In time, Taylor feared the US becoming "Malayed." See Kramer, *Blood of Government*, 207–8.

24. This was after a period of time had elapsed in which to observe how well they worked in Hawai'i, considered as a "training school" for Filipinx workers. See Reinecke, *Feigned Necessity*, 608. See also Emily S. Bogardus, "American Attitudes towards Filipinos," *Sociology and Social Research* 14 (1929): 63–67; and Bruno Lasker, *Filipino Immigration* (New York: Arno Press and The New York Times, 1969), 33–76.

ELEVEN

Labor and Carework

Anna Romina Guevarra

Carework has long been a prized commodity of the Philippines, formally produced, marketed, and sold by the Philippine state machinery since 1974, when the country's labor export economy was formally established. Carework is defined here as unpaid or paid labor in the form of work and service to another individual or community. In the context of the Philippines, carework—and especially gendered carework—is central to the economy and the political machinations of a constellation of state and nonstate actors—the labor brokers and "public managers,"[1] suturing the labor of its workers both to the contemporary neoliberal order as well as its colonial past. As such, an exploration of this analytic is central to revealing not only the workings of the Philippine state, but also the logics of US empire that continue to govern the Philippine political economy and position Filipinxs as laboring subjects connecting the Global North and South. Carework, therefore—and through it, Filipinx American studies—emerges as a key theoretical site and analytic that allows for the exploration of the global reach of US empire, while showcasing the gendered moral economy of migration.

The Philippines' labor export economy is the product of a state broker-ing apparatus; it functions through the work of the Philippine Overseas Employment Administration (POEA) and the Overseas Workers Welfare Administration (OWWA), which emerged as key bureaucratic organizations following the passage of the 1974 Philippine labor code.[2] In addition, the private sector, represented by hundreds of state-licensed private employment agencies, works in coordination with this marketized statecraft to broker and facilitate the migration process and the governmentality of overseas Filipinx workers.[3] While this 1974 policy was meant to be temporary, succeeding ad-ministrations could not overlook the significant remittances that flowed into Philippine banking channels; by the 1980s they became so vast that Overseas Filipinx Workers (OFWs) were crafted as the "modern day heroes" (*bagong bayani*). But it also pushed the state to address the high price of this heroism as coffins containing bodies of OFWs began their homecoming as a result of abuses experienced by workers overseas. To appease a growing public outcry, the Philippine state responded with the Migrant Workers and Overseas Filipinos Act of 1995, which outlined a multipronged promise of welfare protection. It also mirrored a change in policy that reconceptual-ized the country's overseas employment program in terms of managing labor migration. It is this framework and these policies that gave birth to these public managers and labor brokers who would anchor the state through this neoliberal turn, while catapulting Filipinxs' dreams and aspirations for the country's economic comparative advantage.

Carework and Gendered Moral Economies

Undergirding this institutionalized system of labor export is also a gendered moral economy of migration represented by Filipinx careworkers—the iconic figures that haunt the Philippine social imaginary. In fact, when OFWs were proclaimed to be the *bagong bayani* (modern day heroes) of the nation in 1988, then-president Corazon Aquino was standing in front of Fili-pinx domestic workers in Hong Kong in recognition of the role that remit-tances have played in the Philippines economy, accounting for 2 percent of the country's GNP at the time.[4] I have argued in my work that this gendered and racialized moral economy of the Filipinx migrant underscores the cultural logic that governs how OFWs are supposed to behave, as "model" Filipinx who embody an ethic of responsibility toward their families and nation and represent the "Great Filipino Worker" while maintaining their commodification to a neoliberal state.[5] Mediated by state and nonstate actors, this logic becomes hypervisible through the discursive representations of Filipinx workers' caring labor, which is promoted as their *added export value*—a racialized form of productive labor that is pitched as the comparative advantage of Filipinxs.[6] In the context of the labor recruitment of nurses from the Philippines, for example, Filipinx nurses are recruited on the basis of specific qualities that ostensibly make them ideal working subjects—ranging from their readiness to leave the country, their "TLC" (tender loving care) qualities, and their willingness to assume any responsibility in the context of work. This can also be seen in the ways that educational institutions produce "ideal" nurses through the practice of bodywork, whereby Filipinx nurses who aspire to work overseas develop their comparative advantage by working on/manipulating their patients' bodies for practice.[7]

Similarly, Filipinx domestic workers are represented as obedient, God-fearing, and educated—all of which makes them the "Mercedes Benz" of the domestic labor industry. But labor brokers also work to ensure that these discursive representations become a reality by mandating that prospective overseas workers undergo formal training where they are taught to be docile and compliant.[8] It is not uncommon to hear labor brokers note that with Filipinx workers, one is able to obtain a "maid and a tutor" for the price of one. Brokers do not hesitate to highlight applicants' educational background or additional training as bringing "added value" to their work as maids. Consider the following notations found in the domestic work applications: "Her experience and training in the Philippines put her in a good position as childcarer"; "she took a 2-year course of Computer Secretarial"; or "she is attending nursing aid courses."[9] Labor brokers ensure this comparative advantage by headhunting in specific places where they are able to find workers with these particular "added value" skills and sensibilities, or by mandating that household work training programs provide these skills in order to compete in the global market.

The Philippine state, in response to the demand of foreign employers for technically trained domestic workers, allows private employment agencies to require workers to undergo these training programs within state-accredited training centers. State officials affirm that upgrading work skills may be a means of reducing the vulnerability of workers to workplace violence and maltreatment. A number of policy reforms were implemented, beginning in 2006, to professionalize domestic work including new forms of certification from the Technical Education and Skills Development Authority (TESDA). This certification entails attending 216 hours of training through a TESDA-accredited training center, which aims to produce domestic workers who have the appropriate and standardized skills for housecleaning, operating a range of household appliances, and practicing occupational health and safety protocols.

The focus on upgrading domestic workers was pushed even further with the creation of the Supermaid training program, which was a response to some thirty thousand Filipinx workers (a majority of whom were domestic workers) being repatriated from the war in Lebanon in the summer of 2006. Introduced by former Philippine president Gloria Macapagal Arroyo, the program is supposed to enhance the technical capabilities of Filipinx domestic workers, enabling them to land higher-paying jobs as they offer employers expertise that goes beyond household chores. In addition to her enviable domestic work skills, a Filipinx Supermaid can respond to medical emergencies and accidents with appropriate first-aid treatment. She is able to execute procedures for responding to physical threats and dangers such as evacuations from high-rise buildings. She is able to mediate conflicts in the household and attend to various behavioral issues. She is able to care for both human and nonhuman members of the family. As Augusto Syjuco, the head of TESDA succinctly put it, domestic workers "will become upgraded domestic helpers with a higher price."[10] It is as if these skills provide them with extraordinary powers to elevate their social and professional status, and help them deal with the vulnerability they experience given the nature of their job.[11]

Carework and Colonial Legacies

Undergirding the gendered moral economy of Filipinx migration is the history of colonization that the Philippines has been subjected to, which has had an influential role in the organization of carework between the Global

South and North. Arguably, the global presence of Filipinx nurses to fulfill labor shortages stems, at least in part, from the Americanized curriculum and nursing training that the US imposed, following its colonization of the country from 1898 to 1945.[12] As Catherine Ceniza Choy notes, the institutionalization of US nursing programs in the Philippines, beginning in 1907, was an essential "precondition" of the contemporary migration of Filipinx nurses in the US insofar as it provided them US-based nursing training and familiarity with a US work culture.[13] This "Western" nursing curricular framework is pivotal to the ways that labor brokers promote the *added value* of Filipinx nurses, which also helps explain their overwhelming presence in the UK, Australia, and Ireland. Recently, for example, a Filipinx nurse working at the Royal London Hospital received an award as an Officer of the Most Excellent Order of the British Empire (OBE) for her exemplary work during the 2017 London Bridge incident that injured and killed more than thirty individuals.[14]

In addition to influencing the nursing curriculum of the Philippines, the US colonization of the country also fundamentally restructured the country's higher education system. This process began with the deployment of American teachers—the Thomasites in 1901—who embodied America's attempt to transform Filipinxs into a particular type of American citizen, one who was not only "educated" but also emulated the American way of life.[15] The Thomasites, and the US imperial project more generally, provided education that shifted the emphasis from religion to "civilizing" Filipinx through American democratic principles of rules and the law, while institutionalizing the English language as a medium of instruction and "conversion."

Over a hundred years later, we see these colonial legacies manifest in the continuing recruitment of Filipinx teachers in US public schools across the country from Maryland, California, Nevada, to Arizona and New Mexico.[16] Not only are they filling positions that many American teachers are turning away from due to the low wages, but they enter the US as contingent labor on a three-year J1 visa, which does not carry any pathway for permanent residency. Their contingent and precarious status parallels those of the thousands of caregivers working in the US—those who fall into the category of personal attendants and home-care aides—many of whom work as part of an underground informal economy.[17]

The Global Care Chains

The position that the Philippines occupies as a primary source of care labor is what sustains the phenomenon referred to as a *global care chain*—namely, a global transfer of caretaking that fuels the dependence of the Global North on the Global South.[18] It is a process that reifies the current division of reproductive labor, reflecting and perpetuating a class-based hierarchy between the providers and consumers of care and between the Global North and South. In this care chain, the woman who possesses the most economic resources is able to purchase the low-wage labor of a woman with lesser economic resources from the Global South. This woman, as a consequence of leaving her family behind in order to provide this labor, may then also end up having to purchase the low-wage labor of another "poorer" woman in her home country. Thus, this care chain reflects a structural condition that not only links the Global North and South economically, but also characterizes a hierarchy of class privilege that consequently provokes a reexamination and reevaluation of the nature of economic empowerment to be gained in this process. After all, while the lives of the women who are part of this chain are closely intertwined, the process has varied stakes for each, and the benefits they derive from this process are uneven.

This unevenness is especially evident in the growing number of transnational families,[19] which result when members of these families live apart from one another in more than one nation-state. For migrant mothers, this parenting comes at a huge emotional strain for both the migrant parents and their children, at the same time that migrant women/mothers are often held solely accountable by the public and the Philippine state for the "broken homes" or the nation's "care crisis."[20] In this public discourse, migrant women are scrutinized, and often blamed, for the emotional strain that their children experience due to the extended time they spend working overseas, but also for the insufficiency of the material rewards that result from this work. Far from being supported by the state and other labor brokers, these migrant women often end up facilitating the care of one another from a distance, further complicating the understanding of transnational family formations. In this context, Valerie Francisco-Menchavez's work, which explores care networks *among* migrant women working overseas, is important. Referring to "communities of care," Francisco-Menchavez accounts for the migrant networks of support that stem from the connections, interpersonal relationships, and fictive kinship ties that form among migrants that allow them to provide care for one another.[21] Thus, the carework that sustains the global care chains are enacted by a number of actors who are not only in the Philippines, but also in the countries where they work.

Mediations of Care

In recent years, the work of sustaining transnational families is increasingly facilitated by technology, especially digital technology such as Facebook, Skype, FaceTime, and video conferencing. They allow for the creation of "Skype mothers" who can monitor their children from a distance and "Facebook children" who forge new relationships and interactions with their mothers through this technologically mediated platform.[22] Thus, these digital technologies are able to bridge geographic distance and help facilitate the delivery and performance of carework, albeit virtually.

The place of technology, writ large, in mediating and extending global care chains is exemplified most recently by the entrance of a new laboring body in the realm of education—"robot teachers."[23] These robot teachers first emerged in the context of South Korea's robotic innovation—Engkey, the English teaching robot—designed to provide educational assistance in elementary schools. Produced by the Korean Institute of Science and Technology, Engkey is an avatar tele-education robot that is premised on the concept of "distant-teaching" or "e-learning," and represents the South Korean state's commitment to improve the English-language proficiency of its citizens. Its operation, however, is facilitated by Filipinx labor; Engkey's "functionality" derives from the fact that "she" is controlled by a remote teacher who, during the pilot tests, was located in the Philippines. At a height of 3.3 feet, Engkey stands as a *white* penguin-shaped robot, with a TV display screen as a head that projects an image of a young white girl with long blond hair. Filipinx teachers, working as online instructors in call centers in the Philippines, circulate as disembodied, yet gendered and racialized robots with white avatar faces, and interact with South Korean students using a microphone device attached to a video camera to telecast lessons and communicate in real time. The teacher directs and manipulates the robot's movements to correspond with her instruction. However, the students who receive her instruction are not able to see the teacher in the Philippines, or distinguish between the "actual" teacher and the machine that is projecting the teacher's intellect. For these students, Engkey, the robot, is their teacher: one with a white face, blond hair . . . and a Filipinx-tinged "American" accent.

This new configuration of care labor complicates not only what it means to provide carework but it troubles the boundaries between human and machine, creating what I refer to as *mediations of care*—gendered and racialized hierarchies that produce new forms of affective labor and sociality that are governed by modes of simultaneous disembodiment and embodiment, immobility and mobility, and marketized statecraft through vocabularies of innovation and exploitation. In this case, Engkey's success in the classroom depends on how the robot teachers in the Philippines can manipulate her so that "she" can continue to be perceived as a plaything, less threatening than an actual human teacher. The kind of labor performed by these robot teachers and the consciousness they inhabit must balance a fine line between being humanlike yet still appearing to be a "thing"—an entertaining gadget. In this latest configuration of commoditized labor, Engkey, through the labor of the robot teachers, serves as an innovation of such carework, disrupting the ways in which this new form of carework operates through *dis*embodiment and *de*racination, even as Engkey calls into question the inherent class-based and gendered hierarchies that the global care chain presumes. That is, the "good enough" laborer in the Global South, dis/embodied by and transmitted through Engkey, is the female skilled online teacher with a higher education and presumably more "authentic" (perhaps whitened) credentials to serve as the globally legitimate provider of English-language instruction. The legitimate and visible body in this configuration is the white female body that occludes the fact that the actual laboring body is a nonwhite body in the Global South. Thus, Engkey is both an extension of *and* a disruption of the so-called global care chains that perpetuate global inequities in a transformed neoliberal gender and racial order.

NOTES

1. Anna Romina Guevarra, *Marketing Dreams, Manufacturing Heroes: The Transnational Labor Brokering of Filipino Workers* (New Brunswick, N.J.: Rutgers University Press, 2010); Anna Romina Guevarra, "The Public Manager," in *Figures of Southeast Asian Modernity*, ed. Joshua Barker, Erik

Harms, and Johan Lindquist (Honolulu: University of Hawai'i Press, 2013), 29–31; Anna Romina Guevarra, "Managing 'Vulnerabilities' and 'Empowering' Migrant Filipina Workers: The Philippines' Overseas Employment Program," *Social Identities: Journal for the Study of Race, Nation, and Culture* 12, no. 5 (2006): 523–41.

2. See Robyn Magalit Rodriguez, *Migrants for Export: How the Philippine State Brokers Labor to the World* (Minneapolis: University of Minnesota Press, 2010).

3. Rodriguez, *Migrants for Export*; Guevarra, *Marketing Dreams*.

4. Rodriguez, *Migrants for Export*; Guevarra, *Marketing Dreams*.

5. Rodriguez, *Migrants for Export*; Guevarra, "Managing 'Vulnerabilities.'"

6. Rodriguez, *Migrants for Export*; Guevarra, "Managing 'Vulnerabilities.'"

7. Yasmin Y. Ortiga and Jenica Ana Rivero, "Bodies of Work: Skilling at the Bottom of the Global Nursing Care Chain," *Globalizations*, 1–14, *https://doi.org/10.1080/14747731.2019.1576321*.

8. See for example, Nicole Constable, *Maid to Order in Hong Kong: Stories of Filipina Workers* (Ithaca, N.Y.: Cornell University Press, 1997); Geraldine Pratt, "Stereotypes and Ambivalence: The Construction of Domestic Workers in Vancouver, British Columbia," *Gender, Place and Culture: A Journal of Feminist Geography* 4, no. 2 (1997): 159–77; Pei-Chia Lan, *Global Cinderellas: Migrant Domestics and Newly Rich Employers in Taiwan* (Durham, N.C.: Duke University Press, 2006).

9. *http://filipinomaids.com*.

10. Sam Mediavilla, "Displaced Domestic Help to Return as Supermaids," *The Manila Times* (2006).

11. Anna Romina Guevarra, "Supermaids: The Racial Branding of Global Filipino Care Labour," in *Migration and Care Labour: Theory, Policy, and Politics*, ed. Bridget Anderson and Isabel Shutes (Houndmills, Basingstoke, UK: Palgrave Macmillan, 2014), 130–50.

12. Catherine Ceniza Choy, *Empire of Care: Nursing and Migration in Filipino American History* (Durham, N.C.: Duke University Press, 2003).

13. Choy, *Empire of Care*.

14. Rose Eclarinal, "Pinay Nurse to Receive British Royal Award for Community Work, ABS-CBN News," March 2, 2019, *https://news.abs-cbn.com/overseas/03/02/19/pinay-nurse-to-receive-british-royal-award-for- community-work*.

15. Mary Racelis and Judy C. Ick, *Bearers of Benevolence: The Thomasites and Public Education in the Philippines* (Pasig City, Manila: Anvil, 2001).

16. See Lora Bartlett, *Migrant Teachers: How American Schools Import Labor* (Cambridge, Mass.: Harvard University Press, 2014); "Highly Qualified

Filipino Teachers Filling APS Teacher Gap—Albuquerque Public Schools," n.d., accessed March 3, 2019, *https://www.aps.edu/news/highly-qualified-filipino -teachers-filling-aps-teacher-gap*; Terry Greene Sterling and Jude Joffe-Block, "The Job Americans Won't Take: Arizona Looks to Philippines to Fill Teacher Shortage," *The Guardian*, September 5, 2018, sec. US news, *https:// www.theguardian.com/us- news/2018/sep/05/arizona-teachers-filipino-schools-low- pay*; Andrew Craft, "School Districts Increasingly Hiring Foreign Teachers to Fill Shortages," Fox News, May 13, 2018, *https://www.foxnews.com/us/school -districts-increasingly-hiring-foreign-teachers-to-fill-shortages.*

17. Charlene Tung, "Caring Across Borders: Motherhood, Marriage, and Filipina Domestic Workers in California," in *Asian/Pacific Islander American Women: A Historical Anthology*, ed. Shirley Hune and Gail Nomura (New York: New York University Press, 2003), 301–15; Anna Romina Guevarra and Lolita Lledo, "Formalizing the Informal: Low Wage Immigrant Highly Skilled Filipina Caregivers and the Pilipino Worker Center," in *Immigrant Women Workers in the Neoliberal Age*, ed. Nilda Flores-Gonzalez, Anna Romina Guevarra, Maura Toro-Morn, and Grace Chang (Urbana: University of Illinois Press, 2013), 247–61.

18. Rhacel Parreñas, *Servants of Globalization: Women, Migration, and Domestic Work* (Stanford, Calif.: Stanford University Press, 2001).

19. Valerie Francisco-Menchavez, *The Labor of Care: Filipina Migrants and Transnational Families in the Digital Age* (Urbana: University of Illinois Press, 2018); Asuncion Fresnoza-Flot, "Migration Status and Transnational Mother- ing: The Case of Filipino Migrants in France," *Global Networks* 9, no. 2 (2009): 252–70; Rhacel Parreñas, "Mothering from a Distance: Emotions, Gender, and Intergenerational Relations in Filipino Transnational Families," *Feminist Studies* 27, no. 2 (2001): 361–90; Parreñas, *Servants of Globalization*.

20. Parreñas, "Mothering from a Distance."

21. Valerie Francisco-Menchavez, *The Labor of Care: Filipina Migrants and Transnational Families in the Digital Age* (Urbana: University of Illinois Press, 2018).

22. Francisco-Menchavez, *The Labor of Care.*

23. Anna Romina Guevarra, "Mediations of Care: Brokering Labour in the Age of Robotics," *Pacific Affairs* 91, no. 4 (2018): 739–58; Anna Romina Guevarra, "Techno-Modeling Care: Racial Branding, Dis/Embodied Labor, and 'Cybraceros' in South Korea," *Frontiers: A Journal in Women's Studies* 36, no. 3 (2015): 139–59.

The Labor of History in Filipinx Historiography

Jody Blanco

When we inquire into the defining features of our immigrant and diasporic histories in the United States, perhaps the first and most prominent category of reflection is that of labor. We would know this on an almost intuitive level: Work binds us together within determinate sectors (the military industrial complex, the medical-industrial complex, the industries of care and personal service, the arts); and provides the analytic for identifying ourselves with or distancing ourselves from others.[1] Work forms the core preoccupation of narratives our parents, grandparents, and extended families told us and each other: why they worked, how long and hard they worked, what would befall them in the absence of work; what work would and would not make possible, what work we would do when we were grown. It signifies for us, more than any other consideration, our "right" to a sense of national belonging in the US, regardless of whether or not it should.[2] Perhaps then, it comes as no surprise that the published histories and historiographies of Filipinx American and Asian Americans more broadly should focus so closely on labor: from the plantation workers of Hawaiʻi to the engineers in Silicon Valley and the seamen working navy ships and trans-oceanic private liners.

Beyond the history of labor, however, very seldomly do we pause to evaluate the labor of history: the work, the task of promoting a narrative that reconciles an affirmation of our belonging *here and now, together*, with our insertion into the larger historical streams of political economy, migration and diaspora, public opinion, social activism, and cultural cosmopolitanism. While this labor has traditionally dedicated itself toward the articulation of a US ethnic and racial identity, my contribution offers several counterexamples of historiography that encourage us to venture beyond this project, and explore the cross-currents of identification and disidentification of which we are also a part.

The Labor of History

Few texts exhibit the radical divergence between the conception of history and role of historical reflection taking place among elite officials in the Philippines during the first half of the twentieth century and among Filipinx US immigrants or "nationals" in the same period than Carlos Bulosan's stirring autobiography *America Is in the Heart*. Bulosan (1913–56) was born not long after the nineteenth-century generation of writers and educated young men, led by national martyr José Rizal and Marcelo H. del Pilar, were politicizing the knowledge of Philippine history as a weapon against a Spanish colonial government opposed to colonial reforms. Bulosan would come of age during the period that the Philippines was struggling to imagine a future involving national independence after being a colonial possession of Spain and the United States. Both the uncertain future of imperialist policies in the US and the continuity of popular resistance to US rule throughout the Philippines led US presidents William McKinley and William Howard Taft to maintain that colonial rule was temporary, and that after a period of "tutelage" in US-styled government and institutions the Philippines would become an independent republic.[3]

With the defeat of the revolution by the US, those who survived or maneuvered themselves to occupy positions of authority and leadership in the

Philippines under US colonial rule (like Pedro Paterno and Trinidad H. Pardo de Tavera) turned their reflections to the larger arc of history's seemingly unchanging laws of evolution and decadence. They reinterpreted the past in a way that would help to explain the present and perhaps forecast the future of a "Saxonized" Philippines, which at times converged, at times conflicted, with the country's presumably Asian (or "Oriental") roots and "Hispanic" colonial heritage.[4] As the revolutionary legacy dwindled among an ever-smaller Spanish-speaking circle of Manileños, the Spanish and Chinese mestizo inheritors of those sugar and tobacco industries (which were originally promoted by Spain's Bourbon reforms) set about consolidating the lineages, landholdings, and regional identities of a new educated elite.[5] With the introduction of a bicameral Philippine legislature (with executive authority still under a US governor general) in 1916, an economic *burgis* or landowning class succeeded in establishing the oligarchic foundations of the country's political economy for the next century. They also became the most prominent spokespeople of what a Phillipine identity would or ought to be with the acquisition of national independence.[6]

Bulosan, in contrast to these figures, hails from the class responsible for the peasant uprisings in the 1920s and 1930s, in which the inchoate millenarian and sometimes apocalyptic leanings of popular protest had become inextricably intertwined with the folklore of the revolution and the memory of *ilustrado* and popular leaders like Rizal.[7] Landless and destitute in a republic-yet-to-be, uprooted by the violent oscillation between the demands of a backwards economy suddenly hitched to the train of preferential trade relations with the US, on the one hand, and the constant outbreak of mass revolt, on the other, many Filipinxs saw starting over in the sugarcane fields of Hawai'i and Alaskan canneries as the only escape from a predetermined fate of poverty and the impunity of authority. Bulosan and his compatriots had little need or use for the debates between Sajonistas, Hispanistas, Tagalistas, and Orientalists, nor did they possess legal papers documenting a patrimony or legacy inherited from the past. It is just such a context that helps to explain how Bulosan would have trouble recognizing his own blood brothers in America, whom he encounters in random dire straits as he treks up and down the West Coast for seasonal employment in agricultural labor. For Bulosan, family and community existed not in the past, but the future; not in the affirmation of long-standing tradition and its values, but rather in the forced alienation from all existing communities and their traditions; not in history, in short, but rather in a desperate aesthetic vision of what a possible history might one day be—a history capable of redeeming the fragments of past recollections, knitting them into the fabric of a new people and a new common land.

Yet to the indifference of Philippine nationalists who were occupied with the politics of national identity in the Philippines, Bulosan expressed his vision of a new people not in the Philippines, but America:

> America is not bound by geographical latitudes. America is not merely a land or an institution. America is in the hearts of men that died for freedom. . . . America is a prophecy of a new society of men. . . . America is also the nameless foreigner, the homeless refugee, the hungry boy begging for a job and the black body dangling on a tree. America is the illiterate immigrant. . . . We are all that nameless foreigner, that homeless refugee, that hungry boy, that illiterate immigrant and that lynched black body. All of us, from the first Adams to the last Filipino, native born or alien, educated or illiterate—*We are America!*[8]

Bulosan's reflection stands at the intersection of two political projects and their attendant historiographies. The first is the campaign to demand that the US take responsibility for the claims it had advanced as a democratic republic, which it had twisted into an argument for imperial expansion at the turn of the twentieth century. After all, America only became a "prophecy of a new society" for many after the US takeover of the Philippines had accelerated a transition from colonial state monopolies in the Spanish period to the rise of a landowning oligarchy.[9] The second project concerns the imagination of the US as a central arena for the rise of modern labor as the horizon of history as Marx characterized it: the limit at which all meaningful connections and obligations to the past are either severed or suspended in our insertion into (US) society and economy as (labor) commodities and consumers. For what most determines the history of Filipinx presence in the US but the shifting demands of the labor market in the twentieth and twenty-first centuries—from low-paid unskilled agricultural and service labor in the 1930s, to military service as seamen and stewards during and after World War II, to skilled service professionals in care industries like nursing and education in the past fifty years?[10]

The history of Filipinx labor unions on the West Coast documents the struggles of poor and rightless subjects intimately tied to the aesthetic vision of Bulosan's America.[11] As members of a US "unincorporated territory," Bulosan and his compatriots were brought to the US without immigration caps or quotas, while remaining unprotected in the US by the fundamental rights of citizenship: the writ of habeas corpus, the right to own land, the right to elect representatives of government, and (in many states) even the right to marry and have families.[12] The America of Bulosan's future thus served as a placeholder for hope in a world where the past had not and would not determine the future all the way to the end.[13]

What renders Bulosan's labor of history so difficult to evaluate and incorporate into our history today has everything to do with the realignments of labor and national identity in both the US and the Philippines during and after World War II. The Tydings-McDuffie Act in 1934 promised a path to Philippine independence over a ten-year period, in exchange for the severe curtailment of immigration to the US. Bulosan's account of migrant workers in the 1920s and 1930s was only published in 1946, ten years after US immigration had dwindled to fifty a year, and one year after the US had "declared" the Philippines an independent nation after "liberating" it from Japanese control. With labor migration to the US largely confined to and channeled primarily through recruitment into the US Navy after 1952, and with Philippine leaders engaged with the task of reconstructing Manila and forging new, unequal alliances with the US, the historical conjuncture outlined in Bulosan's labor of history fell on deaf ears. Students and advocates of creating ethnic studies programs in California would discover Bulosan's writing twenty-five years later, long after Philippine migration to the US ceased to be defined by the agricultural working class.

In its place, the Immigration and Nationality Act of 1965 promoted a profoundly different mass immigration of professionals from Asia, with an invitation for these new workers to petition their families to immigrate as well. For this new generation of workers and their families, America was also "in the heart" but in a very different way. Philippine enthusiasm and patriotism for the US was born not out of struggle but in the US-sponsored Philippine educational institutions promoting medicine and nursing; in the Philippines' decision to maintain English as a lingua franca after World War II; in the US military bases that remained in open defiance of the Philippines' claim to national sovereignty; in the Philippine government's acquiescence to serve as the launch pad for US interventions in Korea and Vietnam; in a commodity culture dominated by US exports; and finally, in an international labor market recognized by Filipinx leaders as a solution to unemployment and poverty at home. While the elder, *manong* generation of immigrants in the US dwindled to an ever-smaller population of predominantly aging bachelors struggling to stay afloat, a new generation of Filipinx immigrants arrived with a surprising familiarity of the United States. They understood it to be the kind of country that their own fledgling republic was on its way to becoming, eventually.

With their great fortune to have avoided the struggles and shortcomings of other Asian immigrants, such as their relative unfamiliarity with English as well as their greater ambivalence about US wars in Asia—the post-1965 generation also missed an opportunity to forge a concrete connection between themselves and the preceding, "lost" generation of Bulosan and his compatriots. The new immigrant professionals found themselves able to enjoy the benefits of citizenship rights and inclusion without ever having had to take part in the struggles for civil rights for women and racial minorities, or in the imagination of an America as the aesthetic vision of a redeemed labor class. Cut loose from a homeland marked by increasing civil strife, student radicalism, and the turn to martial law under President Ferdinand Marcos (beginning in 1972), and estranged from the struggles of the early Filipinx laboring class, these new immigrants settled in America without the pressure to "be," "become," or "act" American. The colonial past, the experience of Filipinxs and Americans fighting side by side against the Japanese empire, the enfranchisement of Filipina "war brides" of US servicemen, and the mutual benefit of overseas employment between countries, all gave these new immigrants, as well as the family members they petitioned for US citizenship, the confidence that they partook of a shared culture with the US, of global pretensions. It would take the few members of the second and third generations to rediscover the labor of history in Bulosan's work and promote the reading of *America Is in the Heart* in colleges and universities.[14]

The profound disconnect between Filipinx experiences of immigration between the first and second half of the twentieth century could not but produce equally contradictory historical legacies. One remains inextricably tied to the labor and racial struggles for the full rights of citizenship and belonging, which saw Filipinxs bound by solidarity and compassion with other US ethnic minorities; the other draws inspiration from the perceived reciprocal privileges and obligations of a shared international market and a shared global culture. The roots of the first are entangled in the darkest chapters of US history out of the West: from subjection to Lynch and anti-miscegenation laws during the years of the Depression to the perpetual transience of labor camps and urban flophouses. The second sees its roots in the expanding horizons of US military supremacy, economic markets, and diplomatic goodwill—from the formation of the United Nations and the US Marshall Plan to the opening of quotas for immigrants to power the postwar economy.

The disjointed strands of Filipinxs in America lead us to regard Bulosan's words as not only a source of inspiration but also an ever-evolving unsolved mystery. If America is indeed "not bound by geographical latitudes," where does it end and where do other histories begin? How do Filipinxs themselves distinguish between Philippine and US patriotism during the decades of the Cold War?[15] And if the institutionalization of ethnic studies in the early 1970s guaranteed Filipinx students the patrimony of their historical pasts in the US, what did it offer to their immigrant parents and relatives, whose lives remained inextricably tied—by remittances, language, religion, regional politics, and sometimes even lineage, property, and financial investments, as well as traditions—to a republic still struggling to overcome the vicissitudes of the colonial legacy?

Empire and Emporium: Recent Historiographies of Globalization

The intersection of imperial state violence in the US takeover of the Philippines and the deterritorializing trajectory of labor migration and labor markets from the Philippines to the US crystallizes for many scholars the inextricable relationship between oppression and exploitation, impunity and *homo sacer*, segregation or outright exclusion and "differential inclusion."[16] Indeed, one may argue that the uniqueness of Filipinx studies stemmed at least initially from the way in which the history of the Philippines and Philippine diaspora corresponded so closely with new theories of modern empire and a "postmodern" political economy. Yet for scholars of Filipinx studies, the theme of US imperialism also provides an interface with Philippine history that allows us to examine the specificities of our experiences with racial discrimination, de facto segregation, glass ceilings, and unequal opportunity in a new light and under a new lens.[17] Racism, for one thing, turns out to exist not only as a *structure* that conditions the day-to-day lives of US historically underrepresented minorities, but also as a *history* by which politicized acts of translation (such as the portrayal of Filipinxs as stereotyped African Indigenous peoples, Native Americans, or in blackface; or the conflation of Jim Crow legislation in the US as evidence of "race war") became naturalized as the status quo. Once such acts of translation became recognized as such, a whole new field of comparative analysis emerged.[18] Finally, this historical understanding of diverse structures of inequality and subjection under the umbrella concept "Empire" went hand in hand with a related program: the narration of marginalized US diasporic voices—which also go under the name of postcolonial, gendered/queer, racialized, and/or microhistories.[19]

The 1989 publication of Stanley Karnow's popular history of the 1898–1902 US-Philippine War (also called the Philippine-American War) *In Our Image* was certainly not the first history to investigate the contribution of US expansion overseas to the age of nineteenth-century European imperialism in Africa and Asia. Nor was Karnow the first author to explicitly link the discourses and strategies of that period with the imperialist character of the US interventions in Korea and Vietnam. Yet, coinciding as it did with the end of the Cold War and the termination of lease agreements for the US bases in the Philippines, Karnow's work provided Filipinxs an entry point toward the articulation of US empire studies, which would expose young students to the academic work on US empire by Amy Kaplan, Donald Pease, Lisa Lowe, and others. Conversely, the termination of the US military bases agreement between the Philippines and the United States also freed up Philippine-based scholarship to explore the truncated threads of cultural nationalist historiography, inspired by the likes of Teodoro Agoncillo, Milagros Guerrero, Renato Constantino, and Reynaldo Clemeña Ileto.[20] The emergence and counterpoint between these two pivots—toward on the one hand a post–Cold War "empire studies" and on the other a post–martial law, Indigenous-centered cosmopolitanism (characterized by projects like Zeus Salazar's Tagalog translation of Marx and Engels's *Manifesto of the Communist Party* from the original German)—has provided new opportunities to develop programs of historical research, translation, and collaboration that cross the boundaries of national, linguistic, and institutional affiliations. It has also given rise to serious disagreements regarding the administration of "official" versus "unofficial" and unorthodox methods of historical inquiry, as well as the ethics of knowledge-production: the question of who gets to tell the (hi)story of Philippine pasts, as well as the kind(s) of evidence that would supplement empirical data.

Once we identify the existence of two pivots in Philippine and Fil-Am historiography, however, one begins to wonder whether there are, in fact three, or even four? If debates over the status of "(US) empire talk" and new nativisms appear to exhaust the attention and energy concerning the emerging historiographies of globalization today, they certainly do not exhaust the laboratory of comparative empire studies and microhistories of Iberian globalization taking place both within the US and in the (predominantly) Spanish-speaking world today. Academic works by Rudy P. Guevarra Jr.[21] and Anthony Christian Ocampo[22] bring collective histories and sociologies of race to the experiences of the Camacho family in the fiction of Donna Miscolta,[23] linking Latinx and Filipinx legacies of colonialism and labor diasporas in the US. In world history, Josep M. Fradera[24] links the histories of the Philippines, Cuba, and Puerto Rico through the global scale production of agricultural exports like tobacco and sugar. And research programs like the one taking place in Madrid's CSIC (Centro Superior de Investigaciones Científicas) under the direction of María Dolores Elizalde, as well as Kyoto University's CSEAS (Center for Southeast Asian Studies) have not only served to decenter the traditional centers of knowledge-production in the US and Philippines. They have elaborated and unfolded new iterations of what was once called Southeast Asian area studies for an intellectual community and reading public whose members find themselves at once scattered throughout the globe and connected to each other through open-access journals like Kyoto University's *Journal of Southeast Asian Studies*, Ateneo de Manila's *Kritika Kultura*, and University of California, Merced's *Transmodernity* as well as social media platforms. If world empire begets one model of narrating the past, perhaps the world *emporium* made possible by the Manila-Acapulco galleon trade in the sixteenth century begets another.

Still in the distance, however, remains the resumption of that difficult, twisted, and oftentimes self-contradictory labor of history that Bulosan understood to entail the redefinition of America through the histories of its working peoples. In our era of disidentifications and dissent, does the "x" in Filipinx signify a placeholder or permanent fixture? And if America is not in the heart, what name do we give to the future fruit of our labor?

NOTES

1. For overviews of labor migration, see Anthony Pido, "The Macro/Micro Dimensions of Pilipino Immigration to the United States," in *Filipino Americans: Transformation and Identity*, ed. Maria P. P. Root (Thousand Oaks, Calif.: Sage, 1997), 21–38; Yến Lê Espiritu, *Filipino American Lives* (Philadelphia: Temple University Press, 1995), 1–36; Yến Lê Espiritu, *Home Bound: Filipino American Lives across Cultures, Communities, and Countries* (Berkeley: University of California Press, 2003), 127–56; and Robyn Magalit Rodriguez, *Migrants for Export: How the Philippine State Brokers Labor to the World* (Minneapolis: University of Minnesota Press, 2010). For some specific case studies, see Catherine Ceniza Choy, *Empire of Care: Nursing and Migration in Filipino American History* (Durham, N.C.: Duke University Press, 2003); Martin F. Manalansan IV, *Global Divas: Filipino Gay Men in the Diaspora* (Durham, N.C.: Duke University Press, 2003), 89–125; and Kale Bantigue Fajardo, *Filipino Crosscurrents: Oceanographies of Seafaring, Masculinities, and Globalization* (Minneapolis: University of Minnesota Press, 2011).

2. See Harrod Suarez, *The Work of Mothering: Globalization and the Filipino Diaspora* (Urbana: University of Illinois Press, 2017), 5–30.

3. See Oscar Campomanes, "The New Empire's Forgetful and Forgotten Citizens: Unrepresentability and Unassimilability in Filipino-American Postcolonialities," *Critical Mass* 2, no. 2 (1995): 145–200.

4. For an elaboration of this history, see John D. Blanco, "Orientational Enlightenment and the Colonial World: A Derivative Discourse?," in *Filipino Studies: Palimpsests of Nation and Diaspora*, ed. Martin F. Manalansan IV and Augusto F. Espiritu (New York: New York University Press, 2016).

5. For profiles of many of these families, see the essays in *An Anarchy of Families: State and Family in the Philippines*, ed. Alfred McCoy (Madison: University of Wisconsin Press, 2009).

6. See, for example, the collection of speeches and essays in *Thinking for Ourselves: A Collection of Representative Filipino Essays*, ed. Eliseo Quirino and Vicente Hilario (Manila: Cacho Hermanos, 1985 [originally published 1924]).

7. These uprisings included the Colorum uprisings in Surigao del Norte (1924), Panay (1927), and the provinces of northern and Central Luzon (1931); the Sakdalista revolts in Central Luzon (1935); and the Hukbalahap rebellion after the Pacific War (1946). See David Sturtevant, *Popular Uprisings in the Philippines, 1840–1940* (Ithaca, N.Y. Cornell University Press, 1976); and Steffi San Buenaventura, "Hawaii's '1946 *Sakada*,'" *Social Process in Hawai'i* 37 (1996): 74–90. Kerima Polotan's *Hand of the Enemy* (Quezon City: University of the Philippines Press, 1998) famously recounts the legacy of the Sakdalista uprising in Tayug through the (fictional) son of two prominent leaders.

8. Carlos Bulosan, *America Is in the Heart* (Seattle: University of Washington Press, 1977), 189.

9. See James Putzel, *A Captive Land: The Politics of Agrarian Reform in the Philippines* (New York: Monthly Review Press, 1992).

10. See Rodriguez, *Migrants for Export.*

11. Stephanie Hinnershitz, "'We Ask Not for Mercy, but for Justice': The Cannery Workers and Farm Laborers' Union and Filipino Civil Rights in the United States, 1927–1937," *Journal of Social History* 47, no. 1 (2013): 132–52.

12. See Rhacel Salazar Parreñas, "'White Trash' Meets the 'Little Brown Monkeys': The Taxi Dance Hall as a Site of Interracial and Gender Alliances between White Working Class Women and Filipino Immigrant Men in the 1920s and 30s," *Amerasia Journal* 24, no. 2 (1998): 115–34; and Leti Volpp, "American Mestizo: Filipinos and Antimiscegenation Laws in California," *University of California, Davis Law Review* 33, no. 795 (2000): 795–835.

13. These unions included the United Packing and Cannery Workers of America (UPACAWA), the American Federation of Labor–Congress of Industrial Organizations (AFL-CIO), and most notably, the United Farm Workers (UFW) under the shared leadership of Philip Vera Cruz and Cesar Chavez. *America Is in the Heart* inspired the protests and demands of Filipinx and other minority students in California to create an ethnic studies program and curriculum in higher education during the 1970s, even as the children of migrant workers like Fred and Dorothy Cordova went on to create the Filipino American National Historical Society (FANHS), dedicated to preserving the histories of a Filipinx American identity. See Fred Cordova, Dorothy Laigo Cordova, and Albert A. Acena, *Filipinos, Forgotten Asian Americans: A Pictorial Essay 1763–Circa 1963* (Dubuque, Iowa: Kendall Hunt, 1983). Recently, the California legislature has passed a bill (AB 123) to mandate the inclusion of the Filipinx in the teaching of US history in secondary education.

14. See Susan Evangelista, "Filipinos in America: Literature as History," *Philippine Studies: Historical and Ethnographic Viewpoints* 36, no.1 (1988): 36–53.

15. This question is illustrated in a telling episode of Bienvenido Santos's *The Man Who (Thought He) Looked Like Robert Taylor* (Quezon City, Philip-

pines: New Day Press, 1986), in which the characters debate the actual date of Philippine Independence Day.

16. See Renato Constantino, "Society without a Purpose," in *Dissent and Counter-Consciousness* (Manila: Malaya Books, 1970); Giorgio Agamben, *Homo Sacer: Sovereign Power and Bare Life* (Stanford, Calif.: Stanford University Press, 1995); and Espiritu, *Home Bound*, 46–69. For the intersection of state and capital in the genesis of modern empire, see Michael Hardt and Antonio Negri, *Empire* (Cambridge, Mass.: Harvard University Press, 2000); and Kojin Karatani, *The Structure of World History: From Modes of Production to Modes of Exchange* (Durham, N.C.: Duke University Press, 2014).

17. For a partial list of these authors, see the introduction to this volume. Many of these texts explore a revision of US history in and through the study and close reading of literary texts and cultural artifacts.

18. See *The Forbidden Book: The Philippine American War in Political Cartoons*, ed. Abe Ignacio, Helen Toribio, and Jorge Emmanuel (Berkeley: T'Boli/Eastwind Books, 2014); Vicente L. Rafael, *White Love and Other Events in Filipino History* (Durham, N.C.: Duke University Press, 2000); and Paul Kramer, *Blood of Government: Race, Empire, the United States, and the Philippines* (Chapel Hill: University of North Carolina Press, 2006). No novel in English better captures the exuberance and shortcomings of this conjuncture than Karen Tei Yamashita's *I-Hotel* (Minneapolis: Coffee House Press, 2010), which explores ten years (in ten novellas) of the famous tenement hotel located on the outskirts of San Francisco's Chinatown. In it, the itineraries and ideologies of Red Guards, Black Panthers, "Leway Girls," the US-based anti-martial-law organization KDP (Kilusang Demokratikong Pilipino, Philippine Democratic Movement), and young student activists alternately converge and become juxtaposed to one another, against the backdrop of urban gentrification and FBI surveillance.

19. See, for example, Linda Basch, Nina Glick-Schiller, and Christina Szanton-Blanc, *Nations Unbound: Transnational Projects, Postcolonial Predicaments, and Deterritorialized Nation States* (London: Routledge, 1993); Rick Bonus, *Locating Filipino Americans: Ethnicity and the Cultural Politics of Space* (Philadelphia: Temple University Press, 2000); Manalansan, *Global Divas*.

20. Ileto's essay "On the Historiography of Southeast Asia and the Philippines: The 'Golden Age' of Southeast Asia Studies—Experiences and Reflections" (Proceedings of the workshop on "Writing History: Between Coarse Nationalism and Postmodernism," Meiji Gakuin University, Yokohama, March 2002; *https://www.academia.edu/19040349/The_Golden_Age_of_Southeast_Asian_Studies_Experiences_and_Reflections*) provides some invaluable insights on the formation of Philippine studies within the larger orbit of Southeast Asian studies, particularly the emphasis on developing the field as a kind of "Third Way" of historical study that would avoid the ethnocentrism

of colonialist scholarship and the overtly political and polemical claims of
nationalist scholarship during an era of decolonization and Third World
nonalignment projects. See also Ileto, *Filipinos and Their Revolution: Event,
Discourse, and Historiography* (Quezon City, Philippines: Ateneo de Manila
University Press, 1999), 98–131.

21. They P. Guevara Jr., *Becoming Mexipino: Multiethnic Identities and
Communities in San Diego* (New Brunswick, N.J.: Rutgers University
Press, 2012).

22. Anthony Christian Ocampo, *The Latinos of Asia: How Filipino Americans
Break the Rules of Race* (Stanford, Calif.: Stanford University Press, 2016).

23. Donna Miscolta, *Hola and Goodbye: Una Familia in Stories* (Durham,
N.C.: Carolina Wren Press, 2017).

24. Josep Fradera, *Colonias para después de un imperio* (Barcelona: Bella-
terra S.A. Ediciones, 2005).

SECTION B

Reclamation

PART THREE

Across Language, Sex-Gender, and Space-Time Geographies

Pag-uugat at Paglalayag (Roots and Journeys): Filipino Language Learning and Activism

Joi Barrios

In an interview published in the book *On Language: Chomsky's Classic Works*, Noam Chomsky, well known for both his linguistic theories and his Marxist politics, was asked: "Do you see a link between your scientific activities—the study of language—and your political activities?" Chomsky replied: "If there is a connection, it is on a rather abstract level."[1]

For many Filipinx Americans, however, language-learning is a political choice. Some study the language because it is a way of connecting to family members and to their roots. Others do so because knowledge of Filipino is essential to activist work. Leny Strobel asserts the importance of language in the process of decolonization: "If language is the site of ideological struggle, it can also be a site of negotiation. . . . Therefore language can also create new identities capable of challenging the conditions that negate the voices, desires and histories of silenced people."[2]

But who can be considered as activists? For Filipinx Americans, activism comes in many forms: involvement in community issues such as veteran, healthcare, and labor rights; advocacy for Filipinx/Philippine studies, as well as college recruitment and retention programs for Filipinx Americans; volunteerism in medical missions, relief efforts, and housing; and organized resistance, particularly in the national democratic movement in the Philippines.

As we study the dynamics between language acquisition and politics, we can pose the following questions: What are their learning processes? What words are important for them to learn? How is the learning process affected by activism? Similarly, we need to look at two other aspects of language acquisition and politics: language teaching and language use. What informs teaching strategies? How can we implement a critical pedagogy? How can we analyze texts produced in the context of activist work?

Learning the Language

My research on language acquisition is informed by Agnes He's article "An Identity-Based Model for the Development of Chinese as a Heritage Language."[3] In the article, He creates the composite character of Jason, a Chinese heritage learner (HL), and presents several assumptions from a language-socialization and a conversation-analytic perspective: the symbiosis of language and identity; language as a resource for shaping, maintaining, and transforming identity; HL acquisition and HL literacy acquisition processes as identity processes; and ordinary, everyday interaction as the primary locus for language and cultural development.

Similarly, in my essay entitled "Understanding 'Margie': The Filipino Heritage Learner,"[4] I trace the life span of my own composite character—Margarita Louella, or Margie (born to parents Lourdes and Joel in 1973, the year Filipina Margarita Moran won Miss Universe), based on interviews with activist heritage learners.

Margie was born in the US. Her mother speaks to her grandmother in Visayan, her parents speak to each other in Filipino, but they speak to her in English and the code-switching Taglish. For example, at the age of four, Margie's mother would speak to her saying, "Let *ninang* [godmother] make *subo* [feed] you." Her mother code-switches because as a child, she was fined for speaking Filipino in school, and in speech classes had to repeat the sentence "This is an apple" to get the perfect American accent.

There are three possible reasons for code-switching: the neocolonial relationship between the US and the Philippines; the hegemony of English, underlining disparities in class and status; and discrimination in the site of migration, with the Filipino accent marking ethnic identity and otherness.

In contrast, her father struggles with the language because he attended a public school in Cagayan. He could read and write in English, but hesitates when he speaks because he is afraid of pronouncing words incorrectly. One time, he got angry at Margie's brother and said, "Lintik kang bata ka" (literally: "You are [like] lightning," used to manifest anger). Years later, Margie would ask, "Why did my father call my brother a lightning?"

Margie grows up knowing the Filipino words for objects, a few body parts, and people: *kalamansi, adobo, lola*. She knows that the prefix *mag-*, when accompanied by a verb in English, renders the verb Filipino—"magtoothbrush ka na"—especially when commands are given. She knows basic greetings like *Kumusta* (How are you?), *Magandang umaga* (Good morning), and *salamat* (thank you). Her mother tells her: "Mahal kita" (I love you).

It is in college that life changes for Margie. She enrolls in a Filipino class. She watches Filipino plays: One is entitled "Tunggalian" (Conflict); the other is based on Freddie Aguilar's song "Anak" (Child). As she dances the *tinikling* (bamboo dance) at the Philippine Cultural Night (PCN), she also learns her favorite word, *diwa* (spirit). She becomes fascinated with the word *saing* (to cook rice)—*sinaing* (cooked rice), *magsaing* (to cook rice)—"Ah," she says to herself, "there are many words about rice" (*sinangag* or fried rice, *bahaw* or cold rice, *ampaw* or poprice, etc.). She tries to learn the *baybayin* (indigenous writing system) and considers getting a tattoo for the word *Malaya* (Free). She becomes aware of student issues and joins the campaign for Filipinx and Philippine studies.

She learns about Filipinx American history and the struggle of the farm workers. She becomes more involved in community organizing. At the community center, she greets the older Filipinxs with "Kumusta na po kayo?" (How are you now?), proud of knowing the honorific word *po*.

Margie joins a Filipinx American political group, and as her consciousness grows, she learns the word *hustisya* (justice), and can shout slogans such as *Makibaka, Huwag Matakot* (Struggle, Do Not be Afraid)! and *Ibagsak ang Imperyalismo* (Down with Imperialism)! However, when one speaks to her in Filipino, her conversational ability is limited to five minutes.

Margie travels to the Philippines three times. First, to visit family during Christmas. She then returns for three weeks, spending half the time with family, and the other half with Karapatan, a human rights organization. However, when she attends a celebration hosted by the Amado V. Hernandez foundation (an NGO that gives writing workshops to workers and peasants) and listens to poetry, she realizes that she does not know the language. She says to herself, "I do not want to end up like this person who does not know *Inang Wika*" (Mother Language).

On her third visit, she stays for five months, spending most of her time with peasant communities. She learns more about the struggles of the Filipinx people—and calls it *paglalamay sa dilim* (to work in the darkness of night). She now has a better word for justice: the indigenous word *katarungan*. She learns to sing songs such as "Rosas ng Digma" (The Rose of War).[5] She is touched as she leaves the community when they give her a *despedida* (farewell party) for *Maligayang Paglalakbay* (Happy Travels). Back in the United States, she corresponds with people in the Philippines, thus practicing her written Filipino.

Thus, the activist FHL is an extremely motivated HL, who needs the language as he/she becomes more politically involved. Filipino is his/her language because it is the language of the national democratic movement. This reason echoes the fifth reason given for choosing Tagalog as the basis of the national language in 1935: It was the language of the Katipunan and the revolution.[6]

Teaching the Language

Similarly, the teaching of language is not an apolitical act. The choice of teaching materials, language textbooks, and classroom strategies are informed by the instructor's ideological framework. As students learn the language, including the history of its orthography, they can learn about precolonial Philippine society, and the changes brought about by colonialism. In contrast, the lack of a critical pedagogy can lead to misinformation and generalizations.

Consider, for example, the teaching of the indigenous script, *baybayin*, and words in the Filipino language. As students learn that there is only one symbol for the letters i/e, o/u, and d/r, they understand not only the interchangeable use of these letters in words (for example, *din* and *rin* [also]) and pronunciation (*babae/babai* [woman]), but also the unfixed characteristic of meaning in Philippine culture. Moreover, by studying language, they can discuss notions of gender (*siya* is equivalent to he/she) and class (the word *hampaslupa*—literally: to strike the ground—is used only by the affluent to refer to the poor).

However, a class that teaches *utang na loob* (debt of gratitude), *pakikisama* (yielding to the will of the leader or the majority), and *hiya* (shame) as core Filipinx values contributes to the "essentialization" of the Filipinx.[7] Many teachers fail to mention that the emphasis on "Filipino values" comes from the book *Four Readings on Philippine Values*, 1970, edited by Frank Lynch and Alfonso de Guzman III.

In recent years, scholars of Philippine psychology have revisited these values, producing a clearer understanding of social interaction among Filipinxs. Virgilio Enriquez and Carmen Santiago propose a more comprehensive analysis of Filipinx social interaction by using the language in identifying eight levels and modes:[8] (1) *pakikitungo* (transaction/civility with); (2) *pakikisalamuha* (interaction with); (3) *pakikilahok* (joining/participating with); (4) *pakikibagay* (in conformity with/in accord with); (5) *pakikisama* (getting along with); (6) *pakikipagpalagayan/pakikipagpalagayang loob* (being in rapport/understanding/acceptance with); (7) *pakikisangkot* (getting involved); and (8) *pakikiisa* (being one with). From Enriquez's point of view, Filipinx psychology is best understood by searching for the "right words in vernacular languages."[9]

Furthermore, the teaching of Filipino language culture can be limited to learning folk songs, folk dances, and the end of the semester, a *barrio fiesta* (town celebration). This can possibly result in fixed, idealized images of Philippine society, not unlike that of the ever-smiling farmers of a Fernando Amorsolo painting.[10] However, should teachers choose to integrate literary texts that describe and narrate the struggles of Filipinx peasants, student can learn more about issues related to land ownership.

Using the Language

Let us now turn to the more specific use of the language by heritage learners by using as case study the oral and written texts of Melissa Roxas. Roxas, a Filipinx American from San Diego, California, was abducted in May 2009 as she was conducting medical surveys in preparation for a medical mission in La Paz, Tarlac, Philippines.

In her affidavit drafted in May 2009, Melissa Roxas relates her experience—the beatings she received for seven days, how she was suffocated using plastic bags, and drugged using orange juice. The affidavit is peppered with Tagalog words—words spoken to her, conversations heard, and answers she gave.

As she was being abducted, Melissa asks the owner of the house for help, calling him *Kuya* (Elder Brother). When she asked for a lawyer, her abductors said: "Walang abugado-abugado dito. Malinis ka naming nakuha at alam mo naman kung bakit ka nahuli." (No lawyers. We got you "smoothly" and you know why you were captured.)

During her torture, they continued to speak to her in Filipino. These dialogues she does not translate into English. "Ang tigas ng ulo mo. Sasagot ka na sa mga tanong." (You are hard-headed. You will answer our questions.) Unable to break her, they said, "Matigas 'to. Barilin na lang natin." (She is unrelenting. Let us just shoot her.)

And again, on a late night or early dawn, as she was blindfolded, a man asked, "Handa ka bang mamatay?" (Are you ready to die?) To which she answered, "Opo." (Yes [formal].) And he said, "Bago namin patayin ang isang tao, mapapaihi at mapapatae muna namin siya." (Before we kill a person, we can make him/her pee in his/her clothing, and defecate.)

It is interesting to emphasize the contrast of the heritage learner's polite and formal Filipino to the rude language of her torturer. Is it because the first lesson in the Filipino language is politeness (use of the honorifics *po* and *opo*)? The torturer uses words such as *ihi* (urine) and *tae* (feces)—words that are considered *bastos* (rude). The contrast in language not only reflects the relationship between the torturer and the tortured, or the person in power and the powerless, but also shows the activist's adherence to the importance of respect in language.

Melissa is only one of the hundreds of activists that have become statistics in the anti-insurgency campaigns of the Philippine government during the presidencies of Gloria Arroyo, Benigno Aquino Jr., and Rodrigo Roa Duterte.

The collection of poems entitled "*Kundiman* for Melissa,"[11] written for Melissa by fellow poets, echo her words. Kundiman describes itself as an organization dedicated to providing a nurturing space for Asian American poets. Upon learning of Melissa's abduction, Kundiman issued a call: "Let us participate in a community of cymbals through poems—bringing noise and sound and outrage and unremitting memory to what has happened to Melissa and what continues to happen to activists and artists around the world who dare to take a stand against injustice."

All of the poems start with "If I speak for Melissa . . ." Kimberly Alidio quotes her: "When asked, '*Handa ka na bang mamatay?*' [Are you ready to die?], / I give my name: Melissa." Yael Villafranca uses Filipino:

> We rise
>
> as Melissa, *anak na babae*, kapatid na babae,
> *taga Maynila, taga* Los Angeles, *taga Habi,*[12]
> *taga Kundiman.* We name ourselves
> the river carving unyielding stone and speak
>
> for each other, together at once.
>
> *Para sa bayan.*
>
> [We rise
>
> as Melissa, daughter, sister,
> from Maynila, from Los Angeles, from Habi,
> from Kundiman. We name ourselves
> the river carving unyielding stone and speak
>
> for each other, together at once.
>
> For the country.]

The poem employs code-switching, mimicking the HL's interrogation of her own citizenship. Melissa is not defined by a single place. She seems to embark on a journey for the *bayan*, which in Filipino is a flexible term: town, country, people.

In the same way that Margie speaks of *paglalakbay* (journey), echoing epic journeys of Lam-ang[13] and Labaw-Donggon,[14] and the *lakaran* (literally: "to walk; journey") of both the *pasyón* and Andres Bonifacio, so does Melissa. In her poem entitled, "Humus," she says: "When you tell the mountains to be moved, it is not at your call that they obey. But journey and take even a spoonful of earth from its mountaintop and place it on flat ground and you would have changed the world a little bit already." And this is how I know that she now speaks Filipino even as she speaks English. She uses "already" because she is thinking of the Filipino *na*.

A photograph of the organization Anakbayan (Children of the People)[15] shows their members with hats marked by the letter K, symbolizing the late 1890s revolutionary group, the Katipunan. K is a letter that in 1896 was not even in the Roman alphabet introduced by the Spaniards, but as Megan C. Thomas asserts, it has a symbolic significance as it "flags the nation."[16] In the photograph, the activists hold a streamer with the indigenous *baybayin* symbol for K, a signifier that could be recognized by other activists as representing the underground Kabataang Makabayan.[17]

The Filipinx American activist's journey is not unlike that of the letter K—a story rooted in history, colonialism, and struggle for sovereignty.

NOTES

1. Noam Chomsky, *On Language: Chomsky's Classic Works: "Language and Responsibility" and "Reflections on Language"* (New York: The New Press, 2019), 5–6.

2. Leny Mendoza Strobel, *Coming Full Circle: The Process of Decolonization among Post-1965 Filipino Americans* (Ann Arbor: University of Michigan, 2001), 82.

3. Agnes Weiyun He, "An Identity-Based Model for the Development of Chinese as a Heritage Language," in *Chinese as a Heritage Language: Fostering Rooted World Citizenry*, ed. Agnes Weiyun He and Yun Xiao (Manoa: University of Hawai'i, 2008).

4. Joi Barrios, *Tagalog for Beginners: An Introduction to Filipino, the National Language of the Philippines* (Clarendon, Vt.: Tuttle, 2011).

5. The song "Rosas ng Digma" was composed by Danny Fabella and included in the album *Rosas ng Digma* (Musikang Bayan, 2001).

6. From "Proclamation of Tagalog as the Basis of the National Language" by Manuel Quezon, 1938.

7. E. San Juan Jr., *The Philippine Temptation: Dialectics of Philippines–US Literary Relations* (Philadelphia: Temple University Press, 1996).

8. C. Santiago and V. G. Enriquez, "Tungo sa maka-Pilipinong pananaliksik," *Sikolohiyang Pilipino: Mga Ulat at Balita* 1, no. 4 (1976): 3–10.

9. E. Enriquez, quoted in in San Juan, *The Philippine Temptation*, 224.

10. Fernando Amorsolo (1892–1972) was a Filipino painter known for Philippine landscapes. While some critique his works as portraying an idealistic view of the countryside, others also note that the privileging of the "rural" was a rejection of the modernity equated with American colonialism.

11. The word *kundiman* refers to a traditional Filipino love song, popular in the nineteenth century in the Philippines. The sad melody echoes the tragic love for the significant other, as equated with freedom unattained. Kundiman, the group, is a nonprofit organization of Asian American writers. "Kundiman for Melissa" is the set of poems written in support of the "Justice for Melissa Roxas" campaign in 2009.

12. The word *habi* means "to weave" in Filipino.

13. Lam-ang is the epic hero of *Biag na Lam-ang* (The Life of Lam-ang), an Ilocano epic.

14. Labaw Donggon is the epic hero of the *Hinilawod* (Tales from the Mouth of the Halawad River) epic of Panay island.

15. Anakbayan is a youth organization established in the Philippines in 1998. It currently has US chapters in New York, New Jersey, Chicago, Hawai'i, Los Angeles, San Diego, Silicon Valley, and the East Bay.

16. Megan C. Thomas, "'K' is for De-Kolonization: Anti-Colonial Nationalism and Orthographic Reform," *Comparative Studies in Society and History* 49, no. 4 (2007): 938–39.

17. The Kabataan Makabayan is a youth organization founded in 1964. It was forced to go underground upon the declaration of martial law in 1972. It is currently one of the organizations comprising the National Democratic Front (NDF).

FOURTEEN

In an Archipelago and Sea of Complexities:
Contemporary Intersectional / Transpacific / Decolonial
Queer and/or Trans Filipinx American Studies

Kale Bantigue Fajardo

Situated largely in North America, Filipinx American studies is an indispensable field because the field's past and present scholars, educators, writers, cultural workers, and activists invite and compel us to address histories and present-day realities of colonialism, postcolonialism, neocolonialism, and decolonization in transpacific, transnational, translocal, and/or diasporic contexts. As scholars, students, educators, activists, artists, etc., we are generally expected to consider multiple historical contexts, moments, and experiences—and usually in more than one geographic context. As such, Filipinx American studies also often demands (in a good way) that we juggle, learn, and write about multiple sets of knowledge, and complexly interconnected cultural, social, political, historical, and economic phenomena, logics, processes, and experiences.

Due to the Philippines' long history of colonialism (by Spain, the US, and Japan) and the ways that Filipinx migrants and immigrants have been treated in a colonial manner in the US, the field also demands a necessary radical attention to race, racialization, and racial formations because colonialism relies on particular racial hierarchies—for example, between Spaniard and Native/Indio; or US American and Filipinx (among others); and usually, Filipinxs are racially marginalized in these racialized socioeconomic contexts.

Filipinx American studies scholars are especially strong in articulating and revealing *how and why racialization happens precisely through sex, gender, and sexuality*. Indeed, the field has been precisely established and defined by scholars whose research provides case studies in how to closely read or account for Filipinx "racialized masculinities" and "racialized femininities," as well as how gender nonconforming and/or trans Filipinxs are also racialized.

To understand heterogenous racialized Filipinx genders and sexualities, Filipinx American studies scholars also stress economic capitalist structures and resulting socioeconomic differences, hierarchies, and disparities in local, regional, and transnational and transpacific contexts because economic position and labor status in various industries (such as agriculture, domestic service, and shipping, among others) simultaneously co-constitute racialized genders and sexualities. Thus, with an attention to race, gender, sexuality, class, and geographic location, Filipinx American studies scholars, like those situated in other areas of Asian American studies, Black studies, queer of color critique, Native studies, Chicanx and Latinx studies, ethnic studies, and American studies, prioritize and practice intersectional thinking, research, and writing.

To give examples of these contributions and interventions, Filipinx American studies writers and scholars have emphasized race, racialization, and anti-Filipinx racism, for example, in the US or in the context of colonialism or neocolonialism in the Philippines, when considering or unpacking Filipinx sex, gender, and sexuality—in the Philippines, US, or transnationally. Race, racialization, and anti-Filipinx racism have historically been expressed and operationalized by white Americans in the US and in the US empire (including the Philippines) through white dominated institutions, and scholars have critically asserted that racialization happens through sex-gender and sexuality.[1]

In Filipinx American studies, we can see the intersections of race, sex-gender, sexuality, class, nationality, citizenship status, and location quite prominently in Carlos Bulosan's foundational text, *America Is in the*

Heart.[2] Republished in 1977, *America Is in the Heart* is a composite semi-autobiographical and collective social history of Filipinx migrants in the US in the first half of the twentieth century. In this book, Bulosan poignantly describes his (Ilocano) cisgender boyhood in Binalonan, Pangasinan (Philippines), and later, his story shifts to the US colonial metropole, where Bulosan discusses his experiences living and working as a migrant Filipinx cisgender man in the Pacific Northwest, Alaska, and California at a time when the US was in colonial control of the Philippines. In this context, Bulosan and other Filipinx men (as well as women—but note that the numbers of Filipina migrants present in the US were lower) traveled as US "nationals," but not citizens of the US or citizens of the Philippines. This was due to the colonial political situation in the Philippines and how citizenship was defined by the US colonial state. Bulosan writes about the anti-Filipinx racism he and his compatriots experienced as brown working-class (cisgender) migrant men in the US/metropole. Bulosan, for example, writes about how agricultural landowners exploited and mistreated Filipinxs who worked on farms and in fields, as well as the white police who racially harassed them on the West Coast.

This highly gendered, racialized, classed, and sexualized history is strongly supported by the Filipinx migrant men included in Geoffrey Dunn's film, *Dollar a Day, Ten Cents a Dance.*[3] Elderly Filipinx men in this classic documentary recall, for example, their time in the taxi dance halls where they danced with white women for "10 cents a dance." The film also includes footage of historian Fred Cordova describing how dashing the Filipinx men were and how white men felt (sexually) threatened by how Filipinx migrant men crossed the racial-sexual color line when they were socially and sexually intimate with white women. Due to white men's racial, sexual, and economic resentments, white vigilante men targeted Filipinxs in places such as Watsonville, California on the Central Coast. Fermin Tobera was one of the young Filipinx men killed. Filipinx American poet Jeff Tagami memorializes Tobera and his murder in a poem in his collection *October Light* (1990). Sociologist Rhacel Salazar Parreñas in her early essay "'White Trash' Meets the 'Little Brown Monkeys': The Taxi Dance Hall as the Site of Interracial and Gender Alliances between White Working Class Women and Filipino Immigrant Men in the 1920s and 30s" (1998) explains how migrant

Filipinx men were racialized as "brown monkeys." Through this primitivist insult and racial slur, white supremacists and racists sought to primitivize Filipinxs and also liken them to Black Americans who were being subjected to Jim Crow laws and systemic racism. The white working-class women the Filipinx men danced with, dated, had sexual intimacies with, and in some cases married, were also marked and stigmatized as "white trash." Historian Linda España-Maram in *Creating Masculinity in Los Angeles's Little Manila: Working Class Filipinos and Popular Culture, 1920s–1950*[4] documents how working-class migrant Filipinx men used popular culture to resist racism and classism and to create, style, and perform their own (cisgender) masculinities and manhoods during a time when Filipinxs experienced dehumanization in the context of colonial relations and white supremacy, both in the Philippines and the US. They participated in the sport of boxing, they wore stylish Macintosh suits, they experienced the pleasures and freedoms of migrant travel, they developed same-sex/homosocial communities and networks, and as mentioned, they engaged in sexual, romantic, and social intimacies with white women and also women of color (Filipinas, Mexicans, and Chicanas). Melinda L. de Jesús, in an important essay, "Rereading History, Rewriting Desire: Reclaiming Queerness in Carlos Bulosan's *America Is in the Heart* and Bienvenido Santos' *Scent of Apples*,"[5] also explains how and why the homosocial, and at times, homoerotic—and/or queer—relations in Bulosan's and Santos's texts, and presumably in the lives of Filipinx migrant men in the first half of the twentieth century in the US, were important in mobile Filipinx communities. De Jesús's essay is ground-breaking because she exposes the homosocial and homoerotic social conditions and interpersonal relationships in *America Is in the Heart*, and she draws our attention to the possibilities and spaces for (cisgender) masculine/male intimacies. Rather than simply reading or assuming *America Is in the Heart* is a straight and/or macho canonical Filipinx American text, de Jesús reveals the nonheteronormative or queer Filipinx ways of being narrated in Bulosan's important text. De Jesús ultimately teaches us that there are queer ways to read and understand Filipinx migration to the US in the first half of the twentieth century, at a time when the US was in colonial control of the Philippines.

Victor Román Mendoza's *Metroimperial Intimacies: Fantasy, Racial-Sexual Governance, and the Philippines in U.S. Imperialism, 1899–1913*[6] continues this kind of queer Filipinx reading of histories and literatures. Mendoza documents and analyzes how Filipinx Natives in the Philippines in the early years of the US occupation *and* in the context of the US empire were socially constructed as racially and sexually queer. Mendoza highlights how important it is to understand how US colonial racial-sexual ideologies were imposed on the Philippines and Filipinxs in the archipelago, as well as in the US colonial metropole. This transpacific geographic and political approach is what Mendoza theorizes as "metroimperial." In this metroimperial power relationship, US colonial figures interpreted Native Filipinx bodies and behaviors as nonnormative and/or nonheteronormative and/or again queer. In counterdistinction to dominant white US (hetero)sexualities, local and Native Filipinxs engaged in a more diverse, creative, and sex-positive repertoire of sexual-gender practices that went beyond reproductive and heterosexual penetrative sex. Mendoza, for example, suggests that Spanish and American colonial authorities had a difficult time enforcing conventional and compulsory heterosexual behaviors, that is, through the enactment of sodomy laws. US colonial figures and political leaders also used discourses and imaginaries of race, indigeneity, and gender to pathologize and degrade Filipinx revolutionary leaders, such as General and later President Emilio Aguinaldo. Most notably, in *Metroimperial Intimacies*, Mendoza analyzes an important court-martial case concerning a white US officer who was accused of having inappropriate sexual relations with Philippine Scouts, and in another chapter, he analyzes the racial-sexual logics of political cartoons during the early years of US occupation in the Philippines.

Sex-gender is also an important embodied formation and axis of difference, as sex-gender—more specifically, "femaleness," "girlhood," "womanhood" and "femininity"—is often the site of heteropatriarchal institutionalized power, where historically "men" and/or masculine subjects have social and economic power when compared to "women" or feminine/feminized subjects. Philippine studies scholar Neferti Xina M. Tadiar highlights this kind of intersectional feminist and postcolonial reading in her important essay "Sexual Economies in the Asia/Pacific Community."[7] Tadiar focuses on female and feminine subjects (cisgender Filipina women) and their experiences of hypersexualization and the way in which they are racialized and classed and socially constructed as exportable "commodities" due to their work as entertainers, sex workers, and domestic helpers in Asia and around the world. Tadiar underscores the life of Flor Contemplacion, an Overseas Filipinx Worker (OFW) who was employed as a domestic helper in Singapore and was unjustly executed by the Singaporean state in 1995. Tadiar elaborates how the Contemplacion case reveals the extreme inequality female OFWs experience in Asia and in other regions of the world. Moreover, she discusses how in dominant late twentieth-century US discourse, the US is configured as the patriarchal dominant "husband"; Japan is his docile and respectable "wife"; and the Philippines is socially and politically constructed as the US's fuck-able "mistress" or "hooker." Sociologist Rhacel Salazar Parreñas further reveals how female OFWs are literally the "servants of globalization."[8] Parreñas ethnographically documents the everyday lives and struggles of Filipina domestic helpers in Los Angeles, USA, and Rome, Italy, at the end of the twentieth century.

Dialoguing with scholars such as Tadiar and Parreñas, who first revealed how the global economy and globalization are always highly gendered, sexualized, racialized, and classed processes and phenomena, my own ethnographic research in *Filipino Crosscurrents: Oceanographies of Seafaring, Masculinities, and Globalization*[9] takes the previously mentioned Filipina feminist scholarship on sex-gender and economics seriously, to investigate the cultural politics of migrant and maritime masculinities and manhoods of Filipino cisgender male OFWs, specifically Filipino cisgender seamen who worked in the global shipping industry (1999–2002). At the time of my research, much of the contemporary scholarship on OFWs focused on the situation of cisgender women. As noted, though, cisgender male migrants (a la Bulosan) are important historical subjects and literary figures in Filipinx and Filipinx American studies. My cultural studies inflected anthropological research and book sought to bring these two strands of sex-gender based scholarship and literature together. *Filipino Crosscurrents* provides another example of how to think and write intersectionally when addressing contemporary Filipinx mobile and migrant subjects.

Based on transnational and transpacific fieldwork in Manila, Oakland, and at sea, in *Filipino Crosscurrents* I argue that because Philippine overseas migration and labor have been feminized since the 1980s and because the Philippines as a nation has also been feminized (a la Tadiar), at the end of the twentieth century and beginning of the twenty-first, sea-based migration, maritime industries and spaces, as well as Filipinx seamen, emerged as key sites, spaces, and figures for Filipinx state actors to assert Philippine masculinist nationalism and promote neoliberal economic policies. Rather than buttressing dominant state-sanctioned Filipino migrant and maritime masculinities, in *Filipino Crosscurrents*, I ethnographically revealed the contingencies and fissures of dominant Filipino masculinities, while also highlighting marginalized or alternative Filipino maritime and migrant masculinities. For example, I discussed seamen who were frustrated with their OFW lives and who "jumped ship"; seamen who criticized the Philippine state's overreliance on OFW remittances; seamen who were unemployed in Manila; Filipino seamen who expressed care and friendship, not dominant or violent machismo; and Filipino seamen who engaged in social relations with Filipinx tomboys, who I analyze as being on the female-to-male trans spectrum and who also live as men.

My ethnographic account also included significant reflexivity and discussion of my own masculinity. That is, I wrote about my own subject-position, identity/identities, life experiences, and I included auto-ethnographic accounts in order to address how these things affected my fieldwork experiences, research, and the writing of *Filipino Crosscurrents*. This approach was important because through the process of conducting fieldwork on shipping, seamen, and globalization, I strongly realized that throughout my transnational and immigrant life, I had been balancing (at least) two sets of cultural logics on sex-gender: a Tagalog/Philippine cultural logic and a dominant white US set of logics (both introduced earlier). Thus, thinking and writing reflexively was a key practice for me to unpack, explain, and/or translate my own sex-gender and trans masculinity during my fieldwork encounters with Filipinx cisgender seamen.

An attention to reflexivity and place resulted in my essay and later chapter, "Transportation: Translating Filipino/Filipino American Tomboy Masculinities through Seafaring and Migration."[10] In this essay/chapter, I discussed my initial reactions to how Filipinx seamen in ports, ships, and sea wanted to talk to me about Filipinx tomboys they knew in their lives (for example, cousins, other relatives, school friends, and neighbors). As I discuss in this essay, tomboys can be understood as a form of fe/male masculinity and manhood. Seamen's discussions surprised me because my research was on seamen, not tomboys (!) and I had not fully anticipated how my own embodied positionality and identity as a queer masculine (e.g., tomboy in the Philippines and trans in the US) Filipinx American immigrant would affect the kinds of conversations Filipino seamen initiated with me. Conversations with seamen about tomboys happened enough times, though, that I decided it was important to discuss, explain, and theorize these encounters in the field. In "Transportation," I responded and critiqued Philippines-based and diaspora-based Filipina feminists who exclusively wrote about tomboys as if they/we were all women or lesbians. While women- and lesbian-identified tomboys exist, I sought to counterbalance the scholarship by focusing on how Filipino seamen were articulating a more trans understanding of tomboys. Since this essay was published, the language of trans now circulates more significantly in the Philippines, US, and around the world. However, at the time of my writing "Transportation" and getting it published, I felt that tomboys were being misunderstood and that people in the Philippines and diaspora needed to see and understand and respect that tomboys were also transmen/guys/boys.

To further knowledge about Filipino trans masculinities in transnational, translocal, and transwaters, my essay, "Queering and Transing the Great Lakes: Filipino/a Tomboy Masculinities and Manhoods across Waters" (2014) highlights Nice Rodriguez's fiction in *Throw It to the River*,[11] to show how this immigrant tomboy author navigates multiple sets of cultural logics related to (racialized and classed) sex-gender. In Rodriguez's case, she/he[12] was grappling with Philippine, Canadian, and US cultural logics related to immigrant/migrant tomboys/butches/lesbians. Rodriguez also comments and reflects on tomboy-as-trans in an interview with me when he/she reflected on her/his collection of short stories. In this essay, I attempt to show how and why Rodriguez's writing was hybrid in terms of her/his multiple and complex understandings of tomboy in different geographic contexts.

Compared to the early 1990s (when Rodriguez's collection was published), transgender discourse now circulates more widely in the US, Philippines, and Canada. However, from my vantage point, I still see a kind of tomboy erasure. Filipinx transmen who have transitioned or are medically transitioning (for example, through gender-affirming chest reconstruction surgeries and hormone therapies) sometimes still repeat and/or mimic Filipina feminists who socially construct tomboys as women, and in so doing, they exclude tomboys from queer and trans understandings of Filipinx maleness and masculinities. For example, I attended an LGBTQ event at the University of the Philippines in the early 2010s and I heard and observed these types of perspectives from local, self-identified Philippine-based Filipino transmen. Their definitions of who and what constitutes transness appear to be highly informed by dominant white and trans discourse coming out of the US and Europe. This is similar to what anthropologist Martin F. Manalansan IV documents and analyzes in *Global Divas: Filipino Gay Men in the Diaspora*.[13] Manalansan ethnographically shows how Filipinx gay men in New York City resist "global (white) gay discourse and cultural politics through their everyday practices as immigrant Filipino gay men and baklas." The global (white) trans discourse that I caution us from uncritically reinforcing strongly—or only—emphasizes medical transitions and a gender binary where one moves unequivocally from "female" to "male" or "male" to "female." Indigenous Philippine and Filipinx diasporic cultural logics around sex-gender *already allow* for gender fluidities, gender transitions, or gender change, or diverse forms of sex-gender *recognition*. While gender-affirming surgeries and therapies are important to many trans people (including myself), I caution us from uncritically adopting Eurocentric definitions of trans and other sexes-genders. My work has sought to initiate, provoke, and complicate discussions of sexes-genders in Filipinx and Filipinx American studies. My body of work, thus far, seeks to decolonize knowledge about Filipinx sexes-genders, especially cis and trans migrant masculinities and manhoods in transnational Philippines-US contexts.[14]

Intellectual ancestors like Carlos Bulosan gave us a powerful first mapping and itinerary of both the Philippines *and* Filipinx America, to follow and investigate. Additionally, the contemporary Filipinx American studies scholars reviewed here—among *many others* who I was unable to address due to space limitations, but who, thankfully, are also powerfully present in this volume—also urge us, as well as future generations, to see and write about our heterogenous pasts and presents, as well as diverse Filipinx subjects, bodies, politics, cultural forms, and communities in new and more compelling ways—through intersectional, transpacific, decolonial, feminist, queer and/or trans knowledge, theory, writing, and methodologies.

How will you contribute to Filipinx American studies? What historical and contemporary events, politics, cultural forms, experiences of injustice and resistance provoke and inspire you? How does your positionality, as well as your personal / familial / community experiences, affect how you see, write, and create around these provocations and inspirations?

Philippine and Filipinx American archipelagos and seas possess vast multiplicities and complexities of past and present realities of racial-sexual-gender-class-geographic-cultural differences. Come join us in our large Filipinx American studies *bangka* (canoe). It is time to paddle and sail . . .

NOTES

1. This is a foundational concept of women of color feminist theory and queer of color critique. See, for example, Audre Lorde, *Sister Outside: Essays and Speeches* (Trumansburg, N.Y.: Crossing Press, 1984); Gloria Anzaldúa, *Borderlands / La Frontera: The New Mestiza* (San Francisco: Aunt Lute Press, 1987); and Roderick Ferguson, *Aberrations in Black: Towards a Queer of Color Critique* (Minneapolis: University of Minnesota Press, 2004), among others.

2. Carlos Bulosan, *America Is in the Heart* (Seattle: University of Washington Press, 1977).

3. Geoffrey Dunn, *A Dollar a Day, Ten Cents a Dance: A Historic Portrait of Filipino Farmworkers in America* (New York: The Cinema Guild, 2007).

4. Linda España-Maram, *Creating Masculinity in Los Angeles's Little Manila: Working-Class Filipinos and Popular Culture, 1920s–1950s* (New York: Columbia University Press, 2006).

5. Melinda L. de Jesús, "Rereading History, Rewriting Desire: Reclaiming Queerness in Carlos Bulosan's *America Is in the Heart* and Bienvenido N. Santos' *Scent of Apples*," *Journal of Asian American Studies* 5, no. 2 (2002): 91–111.

6. Victor Román Mendoza, *Metroimperial Intimacies: Fantasy, Racial-Sexual Governance, and the Philippines in US Imperialism, 1899–1913* (Durham, N.C.: Duke University Press, 2015).

7. Neferti Xina M. Tadiar, "Sexual Economies in the Asia/Pacific Community," in *What Is in a Rim? Critical Perspectives on the Pacific Region Idea*, ed. Arif Dirlik (Lanham, Md.: Rowman and Littlefield, 1998).

8. Rhacel Salazar Parreñas, *Servants of Globalization: Women, Migration, and Domestic Work* (Stanford, Calif.: Stanford University Press, 2001).

9. Kale Bantigue Fajardo, *Filipino Crosscurrents: Oceanographies of Seafaring, Masculinities, and Globalization* (Minneapolis: University of Minnesota Press, 2011).

10. Kale Bantigue Fajardo, "Transportation: Translating Filipino/Filipino American Tomboy Masculinities through Seafaring and Migration," *GLQ: A Journal of Lesbian and Gay Studies* 14, no. 2–3 (2008): 403–24.

11. Nice Rodriguez, *Throw It to the River* (Toronto: Women's Press, 1993).

12. As mentioned in "Queering and Transing the Great Lakes," she/he are Rodriguez's preferred pronouns.

13. Martin F. Manalansan IV, *Global Divas: Filipino Gay Men in the Diaspora* (Durham, N.C.: Duke University Press, 2003).

14. For other examples of contemporary scholarship on trans in Filipinx/Filipinx American studies, see also Emmanuel David, "Transgender Archipelagos," *Transgender Studies Quarterly* 5, no. 3 (2018): 332–54; Emmanuel David, "Purple-Collar Labor: Transgender Workers and Queer Value at Global Call Centers in the Philippines," *Gender and Society* 29, no. 2 (April 2015): 169–94; and Robert Diaz, "The Limits of Bakla and Gay: Feminist Readings of *My Husband's Lover*, Vice Ganda, and Charice Pempengco," *Signs* 40, no. 3 (2015): 721–45.

FIFTEEN

Dating as Affect in Filipinx Migration

Allan Punzalan Isaac

In informal conversation, when someone is noticed for her bearing in a social setting, she is said to *have* or possess *dating* (dah-teeng'). *Dating* describes the force or impression a person or object brings by appearing in the world. Philippine writer-critic Bienvenido Lumbera defines it as "ang impresyong iniiwan sa isang tao na pagmumukha, bihis, pananalita at kilos ng isang indibidwal" (the impression left by a person's looks, dress, address, and movement).[1] Later, Lumbera applies this definition to Philippine literary works to name the effects of artistic objects that place individual and audience in relationship to each other.

> Pag nahaharap tayo sa isang likhang-sining, sa ganyan ding paraan pumapasok sa ating kamalayan ang mga katangiang umaakit na magustuhan o ayawan natin ang trabaho ng manlilikha. Ang isang painting, tugtugin, o pagtatanghal ay dumarating sa audience na nakaabang, parang destinasyon sa isang paglalakbay, sa magaganap na kamalayan nito. Ang kaganapan ng pagsapit ng

likha, ang dating ng likha, nagbibitiw ang audience ng pahayag ng pagkatuwa, pagkasaya o paghanga.

[When we face a work of art, the qualities that make us like or dislike the artist's work enter our consciousness in this manner. A painting, piece of music, or stage-play reaches the consciousness of the audience who awaits like a destination in a journey. At the experience of this arrival, the impact/arrival of the work, the audience reacts with laughter, joy or admiration.[2]]

Lumbera describes *dating* as the movement of artistic qualities to the consciousness of the observer or listener. *Dating* is aesthetics, as literary critic David Bayot explains in his reading of Lumbera: "The word has the denotation and connotation of both appeal and impact."[3] In this movement from object to audience, Lumbera deploys the metaphor of the haptic in speaking about "impressions" left on the observer's consciousness. Thus, *dating* is a type of affect.

Ascribed to persons, *dating* is not necessarily about being conventionally beautiful but having social potency, which the English word "attractive" in part suggests. However, rather than a centripetal force like attraction, *dating* issues from the body to a specific locale and its circulation within it. *Dating* names how a body or object exudes centrifugal force, negative or positive, to generate feeling in this locale. When Filipinxs translate *dating* into its more conventional root meaning as "arrival," both social bearing and point of entry merge. Therefore, one can say in Taglish that if one has *dating*, one possesses arrival (humorously: *may arrive!*). *Dating* as a way of appearing in the world is a mode of arrival.

Affective Labor and the World

Revolving around feelings, moving bodies, bodies being moved, and bodies going outside its putative boundaries, affect conceptually captures the operations and relations emerging from Philippine global migration of labor and the new socialities generated by these movements. Given the tremendous gendered labor force of nurses, teachers, caregivers, domestics, and other Filipina service workers exported throughout the world by the Philippine brokerage state, to use sociologist Robyn Magalit Rodriguez's term, affect as a concept in Filipinx studies has in large part been touched upon by social science inquiries around care and carework. Quantified, monetized, exported, imported, and managed, affective labor like carework does not produce material commodities, but cultivates relationships to sustain the reproduction of capital. Rhacel Salazar Parreñas, Catherine Ceniza Choy, and Robyn Magalit Rodriguez, among others, have all explored the political economy and history of labor export and the ways by which workers negotiate multiple emotional obligations transnationally. Their scholarship signals the changes this industry has wrought in national economies but also to the quotidian and structural lives of predominantly Filipina labor living abroad. In her pioneering comparative study of caregivers and domestics in Rome and Los Angeles, Parreñas points to the transformation of Filipinx family structure and gender roles among these migrants and the families they have left behind. At the same time the ethnography demonstrates how Filipina migrants negotiate their contradictory financial and social status vis-à-vis the Philippines and the host country. Looking at the nursing industry, Choy provides the history and institutionalization of nursing education in US-administered colonial Philippines that have shaped later migratory policies in both the US and the Philippines and the future orientation of subsequent migrants. These colonial convergences have resulted in the occupational and migratory pipeline leading to an ethnic cadre of Filipina nurses in the US. In understanding the Philippines as a brokerage nation-state, Rodriguez brings out not only the economic but also the emotional ties engineered by the Philippine state to ensure remittances so vital to the national economy, despite the minimal protections the state provides to its citizens abroad.

While sending and receiving nation-states manage and enforce flow and new proximities, subjects too exert force and shape how events, spaces, and other people relate to one another. In the context of queer migrant lives, Martin F. Manalansan IV in cultural anthropology has described the posture of disaffection as one affective register necessary for survival among these workers. Disaffection describes a defensive posture directed at, against, and away from the authorities of the place of migration in order for the worker to have a semblance of control to the rhythms of labor. Disaffection means "not only emotional distance, alienation, antipathy, and isolation but also this word's other connotation of disloyalty to regimes of power and authority" Thus, "disaffection emerges out of the need for survival and persistence in the midst of tribulations."[4] These granular shifts nuance how we understand subjects interpellated by multiple locations and identities in terms of nation, gender, race, and class, but remain irreducible to these categories. Affect thus limns the subtle and not so subtle shifts in mood and modes that frame relationships and ways of being in the world.

Many scholars of Filipinx studies have focused on the "in-between" and the conditions that make the in-between possible. The focus on affect highlights the transsubjective experience that bodies, objects, and social conditions make possible. While affect articulates the capacity and possibility of bodies, sometimes intentional but oftentimes not, it also traces noncorporeal forces like ambience, feel, and atmosphere. Affect, according to Brian Massumi, is emotion not yet processed or quantified; rather it is a felt intensity within and beyond the individual.[5] Indeed, affect is the cumulation of effects impacting and generating emotions, feelings, and conditions around work and migration that issue from the social and political as well as from the local and granular.

Filipinx cultural criticism has explored the production of fantasy, feeling, and affect in visual and performative productions on the transnational order. "Fantasy-production," as Neferti Xina M. Tadiar contends, is the process of shaping individual fantasies and national dreams mired in power relations. Enmeshed in the affective attachments to US empire historically, "fantasies are alienated means of production" and fantasy-production "names this international order of actions."[6] Nerissa S. Balce in her work around early twentieth-century US occupation of the Philippines mines visual archives of death and imperial violence, a past that continually produces the terms of visualizing empire.[7] Vernadette Gonzalez in investigating touristic spaces in Hawai'i and the Philippines shows the afterlife of military imperial violence and how it shapes and conditions how tourists experience pleasure and discovery.[8] Alongside the corporeal archive, in performance studies, Lucy MSP Burns's work ruminates upon "puro arte" as a gendered and racialized subject's "mode of self-presentation to exceed their erasure as subjects." Despite structures of domination, these continue to "appear as difficult subjects who press against the accepted norms of gender and performance."[9] Christine Bacareza Balance explores the interstices of performance to work through the traps of representation in her notion of "disobedient listening," practices that circulate and outline translocal auditory lives as an alternative spatial geography.[10] In all these cases, Filipinx subjects and their various emergences (arrival and impact) on stage, film, photographs, music, and everyday life also produce affective worlds. Bodily senses and sense-making become an interface for ways to be in the world to mark durations and spaces.[11]

Dating *and Communal Futures*

A person's *dating*, or "appeal and impact," to use Bayot's phrase, creates conditions for sociality. *Dating* is a form of address that generates and defines the terms of collectivity at the same time that it generates pleasure. A person might be unaware of her *dating* but she is admired usually by way of group acknowledgment, so individuals might be bonded through admiration of the person as achieved state, creating a temporary sociality. Anthropologist Fenella Cannell has described how local beauty pageants in lowland Christian Philippine cultural practices are a form of communal power, not only in the act of holding the crowd's attention but also in making a social network manifest and visible through audience acclamation. *Biyuti*, using the vernacular spelling, defines personhood, as Manalansan has argued, evoking its queer sensibilities. Relatedly, "bakla," Manalansan signals, "invokes particular kinds of scripts that point to notions of self, embedded in social relations . . . bakla is not an identity that is assumed by particular men but more accurately a slippery condition, a performative event or series of events of self-formation." Self-formation according to social scripts and setting is tactical. Thus, *biyuti* as personhood beyond personal appearance comes to light only *in communality*. Further, I would argue that a person's *dating* is a tactical and tactile redirection of space and time.

Dating generates value in atmosphere and event as ends in themselves. Let us recall Lumbera's description of arrival as event: *"Ang kaganapan ng pagsapit ng likha*, ang dating ng likha, nagbibitiw ang audience ng pahayag ng pagkatuwa, pagkasaya o paghanga"* (*At the experience of this arrival*, the impact or arrival of the work, the audience reacts with laughter, joy or admiration [my italics]). Arrival is an experience in itself. It is a disruptive event that marks possibility. I would thus connect arrival to futurity in the fullness of present possibility. If return is framed as an iteration of arrival, the past as a discrete temporal comparison recedes. Arrival is a disruption of the present so that another vision of the future emerges. Time here is not about chronology on which return depends—a sequence of events that could be recalled or be made discrete. In other words, *dating* is not so much about time as duration but about timing and the opportune, that intangible eventuality not wholly about individual intention but the deployment of social conditions to configure possibility. If *dating* is about bending time and space of the present, someone's presence becomes a moment of other possibilities that were not there before the arrival.

Much Filipinx American and diasporic literature, not just scholarship, take return, figuratively or literally, as one of its thematic concerns. The theme is not always only about the fantasy of return but the very conditions of contemporary contract labor and expirations of visas. Return could be a function of desire but might be mandatory for some and even impossible for many, as is the case for undocumented and illegally overstaying migrants around the world.[12] Returning subjects are caught between continuity and the fear of its impossibility. The former assumes static subjects and relationships, and the latter assumes a complete erasure of history, a re-creation myth. A return intimates looping back not just to the Philippines but also a recovery of lost time and relationships. However, this recovery assumes that there is a discrete and static past to return to. Both are premised on overvaluation of the individual as autonomous rather than always already integrated in a social and historical network. By shifting the viewing frame from one of return home to another iteration of arrival, *dating* disrupts chronology itself. Communal observers are able to access the new arrival, as she reconfigures the space around her.[13]

Indicating this interconnectivity among bodies, *dating* is the effect of reshaping time and place for communal pleasure and creates the condition for sociality. Arrival or *dating* may be thought of as interruption of time by the act of entry. What emerges in arrival understood in this way is the immaterial forces that circulate to create the terms of the local community and its legibility to itself. Together arrival and impact may be understood through this emergence. Ruminating on *dating* in this essay, I suggest that *dating* as affect could describe the interruptive spaces and time within global migration by which overseas Filipinxs craft their own departures, returns, and arrivals.

NOTES

1. Bienvenido Lumbera, "'Datíng': Panimulang Muni sa Estetika ng Panitikang Filipino," *Lagda* 1 (1999): 34.

2. Lumbera, "Datíng," 35: Translation mine.

3. David Jonathan Bayot, "Bienvenido L. Lumbera on Revaluation: The National Stages of Philippine Literature and Its History," *IDEYA: Journal of Humanities* 8, no. 1 (2006): 106.

4. Martin F. Manalansan IV, "Queering the Chain of Care Paradigm," *S&F Online* 6, no. 3 (Summer 2008): 5.

5. Brian Massumi, *Parables of the Virtual: Movement, Affect, Sensation* (Durham, N.C.: Duke University Press, 2002), 25.

6. Neferti Xina M. Tadiar, *Fantasy-Production: Sexual Economies and Other Philippine Consequences for the New World Order* (Quezon City, Philippines: Ateneo De Manila University Press, 2004), 2.

7. Nerissa S. Balce, *Body Parts of Empire: Visual Abjection, Filipino Images, and the American Archive* (Ann Arbor: University of Michigan Press, 2016).

8. Vernadette Gonzalez, *Securing Paradise: Tourism and Militarism in Hawai'i and the Philippines* (Durham, N.C.: Duke University Press, 2013).

9. Lucy MSP Burns, *Puro Arte: Filipinos on the Stages of Empire* (New York: New York University Press, 2013), 2.

10. Christine Bacareza Balance, *Tropical Renditions: Making Musical Scenes in Filipino America* (Durham, N.C.: Duke University Press, 2016).

11. In literary studies, Jeffrey Santa Ana investigates production of emotion as coterminous with production of race, particularly Asian racialization. See Jeffrey Santa Ana, *Racial Feelings: Asian American in a Capitalist Culture of Emotion* (Philadelphia: Temple University Press, 2015).

12. See Jose Antonio Vargas's documentary film, *Documented* (2014), and subsequent memoir, *Dear America* (2018). My thanks to Lucy Burns for this insight regarding return narratives.

13. *Datíng* is often ascribed to male subjects. For my purposes, I want to redirect this ascription to women as well as queer and feminized migratory subjects.

SIXTEEN

Gender: A Transpacific Feminist Approach to Filipinx Studies

Denise Cruz

A pivotal moment in Bienvenido N. Santos's much-anthologized short story, "Scent of Apples" (1955), centers on a faded and worn photograph of a Filipina. Published in the midcentury but set in the 1940s, "Scent of Apples" engages with the complexities of gender, class, labor, and transnational migration. The story's narrator, an elite Filipino who is touring the United States as part of a public relations goodwill tour during World War II, is in the home of Celestino Fabia, an older, migrant Filipino laborer.[1] The narrator notices the photograph on the dresser, "yellow and soiled with many fingerings. The faded figure of a woman in Philippine dress could still be distinguished though the face had become a blur."[2] When the narrator asks Fabia who the woman is, the older man admits that he doesn't know. "I found that picture," he admits, "many years ago in a room on La Salle street in Chicago. I have often wondered who she is." The narrator asks Fabia if the face in the photograph was originally blurred, and Fabia replies, "Oh no. It was a young face and good." In the story, the connection between two men, who are separated by generation, class position, and education, is brokered in part by their relationship to the blurred image of an idealized Filipina.

As an intersectional, critical framework, gender has been both *formative* and *transformative* to the development of Filipinx and Filipinx American studies. I open this essay with Santos's Filipina because she is part of a larger cast, populated by other iconic figures that have been pivotal to studies of Filipinx American literature and culture. This roster includes the chaste and sacrificial María Clara of José Rizal's nineteenth-century novel *Noli Me Tangere*; the eroticized images of bare-chested Filipinas circulated during the US occupation; the left-behind Filipina mother as figure of the nation (*Inang Bayan*) in Carlos Bulosan's *America Is in the Heart*; and allusions to Imelda Marcos's oppressive manipulation of beauty in Jessica Hagedorn's *Dogeaters*. In more recent years, this list has included more contemporary "fantasy-productions" of Filipina women as shaped by neocolonial and global forms of power (Neferti Xina M. Tadiar); the nurses, caregivers, and "servants of globalization" featured in popular discourse about contemporary Filipinx labor and studied by Catherine Ceniza Choy, Rhacel Salazar Parreñas, Robyn Magalit Rodriguez, Kale Bantigue Fajardo, and Allan Punzalan Isaac; and the global queens and divas featured in the work of Martin F. Manalansan IV or Robert Diaz.

It is therefore difficult to narrow down the ways in which gender has shaped and framed Filipinx studies, in part because gender has been so central to the development of this interdisciplinary field. In this essay, I narrate the complicated ways in which gender emerges when applied as part of a broader transpacific and feminist framework. A transpacific feminist approach to gender in Filipinx studies reveals both the critical engagement of constructions of masculinity and femininity across varied forms of cultural production, and second, the importance of a strong tradition of Filipinx feminist literary and cultural production. Throughout the essay, "gender" operates in two ways: first, to name masculinity and femininity as historically inflected and culturally specific constructions; and second, to underscore the importance of the feminist scholarship that has been critical to recognizing, documenting, and analyzing constructions of gender and its relationship to historic and persistent inequities.[3]

When I first began my work on gender and Filipinx American studies, I was struck by what I perceived to be a significant chronological division between the early to mid-twentieth-century examinations of the term and more contemporary studies. While Filipinas were clearly central to the narration of Filipinx history, culture, and experience, I found that accounts of the early twentieth century featured—for good reason—Filipinas as reified icons (the mother as nation, for example), while late twentieth-century work centered on transgressive women who flouted limiting terms of gender and sexuality, illustrated most famously by the publication and success of Jessica Hagedorn's influential feminist novel *Dogeaters* (1990).[4] In terms of the development of the field, this contemporary slant makes sense given the efflorescence of Filipina feminist work in the Philippines and the United States from the 1980s to the 2000s. This period was a watershed moment for approaches that involved both the development of Filipinx studies as an interdisciplinary field, and for feminist work that explicitly focused on either recovering, documenting, and analyzing the experiences of Filipina women as important to a broader academic feminist project.

These years saw the concerted interventions and new scholarship from the critics cited above, but they also emerged in conversation with Pinay peminism/feminism, theorized by scholars such as Melinda L. de Jesús and Allyson Tintiangco-Cubales, and the forms of feminism that emerged in novels, short stories, and poetry: Hagedorn, M. Evelina Galang, Barbara Jane Reyes, Jean Vengua Gier, Catalina Cariaga, Cecilia Manguerra Brainard, Evangeline Canonizada Buell, and R. Zamora Linmark. It is important to underscore that these U.S.-based developments did not occur in a vacuum, for these publications intersected with the long standing work of Filipina feminist scholars in the Philippines, including Soledad Reyes, Mina Roces, Cristina Pantoja-Hidalgo, Thelma B. Kintanar, Maria Luisa T. Camagay, and Joi Barrios.[5]

The faded image of the Filipina in Santos's short story recalls how the haunting presence of the Filipina shaped early to mid-twentieth-century Filipinx experience. As Nerissa S. Balce has argued, representations of the "Filipina savage," bare-breasted and exposed for imperial viewing and possession, become a "sign of conquest" in early twentieth-century photographic images that were circulated in the years immediately following the Spanish-American War.[6] The absent presence of the Filipina also informs accounts of Filipinx migrants, the bachelor communities on the West Coast, and the emphasis in legal and journalistic discourse on Filipinxs' interracial relationships.[7] Scholarship on this period initially centered on the migrant Filipinx communities that occupied the West Coast of the United States; a wave of tens of thousands of Filipinx workers who arrived in Alaska, Hawai'i, and the West Coast of the mainland during the 1920s.[8] Ronald Takaki's emblematic history of Asian Americans, *Strangers from a Different Shore*, for example, notes the scarcity of Filipinas in the United States during the first half of the twentieth century; in 1930, for example, only 6.5 percent of approximately forty-five thousand Filipinxs on the mainland were women.[9] Although women represented a small percentage of the population, their absence nevertheless became a key determining factor in representations of Filipinx migrant communities. Filipino men became associated with forms of hypersexuality, marked, as Linda España-Maram and Rick Baldoz document, by their frequenting of dance halls and by their mixed relations with working-class white and Latina women.[10] Constructions of Filipino masculinity also depicted Filipino men as deviant or inadequate: either hypersexual bachelors or as "little brown brothers," represented by the Philippine Scouts in need of tutelage (Allan Punzalan Isaac and Sharon Delmendo) or the elite pensionados, funded students who were educated in the US and meant to return as leaders (Augusto F. Espiritu).[11]

On one hand this history—which depends upon the scarcity of Filipinas and the hypervisible presence of Filipinos—has been central to how we have understood the development of Filipinx communities in the United States, and it reveals how gendered constructions of Filipinas and Filipinos have been critical to the Filipinx experience and our accounts of it. But scholars have since filled in significant archival gaps, fleshing out the lives of Filipina women previously represented merely as a minority percentage. Historians Dawn Bohulano Mabalon and Dorothy B. Fujita-Rony, for example, have recovered the experiences of women in communities like Stockton's Little Manila, the Pacific Northwest, or rural spaces. Catherine Ceniza Choy, Victor Mendoza, Martin Joseph Ponce, and I have examined the importance of elite diasporic Filipinos and Filipinas who published literature in the early twentieth century.[12] In these developments, broadening the geographic framework beyond US boundaries has revealed the importance of Filipina suffrage to the period of the 1920s, the same years initially dominated by accounts of the male migrant laborer in Filipinx American studies.[13]

While a transpacific approach to gender and sexuality has importantly expanded what we know about gender in Filipinx and Filipinx American experience, this framework also demands awareness of critical conversations and contexts about gender that are located within Asia and the Pacific.[14] Such an approach is especially important given that Filipinx racial formation, gender, and sexuality have been influenced not only by the United States and Europe, but also in conversation with other local, regional, and national modalities.[15] Scholars such as Caroline S. Hau, Reynaldo Clemeña Ileto, Vicente L. Rafael, Resil B. Mojares, J. Neil C. Garcia, and others have underscored how knowledge production and circulation are shaped not only by histories of empire and race but also by funding, training, class, politics, and location.[16] For example, as Manalansan, Garcia, Diaz, Fajardo, and Bobby Benedicto have argued, the gender nonconforming identities of the *bakla* or *tomboi* do not fit clearly or uniformly within US-based categories of queer identity.[17] Rafael, Hau, Tadiar, Raquel A. G. Reyes, Fenella Cannell, and Vernadette Vicuña Gonzalez have examined gendered constructions amid the local specificities of language and translation, systems of class and education, religion and regionalisms, and the overlap of colonialism and developing forms of nationalism and modernity.[18] My own work on transpacific femininities was inspired by this work and its call for attention to how gender must be read in the context of relationships not only between the United States and the Philippines but also with Japan, Spain, or China, or amid the discourses of Catholicism, Islam, and animism.

Transpacific research on gender has also been developed by increased scholarly attention to digital and multimedia forms. Multimedia and digital production has been absolutely critical to innovative scholarship on how Filipina, Filipino, and Filipinx artists and cultural producers have countered dominant, mainstream, and normative representations of gendered identities and expressions. Examples include Robert Diaz's analysis of YouTube-celebrity-turned-pop-superstar Jake Zyrus, Lucy Mae San Pablo Burns's examination of multimedia performance artists Barrionics and Mail Order Brides (M. O. B.), Bliss Cua Lim's theorization of queer time in Philippine cinema, and the work of feminist scholar and filmmaker Celine Parreñas Shimizu.[19]

In a time of limited resources and funding, digital archives can facilitate transpacific research on gender, allowing researchers to access records, publications, texts, and or photographs that are not always easily available or that would require significant costs. But as I have discussed in more detail elsewhere, our use of increased access to digital archives and scholarly repositories, however, also requires continued self-reflexivity, for even though online repositories and search engines widen our access to more materials about gender, this increased accessibility does not always equate with visibility.[20]

If anything, these twenty-first-century developments in how we conduct scholarship also present a reminder of just how important—and complicated—gender has been and continues to be to Filipinx studies. At the same time, for scholars of gender and sexuality more broadly, Filipinx studies offers a stunning range of examples of interdisciplinary and intersectional analysis, a framework that has for quite some time considered the entwined roles of race and empire, activism and resistance, class and labor, culture and media, and humanities and social sciences approaches. In my own primary discipline, authors continue to publish works that revise that fading and blurred image of the Filipina in "Scent of Apples." Elaine Castillo's novel *America Is Not the Heart* (2018) and Gina Apostol's *Gun Dealers' Daughter* (2010) and *Insurrecto* (2018), imaginatively return to the fraught past: the legacies of martial law, continued corruption in the Philippines, and the Philippine-American War. The stories in Mia Alvar's collection *In the Country* (2015) explore new geographies of Filipinx experiences, tracing a map of gendered global labor that connects the Philippines, the United States, and Gulf Coast. Barbara Jane Reyes's *Invocation to Daughters* (2017) is a collection that uses experimental poetics as a form of feminist praxis. These texts represent only a small selection of a vibrant list of authors who are, once again, asserting the importance of gender and feminist practices to imagining the past, present, and future of Filipinx studies.

NOTES

1. Throughout this essay, I use the term "Filipinx" to refer to Filipino/a/x people as a general case. I sometimes use the more specific terms Filipino or Filipina to refer to particular literary or historical cases.

2. Bienvenido N. Santos, "Scent of Apples," in *You Lovely People* (Manila: Bookmark, 1991 [1955]), 179–90, 188.

3. The paradigmatic text defining this use of gender is of course Judith Butler's *Gender Trouble* (New York: Routledge, 1990).

4. This paragraph distills some of the key interests of Denise Cruz, *Transpacific Femininities: The Making of the Modern Filipina* (Durham, N.C.: Duke University Press, 2012).

5. I cite a long list of these scholars in an attempt to draw attention to their work, but please note that this list is not exhaustive. Pennie S. Azarcon, ed., *Kamalayan: Feminist Writings in the Philippines* (Quezon City, Philippines: Pilipina, 1987); Merlie M. Alunan, *Fern Garden: An Anthology of Women Writing in the South* (Manila: Committee on Literature, National Commission on Culture and the Arts, 1998); Mila Astorga, Marra P. L. Lanot, and Lilia Quindoza Santiago, eds., *Filipina I: Poetry, Drama, and Fiction* (Quezon City, Philippines: New Day, 1984) and *Filipina II: An Anthology of Contemporary Women Writers in the Philippines: Essays* (Quezon City, Philippines: New Day, 1985); Maria Luisa Camagay, *Working Women of Manila in the 19th Century* (Diliman: University of the Philippines Press and the University Center for Women's Studies, 1995); Erlinda Kintanar-Albuyo, Erma M. Cuizon, Ma. Paloma A. Sandiago, eds., *Centering Voices: An Anthology* (Cebu City: Women in Literary Arts, 1995); Estrella D. Alfon and Amelia Lapeña Bonifacio, eds., *Twelve Philippine Women Writers* (Quezon City: University of the Philippines Press, 1995); Thelma Kintanar, *Women Reading: Feminist Perspectives on Philippine Literary Texts* (Quezon City: University of the Philippines Press / University Center for Women's Studies, 1992); Soledad S. Reyes, *Ang Silid na Mahiwaga: Kalipunan ng Kuwento't Tula ng mga Babaeng Manunulat* (Pasig City, Manila: Anvil, 2003); Maria Villanueva, *Going Home to a Landscape: Writings by Filipinos* (Corvallis, Oreg.: Calyx Books, 2003); Edna Zapanta-Manlapaz, ed., *Songs of Ourselves: Writings by Filipino Women in English* (Pasig City, Manila: Anvil, 1996); Nick Carbó and Eileen Tabios, eds., *Babaylan: An Anthology of Filipina and Filipina American Writers* (San Francisco: Aunt Lute Books, 2000); Sol Juvida, *Pinay* (Pasig City, Manila: Anvil, 1995).

6. Nerissa S. Balce, "The Filipina's Breast: Savagery, Docility, and the Erotics of the American Empire," in *Positively No Filipinos Allowed*, ed. Antonio T. Tiongson Jr., Edgardo Valencia Gutierrez, Ricardo Valencia Gutierrez (Philadelphia: Temple University Press, 2006).

7. Vicente L. Rafael discusses haunting and spectral presence in "Your Grief Is Our Gossip," in his *White Love and Other Events in Filipino History* (Quezon City, Philippines: Ateneo de Manila University Press, 2000).

8. Rick Baldoz, *The Third Asiatic Invasion: Migration and Empire in Filipino America, 1898–1946* (New York: New York University Press, 2011). See also Fred Cordova, Dorothy Laigo Cordova, and Albert A. Acena, *Filipinos, Forgotten Asian Americans: A Pictorial Essay, 1763–Circa 1963* (Dubuque, Iowa: Kendall/Hunt, 1983) and Antonio T. Tiongson Jr., Edgardo Valencia Gutierrez and Ricardo Valencia Gutierrez, eds., *Positively No Filipinos Allowed* (Philadelphia: Temple University Press, 2006).

9. Ronald Takaki, *Strangers from a Different Shore: A History of Asian Americans* (Boston: Little Brown and Co., 1998), 58.

10. Baldoz, *Third Asiatic Invasion* and Linda España-Maram, *Creating Masculinity in Los Angeles's Little Manila: Working Class Filipinos and Popular Culture, 1920s to 1950s* (New York: Columbia University Press, 2006). For other characterizations of Asian men, see Nayan Shah, *Contagious Divides: Epidemics and Race in San Francisco's Chinatown* (Berkeley: University of California Press, 2001).

11. Allan Punzalan Isaac, *American Tropics: Articulating Race in Filipino America* (Minneapolis: University of Minnesota Press, 2006); Sharon Delmendo, *The Star-Entangled Banner: One Hundred Years of America in the Philippines* (New Brunswick, N.J.: Rutgers University Press, 2004); and Augusto F. Espiritu, *Five Faces of Exile: The Nation and Filipino American Intellectuals* (Stanford, Calif.: Stanford University Press, 2005).

12. Catherine Ceniza Choy, "Filipino Woman in America: The Life and Work of Encarnacion Alzona," *Genre* 39, no. 3 (2006): 127–40; Cruz, *Transpacific Femininities*; Victor Mendoza, *Metroimperial Intimacies: Fantasy, Racial-Sexual Governance, and the Philippines in U.S. Imperialism, 1899–1913* (Durham, N.C.: Duke University Press, 2015); Martin Joseph Ponce, *Beyond the Nation: Diasporic Filipino Literature and Queer Reading* (New York: New York University Press, 2012). For examples of early Filipina authors, see Denise Cruz, "The Case of Felicidad Ocampo," in Martin F. Manalansan IV and Augusto F. Espiritu, eds., *Filipino Studies: Palimpsests of Nation and Diaspora* (New York: New York University Press, 2016), 274–96; and Yay Panlilio, *The Crucible: An Autobiography of Colonel Yay, Filipina American Guerrilla* (New Brunswick, N.J.: Rutgers University Press, 2010). On early women's literature in the Philippines, see Edna Zapanta-Manlapaz, *Our Literary Matriarchs, 1925–1953: Angela Manalang Gloria, Paz M. Latorena, Loreto Paras Sulit, and Paz Benitez* (Quezon City, Philippines: Ateneo de Manila University Press, 1996).

13. See Mina Roces and Louise Edwards, eds., *Women's Suffrage in Asia: Gender, Nationalism, and Democracy* (New York: Routledge, 2004); and Cruz, *Transpacific Femininities*.

14. J. Neil C. Garcia, *Philippine Gay Culture: Binabae to Bakla, Silahis to MSM* (Hong Kong: Hong Kong University Press, 2008); and Kuan Hsing-Chen, *Asia as Method: Towards Deimperialization* (Durham, N.C.: Duke University Press, 2010).

15. See for example Raquel A. G. Reyes, *Love, Passion and Patriotism: Sexuality and the Philippine Propaganda Movement, 1882–1892* (Seattle: University of Washington Press, 2008); Mina Roces and Louise Edwards, eds., *Women's Suffrage in Asia: Gender, Nationalism, and Democracy*; Tadiar, *Fantasy-Production*; and Vicente L. Rafael, *White Love and Other Events in Filipino History* (Durham, N.C.: Duke University Press, 2000) and *The Promise of the*

Foreign: Nationalism and the Technics of Translation in the Spanish Philippines (Durham, N.C.: Duke University Press, 2005).

16. See for example Reynaldo Clemeña Ileto, "Orientalism and the Study of Philippine Politics," *Philippine Political Science Journal* 22, no. 45 (2001): 1–32; Caroline Hau, "Privileging Roots and Routes: Filipino Intellectuals and the Contest Over Epistemic Power and Authority," *Philippine Studies: Historical and Ethnographic Viewpoints* 62, no. 1 (2014): 29–65; Resil B. Mojares, "The Spaces of Southeast Asian Scholarship," *Philippine Studies: Historical and Ethnographic Viewpoints* 61, no. 1 (2013): 105–24; and Vicente L. Rafael, "Reorientations: Notes on the Study of the Philippines in the United States," *Philippine Studies: Historical and Ethnographic Viewpoints* 56, no. 4 (2008): 475–92.

17. Bobby Benedicto, *Under Bright Lights: Gay Manila and the Global Scene* (Minneapolis: University of Minnesota Press, 2014); Garcia, *Philippine Gay Culture*; Kale Bantigue Fajardo, *Filipino Crosscurrents: Oceanographies of Seafaring, Masculinity, and Globalization* (Minneapolis: University of Minnesota Press, 2011); Martin F. Manalansan IV, *Global Divas: Filipino Gay Men in the Diaspora* (Durham, N.C.: Duke University Press, 2003).

18. In addition to previously cited work by Rafael, Reyes, Tadiar, and Roces, see Vernadette Vicuña Gonzalez, *Empire's Mistress: Starring Isabel Rosario Cooper* (Durham, N.C.: Duke University Press, 2021); Fenella Cannell, *Power and Intimacy in the Christian Philippines* (Cambridge: Cambridge University Press, 1999); and Caroline S. Hau, *The Chinese Question: Ethnicity, Nation and Region in and beyond the Philippines* (Quezon City, Philippines: Ateneo de Manila University Press, 2014).

19. Robert Diaz, "The Limits of Bakla and Gay: Feminist Readings of My Husband's Lover, Vice Ganda, and Charice Pempengco," *Signs: Journal of Women in Culture and Society* 40.3 (Spring 2015): 721–45; Bliss Cua Lim, "Queer Aswang Transmedia: Folklore as Camp," *Kritika Kultura* 24 (2015): 178–225; Lucy MSP Burns, *Puro Arte: Filipinos on the Stages of Empire* (New York: New York University Press, 2012). For a catalog of Shimizu's films, see *http://www.celineshimizu.com/filmmaker/*.

20. Teachers, researchers, and students who employ a transpacific approach to gender in a digital age might therefore do the following: (1) become familiar with presses and journals based outside of the United States; (2) meet with research librarians in order to learn effective strategies for conducting searches (especially since we gravitate to Google-type search terms); (3) use global catalogs (such as Worldcat) in addition to catalogs based in the United States and Europe; and (4) explicitly teach the difference between databases and repositories (which require subscriptions in order to be featured). See Denise Cruz, "Notes on Transpacific Archives," *Gender in the Transpacific World*, ed. Judy Wu and Catherina Ceniza Choy (Leiden and Boston: Brill Press, 2017), 10–19.

SEVENTEEN

The Contingencies of *Kasarian*

Robert Diaz

In her provocative film *Imelda* (2003), Ramona Diaz reimagines Marcosian martial law's impending demise through the creative camp that saturates Manila's queer nightlife.[1] While featuring footage of urban masses marching down Epifanio de los Santos Avenue (or EDSA) to demand political change, the documentary glimpses an intimate scene from the "The Aquino/ Marcos Drag Show." Held at the Politixx Niteclub, this act begins with a drag queen dressed as Corazon Aquino standing center stage. She holds a large wooden rosary and silently pleads with a Catholic priest standing beside her. He nods in agreement while the classic ballad "Does He Love You?" (1993) plays throughout their exchange. Originally sung by Reba McEntire and Linda Davis, this duet dramatizes the angst between two women as they ponder who's more deserving of one man's love. When Faux Aquino lip-synchs McEntire's part, another queen dressed as Imelda Marcos saunters on stage with bodyguard in tow. Faux Imelda lip-synchs Davis's part while exuding both condescension and indifference. When she reaches center stage, Aquino turns to Imelda to continue her silent pleading. The latter looks away, emphasizing her unwavering disinterest.

At its core, this queer interlude subtends historical archive by exposing the gendered dynamics that shape Philippine nationalisms during dictatorial duress. By parodying unrequited love between two women, this performance critiques how Imelda Marcos and Corazon Aquino strategically consolidated political power through heteropatriarchal articulations of respectable womanhood. As the critic Mina Roces has argued, both Aquino and Marcos moralized their role as nationalist figures by espousing contradictory versions of Filipinx femininity. Marcos used lofty visions of beauty as the rationale for maintaining fascistic will and pursuing dictatorial dreams. Aquino offered herself as the vessel of postdictatorial hope for freedom by leaning into her domestic simplicity and maternal piousness.[2] "The Aquino/Marcos Drag Show" thus hyperbolizes these overdetermined scripts. It parodies two women's repetitive invocation of love and it turns into a metaphor for how Marcos and Aquino tactically deployed love—for their husbands, countrymen, and the Catholic Church—to moralize their relationship to power. *Imelda* ultimately turns to performance of queer life to revisit the broader constitutive relations between gender and sexuality, as it qualifies the political limits of Philippine nationalisms when buttressed by heteronormative notions of women's agency and desire.

I thus begin with this queer moment from Diaz's film since it highlights the many contributions of theorizing gender and sexuality constitutively when understanding Filipinx histories more broadly. The closest vernacular word for gender and sex in Tagalog is *kasarian*, a term whose root word *sari* (kind) offers us much more capacious ways to frame gender and sexuality beyond their often binaristic qualities in English. While such a binary has and continues to be challenged by activists and scholars in the West, recentering a vernacular term from the Global South like *kasarian* enables us to glean how the region's vernacularism can productively unsettle the forms of knowledge we currently have to identify and index marginalized subjectivities and experiences. As they emphasize *kasarian*'s mutability for instance, Lilia Santiago and J. Neil C. Garcia have emphasized how the word *sari* in its colloquial usage demands a more diverse concatenation of typologies, objects, and frameworks for rendering gender and sexuality in the everyday. *Sari* requires that we not only see gender and sexuality as co-constitutive realities. It also asks that we understand *sari*'s expansive mutability as engendering opportunities to rework, undo, and reimagine subjectivities in process as these emerge across the many elsewheres diasporic Filipinxs inhabit.

I would argue that it is precisely this contingent yet capacious nature of *kasarian* that fuels diverse renditions of Filipinx marginalization and empowerment across a wide range of artistic and cultural expressions. In Filipinx American literature for instance, it would be difficult to fully comprehend Allos's marginalization in Carlos Bulosan's *America Is in the Heart*, or Joey Sands's strategic deployment of sex in Jessica Hagedorn's *Dogeaters*, or overachiever Orling Domingo's desire to dress up as Farrah Fawcett in R. Zamora Linmark's *Rolling the R's*, or Hero's insurgency and precarity in Elaine Castillo's *America Is Not the Heart* without framing their gendered and sexual disempowerment through the shifting aftermath of colonialism, sexism, and racism.[3] Or, in the writings of Ronald Baytan, Danton Remoto, and J. Neil C. Garcia, it is precisely the fluidity of the *bakla*—a term that denotes feminine and nonnormative gender identification—that becomes a crucial entry point from which these authors center Global South psychosexual dynamics and knowledge formations as a response to the exclusionary effects of Western biomedical terms for sexual marginality such as lesbian, gay, bisexual, and transgender identity.[4] Beyond these authors' interventions, the consistent reemergence of a precolonial figure like *babaylan* in contemporary diasporic art and political activism across the diaspora also signifies the need to refuse the collapse of precolonial and Indigenous identities and intimacies with European and colonial ones.

Moving beyond diasporic literature, *kasarian*'s contingent nature could also be seen as fueling the many contributions of Philippine New Cinema, an artistic movement from the 1970s until the early 1990s that directly turned the intersections of gender and sexuality to frame the necropolitical and classist practices of dictatorship. Canonical films in the movement like *Manila By Night*, *Manila Sa Kuko Ng Liwanag*, *Tubog sa Ginto*, *Insiang*, *Alyas Baby Tsina*, *Oro Plata Mata*, and *Batch 81* collectively reframe the aftermath of martial law, as well as Spanish, American, and Japanese colonialisms, by approaching these histories from the vantage point of the country's most economically disenfranchised. Focusing on New Cinema's subversive story lines and aesthetics, critics like Roland B. Tolentino, José B. Capino, and Bliss Cua

Lim have argued that New Cinematic films foreground nonnormative intimacies and social relations to then connect the country's violent histories with the kinds of resistances and lives lived despite these histories.[5]

In terms of critical work in the field of Filipinx American and diaspora studies, *kasarian* also animates analyses of empire, migration, and globalization. Victor Román Mendoza, for instance, returns to the American colonization of the Philippines to track how various intimacies between US subjects and Filipinxs threatened the racialized schemas of colonization.[6] These wayward intimacies then effected disciplinary practices that policed Filipinx domesticity and sexuality. Examining the movement of Filipinxs between the United States and the Philippines at the turn of the twentieth century, Denise Cruz and Martin Joseph Ponce investigate how Filipinx writers intervened in discourses around national belonging through articulations of sexuality.[7] Cruz argues for the significance of the "transpacific Filipina" to transnational ideas about both colonialism and modernity. Ponce focuses on the works of authors who, through their novels and poetry, redefine and to some extent undo the boundaries of nationhood, thus queering its iterations. Connecting empire's ghosts to globalization, Neferti Xina M. Tadiar suggests that the specific concatenations between sexuality and gender in the Philippines produces what she calls "fantasy-productions," or versions of nationhood transnationally oriented toward the false promises of capitalist accumulation.[8]

Contributing to Tadiar's analysis, Robyn Magalit Rodriguez, Rhacel Salazar Parreñas, Valerie Francisco-Menchavez, and Ethel Tungohan further contextualize globalization's effects as they collectively trace how "labor brokerage" practices depend upon gendered assumptions around caregiving and sex work.[9] These writers remind us that the line between hyperdomesticity and hypersexuality is a thin one, as labor is feminized in an era of expanding transnational capital. Martin F. Manalansan IV cautions against such gendered assumptions around migrant labor. Aside from his significant ethnographic work on gay Filipinxs in New York, Manalansan also studies how the "chain of care" model (which imagines women in the Third World as the key caretakers of bodies in the First World) fails to account for the ambivalent experiences of queer and nonnormative Filipinxs in these same roles.[10] These workers compose themselves in the act of care to register disaffection, routine-ness, and disinvestment. Queerness then—as affect, kinship, and sexuality—challenges normative assumptions about womanhood that dominant notions of carework tend to reproduce. Extending Mana-lansan's analysis, Allan Punzalan Isaac offers a useful corrective to nationalist narratives of care.[11] Isaac suggests that a "refusal to wallow" in representations of queer caregivers in Israel offers new ways for us to conceive of the logics of care often reproduced through migrant sacrifice, as a kind of queer kinship that transects national borders.

As he investigates the cultural manifestations of masculinity in the lives of seafarers, Kale Bantigue Fajardo reflects on how "tomboy"—a word synonymous with lesbian and trans identity—is often used to describe the working class as well.[12] Jan M. Padios and Emmanuel David further examine the significance of sexuality to Philippine class and labor politics by focusing on the growing call center industry, particularly its upending effects on seemingly fixed local class dynamics.[13] These effects can then be seen in how the bodies working in these industries are portrayed generally. Call center agents have been depicted negatively as vectors of HIV (in the case of Padios's research), or have celebrated their sexuality as a means to reflect a more Americanized (and thus presumably more progressive) industry (which David further unpacks). Across these scholarly works, sexuality functions as a framing mechanism for understanding the contingent relations of gender and class as they constitute each other in the lives of Filipinxs across different historical, geographic, and political contexts.

Kasarian's reframing of gender and sexuality are arguably most visibilized through diasporic and popular representations of queer life. One of the most enduring forms of queer cultural expression that continues to proliferate in television, film, and other forms of new media is *kabaklaan*. Although connected to the identity *bakla*, *kabaklaan* exceeds this category. *Kabaklaan* can be seen as a performance, a posture, a way of acting, a style of being over the top, and a means to assert a distinctly queer Filipinx sensibility. *Kabaklaan* is often humorous, and at times dares to poke fun at what is solemn, divine, and sacrosanct. It has its own ethics, and thus is often reined in, disciplined, and policed precisely because it does not choose the right subject to direct its energies to. It can force itself onto its intended audience even at the borders of its erasure. *Kabaklaan* evinces what Lucy MSP Burns calls *puro arte*, or the histrionic modes of cultural expression that Filipinx subjects animate.[14]

Because of all these characteristics, *kabaklaan* is an important site from which to index the contradictory effects of globalization on diasporic sexualities. Bobby Benedicto, for instance, tracks how discourse that aspires for "gay globality" in the Philippines, or elite forms of homonormativity grounded in Western constructs of LGBTQ identities, have begun to invisibilize practices of *kabaklaan*.[15] In dialogue with Benedicto's research, my work examines how *kabaklaan*, because of its links to the identity *bakla*, becomes an important site from which to understand the shifting nature of transgender and feminist politics in the diaspora.[16] As I analyze Philippine celebrities, soap operas, and films, I also note how *kabaklaan* hybridizes trans politics and discourses, marking the uneven forms of knowledge exchange between the Global South and the Global North. Along with Denise Cruz, I also examine how *kabaklaan* appears in diasporic spaces like Canada as a means to diagnose and critique the specific demands of Canadian multiculturalism and settler colonialism.[17] *Kabaklaan* rescripts Filipinx presence in Canada away from a history of service and carework, which Cruz's analysis of Canada Philippine Fashion Week in Toronto shows. It also becomes crucial in performances of pageantry and drag that challenge respectable forms of cultural belonging. *Kabaklaan* enables queer Filipinx artists to critique the centrality of both whiteness and the nuclear family in conceptualizations of ideal Canadian citizenship.

As the diaspora continues to grow, the vocabularies for how we denote gender and sexuality continue to foreground the expansiveness of *kasarian*. For instance, echoing the openness of the term "Latinx," many scholars and activists have begun to use "Filipinx" as a way to rescript nationality and ethnicity. "Filipinx" is a gender-neutral term that perhaps echoes the desire for multiplicity that *kasarian* offers. "Filipinx" similarly invites us to think beyond the linguistic genealogies of colonialism we have come to continually rely upon. Similar to the *sari* in *kasarian*, it offers contingency as a means to transform the vernacular. It highlights the creative energies with which diasporic Filipinxs continue to reimagine what defines us. It thus reflects the generative ethos imbedded in *kasarian*.

NOTES

1. *Imelda*, directed and produced by Ramona Diaz (United States: United Pictures, 2004).

2. Mina Roces, *Women, Power, and Kinship Politics* (Westport, Conn.: Praeger, 1998).

3. Carlos Bulosan, *America Is in the Heart* (Seattle: University of Washington Press, 1973); Jessica Hagedorn, *Dogeaters* (New York: Penguin Books, 1990); R. Zamora Linmark, *Rolling the R's* (Los Angeles: Kaya Press, 1995); Elaine Castillo, *America Is Not the Heart* (New York: Penguin Books, 2019).

4. Ronald Baytan, *The Queen Lives Alone* (Quezon City: University of the Philippines Press, 2012); J. Neil C. Garcia and Danton Remoto, eds., *Ladlad: An Anthology of Philippine Gay Writing* (Mandaluyong: Anvil Press, 1996).

5. Roland Tolentino, *National/Transnational: Subject Formation and Media in and on the Philippines* (Loyola Heights, Philippines: Ateneo De Manila Press, 2001); Bliss Cua Lim, *Translating Time: Cinema, the Fantastic, and Temporal Critique* (Durham, N.C.: Duke University Press, 2009); Jose B. Capino, *Dream Factories of a Former Colony: American Fantasies in Philippine Cinema* (Minneapolis: University of Minnesota Press, 2010).

6. Victor Mendoza, *Metroimperial Intimacies: Fantasy, Racial-Sexual Governance, and the Philippines in U.S. Imperialism, 1899–1913* (Durham, N.C.: Duke University Press, 2015).

7. Denise Cruz, *Transpacific Femininities: The Making of the Modern Filipina* (Durham, N.C.: Duke University Press, 2012); Martin Joseph Ponce, *Beyond the Nation: Diasporic Filipino Literature and Queer Reading* (New York: New York University Press, 2012).

8. Neferti Xina M. Tadiar, *Fantasy-Production: Sexual Economies and Other Philippine Consequences for the New World Order* (Hong Kong: Hong Kong University Press, 2004).

9. Robyn Magalit Rodriguez, *Migrants for Export: How the Philippine State Brokers Labor to the World* (Minneapolis: University of Minnesota Press, 2010); Rhacel Salazar Parreñas, *Illicit Flirtations: Labor, Migration, and Sex Trafficking in Tokyo* (Stanford, Calif.: Stanford University Press, 2011); Valerie Francisco-Menchavez, *The Labor of Care: Filipina Migrants and Transnational Families in the Digital Age* (Urbana: University of Illinois Press, 2018).

10. Martin F. Manalansan IV, *Global Divas: Filipino Gay Men in the Diaspora* (Durham, N.C.: Duke University Press, 2003); "Queering the Chain of Care Paradigm," *S&F Online* 6, no. 3 (2008). Retrieved from: *http://sfonline .barnard.edu/immigration/print_manalansan.htm*.

11. Allan Punzalan Isaac, "In a Precarious Time and Place: The Refusal to Wallow and Other Migratory Temporal Investments in Care Divas, the Musical," *Journal of Asian American Studies* 19, no. 1 (February 2016): 5–24.

12. Kale Fajardo, *Filipino Crosscurrents: Oceanographies of Seafaring, Masculinities, and Globalization* (Minneapolis: University of Minnesota Press, 2011).

13. Jan M. Padios, *A Nation on the Line: Call Centers as Postcolonial Predicaments in the Philippines* (Durham, N.C.: Duke University Press, 2018); Emmanuel David, "Purple-Collar Labor: Transgender Workers and Queer Value

at Global Call Centers in the Philippines," *Gender & Society* 29, no. 2 (April 2015): 169–94.

14. Lucy MSP Burns, *Puro Arte: Filipinos on the Stages of Empire* (New York: New York University Press, 2012).

15. Bobby Benedicto, *Under Bright Lights: Gay Manila and the Global Scene* (Minneapolis: University of Minnesota Press, 2014).

16. Robert Diaz, "Biyuti from Below: Contemporary Philippine Cinema and the Transing of Kabaklaan," *TSQ* 5, no. 3 (2018): 404–24.

17. Denise Cruz, "Global Mess and Glamour: Behind the Spectacle of Transnational Fashion," *Journal of Asian American Studies* 19, no. 2 (2016): 143–67; Robert Diaz, "Queer Unsettlements: Diasporic Filipinos in Canada's World Pride," *Journal of Asian American Studies* 19, no. 3 (2016): 327–50.

PART FOUR

Critical Schooling and Justice in Other Words

EIGHTEEN

Filipinx Americans and Higher Education

Dina C. Maramba

My role as a former student affairs educator and my current position as a university professor have provided me with many lessons and insights about Filipinx American identity and higher education. As a student affairs practitioner for over ten years, I worked closely with first-generation college and underserved students of color, including Filipinx Americans. They often shared with me their challenges of negotiating their social identities. More specifically, students often talked about struggling to navigate unwelcome college terrain while also trying to make sense of their ethnic identity and the intersection of race, socioeconomic status, gender, sexuality, and immigration status. Undoubtedly, these dynamics played prominent roles in their collegiate experience. As I continued to work with Filipinx American students, I also observed that higher education institutions (and secondary education institutions) have yet to fully recognize and understand the influence of intersecting identities on the college students' lives and the vital connection to their academic success and personal growth in college. In my current position as a university professor, I have the opportunity to continue to interact with underserved students of color and conduct research on topics about how their intersectional identities interact with college environments. Equally, if not more important, I examine how the existing hegemonic power structures of higher education institutions have consequences on how students negotiate their intersecting identities. I also consider how these power structures influence students' college access, retention, persistence, access to resources, and overall sense of well-being and belonging on college campuses. At this juncture, I will briefly reflect on the criticality of engaging these issues as they relate to Filipinx Americans.

I will focus on the complexities of racial and ethnic identities of Filipinx Americans within the context of higher education. While I focus on ethnic identity (Filipinx American), I still recognize the extricable and complicated links with other social identities like race, gender, sexuality, socioeconomic status, and immigration status, and consider the overall role of hegemonic power within higher education campuses. Filipinx Americans bring to the table a unique and multifaceted piece to identity and education discussions by the very fact that the Philippines began its interaction with the US through a colonial and currently a postcolonial relationship. For many historical and political reasons, not to be discussed here due to limited space, the perception that all Filipinx Americans are highly educated "immigrants," well versed in English, and well adjusted to American life, still exists. It has certainly brought on direct and indirect ways in which Filipinx American students are perceived and treated by educational institutions and how they challenge these educational issues.

First, I will problematize higher education institutions' practice of categorizing social identities, mainly concerning race and ethnicity and notions of success. Next, I will highlight areas of the literature relevant to students of color and, in particular Filipinx American students. Lastly, I will share my critical reflections on the complexity of the precarious (non)positioning and (non)inclusionary practices by collegiate institutions regarding Filipinx American students. I will also briefly discuss, as examples, access to college and affirmative action, K–12 education, and reflections of Filipinx Americans reflected in curriculum and faculty. I will further explore how counternarratives of Filipinx American college students, and intersections of their social identities, provide a platform to address the need for higher education institutional change.

Among the many assumed benchmarks of success for higher education institutions is retaining and eventually graduating their student population, which includes but is not limited to Filipinx Americans. The road to accomplishing this goal involves having an understanding of the students who attend their institutions. Universities and colleges generally operate under limited theoretical knowledge that students are successful and retained when they are involved socially and academically on campus, feel validated, and find meaning and purpose in their college experience.[1] Universities also use college student development theories—e.g., cognitive, psychological, and social—to help explain the nature of and the influence of context and environment on students.[2] These theories and studies largely guide colleges and universities to better understand students they are serving. But research has also shown there is still a need to understand the experiences of college students of color. For the point of this essay, in particular, there is little focus on Filipinx American students. All of these taken together, higher education institutions are generally guided by a "one size fits all" understanding of college student success, retention, and overall college experiences. While these current general understandings about college students are useful, critical scholars, practitioners, and researchers challenge the applicability of these theories and studies to underserved, racially and ethnically diverse populations.[3]

Those who conduct K–12 and college research studies for and about Filipinx American students will agree that critical research is still lacking and remains underexplored. Hence, Filipinx Americans have been described as "forgotten Asian Americans," colonized subjects, betwixt and between invisible subjects, the middle, the "other" students, and the Latinos of Asia.[4] These descriptions reflect the intricacies of the social identities of Filipinx Americans.

There are many ways in which higher education institutions engage with social identities. One of the most conventional approaches is when an institution reports its demographic numbers via social identities like race, gender, first-generation, and socioeconomic status. Socioeconomic status is often indirectly stated by the number of recipients receiving certain types of financial aid, and on occasion, institutions might also juxtapose their student population's social identities with the number of students admitted, enrolled, retained, and their graduation rates. Comparing these social identities with admission, enrollment, and retention rates are often used as evaluative forms of success for both the institution and its student population.

These connections fall short of providing a real understanding of college students of color experiences and characteristics because of, among many reasons, institutions' power to name, categorize, and define success. Moreover, it is a major shortcoming not to recognize that social categories come with real sociopolitical and racial consequences and must be contextualized when evaluating modes of success within educational institutions. Although the numbers of certain racial information might vary, they are often presented as four main categories (African American / Black, Chicanx / Latinx, Asian American / Pacific Islander, and sometimes American Indian). According to the US Census, the Asian American population has grown from 11.9 million (2000) to 20.4 million (2015), a 72 percent increase. As of 2017, within the Asian American group, the three largest remain the Chinese at 4.9 million (24 percent), Asian Indian at 4 million (20 percent), and Filipinxs at 3.9 million (19 percent).[5] The Asian American category comprises more than twenty ethnic groups (this number does not include Native Hawaiian and Pacific Islanders, who are still often inaccurately lumped in with the Asian American category). Within the Asian American category is a wide range of diversity in socioeconomic class, language, history, immigration status, and religion (CARE, 2016).[6]

Given these vast differences among the ethnic groups, we cannot paint an accurate picture of the Filipinx American experience. Even though the Filipinx population is the third-largest Asian American population in the US, and California has the largest Filipinx community (US Census, 2015), schools and colleges still have limited knowledge about Filipinx Americans. While aggregate numbers of the Asian American group can be helpful, they can also be misleading if not used carefully. By disaggregating ethnic groups within the Asian American grouping, along with a critical understanding of the relationship among the other social identities, we can better understand the contexts of Filipinx Americans. Although some states and universities already disaggregate Asian American ethnic groups, e.g., California, Hawai'i, and Washington, many have yet to incorporate this practice into their university institutional data collecting. Without disaggregated data, we have an incomplete picture of Filipinx American students. But this process of disaggregation into ethnic groups should not end there. It is not only essential to know that institutions disaggregate, but even more critical is how institutions should use the data.

This next section touches upon college access / affirmative action, K–12 education, curriculum, and faculty issues as they pertain to Filipinx Americans. Within the affirmative action debate, opponents of affirmative action are pushing for admissions to be race-neutral. This line of thinking fails to consider particular contexts (historical and current) of specific groups, ignores the intersectionalities of ethnicity, immigration status, gender, sexuality, and socioeconomic class; more insidious are the institutional racist practices and policies that further widen the access gap for underserved groups. Despite the stereotype that Asian Americans are overrepresented and faring well academically in colleges and universities, Filipinx American students do indeed face college-access challenges.[7]

Filipinx American students, as of 1987, were removed from any consideration under affirmative action policies because they were deemed as no longer a population of concern.[8] As a result, they were negatively affected as it excluded them within the discourse of college access and affirmative action. An example of the negative consequence was at the University of Hawai'i. During the same year that Filipinx American students were removed from the list of populations under affirmative action, the University of Hawai'i system also raised tuition dramatically, and the numbers of Filipinx American students substantially decreased at the flagship University of Hawai'i at Manoa. They also experienced lower graduation rates compared to the average graduation rate at the university.[9] Although some Asian American ethnic groups are well represented in the University of California (UC) system-wide, another study indicated that with the passage of Proposition 209 in 1996, which removed affirmative action race-conscious admissions, Filipinx Americans are underrepresented at the more selective UC campuses such as UC Berkeley and UCLA.[10] For example, admittance rates for Filipinx Americans decreased from 201 in 1989 to 80 in 2010 at UC Berkeley. In addition, Asian Americans, a grouping that includes Filipinx students, are often wedged in the middle of the college admissions debate between white students and African American and Chicanx/Latinx students.[11]

On the K–12 education level, there also exist several issues that affect Filipinx Americans. In their examination of prominent secondary school history textbooks, Roland Coloma found that less than 1 percent of them mentioned any Philippine or Filipinx topics.[12] In a complementary study, Allyson Tintiangco-Cubales discussed how poverty heavily influenced Filipinx youth's school experiences and negatively affected their potential for academic success.[13] Robert T. Teranishi found that high schools and teachers characterized Filipinx American youth as gang members who lacked aspirations to pursue further education.[14] High school teachers' lower expectations also lower the potential for Filipinx American students to pursue higher education goals.

Further studies show the need for a culturally sensitive curriculum and better teacher training. As previously mentioned, Filipinx Americans are not consistently reflected in the existing K–12 curriculum.[15] An example of an effort to address this is Patricia Halagao's codevelopment of two Filipinx American curricula and pedagogy programs called Pinoy Teach and iJeeepney.com. This development eventually led to the creation of the Sistan C. Alhambra Filipino American Education Institute, which serves as a conduit to assist professors, teachers, and community members in meeting Filipinx students' needs. Allyson Tintiangco-Cubales, the founder of the Pin@y (Pinay/Pinoy) Educational Partnerships (P.E.P.), created a strong pipeline partnership between the university, K–12 schools, and the community. This groundbreaking and long-standing program critically addresses the lack of curriculum, pedagogy, and representation within the educational system for and about Filipinx Americans.[16]

Relevant to higher education, Dina C. Maramba and Kevin L. Nadal's analysis of the Filipinx American faculty pipeline indicated that faculty are not well represented at the full-time tenure-track level in the social science disciplines.[17] Their national study showed that 114 Filipinx American professors teach in the social science disciplines and included only 46 associate professors and 16 full professors. The vast majority of faculty are nontenured assistant professors. The study also indicated that Filipinx professors are mostly located in universities on the West Coast and heavily represented in the disciplines of ethnic studies and American studies and less in education, anthropology, and economics. These findings have significant repercussions for Filipinx college students who look to Filipinx American faculty who might serve as a support system and as role models.

Lastly, in my current observations and research about Filipinx American college students, I reflect briefly on their counternarratives and in relationship to university practices, specifically in the form of those who work directly with college students on campus (e.g., student affairs staff, faculty, and administrators). Student affairs educators, administrators, and faculty must have an understanding of the diverse populations they serve. These interactions can affect their comfort level with university staff and their overall campus experience.

Filipinx American students have experienced unwelcoming college environments. For example, in meetings with career and academic counselors, and school psychologists, some Filipinx American students report feeling unsupported and misunderstood.[18] When they express their concerns about changing their major and agonizing over how to share their apprehension with their parents, they are often met with counselor advice that reflects individualistic approaches that do not consider family dynamics and relationships with their Filipinx immigrant parents.[19] Filipinx students have also had negative interactions with teaching assistants and faculty. For example, in a discussion involving the desire to write their term paper on Filipinx topics, a Filipinx American student was told by their professor that they should change their topic altogether because it was not a viable topic nor was there enough evidence or references for them to substantiate their thesis statements.[20]

These examples of negative exchanges between Filipinx American college students and university staff who lack knowledge about this population ultimately affect students' college experiences, self-esteem, and overall well-being.[21] Many research studies have explained that these interactions occur because of the misperception that Asian Americans are not a population that needs much attention because they are already well-adjusted in school.[22] The perpetual model minority stereotype discussion continues to be contested by critical researchers. It has challenged higher education institutions to reframe this discourse as it has negative consequences for all groups included within the Asian American category.[23]

Indeed, Filipinx Americans continue to challenge and interrogate identities within the context of education. To recap, they expose the limitations in the ways we consider collecting accurate student demographics and disaggregating data within the Asian American category. As mentioned previously, Filipinx Americans also pose as good examples of what happens when a population is unfairly excluded from race-conscious policies such as affirmative action. Also, the existing research for and about Filipinx American students has shown the limited ways schools perceive this population in the curriculum and the low representation of those who teach and are tenured at the higher education level.

The case of Filipinx American students offers an essential site for critical analysis and provides opportunities to improve our higher education institutions. They challenge higher education to reconsider taken-for-granted social identities and definitions of college student success. Such examples include how we think about Filipinx Americans as part of a racial group (Asian American) and part of a unique and complex ethnic group (Filipinx). Unlike other ethnic groups in the Asian American category, we must also consider how the vestiges of US colonization play a role in the educational experiences of Filipinx American populations. Even when race, ethnicity, class, gender, sexuality, and immigrant status are recognized, there remains a void of true understanding and contextualizing of students' holistic experiences in college. There is indeed a void in terms of how higher education understands Filipinx American students. Through engaging Filipinx Americans in and with the areas discussed in this essay—e.g., intersections of social identities, affirmative action, curriculum, university faculty, and staff—we can continue to institutionalize critical knowledge about this population and for other marginalized communities. Therefore, it becomes crucial that we study and identify the universities' role in perpetuating the privileging of master narratives that do not reflect underserved populations at both the secondary and postsecondary levels.[24] To conclude, the positionalities of Filipinx Americans have certainly provided more opportunities for further research and have offered nuanced complexities and possibilities for critical interventions and discourse on identities and higher education.

NOTES

1. A. W. Astin, "Student Involvement: A Developmental Theory for Higher Education," *Journal of College Student Personnel* 25 (1984): 297–308; L. I. Rendón, "Validating Culturally Diverse Students: Toward a New Model of Learning and Student Development," *Innovative Higher Education* 19 (1994): 33–51; Marcia B. Baxter Magolda, *Authoring Your Life* (Sterling, Va.: Stylus, 2009).

2. V. Torres, S. R. Jones, and K. Renn, "Identity Development Theories in Student Affairs: Origins, Current Status, and New Approaches," *Journal of College Student Development* 50, no. 6 (2009): 577–96.

3. Rendón, "Validating Culturally Diverse Students"; M. P. Johnston-Guerrero, "Embracing the Messiness: Critical and Diverse Perspectives on Racial and Ethnic Identity Development," *New Directions for Student Services* 2016, no. 154 (2016): 43–55, doi:*10.1002/ss.20174*; R. T. Teranishi, *Asians in the Ivory Tower: Dilemmas of Racial Inequalities in American Higher Education* (New York: Teachers College Press, 2010); O. Poon, D. Squire, C. Kodama, A. Byrd, J. Chan, L. Manzano, S. Furr, and D. Bshundat, "A Critical Review of Model Minority Myth in Selected Literature on Asian American and Pacific Islanders in Higher Education," *Review of Educational Research* 86, no. 2 (2016): 469–502; D. Solorzano, M. Ceja, and T. Yosso, "Critical Race Theory, Racial Microaggressions, and Campus Racial Climate: The Experiences of African American College Students," *Journal of Negro Education*, 68, no. 1/2 (2000): 60–73.

4. F. Cordova, D. L. Cordova, and A. A. Acena, *Filipinos, Forgotten Asian Americans: A Pictorial Essay, 1763–Circa 1963* (Dubuque, Iowa: Kendall/Hunt, 1983); L. M. Strobel, *Coming Full Circle: The Process of Decolonization among Post-1965 Filipino Americans*, 2nd ed. (Santa Rosa, Calif.: Center for Babaylan Studies, 2016); Z. Leonardo and C. E. Matias, "Betwixt and Between Colonial and Postcolonial Mentality: The Critical Education of Filipino Americans," in *The "Other" Students: Filipino Americans, Education, and Power*, ed. D. C. Maramba and R. Bonus (Charlotte, N.C.: Information Age Publishing, Inc., 2013), 3–18; R. S. Coloma, "Invisible Subjects: Filipinas/os in Secondary History Textbooks," in *The "Other" Students*, ed. Maramba and Bonus, 165–82; A. Tintiangco-Cubales, "Struggling to Survive: Poverty, Violence, and Invisibility in the Lives of Urban Filipina/o American Youth," in *The "Other" Students*, ed. Maramba and Bonus, 123–43; T. L. Buenavista, "Philipinos in the Middle: Higher Education and a Sociocultural Context of Contradictions," in *The "Other" Students*, ed. Maramba and Bonus, 259–75; A. C. Ocampo, *The Latinos of Asia: How Filipino Americans Break the Rules of Race* (Stanford, Calif.: Stanford University Press, 2016).

5. Pew Research: G. Lopez, N. G. Ruiz, and E. Patten, *Key Facts about Asian Americans, a Diverse and Growing Population* (Sept 8, 2017), *http://www.pewresearch.org/fact-tank/2017/09/08/key-facts-about-asian-americans/*.

6. CARE, 2016.

7. J. Y. Okamura, "Filipino American Access to Higher Education in California and Hawai'i," in *The "Other" Students*, ed. Maramba and Bonus, 213–35.

8. Okamura, "Filipino American Access to Higher Education."

9. Okamura, "Filipino American Access to Higher Education."

10. Asian American Advancing Justice, "Asian American and Affirmative Action: We Will Not Be Your Wedges," *https://www.advancingjustice-la.org/what-we-do/policy-and-research/educational-opportunity-and-empowerment/affirmative-action/not-your-wedge*.

11. Asian American Advancing Justice, *Asian American and Affirmative Action*.

12. Coloma, "Invisible Subjects."

13. Tintiangco-Cubales, "Struggling to Survive."

14. R. T. Teranishi, M. Ceja, A. L. Antonio, W. R. Allen, and P. Mc-Donough, "The College-Choice Process for Asian Pacific Americans: Ethnicity and Socioeconomic Class in Context," *Review of Higher Education* 27, no. 4 (2004): 527–51.

15. Coloma, "Invisible Subjects."

16. Pin@y Educational Partnerships (P.E.P.), *http://www.pepsf.org/about .html*.

17. D. C. Maramba and K. L. Nadal, "Exploring the Filipino American Faculty Pipeline: Implications for Higher Education," in *The "Other" Students*, ed. Maramba and Bonus, 297–307.

18. D. C. Maramba, "Immigrant Families and the College Experience: Perspectives of Filipina Americans," *Journal of College Student Development* 49, no. 4 (2008): 336–50.

19. D. C. Maramba, "Family and Education Environments: Contexts and Counterstories of Filipino Americans," in *Educating Asian Americans: Achievement, Schooling, and Identities*, ed. Russell Endo and Xue Lan Rong (Charlotte, N.C.: Information Age Publishing, Inc., 2013), 205–31; Maramba, "Immigrant Families and the College Experience"; K. L. Nadal, "Counseling Filipino American College Students: Promoting Identity Development, Optimal Mental Health, and Academic Success," in *The "Other" Students*, ed. Maramba and Bonus, 103–19.

20. D. C. Maramba, "Understanding Campus Climate through Voices of Filipino/a American College Students," *College Student Journal* 42, no. 4 (2008): 1045–60.

21. R. I. Monzon, "Collective Self-Esteem and Perceptions of Family and Campus Environments among Filipino American College Students," in *The "Other" Students*, ed. Maramba and Bonus, 237–58.

22. D. C. Maramba and R. Bonus, eds., *The "Other" Students: Filipino Americans, Education, and Power* (Charlotte, N.C.: Information Age Publishing, Inc., 2013); Teranishi, *Asians in the Ivory Tower*.

23. Poon et al., "A Critical Review of Model Minority Myth."

24. D. C. Maramba and C. Kodama, eds., *Bridging Research and Practice to Support Asian American Students*, *New Directions for Student Services*, no. 160 (Winter 2017); D. C. Maramba and P. Velasquez, "Influences of the Campus Experience on the Ethnic Identity Development of Students of Color," *Education and Urban Society* 44, no. 3 (2012): 294–317, doi: *10.1177/0013124510393239*.

NINETEEN

Filipinx American College Student Identities:
A Critique of Models

Reuben B. Deleon

In *Keywords for Asian American Studies*, Jennifer Ho noted that identity "opposes concretized and totalizing definitions in favor of an Asian American epistemology that questions essentialist notions of singularity."[1] Identity as a construct is a capricious idea, rooted in historical and global contexts that intermix with ever-shifting realities. Within the field of Filipinx studies, this remains true as it subjects identity to inherited colonial and globalized legacies. This chapter explores these legacies by tracing constructions of identity within the field of Filipinx studies and bridging it to the field of education. Specifically, this chapter argues for several key points: the conceptual shortcomings of student development/identity research in higher education, the utility of examining Asian American and Pacific Islander (AAPI) specific racial/ethnic identity on college campuses, and finally the case for Filipinx American college students as a launching point for reconceptualizing theories of their racial and ethnic identity, especially within Filipinx-centric extracurricular activities.

Tracing a basis for understanding identity within Filipinx studies requires an acknowledgment and examination of Spanish colonialism and imperialism. Philippine scholar Renato Constantino argued that the vestiges of colonialism and Catholicism contributed to both the notion of "static" understandings of culture and the censorship of Filipinx indigeneity.[2] Constantino further noted that "Westernized" constructs pervaded all parts of society, influencing how societal institutions normalized a preference for individualism, meritocracy, and the preference for "the better." Nearly a decade later, texts such as Virgilio Enriquez's *From Colonial to Liberation Psychology* echoed this sentiment through a decentering of European and American constructions of Filipinx identity.[3] Contemporary scholars of Filipinx psychology and colonial mentality such as E. J. R. David's *Brown Skin, White Minds* and Kevin L. Nadal's *Filipino American Psychology: A Handbook of Theory, Research, and Clinical Practice* continue this tradition, echoing both the fluidity of identity and Filipinx's constant negotiation with their colonial past.[4]

Within the larger Asian American studies aggregate, theories such as Jean Kim's Asian American Racial Identity Development Model conceptualizes racial identity development as a process for engaging whiteness, and experiencing politicization as a route to satiation with personal understandings of race.[5] Although models such as Kim's serve as barometers for understanding an individual's position in their racial identity development, they do not adequately address the unique needs of other ethnic groups. Rather, these models serve as a general guide for individuals to match them with experiences to predetermined categories. Conceptually, identity theories have the power to be prescriptive and tend to aid in the contextualization of one's own self-perception. Conversely, they also have the potential to be destructive in the ways they frame identity construction as essentialist, causing certain individuals to feel excluded from their respective group. Generally, identity does not intend to produce a resolution for internal struggle. Rather, it is a stop on a journey through contextualizing one's experiences. Other researchers have explored the intersectional nature of Filipinx identity by centering on the interplay between ethnicity and other identities. The only ethnic identity model for Filipinxs is Kevin L. Nadal's Pilipino American Identity Development Model.[6] Spanning six stages, his model focuses on perceptions of self, other Filipinxs, other Asian Americans, people of color, and whites. Based on the stage of the model, individuals traverse feelings of isolation, assimilation, varying levels of political consciousness, and eventually a comprehensive understanding of their own ethnic identity.

Like other racial/ethnic groups, there is no singular profile of Filipinx identity. Rather, it fluctuates based on situational context, history, and personal experiences. In terms of Filipinx-specific literature, identity is affected by influences stemming from things such as histories of colonization, citizenship status, and existence as racially/ethnically liminal individuals.[7] Anthony Christian Ocampo's works on identity expand on others by drawing linkages between the perplexing relationship between race and panethnicity. In his book *The Latinos of Asia: How Filipino Americans Break the Rules of Race*, Ocampo explores the complex foundation for identity exploration.[8] His approach illuminates the struggle that many Filipinx individuals have with constructing their identity, especially in response to things like colonial mentality, geographical affiliations, and the ever-present struggle to obtain the "correct" kind of Filipinxness. Ocampo reiterates the confusion that comes with defining one's identity, especially when said identity is often in juxtaposition against not only white, but other races and ethnicities as well. In his chapter on collegiate experiences, he echoes this process, noting that racial/ethnic misidentification, individual and collective pursuits of knowledge, and the shifting contexts of "home" serve as an applicable backdrop for examination. It is at this crossroads that I advocate for more nuanced research.

It is important to position this chapter by first understanding why college students serve as an applicable site of examination. Although higher education research has touted the importance of culturally relevant curricula, institutional actors, and literature, spaces regarding identity work continue to be limited.[9] Focusing on the macro-level student body, considerations of race, ethnicity, and culture have a tendency to be overlooked. Broadly, different approaches to student identity have tackled positioning as members of the college community, as a process integrated into student development and meaning-making, and of multidimensional identities.[10] Canonical works like those aforementioned rarely consider race as a centralized factor in college student identity development, nor deeply consider how ethnicity and shared histories of oppression impact the identity formation process. Rather, these works rely on shared experiences to form constructs of identity. Because of the absence of critical examination and integration of concepts such as racism, colonization, imperialism, and other forms of oppression, these theories become critiqued as incomplete and framed as problematic in their present form. To combat this, researchers have been in pursuit of the disaggregation of student experiences. In the case of the AAPI communities, existing works illuminate the relationship between racial/ethnic identity and educational experiences.

Existing literature on AAPI identity and education has revealed its complexity. Several factors can abstract the identity process, including level of affiliation to communities, differing points of access to identity, and varied experiences of racism and marginalization.[11] As one of the largest growing ethnic groups in the United States, Filipinxs continue to be a powerful presence in postsecondary education. As research on Filipinxs continues to aggregate into the larger Asian American racial group, the need for more critical scholarship, especially within the realms of nuance, will increase. At the time of this writing, limited works exist on Filipinx Americans in postsecondary education. One of those texts, Dina C. Maramba and Rick Bonus's anthology *The "Other" Students: Filipino Americans, Education, and Power*, develops the foundation of the field through the intersections of Filipinx students and studies of history, identity, pedagogy, and policy.[12] For example, Third Andresen's chapter on identity states that active work toward a multicultural curriculum can aid in the decolonization of Filipinx students. Doing this work not only liberates students from their colonial bounds but teaches them to produce new knowledge constructions of identity. In line with this call, this chapter develops a case to traverse this landscape further.

It is important to note that examples of this work exist in limited quantity within the field of higher education. For example, Dina C. Maramba's study "Understanding Campus Climate through Voices of Filipino/a American College Students" focused on some emerging concerns of Filipina college students.[13] Students reported feeling underrepresented and they shared desires for increased presence in faculty, staff, and curriculum in their schools. Filipina students shared the differential treatment they received because of their gender, including the inability to socialize with friends and the need to fulfill gendered family roles at home. For many, college was a time for Filipinas to find solace with their peers and critically examine the reasons for their treatment. As a canonical work in Filipinx American college experience, Maramba's work inspires this chapter. Her in-depth look into the students' lives opened up conceptual space to center Filipinxs as a population to examine. It is important to note that the "othering" of Filipinx students starts early, with research showing the divisive treatment they have received when compared to other Asian American groups in high school and the generalized aggregation into the AAPI category later in college.[14] In the introduction chapter of *The "Other" Students*, Maramba and Bonus share the sentiment of note that Filipinxs occupy a liminal space, where they must acknowledge and interact with the histories of colonization, immigration/migration, racialization, and their positioning within larger capitalist global contexts.[15] Attempting to capture how these contexts intermingle in the identity development processes is arduous. Because the construct of identity possesses capricious characteristics, finding a "correct" means of examining Filipinx identity remains complicated. In the case of this chapter, taking a micro-level emphasis to identity development aids in illuminating the need for further research. As many Filipinxs engage with their racial and ethnic identity in college through ethnic studies courses, peer interaction, and extracurricular activities, these examples serve as pertinent settings to explore these topics.

Although a growing number of Filipinxs are attending college, their nuanced experiences and narratives on campuses are still unexplored. It is important to note that limited studies regarding the progress and benefits of Filipinx-centric activities and initiatives exist. For example, studies investigate how Filipinx American studies and language courses continue to show up on college campuses.[16] This potentially aids in developing a feeling of acclimation on campus.[17] Also, research suggests that constant interaction with peers in college aids in dealing with issues surrounding poor campus climate and navigating educational pathways.[18] Some of the spaces that have received a lot of attention in the literature are ethnic organizations and extracurricular activities. Student organizations and extracurricular activities that center on Filipinx history and culture exist in most colleges that have a significant Filipinx population. Research regarding participation within ethnic organizations (such as Filipinx clubs on campuses) suggests a potential space for examining Filipinx identity. For example, Karen Inkelas comments on the benefits of contact with peers with similar backgrounds in her study on ethnic club participation and Asian American racial/ethnic awareness.[19] Additionally, Dina C. Maramba and Samuel D. Museus note that increased ethnic identity awareness also creates a stronger sense of belonging on campus.[20] As both a formal and informal medium, these organizations and activities create a perfect space to look at formations of identity. Although existing outside of the traditional classroom structure, ethnic organizations can serve as safe and comfortable spaces in which students can explore and critique their identity formation.

Because of these experiences of misidentification, these conditions create a fascinating space to explore identity formation. By centering the examination through students, it has the potential to provide rich descriptions of formative moments inside and outside of the classroom. Research has shown that college is a time in people's lives where they research and reconceptualize their ethnic identity.[21] Samuel D. Museus and Stephen John Quaye's article on intercultural perspectives and persistence supports this research, as it illuminates the positive relationship between experiential and interpersonal knowledge and campus integration.[22] As students continue to pursue the knowledge of self, they too become stronger members of their college campuses and ultimately perform better in school. Additionally, for many Filipinxs, this may be the first time that they interact with curriculum and peers that have a shared interest in learning and exploring their Filipinx identity. Although the aforementioned examples create a theoretical basis for exploration, it is important to note that the research on Filipinxs college students and their identities is still developing.

As the field of Filipinx American studies expands into new frontiers, the possibilities for interdisciplinary critical analysis also grow. For this chapter, I complicate existing notions of Filipinx identity through an understudied medium. Considering the various ways Filipinx college students serve as a medium for understanding intersecting meanings of identity, it will become increasingly pertinent to remain close to this population. As the experiences of Filipinxs continue to become more complex, it will be increasingly important to examine individuals within niche contexts such as schooling. Whether through formal and informal coursework, organizations, or theatrical endeavors, Filipinx students provide a vibrant medium for understanding racial and ethnic identity. Furthermore, as the institutions of higher education continue to further integrate themselves and their students into a strongly interconnected global market, it will also be important to give attention to how those influences interact with the complex histories that Filipinxs occupy as well.

NOTES

1. Jennifer Ho, "Identity," in *Keywords for Asian American Studies*, series ed. Cathy J. Schlund-Vials, Linda Trinh Võ, and K. Scott Wong (New York: New York University Press, 2015), 125–27. Retrieved from *https://www.jstor.org /stable/j.ctt15r3zv2*.

2. Renato Constantino, *Insight & Foresight: Selected Excerpts* (Quezon City, Philippines: Foundation for Nationalist Studies, 1977), distributed by Erehwon Bookshop.

3. Virgilio G. Enriquez, *From Colonial to Liberation Psychology: The Philippine Experience* (Quezon City: University of the Philippines Press, 1984).

4. E. J. R. David, *Brown Skin, White Minds: Filipino-/American Postcolonial Psychology (with commentaries) [Kayumanggi balat, puti isip]* (Charlotte, N.C.: Information Age Publishing Inc., 2013); Kevin L. Nadal, *Filipino American Psychology: A Handbook of Theory, Research, and Clinical Practice* (Hoboken, N.J.: John Wiley, 2011).

5. Jean Kim, "Asian American Racial Identity Development Theory," in *New Perspectives on Racial Identity Development: Integrating Emerging Frameworks*, ed. Charmaine L. Wijeyesinghe and Bailey W. Jackson III (New York: New York University Press, 2012).

6. Kevin L. Nadal, "Pilipino American Identity Development Model," *Journal of Multicultural Counseling and Development* 32, no. 1 (2004): 45.

7. David, *Brown Skin, White Minds*; Tracy Lachica Buenavista, "Issues Affecting US Filipino Student Access to Postsecondary Education: A Critical Race Theory Perspective," *Journal of Education for Students Placed at Risk (JESPAR)* 15, nos. 1–2 (2010): 114–26, *https://doi.org/10.1080 /10824661003635093*; Anthony Christian Ocampo, "'Am I Really Asian?': Educational Experiences and Panethnic Identification among Second–Generation Filipino Americans," *Journal of Asian American Studies* 16, no. 3 (2013): 295–324, *https://doi.org/10.1353/jaas.2013.0032*; Anthony Christian Ocampo, *The Latinos of Asia: How Filipino Americans Break the Rules of Race* (Stanford, Calif.: Stanford University Press, 2016).

8. Ocampo, *The Latinos of Asia*.

9. Shaun R. Harper and Sylvia Hurtado, "Nine Themes in Campus Racial Climates and Implications for Institutional Transformation," *New Directions for Student Services* 120 (2007): 7–24, *https://doi.org/10.1002/ss.254*.

10. Vincent Tinto, *Leaving College: Rethinking the Causes and Cures of Student Attrition* (Chicago: University of Chicago Press, 1993); Arthur W.

228   *Reuben B. Deleon*

Chickering and Linda Reisser, *Education and Identity* (San Francisco: Jossey-Bass Publishers, 1993); Marcia B. Baxter Magolda, "Three Elements of Self-Authorship," *Journal of College Student Development* 49, no. 4 (2008): 269–84, https://doi.org/10.1353/csd.0.0016; E. S. Abes, S. R. Jones, and M. K. McEwen, "Reconceptualizing the Model of Multiple Dimensions of Identity: The Role of Meaning-Making Capacity in the Construction of Multiple Identities," *Journal of College Student Development* 48, no. 1 (2007): 1–22.

11. Jason Chan, "Complexities of Racial Identity Development for Asian Pacific Islander Desi American (APIDA) College Students: Complexities of Racial Identity Development," *New Directions for Student Services* 160 (2017): 11–23, https://doi.org/10.1002/ss.20240.

12. Dina C. Maramba and Rick Bonus, *The "Other" Students: Filipino Americans, Education, and Power* (Charlotte, N.C.: Information Age, 2013).

13. Dina C. Maramba, "Understanding Campus Climate through Voices of Filipino/a American College Students," *College Student Journal* 42, no. 4 (2008): 104–560.

14. R. T. Teranishi, "Asian Pacific Americans and Critical Race Theory: An Examination of School Racial Climate," *Equity & Excellence in Education* 35, no. 2 (2002): 144–54; Nolan L. Cabrera, "Beyond Black and White: How White, Male, College Students See Their Asian American Peers," *Equity & Excellence in Education* 47, no. 2 (2014): 133–51.

15. Maramba and Bonus, *The "Other" Students*.

16. Omega Loren Letana, *Sino Ako? (Who Am I?): Exploring Filipino American Identity in Philippine Studies Courses* (San Francisco: University of San Francisco, 2016).

17. Letana, *Sino Ako?*; Panganiban, "Easing the Sophomore Slump."

18. Panganiban, "Easing the Sophomore Slump."

19. K. K. Inkelas, "Does Participation in Ethnic Cocurricular Activities Facilitate a Sense of Ethnic Awareness and Understanding? A Study of Asian Pacific American Undergraduates," *Journal of College Student Development* 45, no. 3 (2004): 285–302.

20. Dina C. Maramba and Samuel D. Museus, "Examining the Effects of Campus Climate, Ethnic Group Cohesion, and Cross-Cultural Interaction on Filipino American Students' Sense of Belonging in College," *Journal of College Student Retention: Research, Theory & Practice* 14, no. 4 (2013): 495–522.

21. Dina C. Maramba and Patrick Velasquez, "Influences of the Campus Experience on the Ethnic Identity Development of Students of Color," *Education and Urban Society* 44, no. 3 (2012): 294–317.

22. Samuel D. Museus and Stephen J. Quaye, "Toward an Intercultural Perspective of Racial and Ethnic Minority College Student Persistence," *The Review of Higher Education: Journal of the Association for the Study of Higher Education* 33, no. 1 (2009): 67–94.

Third World Studies and the Living Archive of US-Based Filipinx Activism

Michael Schulze-Oechtering

It goes without being said that Filipinx American studies was a product of radical student protest. When scholars historicize the field, they often highlight Pilipino American Collegiate Endeavor (PACE), one of the many student groups at San Francisco State University (SFSU) that coalesced into the Third World Liberation Front (TWLF).[1] In an essay entitled "A Non-White Struggle towards a New Humanism," the TWLF coalition members explained the political motivations that guided their demand for a "Third World college":

> We adhere to the struggles in Asia, Africa, and Latin America, ideologically, spiritually, and culturally.... We have decided to fuse ourselves with the masses of Third World peoples, to create, through struggles, a new humanity, a new humanism, a new world consciousness.[2]

According to Gary Y. Okihiro, the radical curricular and pedagogical endeavor of the TWLF, what Okihiro terms "Third World studies," was *doomed from its inception.* As Okihiro contends in *Third World Studies: Theorizing Liberation*, the emergent discipline "never existed because it was extinguished at its birth."[3] In this sense, *Third World Studies* offered incisive critique of the political and intellectual costs of institutionalization for the field of study that came to be known as ethnic studies. By doing so, he opens new terrains of theorization for ethnic studies scholars interested in Third World studies' political vision and enduring legacy. In this chapter, I build upon Okihiro's generative analysis by examining one the central intellectual orientations of Filipinx American studies at its inception. That is, the field's emphasis on *the community* as a *site of radical pedagogy and knowledge production.*

In *Third World Studies*, Okihiro strategically decentered the "community studies" component of Third World studies in order to illuminate the limitations of "theorizing liberation" within the academy. As Okihiro notes, "Turning the Third World curriculum into ethnic studies . . . trivialized that declaration of global solidarity with the liberation and antiracist struggles of Third World peoples. . . . [I]t reduced its revolutionary potential and power by grafting it onto the trunk of race relations and ethnic studies as explicated by sociologists at the University of Chicago."[4] As this passage demonstrates, Okihiro privileged the university in his analysis, only in order to demonstrate the institution's limitations as a home for radical political theory. However, what happens to our understanding of Third World studies when we decenter the university and pay closer attention to the community-based struggles that predated and informed radical visions of education, such as those advanced by the TWLF? I contend that reorienting our attention to the community allows us to uncover and reclaim alternative spaces of political education and radical knowledge production. To illustrate this point, I will examine the community-based learning that occurs as Filipinx American youth in Seattle immersed themselves in antigentrification and labor struggles during the 1970s.

For the youth activists at the center of this chapter's analysis, their community was their classroom and their *manongs* were their teachers. *Manong* is an Ilokano term of respect used to refer to an elderly male. During the 1970s, the use of the word *manong* took on an explicitly political connotation, referring to an earlier wave of Filipinx migrants, many of whom came to the United States as colonial subjects during the 1920s and 1930s. In this period, these first-wave migrants played leading roles in the working-class insurgencies that erupted in the labor-intensive industries of Hawai'i, California, and Alaska.[5] During the late 1940s and early 1950s, many *manongs* were subject to the Cold War surveillance state's constant attempt to deport supposed "alien subversives." By the 1970s, many of these community pioneers faced development-based displacement from the communities they created at the margins of US society.[6] For Filipinx American youth activists of the 1970s who tirelessly searched for their "roots," they came to view their *manongs* as both *radical political subjects* and *targets of racialized state violence.*

There are certainly limits to politically elevating the "*manong* generation." While *manongs* were radical political subjects, they also possessed their share of contradictions. Specifically, the *manong* generation was a product of a largely male wave of migration, and as a result, masculinist rhetoric and imagery permeated their labor history. However, a diverse range of masculinities coexisted in Alaska's salmon canneries. In some instances, resistance did involve physical confrontations with company foremen. Yet, in other cases, *manongs* modeled practices of collective care that allowed their coworkers to survive grueling conditions of life and labor. Writer-activist Carlos Bulosan's cultural production, particular a poem he wrote for his dear friend and fellow cannery union leader, Chris Mensalvas Sr., offered a window into what I refer to as the *manongs' politics of care.*

> They are afraid, my brother,
> They are afraid of our mighty fists, my brother,
> They are afraid of the magnificence of our works, my brother,
> They are even afraid of our songs of love, my brother.[7]

I make the case that this politics of care, what Bulosan referred to as their "songs of love," has a great deal in common with the praxis of "revolution love" embodied in the organizing methods of women of color feminists such as Ella Baker, Madonna Thunder Hawk, and Yuri Kochiyama. Moreover, this diversity of gendered resistance strategies opened a political space for Filipinx women and men and allied workers to shift the dominant political culture in the canneries toward a more explicitly feminist lens.[8] Yet, regardless of the political contradictions and limitations of their community elders, the political entry point for Filipinx American youth activists in the Pacific Northwest was quite often their *manongs.*

Through living and laboring alongside their *manongs*, Filipinx American youth activists encountered a politically generative *living archive of US-based Filipinx activism.*[9] By this, I am referring to the myriad of documents that connected a younger generation of Filipinx American youth activists in the Pacific Northwest to an intergenerational and transpacific "culture of opposition."[10] I use the term "living archive" to refer to Filipinx American youth's political engagement with these documents. As Maylei Blackwell reminds us, "Re-membering is a vital act in creating political subjectivity."[11] Filipinx American youth were not only learning their history, they were creating "new terrains of memory" that firmly placed their parents, relatives, and community members at the center of militant responses to labor exploitation in Alaska's salmon canneries and a repressive Cold War security state. As a result, they came to understand their activist projects in the 1970s not as a break from a community norm of political complacency, but as part of a radical tradition that stretched back at least to the 1930s. The lessons learned from this living archive provided clarity on how to advance their community's tradition of radicalism into the present. Moreover, it demonstrates that community-based struggles were educational spaces where Third World studies thrived amidst the academy's attempts to discipline and domesticate it. In what follows, I provide a brief discussion of Filipinx American youth activists and their politically generative encounter with a key document to the living archive of US-based Filipinx activism: *The International Longshoremen's and Warehousemen's Union Local 37 Yearbook* (hereafter cited as the *Local 37 Yearbook*).

The Living Archive of US-Based Filipinx Activism

In the early 1970s, Seattle's International District (ID) was a community facing erasure. In February of 1972, when King County officials announced that a $40-million domed stadium was to be built in the ID, it produced a panic among the community, which was largely Asian, elderly, and poor. Fears were confirmed two months later as a community newspaper announced that upwards of ten single-resident occupancies (SROs) would be shut down if they did not meet fire safety codes by May 28 of that year. The potential hotel would have led to the displacement of 734 residents, 485 of which were retired cannery workers, and 332 were "old single Filipinos."[12] For the better part of the 1970s, a broad coalition of student radicals, community activists, and allies across the city fought the destructive march of development in the ID. This was the context in which Filipinx American youth activists met Chris Mensalvas Sr., an "old left" labor radical and former cannery union president.

By the 1970s, Mensalvas was in his sixties. At "only five feet tall" and "barely able to stand," the former cannery union president was, at least physically, a shell of his former self. But Mensalvas still possessed an attribute that made him a talented organizer: the ability to captivate audiences. As the struggle to preserve the ID evolved into a social movement, Mensalvas became a vocal leader and, as a result, a fixture within Seattle's broader Asian American movement. He regularly spoke at May Day rallies in the ID, Filipinx American student conferences, and Asian American studies classrooms at the University of Washington.[13] In this context, Mensalvas became a teacher of sorts, whose lessons linked Filipinx American youth activist to their radical roots. In the process, Mensalvas's SRO apartment became a dynamic learning environment.

David Della's memories of that apartment offer a window into the way Mensalvas mentored a younger generation of radicals. Della met Mensalvas for the first time in the mid-1970s, when the Alaska Cannery Workers Association (ACWA), a group of college-aged Filipinx American cannery workers, prioritized building relationships with *manongs* in the ID. As a 1975 ACWA report noted, "We have to do more contact work with manongs in Chinatown. Many still go to Alaska and are active union members. This is the group that could really help us in the union struggle or the court trials."[14] Amidst this political work, Della made his first visit to Mensalvas's apartment. In what became a four-hour meeting, the former Local 37 president proceeded to pull out "papers and books about . . . his experiences . . . in the canneries."[15] This was precisely Mensalvas's pedagogy. As up-and-coming Filipinx American activists discussed their contemporary struggles, Mensalvas used his own experiences, as well as his vast archival collection, to contextualize current inequities and challenge a younger generation to envision new political possibilities.

In Mensalvas's room, Della and his peers encountered the *Local 37 Yearbook*, a political text that served as a road map for the resurgence of US-based

Filipinx radicalism in the Alaskan canneries. To fully appreciate the document, proper historical context is needed. Within Asian American studies, the 1952 McCarran Walter Act is often remembered as the law that marked the formal end of Asian exclusion. However, Rachel Ida Buff noted, "the act asserted a particular vision of imperial space."[16] Here, Buff was referring to a series of provisions within the law that were both inclusionary and exclusionary, and pivoted not necessarily around racial or ethnic categories but ideas of martial patriotism and national security. For one, Buff reminds us, the law conferred the right to citizenship to "a child born abroad to one U.S. military parent," but it also restricted the entry of residents of US territories seeking to enter the continental United States. In addition to hardening borders between colony and metropole, the law built upon the 1940 Smith Act and "provided additional legal basis for the deportation of foreign-born subversives."[17]

The Cold War surveillance state pulled Filipinx workers in the ILWU Local 37 in multiple political directions. For one, between 1949 and 1955, five union leaders faced the threat of deportation for their alleged communist affiliations. Under the provision that allowed immigration officials to screen those entering from US territories, Seattle immigration official John Boyd promised "immigration officers will meet every ship coming to Seattle from Alaska." In true nativist rhetoric, Boyd stated that "anyone on board who can't prove he's an American citizen—and a desirable one, at that—will be refused permission to walk ashore."[18] Given that Filipinx cannery workers traveled to Alaska by boat from the port of Seattle, this policy impacted all union members. In the summer cannery season of 1953 alone, Arleen De Vera writes, "more than a hundred were jailed, and eventually, over a dozen [were] singled out for exclusion."[19] Furthermore, a broader current of Cold War anticommunism left its imprint on union elections. In response to the US government labeling the ILWU Local 37 a "subversive organization," Trinidad Rojo ran for president in 1953 in opposition to Mensalvas. Rojo campaigned under the banner that the union should focus on what he called "real union issues," meaning expanding union numbers and above all not affiliating with subversives that "irritate Uncle Sam."[20] While Rojo was defeated, his election exposed ideological tensions within the union that Cold War policies exacerbated.

If the McCarran Walter Act "asserted a . . . vision of imperial space," the *Local 37 Yearbook* offered a decolonial spatial imaginary. The yearbook's editor, Carlos Bulosan, set the document's radical tone as he stressed the importance of the "unconditional unity of all workers . . . against the evil designs of imperialist butchers and other profiteers of death and suffering."[21] Bulosan's proletarian internationalism was chiefly concerned with the conditions of Filipinx workers across the Pacific. In an article written by Bulosan, "Terrorism Rides the Philippines," he describes a stark picture of state violence in the neocolony. In the first two months of 1951, Bulosan estimated that 540 labor activists were arrested in the Philippines and "death sentences were passed on six people, including a young woman of 24."[22] While Bulosan's article shed a light on a labor struggle that Bulosan declared was "unbeknown to the world," an article by poet and labor organizer Amado Hernandez further created lines of communication between Filipinx workers and the US working class. Moreover, the *Local 37 Yearbook*'s dual attention to the "deportability" of Filipinx workers in the US and the repressive conditions faced by workers in the Philippines signaled the union's diasporic labor politics. When read together, each case represented a "domestic" and "foreign" manifestation of counterinsurgency that reinforced the US Cold War security state's "vision of imperial space." More importantly, even as Mensalvas and other union leaders fought pending deportation orders from US authorities, the *Local 37 Yearbook*, much like the TWLF, embraced "spatial and ideological affiliations with the Third World and its people" where worker movements across the Pacific were unified in their political opposition to US empire.[23]

Embracing and Extending Their Radical Tradition through Study and Struggle

The fact that Filipinx American youth discovered the *Local 37 Yearbook* in a time period that ran parallel to Ferdinand Marcos's martial law regime was not lost on them. In fact, it spoke to a broader political current within the Katipunan ng mga Demokratikong Pilipinas (KDP), a radical anti–martial law organization within Filipinx communities across the United States between 1973 and 1986. Augusto F. Espiritu's work on the KDP, particularly its dual line of supporting the National Democratic Movement in the Philippines and building an antiracist, socialist alternative to capitalism in the United States, illuminates the tensions that existed within the organization and constrained its ability to build a transpacific social movement. Specifically, the Chicago chapter of the KDP fractured around the group's competing commitments to grassroots community organizing and international solidarity.[24] However, the *Local 37 Yearbook* demonstrates that the KDP's seemingly disparate political impulses had been historically intertwined. The dual processes of study and struggle were critical to the development of Silme Domingo and Gene Viernes's anti-imperialist politics. As KDP activist Cindy Domingo noted, the *Local 37's Yearbook* provided a political model for bringing the KDP's dual line into the cannery union. Domingo explains, "Well taught by the manongs, Silme and Gene always brought their anti-Marcos politics into the union whenever possible."[25]

In 1981, the political education Domingo and Viernes gained from their *manongs* translated into a concrete program of international solidarity. That year, Viernes took a trip to the Philippines that was facilitated by the KDP and had the explicit goal of building bridges between the ILWU Local 37 and the Kilusang Mayo Uno (KMU), a militant and anti-Marcos labor federation in the Philippines. While Viernes's travels culminated in the passage of an ILWU resolution that sent a fact-finding mission to the Philippines to investigate labor conditions, they also resulted in Marcos orchestrating the political assassinations of Domingo and Viernes in Seattle in 1981.[26] By reading the KDP's solidarity with the KMU alongside the Marcos regime's ability to stretch its long arm of repression into the United States, we are able to observe a protracted struggle over the meaning of a "decolonized Pacific."[27] In this history, disparate geographic spaces were forged together by the political struggles of Filipinx workers on both sides of the Pacific, as well as the violent repression of their radical imaginaries.

NOTES

1. Michael Viola et al., "Carlos Bulosan and a Collective Outline for Critical Filipina and Filipino Studies," *Kritika Kultura* 23 (2014): 255–76.
2. Gary Y. Okihiro, *Third World Studies: Theorizing Liberation* (Durham, N.C.: Duke University Press, 2016), 16.
3. Okihiro, *Third World Studies*, 1.
4. Okihiro, *Third World Studies*, 19.
5. Moon-Kie Jung, *Reworking Race: The Making of Hawaii's Interracial Labor Movement* (New York: Columbia University Press, 2006); Dawn Bohulano Mabalon, *Little Manila Is in the Heart* (Durham, N.C.: Duke University Press,

2013); Dorothy Fujita-Rony, *American Workers, Colonial Power: Philippine Seattle and the Transpacific West, 1919–1941* (Berkeley: University of California Press, 2003).

6. Estella Habal, *San Francisco's International Hotel: Mobilizing the Filipino American Community in the Anti-Eviction Movement* (Philadelphia: Temple University Press, 2008).

7. Carlos Bulosan, "Song for Chris Mensalvas Birthday," The Words of Carlos Bulosan, accessed August 6, 2020; *https://bulosan.org/in-his-words/*.

8. I develop this point in my forthcoming book, *No Separate Peace: Multiracial Struggles against Racial Capitalism in the Pacific Northwest, 1970–2000*.

9. In this essay, I use two terms somewhat interchangeably: "Filipinx American youth activists" and "US-based Filipinx activism." The former refers to activists of Philippine descent who were born in the United States. The latter is a more comprehensive category that includes immigrant and American born activists. These two groups have distinct relationships to citizenship rights, but, I contend, are part of a collective tradition of resistance.

10. For a discussion of "culture of opposition," see George Lipsitz, *Life in the Struggle: Ivory Perry and the Culture of Opposition* (Philadelphia: Temple University Press, 1995).

11. Maylei Blackwell, *Chicana Power!: Contested Histories of Feminism in the Chicano Movement* (Austin: University of Texas Press, 2011), 11.

12. Michael Schulze-Oechtering, "The Alaska Cannery Workers Association and the Ebbs and Flows of Struggle: Manong Knowledge, Blues Epistemology, and Racial Cross-Fertilization," *Amerasia Journal* 42, no. 2 (2016): 33.

13. Schulze-Oechtering, "The Alaska Cannery Workers Association."

14. "Draft of ACWA Three-Month Plan on Cannery Work Organizing," March 1975, TSP, Box 18, Folder 16.

15. David Della, Interview with Cindy Domingo, tape recording, Seattle, Wash., March 18, 2003.

16. Rachel Ida Buff, *Against the Deportation Terror: Organizing for Immigrant Rights in the Twentieth Century* (Philadelphia: Temple University Press, 2017), 70.

17. Buff, *Against the Deportation Terror.*

18. Arleen de Vera, "Without Parallel: The Local 7 Deportation Cases: 1949–1955," *Amerasia Journal* 20, no. 2 (1994): 1–25.

19. de Vera, "Without Parallel," 15.

20. de Vera, "Without Parallel," 12.

21. Carlos Bulosan, "To Whom it May Concern," *1952 Yearbook*, ILWU Local 37 (Seattle: ILWU, 1952), 21.

22. Carlos Bulosan, "Terrorism Rides High in the Philippines," *1952 Yearbook*, ILWU Local 37 (Seattle: ILWU, 1952), 28.

23. Okihiro, *Third World Studies*, 7.

24. Augusto F. Espiritu, "Journeys of Discovery and Difference: Transnational Politics and the Union of Democratic Filipinos," in *The Transnational Politics of Asian Americans* (Philadelphia: Temple University Press, 2009), 38–55.

25. Cindy Domingo, "Long Road to Justice," in *A Time to Rise: Collective Memoirs of the Union of Democratic Filipinos*, ed. Rene Cruz, et al. (Seattle: University of Washington Press, 2017), 232.

26. Domingo, "Long Road to Justice."

27. For a discussion of the "decolonizing pacific" as an analytic framework, see Simeon Man, *Soldiering through Empire: Race and the Making of the Decolonized Pacific* (Berkeley: University of California Press, 2018).

TWENTY-ONE

Activism Is in the Heart of Filipinx American Studies

Jeffrey Santa Ana

"You cannot save the world," some of my family and friends console me when they sense my frustration. I know I cannot, but I want to try. . . . Anyone can save the world, if one is willing enough to stand tall despite the incoming tides. We are the limestones, we are the islands, and these are our bodies colliding and connecting with one another beneath the water. We are not resilient, no, but we can be unified in our defiance; we are the people of the [Philippine] archipelago and we are here to tell the rest of the world how we have survived and how we will continue surviving and thriving, together.

—RINA GARCIA CHUA

For Rina Garcia Chua, a Filipinx environmental writer and poet from Manila living and working in North America, being Filipinx in our current time of global ecological crisis means surviving collaboratively with Filipinxs both at home in the Philippines and abroad in the diaspora.[1] Surviving, however, is not enough. For Filipinxs whose archipelagic homeland is, according to Garcia Chua, an epicenter of environmental catastrophe, surviving means *thriving* by bearing witness to the disastrous consequences of anthropogenic climate change and, moreover, trying to "save the world" from these consequences.

As Filipinx environmental writer-activists like Garcia Chua point out, one of the most evident and recent events that exemplifies how the Philippines is an epicenter of environmental crisis and catastrophe is Super Typhoon Yolanda (known internationally as Haiyan). When Super Typhoon Yolanda made landfall in Visayas on November 8, 2013, it was the most powerful storm ever recorded to strike land. The Category 5 typhoon wreaked havoc on the central Philippines' telecommunications, agriculture, and transportation infrastructure, delaying recovery and relief operations for several weeks. Entire provinces and cities on the islands of Samar and Leyte suffered massive destruction and devastation. In addition to leaving 7,360 people dead or missing on these islands, Yolanda swept away more than 1.1 million houses and displaced 4.1 million people.[2]

Immediately in the wake of Yolanda, Filipinx writers and artists both in the Philippines and in the diaspora expressed their grief and anger about the catastrophe. They collectively channeled their grief and anger by collaborating to produce poetry and prose that centered the emotional gravity of their response to Yolanda as an environmental disaster affecting Filipinxs both in the Philippines and in the diaspora.[3] In this regard, their writings articulate what Garcia Chua has argued is a moral obligation of Philippine poetry about environmental disasters: to express "that you are doing something about it and that you are, ethically, addressing what had happened."[4] Philippine poems about environmental disasters bear witness to these calamities, and subsequently, they not only "help us remember and commemorate disasters and deaths,"[5] but also "heal the trauma through communal feeling of survival."[6] In the effort to express their anguish and also raise money to help the people of Samar and Leyte who were devastated by Yolanda, Filipinx writers and artists worked cooperatively to produce literary anthologies that attempted to make sense of the catastrophe not only in the context of the Philippines' history as a country formerly colonized by the United States through economic, military, and cultural influences,[7] but also in the present situation of the Philippines' neocolonization by global capitalist policies of development.[8] By making sense of Yolanda's calamitous impact on the Philippines in the context of the country's subjection to past and present imperialist incursions and colonial powers, Filipinx writers and artists created a space for ecological consciousness, one that enables becoming morally and ethically aware of climate change's planetary scale within the realm of understanding the immense historical and geographic scales of imperialism and global capitalist development.

By creating and asserting an ecological consciousness that throws into relief the ways in which histories of US empire and colonialism intersect with environmental violence and devastation, Filipinx writers and artists who worked together to bring international attention to Yolanda's destruction of lives and environment in the Philippines hence articulated a distinctive Filipinx *activism*. This collaborative activism immediately in the aftermath of Yolanda's devastation appealed to human experience in order to bring the vast scale of climate change within the realm of comprehending global warming's provenance in fossil fuel–based colonial powers. Filipinx ecological consciousness accordingly is Filipinx activism that, as Garcia Chua puts it, attempts to "save the world" by positioning us to grasp the concerns of environmental justice that follow from the environmental violence wrought by anthropogenic climate change. This is violence against Filipinx people and their environment caused by the extreme weather events of climate change, whose human creation is largely the material and historical forces of Western empire: the Global North's imperialist resource extractions, militarism and war technologies, the pollution and degradation of physical environments, petrocapitalism (i.e., profit accumulation from the extraction, distribution, and consumption of oil), and the ruinous commodification and commercialization of the natural world in the Philippines and throughout the Global South.

As can be seen in the example of Filipinx writers and artists who brought global attention to the related intersections between Typhoon Yolanda and imperialism, activism is in the heart of Filipinxs in the Philippines and in the diaspora. *America Is in the Heart* by Carlos Bulosan (c. 1913–56) is deliberately invoked here because his classic personal narrative articulates an antiracist and anti-imperialist politics that inspires both explicitly and obliquely all contemporary leftist-activist expressions of diasporic Filipinxs in the United States.[9] Bulosan was one of several children born into a peasant farming family in Binalonan, Pagasinan province in the Philippines. His parents became impoverished in the 1920s after losing their land to a rich and elite class of landowners who acquired and maintained their wealth through an exploitative system of absentee property ownership.[10] At the age of seventeen and with the support of his family, Bulosan left the Philippines in 1930 and migrated to the United States as a "noncitizen national."[11] Traveling by ship, he landed in Seattle, Washington, where he immediately found himself in a desperate situation to find work at the beginning of America's worst economic crisis, the Great Depression. Encountering racial hostility from whites that was intensified by the country's economic crisis, Bulosan became desperate to survive and was forced to work in various low-paying jobs: cleaning and packing fish in canneries, servicing in hotels, washing dishes in restaurants, and harvesting fruit and vegetables in farm fields. Bulosan's anticapitalist politics and his socialist vision were thus rooted in both the impoverishment of his family in the Philippines and the suffering of fellow migrants and the working poor during the Great Depression.

In 1946, fifteen years after arriving in the United States, Bulosan published *America Is in the Heart*, his semi-autobiographical novel that documented for the world to see how the early generation of diasporic Filipinx workers in the US struggled to survive in the "capitalist colonial nightmare of the American Dream."[12] As E. San Juan Jr. asserts, Bulosan went on to achieve international recognition as a great writer, poet, and activist who spent most of his life representing and documenting "the heroic struggles and sacrifices of the Filipino community as a colonized and an emergent national agency in world history."[13] Clearly, the progressive activism of Filipinx Americans would not be intelligible or even realizable today without Bulosan and the first wave of Filipinx women and men who left the Philippines and migrated to the United States from the 1920s to the 1950s. The socialist vision among the worker-activists of this early generation inspired the Filipinx labor organizers of the United Farm Workers and the student activists of the Third World Liberation Front in mid-twentieth-century America.

For Filipinx writers, artists, and scholars in the United States who link struggles in the Philippines to US grassroots campaigns against racism, labor exploitation, anti-immigrant bias, and the prison industrial complex, activism is undoubtedly in the heart of Filipinx American studies. Consequently, the Filipinx intellectuals and artists in the US whose work throws into sharp relief matters of injustice, corruption, and human rights violations show how their activism serves as an indispensable and unique site for the trenchant critical analysis that is also in the heart of Filipinx American studies. Comprising "policy or action of using vigorous campaigning to bring about political or social change,"[14] activism is both the provenance and a continuing focal point of inquiry in the field of Filipinx American studies. As Martin F. Manalansan IV and Augusto F. Espiritu note, Filipinx American studies traces its origins to the 1960s when "Filipinos in the United States were swept up in several overlapping strands of political activism, from the anti-dictatorship struggle against Ferdinand Marcos to the Asian American movement to the Filipino American movement to sporadic participation in American Indian, Puerto Rican, African American, and anti–Vietnam War activism."[15] In the 1960s decade of dissent and social protest, "Filipino American women and men were also actively involved in gay liberation, feminist, and Third World feminist movements."[16] In particular, Filipinx women and men who were migrant, immigrant, and US-born fought for workers' rights both on the West Coast and in Hawai'i's agricultural labor movements. Forming coalitions with African American, Mexican American, Native American, and Asian American student groups, Filipinx Americans struggled against war, imperialism, and social injustice in the Third World Liberation Front on California's university campuses. Their activism against the US imperialist wars in Southeast Asia and their stand against white supremacy in these coalitions helped initiate and sustain the longest student strikes in US history, leading to the establishment of ethnic studies departments and programs and the hiring of and granting tenure to ethnic studies faculty. From Filipinx American activism in the 1960s, "Filipino American identity, culture, and institutions emerged during the 1970s and 1980s in response to this surge in mass democratic politics, its critique of American racism, and its positive embrace of racial identity."[17] Today's Filipinx American student activists such as the university students in the Critical Filipina and Filipino Studies Collective (CFFSC) in California owe their origins to the Filipinx student activists of the 1960s who comprised the Pilipino American Collegiate Endeavor (PACE). Contemporary Filipinx American activists who organize and empower low-wage Filipinx workers to fight for their labor, health, gender, and immigrant rights carry on the work of Filipinx activists in the 1970s who joined with the residents of the International Hotel in San Francisco to resist new development projects that threatened this home of primarily elderly Chinese and Filipinx men in the city's Manilatown.[18]

Filipinx American activists today therefore take their inspiration from the students and activists of the 1960s and 1970s who joined forces with other civil rights and racial minority groups in the Third World Liberation Front and in the Battle for the International Hotel. In addition to demanding the establishment of Black studies and ethnic studies at public universities and colleges, these activist organizations insisted on ending US imperialist wars and militarist occupations in the non-Western world and recognizing the right of self-determination and sovereignty for Indigenous people in North America and formerly colonized people of the Third World.

Although Filipinx American studies apparently originates in the countercultural and social revolutionary movements of the 1960s and 1970s, much of the field's scholarship has focused and continues to concentrate on the experiences of Filipinxs in the United States in the decades preceding the 1960s, specifically from the 1920s to the 1950s when many Filipinxs in the US came to the country as diasporic workers, arriving on the West Coast and making their way to the American Midwest and Eastern Seaboard. This scholarship has focused most pertinently on the Filipinx worker activists of the West Coast who formed, led, and participated in agricultural labor organizations that fought for better wages and benefits for farmers, field hands, and factory workers. In particular, this scholarship has shown how the work of Filipinx laborers and community activists such as Carlos Bulosan, Larry Itliong (1913–77), Philip Vera Cruz (1904–94), Violeta "Bullet" Marasigan (1939–2000), and Thelma Garcia Buchholdt (1934–2007) has been indispensable to the project of Filipinx American studies. As Dawn Bohulano Mabalon and Gayle Romasanta show in their book *Journey for Justice: The Life of Larry Itliong*, Filipinx farmers and field hands played crucial roles as leaders and coordinators of the agricultural labor organizations in California's Central Valley.[19] These Filipinx worker activists collaborated with Mexican immigrant and migrant farmers to bring to the American public's attention (and further, the world's attention) the plight of Filipinx and Mexican migrant agricultural laborers on the US Pacific Coast: their sufferings under decades of racial discrimination, substandard and unhealthful working conditions, and impoverishment from exploitative labor practices and lower-than-average wages.

Among these Filipinx labor activists, Larry Itliong stood out as a dynamic organizer, arranging and leading cannery and agricultural unions in Alaska, Washington, and throughout California. Itliong was born on October 25, 1913, in Pangasinan province in the Philippines. In 1929 when he was fifteen years old, he migrated to the US and found work as a cannery laborer in Alaska and a farmworker in California. He joined his first strike in 1930. In 1956, he was a leader of the Filipinx contingent in the Agricultural Organizing Committee (AWOC), recruiting a number of other skillful organizers, among them Peter Velasco and Philip Vera Cruz who were critical to the success of the United Farm Workers. As Mabalon explains, Itliong was "instrumental, along with the more well-known Mexican-American labor leader Cesar Chavez, in gaining rights for farm laborers and setting the stage for immigrant labor activism and union building in the U.S."[20] On September 8, 1965, Itliong gathered with the Filipinx workers of AWOC in the Filipino Community Hall in Delano, California to discuss taking action against years of poor pay and abuse by white farm owners and growers. Itliong and the workers voted to go on strike, and they asked Chavez, who led a mostly Latinx farm workers union, the National Farm Workers Association, to join their strike.[21] With Itliong and Chavez as the leaders, the Filipinx and Latinx workers collaborated to walk out on strike against the farm owners and growers in what became known as The 1965–70 Delano Grape Strike, one of most successful and significant campaigns of civil resistance and labor activism in US history.[22]

In addition to being a labor activist, Itliong was also a communist and an anti-imperialist, who spoke out vociferously against the dictatorship of Ferdinand Marcos in the Philippines and the support of the US for Marcos's authoritarian regime. In this regard, Itliong's activism was inspired by Carlos Bulosan, who was also a communist and an anti-imperialist activist involved in the worker movement and organizing unions along the Pacific Coast. As Mabalon contends, the labor activism of Itliong and Bulosan cannot be understood apart from their leftist socialist politics. Itliong, Bulosan, and many other members of Filipinx labor unions were "tough leftists, Marxists, and Communists. . . . They met the violence of the growers with their own militance. They carried guns and knives for self-defense. They were feared within the labor movement, and the FBI had several of the Local 7 Filipino labor leaders under surveillance by the late 1940s for their Communist Party membership and/or leftist politics."[23]

Another significant activist organizer from the early generation of Filipinx Americans is Violeta "Bullet" Marasigan. As a teenager, Marasigan gave herself the nickname "Bullet" because of her directness and fierce determination to "confront anybody, anything, that stands in the way of progress."[24] In the San Francisco Bay Area where she lived and worked for much of her life, she was known among community organizers as "the quintessential activist" with an "internal fire that was constantly burning."[25] Marasigan was born on January 4, 1939, in rural Quezon province in the Philippines. After graduating from the University of the Philippines with a degree in social work, Marasigan went to the United States in 1959 to pursue a master's degree at San Francisco State University, where she became involved in the student strikes for ethnic studies and demonstrations against US war, militarism, and imperialist occupations in the Asia-Pacific and the Global South.[26] Along with Emile De Guzman, a young Filipinx student leader of the Third World Liberation strikes at UC Berkeley,[27] Marasigan was one of the activist leaders in the Battle for the International Hotel. She was employed as a social worker at the United Filipino Association, a nonprofit group organized by the hotel's elderly tenants in response to the real estate company, Milton Meyer & Company, which owned the hotel and wanted to evict the tenants in order to demolish the building and replace the neighborhood's low-cost housing and Asian American community businesses with buildings and structures that Milton Meyer deemed more profitable and attractive for gentrification.[28] Marasigan fought for the rights of the tenants. When she discovered, for instance, that many of the tenants were not receiving their full Social Security benefits and access to social services, she accompanied them "to the SSI office and spoke with their caseworkers. After that, everybody had their full SSI benefits."[29] Although all of the hotel's tenants were evicted in 1977 and the building was demolished in 1981, Marasigan continued to work and fight tirelessly for the rights of Filipinx veterans, retired farmers, and poor and working-class immigrants.

Marasigan is especially known for her antifascist activism against the dictatorship of Marcos and his regime's violations of human rights during the years of martial law (1972–81). When Marasigan returned to the Philippines in the 1970s, she joined the resistance movements against Marcos, advocated for human rights, and championed feminist causes. In 1982, she was arrested and charged with subversion, and spent one year in jail at Camp Crame, the national headquarters of the Philippine National Police in Manila where some of the worst violations and atrocities (tortures and killings) of political dissidents and anti-Marcos activists took place. After Marcos was toppled in 1986, Marasigan and her family returned to the San Francisco Bay Area, where she resumed her work as a social worker, assisting Asian and Filipinx immigrants and young people, and helping Filipinx American veterans of World War II to get equal military benefits.[30]

Like Itliong, Marasigan was both a dynamic organizer and an outspoken community leader who spent most of her life as an activist struggling for the rights of disenfranchised Filipinxs in the Philippines and the United States. She was just as much a "tough leftist" as Itliong, Bulosan, and the mostly male members of the Filipinx American labor unions. Speaking truth to power, her politics and activism were equally radical, confrontational, and unyielding. It is perplexing and something of an enigma, then, that Marasigan and other Filipinx women of the early generation who were hugely important as community leaders and activists largely remain ignored by scholars of Filipinx labor history and Filipinx American studies.[31] To date, there has been much more scholarly attention paid to Filipinx men of the early generation and their radical politics and community activism. Although this scholarship has been and will continue to be essential to the institutionalization and growth of Filipinx American studies, the tendency has been to construe the historiography of Filipinx labor history and community activism in masculinist terms. By not making more central to its scholarship the contributions of early-generation Filipinx women to the history of Filipinx labor history and activism, Filipinx American studies risks setting up a form of labor radicalism that normalizes and naturalizes radical politics and activism as masculine and (hetero)patriarchal.

In the attempt to counteract and challenge masculinist and (hetero)patriarchal constructions of radical activism and community leadership in Filipinx labor history and Filipinx American studies, this chapter now turns attention to Thelma Garcia Buchholdt, a Filipinx American politician, historian, and civil rights activist who fought for the rights of Alaska's Indigenous people. Buchholdt was born on August 1, 1934, in Claveria, Cagayan province in the Philippines. Her father, Eugenio Garcia, was of mountain tribal heritage, with manifestly Negrito features.[32] Observing the townspeople's disparagement of her father as well as their racist treatment of the mountain tribal people when they came down from the highlands to trade in Claveria, Buchholdt grew up resenting the racial denigration and exclusion of Indigenous people, and she resolved to promote the culture and heritage of the Philippines' mountain ethnic groups collectively known as the Igorot people.[33] At fifteen years of age in 1951, she immigrated to the United States and enrolled at Mount Saint Mary's College in Los Angeles, earning a BA degree in zoology in 1956. After college, she began her teaching career in California and "became actively involved in the civil rights movement as it developed in the late 1950s and early 60s."[34] In the late 1960s, she arrived in Alaska "at a time when the Alaska Native land claims movement was just gathering strength, and she and her husband, Jon, became involved advocates of the land claims movement when it was still politically dangerous to champion the land claims of Alaska's Native people."[35] Buchholdt went on to make history in Alaska as an elected representative of the Alaskan legislature, and she always made Native American relations and the rights of ethnic minority groups central to her politics. In 1974, she was elected to the Alaska House of Representatives as an Ad Hoc Democrat, becoming the first Asian American elected to the Alaska State Legislature and the first female Filipinx American elected to a legislature in the United States. She was re-elected to the Alaskan legislature in 1976, 1978, and 1980.

Like Bulosan, Itliong, Marasigan, and other Filipinx activists in mid-twentieth-century America, Buchholdt was an early-generation Filipinx activist who dedicated most of her life to progressive political causes and community leadership, as well as to researching, teaching, and documenting the early history of Filipinx migration and growth in Alaska. Among her academic accomplishments, her work as a scholar and teacher of Filipinx American history and cultural heritage in Alaska stands out. In 1996, she published the first book-length study of Alaska's Filipinx heritage titled *Filipinos in Alaska, 1788–1958.*[36] "Filipino immigration to the United States continues to be an important part of America's story," Buchholdt wrote in her book's introduction. "Yet, while historians in many states have written about Filipinos living in those states, in Alaska, the history of Filipinos and their contributions to the state's social and economic development have thus far been a neglected subject."[37] Buchholdt accordingly wrote her book with the writer-activist intention of making more visible the history of Filipinx people in Alaska and their important contributions to Alaskan culture, ethnic community formation, and Native American relations. In addition to her teaching and scholarship, Buchholdt made significant contributions to promoting Filipinx American history by founding and directing Asian American and Filipinx cultural centers. In 1975, she founded and coordinated the Filipino Heritage Council of Alaska, and in 1980 she was elected the first Asian American president of the National Order of Women Legislators.[38] In 1983, she founded and became the first president of the Asian Alaskan Cultural Center, the first cross-cultural center of its kind in Alaska, and in 1994 she founded the Alaska chapter of the Filipino American National Historical Society (FANHS) and was appointed director of Alaska's Office of Equal Opportunity.[39]

Buchholdt has a digital biography about her life created by family, friends, and others who knew and admired her, "and believed that her story is inspiring and important to Filipino American history."[40] As this biography proclaims, the history of the Filipinx diaspora to North America was important to Buchholdt. "She wrote about history. But more significantly, Thelma Garcia Buchholdt made history."[41] The Alaskan state government made sure to give Buchholdt the historical commemoration she deserves. In 2008, the Alaska Democratic Party awarded her the James "Jim" Doogan Lifetime Achievement Award, and on March 6 of that same year she was inducted into the Alaska Women's Hall of Fame in recognition of her public service to uphold social justice and the values of cultural diversity and respect for all people.[42]

Today's Filipinx writer-activists who are American born and in the diaspora have inherited the leftist politics of the early generation of Filipinx women and men activists and political leaders. Their activism has either directly or implicitly encouraged a contemporary generation of Filipinx American writers and artists, including Jessica Hagedorn, Gina Apostol, Luis H. Francia, R. Zamora Linmark, Eric Gamalinda, Elaine Castillo, Noel Alumit, Sarah Gambito, Lara Stapleton, Sabina Murray, Joseph Legaspi, Han Ong, Mia Alvar, and Rina Garcia Chua. The antiracist, anti-imperialist, anticapitalist, and environmentalist politics in the work of these writers and artists that largely informs Filipinx American studies is historically contingent on the collaborative efforts of diasporic and migrant Filipinx laborers and activists in early- to mid-twentieth-century America. For the early generation of Filipinx women and men who resided in North America for most of their lives, their activism was not bound by nation-state borders or by any nationalist imperative to demonstrate and represent allegiance to such borders. In fact, their capacity and drive to speak truth to power that underly their radical politics and activism should be understood as both a defiance of and a resistance to the race, gender, and class-based exclusionary restrictions of national borders, whose enforcement has been premised on the despotism of authoritarian leaders (e.g., in our current historical moment, Vladimir Putin, Donald Trump, Jair Bolsonaro, and Rodrigo Roa Duterte are tyrannical leaders) and the right-wing populism such leaders perpetuate and exploit.

To the extent that Bulosan, Itliong, Marasigan, and Buchholdt all understood their activism in the US to be inseparable from their speaking out against oppression and injustice against the poor in the Philippines, their activism should accordingly be understood in a transnational framework that situates the history of Filipinx American activism in a larger diasporic context. If Bulosan, Itliong, Marasigan, and Buchholdt were alive today, they would not only speak out against injustice and demand a moral response to the problem of racial discrimination and class exploitation in Trump's America, but they also would publicly confront the massive human rights violations and abuses of Duterte's authoritarian regime in the Philippines. They would find counterparts in women and men in the Philippines today who are activist leaders risking their own lives by organizing dissent against Duterte and calling him to account over his so-called war on drugs that currently has claimed more than 5,000 lives, mostly poor people who have been brutally murdered in extrajudicial killings carried out by the police.[43] Take, for example, Leila de Lima, a human rights activist and senator of the Philippines who, for the past four years, has been imprisoned on dubious drug-trafficking charges after taking a stand against Duterte's dictatorial regime and his bloody drug war. The arrest and jailing of Senator de Lima on February 23, 2017, ignited an international firestorm that has led to global recognition of her defense of human rights. De Lima has been designated a "prisoner of conscience" by numerous international human rights organizations, and in May 2018 Amnesty International conferred on her the first ever Most Distinguished Human Rights Defender award during the Ignite Awards for Human Rights.[44] Filipinxs in the diaspora everywhere have come to know about de Lima's unjust imprisonment and also her defense of human rights, which has become a model for others who hope to turn the tide against dictatorial regimes in the world.

Other Filipinx activists who have confronted Duterte and denounced his regime's human rights violations are Sherwin de Vera, an environmental justice activist and the coordinator of Defend Ilocos, a regional environmental network in the northwest Philippines that represents and advances people's opposition against large-scale and destructive mining,[45] and Maria Ressa, a journalist, author, and cofounder of *Rappler*, an online investigative news website that works as a fact-checker in the Philippines in the fight against fake news on Facebook.[46] Like de Lima, Ressa and de Vera were arrested on dubious charges after publicly speaking out against Duterte. Similar to de Lima's case, Ressa and de Vera's arrest and imprisonment have been seen by the international community as politically motivated acts to silence dissent by the Philippine government. As the work and struggles of these three contemporary activists powerfully reveal, the social movements for human rights by Filipinx activists both in the Philippines and in the diaspora are indispensable to the progressive politics of recent Filipinx writers, artists, and scholars in the United States. The life and work of both past and present Filipinx activists inspires a new generation of activists to collaborate on defending human rights and advancing the cause of social justice. Fighting for civil rights and empowering people to create a more just world are among the most important causes for Filipinx activists today. These are causes, furthermore, that inspire the public and collaborative work of critical analysis for Filipinx intellectuals, artists, and teachers in the Philippines and in the diaspora. In this sense, activism is and always has been in the heart of Filipinx American studies.

NOTES

1. The epigraph comes from Rina Garcia Chua, "Introduction: Living Limestones and the Move to Refuse Resilience," in *Sustaining the Archipelago: An Anthology of Philippine Ecopoetry*, ed. Rina Garcia Chua (Manila: University of Santo Tomas Publishing House, 2017), xlviii, original emphasis.

2. Ted Aljibe, "Philippines Five Years after Typhoon Haiyan," *The Guardian* (November 8, 2018); *https://theguardian.com/artanddesign/2018/nov/06/philippines -five-years-after-typhoon-haiyan*, accessed January 19, 2019.

3. See, for example, published anthologies of literary works from Filipino writers on their recollections of experiences during Super Typhoon Yolanda: Renato Redentor Constantino, ed., *AGAM: Filipino Narratives on Uncertainty and Climate Change* (Quezon City, Philippines: Institute for Climate and Sustainable Cities, 2014); Eileen R. Tabios, ed., *Verses Typhoon Yolanda: A Storm of Filipino Poets* (San Francisco.: Meritage Press, 2014); and Merlie M. Alunan, ed., *Our Memory of Water: Words after Haiyan* (Naga City, Philippines: Ateneo de Naga University Press, 2016).

4. Rina Garcia Chua, "Dismantling Disaster, Death, and Survival in Philippine Ecopoetry," *Kritika Kultura* 25 (2015): 26–45 [33].

5. Chua, "Dismantling Disaster," 42.

6. Chua, "Dismantling Disaster," 42.

7. After the Philippine-American War (1899–1902), the United States ruled the Philippines as the country's colonizer for nearly fifty years (1899–1946). The US colonized the Philippines through military occupation and a

system of political and economic domination that was implemented and maintained through American racial ideologies of white supremacy. See Paul Kramer, *The Blood of Government: Race, Empire, the United States, and the Philippines* (Chapel Hill: University of North Carolina Press, 2006); and Dylan Rodríguez, *Suspended Apocalypse: White Supremacy, Genocide, and the Filipino Condition* (Minneapolis: University of Minnesota Press, 2010).

8. By "global capitalist policies of development," I mean the attempt by wealthy nations of the Global North to benefit poor countries of the Global South with technical and financial assistance that subscribes to the Global North's capitalist growth model. As the postcolonial ecocritics Graham Huggan and Helen Tiffin have pointed out, this form of strategic altruism is, on the surface, meant to close the gap between rich nations of the Global North (many of them former colonizers) and the underprivileged countries of the Global South (most of them former colonies of the Global North) (Huggan and Tiffin, *Postcolonial Ecocriticism: Literature, Animals, Environment* [New York: Routledge, 2015], 30). Yet the benefits of the Global North's capitalist development practices, which are delivered to the Global South under the guise of assisted modernization by economic agencies such as the World Bank and the International Monetary Fund, is ultimately geared to the Global North's own economic and political objectives to control the global capitalist market system (Huggan and Tiffin, *Postcolonial Ecocriticism*, 31). Hence, this form of postcolonial development that is meant "to address the persistence of poverty, environmental degradation and the violation of human freedom in the contemporary globalized world" continues to profit rich nations while spreading inequality among poor countries, but enables the Global North to champion its own "adherence to freedom, democracy and human rights" (Huggan and Tiffin, *Postcolonial Ecocriticism*, 31–32).

9. Carlos Bulosan, *America Is in the Heart: A Personal History* (Seattle: University of Washington Press, 1991 [1946]).

10. Augusto F. Espiritu, *Five Faces of Exile: The Nation and Filipino American Intellectuals* (Stanford, Calif.: Stanford University Press, 2005), 47.

11. As colonial subjects, Filipinxs came to America as "nationals" with some rights of immigration. Although permitted unrestricted entry as nationals until the mid-1930s, Filipinxs could not become citizens. They could travel freely within the territorial domain of the United States, but they had to live under laws that discriminated against them on the basis of race (Espiritu, *Five Faces of Exile*, 47).

12. Sarita Echavez See, *The Filipino Primitive: Accumulation and Resistance in the American Museum* (Minneapolis: University of Minnesota Press, 2017), 104.

13. E. San Juan Jr. quoted in Carlos Bulosan Centennial, Bulosan.org (2014); *https://bulosan.org*, accessed March 11, 2019.

14. "Definition of activism in English by Oxford Dictionaries," in *The Oxford English Dictionary*; *https://en.oxforddictionaries.com/definition/activism*, accessed December 10, 2018.

15. Martin F. Manalansan IV and Augusto F. Espiritu, "The Field: Dialogues, Visions, Tensions, and Aspirations," in *Filipino Studies: Palimpsests of Nation and Diaspora* (New York: New York University Press, 2016), 5.

16. Manalansan and Espiritu, "The Field," 5.

17. Manalansan and Espiritu, "The Field," 5.

18. James Sobredo explains that the Battle for the International Hotel in 1977 "symbolized the Filipino American struggle for identity, self-determination, and civil rights. It was a struggle that involved not only Filipinos but other Asian Americans, African Americans, Mexican Americans, student activists, religious groups and organizations, gays and lesbians, leftists, and community activists." "The Battle for the International Hotel: Historical Essay" (Found San Francisco digital archive; *http://www.foundsf.org/index.php?title=The_Battle_for_the_International_Hotel. Sobredo*, accessed January 26, 2019).

19. Dawn Bohulano Mabalon and Gayle Romasanta, *Journey for Justice: The Life of Larry Itliong* (Stockton, Calif.: Bridge & Delta Publishing, 2018).

20. Dawn Bohulano Mabalon, "There Was Cesar Chavez, and There Was Carlos Bulosan," Interview by Nita Noveno, *The Margins*, Asian American Writers' Workshop (June 11, 2014); *aaww.org/little-manila-dawn-mabalon/*, accessed January 6, 2019.

21. Paula Mejia, "The Forgotten Filipino American Activist behind the Delano Grape Strike," *Atlas Obscura* (May 17, 2018); *https://www.atlasobscura.com/articles/larry-itliong-delano-grape-strike*, accessed January 6, 2019.

22. Inga Kim, "The 1965–1970 Delano Grape Strike and Boycott," *United Farm Workers: ¡Si, Se Puede!* (March 7, 2017); *https://ufw.org/1965-1970-delano-grape-strike-boycott/*, accessed January 19, 2019.

23. Mabalon, "There Was Cesar Chavez."

24. Gregory Lewis, "Filipina 'Bullet' is a straight shooter," *SF Gate* digital archive (May 22, 1995); *https://www.sfgate.com/news/article/Filipina-Bullet-is-a-straight-shooter-3145264.php*, accessed March 10, 2019.

25. Benjamin Pimental, "Filipino American Political Activist Dies/ Marasigan killed in freak accident," obituary, *SF Gate* digital archive (April 19, 2000); *https://www.sfgate.com/news/article/Filipino-American-Political-Activist-Dies-2763673.php*, accessed March 10, 2019.

26. Pamela Burdman, "Bullet Marasigan: A Filipina-American Study in Contradictions," *Wildflowers Institute* digital archive; *http://www.wildflowers.org/community/Filipino/stories.shtml*, accessed March 10, 2019.

27. Sobredo, "The Battle for the International Hotel."

28. Sobredo, "The Battle for the International Hotel."

29. Sobredo, "The Battle for the International Hotel."

30. "Violeta Marasigan; Bay Area Activist for Filipino Americans," obituary, *Los Angeles Times* digital archive (April 20, 2000); *https://articles .latimes.com/2000/apr/20/local/me-21660*, accessed March 10, 2019.

31. A notable exception to this lack of scholarly attention on Filipinx women who were activists and community leaders in the United States is Karen Buenavista Hanna's study of Filipinx women and mothers who worked in the anti-imperialist and anti-Marcos movement in Chicago in the 1980s and 1990s. See Hanna's article "When Mothers Lead: Revolutionary Adaptability in a Filipina/o American Community Theater Organization," in *Amerasia Journal* 45, no. 2 (2019): 188–206. In her article, Hanna develops the concept of "mothering" as a focus in Filipinx American anti-imperialist activism and in supporting Philippine revolutionary politics. Hanna's "mothering" concept is a unique perspective in a body of literature that normally depicts Filipinx revolutionary activists as men who are single intellectuals and/or religious.

32. Thelma Buchholdt Archives: Index; *http://www.thelmabuchholdt.com /GuinaangAlbum.htm*, accessed March 15, 2019.

33. According to Buchholdt's digital biography, when Buchholdt was "elected President of the Anchorage Filipino Community in 1971, she was the first woman to hold that office, and she inherited the responsibility for conducting the annual Founder's Day banquet, at which traditionally the Community featured Filipino folk dancing. There had never been any mountain tribal dancing at these banquets. So Thelma set out to remedy that, and she began insisting that Igorot tribal dances be included in all Anchorage Filipino Community dance performances" (Buchholdt Archives).

34. Buchholdt Archives; *http://www.thelmabuchholdt.com*.

35. Buchholdt Archives; *http://www.thelmabuchholdt.com/GuinaangAlbum.htm*.

36. Thelma Garcia Buchholdt, *Filipinos in Alaska, 1788–1958* (Anchorage, Alaska: Aboriginal Press, 1996).

37. Buchholdt Archives; *http://www.thelmabuchholdt.com/Book.htm*.

38. Women's History Month at the University of the District of Columbia, "Thelma G. Buchholdt" (2019); *https://www.udc.edu/2017/03/03/womens-history -month-thelma-g-buchholdt/*, accessed March 16, 2019.

39. Women's History Month, "Thelma G. Buchholdt."

40. Buchholdt Archives; *http://www.thelmabuchholdt.com*.

41. Buchholdt Archives; *http://www.thelmabuchholdt.com*.

42. Buchholdt Archives; *http://www.thelmabuchholdt.com/LegProclamation.htm*.

43. Sofia Tomacruz, "Duterte gov't tally: 'Drug war' deaths breach 5,000-mark before 2019," *Rappler* online (December 31, 2018); *https://www .rappler.com/nation/220013-duterte-government-tally-killed-war-on-drugs -november-2018*, accessed March 20, 2019.

44. Senate of the Philippines 17th Congress, "AI hails De Lima as Most Distinguished Human Rights Defender," Senate of the Philippines (May 18, 2018); *http://www.senate.gov.ph/press_release/2018/0528_delima3.asp*, accessed March 20, 2019.

45. "Sherwin De Vera Arrested," *Front Line Defenders* (December 18, 2017); *https://www.frontlinedefenders.org/en/case/sherwin-de-vera-arrested*, accessed March 20, 2019.

46. Maria A. Ressa, "Facebook let my government target me. Here's why I still work with them," *Rappler* (January 21, 2019); *https://www.rappler.com /authorprofile/maria-ressa*, accessed March 20, 2019.

TWENTY-TWO

Filipinx American Activism—and Why I Once Loved Manny Pacquiao

Karín Aguilar-San Juan

A line differentiates celebrity philanthropy from collective social action. Celebrity philanthropists want to do something positive for others and they often have good intentions when they donate to a cause. Socially conscious philanthropists sometimes go one step further to connect their efforts with community-based initiatives or programs that add even more impact to their gifts. In contrast, collective social action involves a sustained effort at self-advancement by the aggrieved group. Usually they are trying to address an underlying structural or systemic problem. Ideally, activists are not dependent on an outside benefactor; if there is no outside benefactor, then there is no danger of such a benefactor adopting a "savior" stance; no danger at all of claiming that they are "doing good" at the expense of other people's suffering; and no danger whatsoever of diffusing or corrupting their overall activist agenda.

I do not mean to dismiss the positive effects of celebrities helping others through charitable giving. Like all of his fans, I felt good when the world-champion boxing icon Manny Pacquiao used his prize money to build a hospital for the poor in his home province of Sarangani, Mindanao. Ever since I read about the working-class Filipinx boxers in Little Manila, I've had a soft spot for the PacMan.[1] Once ranked among ESPN's best "pound-for-pound" boxers, he made me so proud. But my pride was practically extinguished a few years ago when he gratuitously offered the fans his embarrassing retrograde homophobic beliefs. I don't expect boxers to be the most sensitive people but it is the twenty-first century, and the competitive sports world has seen many amazing and successful athletes come out in public about their homosexuality, queerness, or gender nonconforming bodies. Did it ever occur to Pacquiao that his words would hurt, and that his statements could smear his celebrity status and cancel out the positive consequences of his money?

Of course, activist groups also have to deal with homophobic views, not to mention myriad other forms of prejudice and human short-sightedness. But a huge part of activist work is precisely to reflect upon the ways we each uphold harmful social dynamics and to push for collectively shaped, democratic agendas to solve those problems. Although they bring attention to an activist cause, one rich celebrity throwing their money around does not necessarily draw attention to the broader context. Indeed, representing activism through Filipinx celebrity and philanthropy promotes an erroneous, distorted formula for attacking deep-seated structural inequities such as the lack of modern healthcare facilities for the poor.

A major purpose of this essay is to uplift specific examples of Fil-Am activism—cannery and farm workers, military veterans, nurses, nannies, and undocumented queers—that follow a historical trajectory without tracing a linear path of progress or liberation.[2] These examples, chosen from hundreds if not thousands of known and unknown (to scholars) instances of collective social action, give evidence of the risks people have taken to improve their lot, whether focused on working conditions; benefits and recognition; examinations and licensure; or state-sponsored violence. Applying frames of "labor," "empire," and "gender/sexuality" allows us to place each group into relationship with the others, taking into account the multiple lenses through which Fil-Am activism might be analyzed and understood. By making the connection across farm labor/cannery organizing to the other realms of activism where questions of identity, desire, and pleasure are both integral and salient, we acknowledge and move beyond Old Left/New Left debates about, for example, the primacy of controlling the means of production versus battles over identity or culture. Instead, we can see Fil-Am activism as a way to grapple with structures of power and identity, to create new systems for meeting human needs, and to affirm life in the face of life-threatening forces on a global scale.

That . . . [is] the hardest thing for us to do, to make ourselves understand that we are one Filipino race.

—PONCE TORRES, *Seattle union organizer*

During the first half of the twentieth century, Filipinx migrant labor enriched US food and agriculture industries from the sugar plantations and loading docks of Hawai'i to the fish canneries of Alaska, and from the apple orchards of Washington to the fields of grapes and cabbages in California.[3] To make their voices heard against harsh working conditions and exorbitantly low wages, laborers needed to act as one. Action based on grievances shared by Ilocano, Tagalog, and Visayan cannery workers helped to construct a unified Filipinx identity, even though those moments of unity were sometimes tenuous. In Seattle in 1936, it took a dual murder of two union leaders to solidify the otherwise fractious solidarity within the Cannery Workers and Farm Labor Union, Local 18257.[4]

The Sugar Strike of 1946, a massive seventy-nine-day event involving twenty-five thousand people led by the International Longshore and Warehouse Union, transformed Hawai'i's economy and politics. At one point, management on the sugar plantations tried to stave off an impending strike by bringing in six thousand workers from Abra, Pangasinan, Ilocos Norte, and Ilocos Sur (the same regions called home by the Filipinx "nationals" already living in Hawai'i). Management's premise was that having just experienced a brutal military occupation of the Philippines by Japanese troops, these new imports would avoid linking arms with their Hawaiian counterparts of Japanese ancestry. Managers were counting on cross-ethnic divisions, but that plan backfired because the ILWU-allied National Union of Marine Cooks and Stewards took it upon themselves to educate the new recruits during their overseas journey. By the time they disembarked in Hawai'i, the new Filipinx workers had already joined the ILWU.[5] Bonding together as Filipinx was one step, but they also had to become unionized.

Engaging the rubric of labor as a frame for Fil-Am activism challenges the cultural and geographic parameters of conventional US labor history and forces to the surface underlying assumptions regarding who is at the center of analysis. Critical Filipinx studies reinvigorates analyses of capitalism and the exploitation of the working class with questions regarding race, ethnicity, gender, and sexuality.[6] In this sense, critical Filipinx studies lays an alternative groundwork, establishing US imperialism as the context in which the energy and aspirations of Filipinx bodies and minds have been and continue to be harnessed and channeled toward diasporic activity.

Who knows what new insights might emerge if the two examples above were reexamined looking for something other than the experience of male-bodied Filipinxs and the extraction of surplus value from their masculine labor? For example, in a fresh and exciting take on the Alaskan canneries, Juliana Hu Pegues uncovers the presence of Native women alongside Asian (Filipinx and Japanese) men. Strategies of "embodied pleasure" and "contestational joy" within Alaska's colonial industries indicate that the Native women played a subordinate yet essential role in the ability of Filipinx men to work and organize.[7] Attending to the lives and efforts of Indigenous women as they have influenced and supported men in the canneries brings into view the "settler colonialism" aspect of US imperialism, revealing the intricacies of migrant labor's relationship to the white settler state.

The year 1946 also brought the Rescission Act, a decision by the US Congress to deny the contributions of Filipinx veterans to US military force during World War II. During the years 1935 to 1945, hundreds of thousands of soldiers in the Philippines were organized into four different categories, each unit serving the United States in different ways to maintain its colonial foothold in Asia. These included the Old Scouts, the Philippine Army, anti-Japanese guerrilla units, and the New Scouts. Tens of thousands of guerrillas enabled US military forces to recapture the Philippines after Japanese occupation; the New Scouts even assisted in the US occupation of Japan after Japan's surrender. During World War II, the US government amended the 1940 National Act precisely to lure noncitizens to fight on behalf of the United States with the promise of citizenship through naturalization. Yet at the conclusion of World War II, the Rescission Act "legally nullified" the status of Filipinx veterans, rendering them ineligible for the recognition, benefits, or path to citizenship that previous laws had assigned them.[8]

The movement for "full equity" among Filipinx veterans achieved an important victory in 2009, using a legislative "reparations" approach based on denied opportunities instead of an organized labor approach. The full-equity movement directed most of its energies toward one of the lost benefits: a path to naturalized citizenship. From the 1960s through the 1980s, veterans attempted to sue the US government for barring Filipinxs from the right to naturalize. Senator Dan Inouye from Hawai'i (a longtime supporter of Filipinx veterans and a World War II veteran himself) managed to author Section 405, a clause in the Immigration Act of 1990 that extended the deadline during which veterans could apply for US citizenship. As a result, nearly 30,000 veterans (by then, many of them septuagenarians) became naturalized US citizens. In 2009 as part of the American Recovery and Reinvestment Act, veterans also received direct financial payments and recognition for their military service.[9]

The movement to bring redress to veterans through legislative reparations emerges out of the historically convoluted relationship of the Philippines to US militarism and imperialism in Southeast Asia. This brings to mind a different but equally convoluted situation faced by Hmong soldiers recruited to fight as guerrilla units in the "secret wars" waged by the CIA in Laos and Cambodia during the 1970s.[10] The Hmong Naturalization Act of 1997 portrays Hmong veterans as friends and allies to the United States, but that portrayal requires putting into motion a complex "refugee analytic" that asserts retroactive citizenship as an adequate and even generous exchange for military service, traumatization, and the rampant loss of life.[11] How might scholarship in critical Filipinx studies, taking its cues from critical refugee studies, look more deeply at the notion of retroactive citizenship as a duplicitous, unfair component of participation in US wars? The effort to expose the racist and imperialist underpinnings of war and combat does not have to discredit Filipinx veterans' desire to serve or their efforts for reparative full equity, as critical Hmong scholars demonstrate with their own examples. Moreover, critical Filipinx studies potentially contributes to global peace and social justice insofar as it is able to connect the realities of lived experience of war and combat—starting as far back as 1898 and continuing into the present—to the discursive or ideological operations of empire. As Camilla Fojas remarks, "[The Spanish-American War] set the national mood and attitude of global superiority. We live in the afterlife of that imperial moment."[12]

We are sick and tired of being subservient and culturally non-aggressive.

—NORMA RUSPIAN WATSON, *nurse leader and activist researcher*

Thinking of activism in terms only of agricultural labor and wartime combat runs the risk of producing a narrative that privileges and normalizes masculinity and the social realms dominated by heterosexual men and male bodies.[13] Moreover, to focus on combat rather than on the totalizing experience of death and destruction prevents nonmasculine forms of activism in response to war from coming into view. In contrast, labor activism in the post-Marcos era in the United States centers on nursing and domestic work. Not all nurses are women, and sometimes nannies are butch; indeed, examining their activist experiences presents an opportunity to elevate female-bodied Filipinx, including Filipina women, and simultaneously to expose and release gendered binaries and assumptions.

Energizing a twenty-first-century globalized "empire of care," nurses and nannies are bound together by the stereotypes they face on a daily basis as well as the "feminization, racialization, and commodification" of their bodies and work lives.[14] The idea that Filipina women are preternaturally disposed to care for others sets up an expectation that they will neither organize nor revolt against even the most obnoxious employers out of gratitude for the opportunity to live and work in the United States. Instead, nurses organized and fought against culturally biased licensing examinations, visa requirements that sought to limit their access to US employment, and hostility from American nurses who saw them as a workplace threat.[15] After two decades of conferencing, petitioning, and picketing, the nurses won significant gains, including the 1989 Immigration Nursing Relief Act, which among other things acknowledged the valuable role Filipinx nurses continue to play in US hospitals and medical facilities. The premature death of Araceli

Buendia Ilagan, along with countless other "frontline" healthcare workers, reminds us of COVID-19's drastic and unequal toll.[16]

But even more so than nurses, domestic workers from the Philippines and other nations of the Global South are literally "doing the dirty work" of the Global North: minding children and elders, cleaning house, cooking meals, washing and ironing clothes, and attending to all that is traditionally gendered female and assigned as unpaid work within the family unit.[17] Searching for illustrations of activism makes it crucial to acknowledge the aspirational collectivity of domestic workers who follow a "hidden script" when, for example, they respond to an employer's insult or seek to negotiate a higher fee.[18] At the same time, this is usually all happening within the "twilight zone of the informal economy" where there are no contracts or permits and where the relationship between trusting employer and loyal employee is both delicate and highly imbalanced.[19] The very nature of the international care economy demands that scholars in critical Filipinx studies reach beyond an ethnic or gender frame to make the large-scale social policy connections that will enable structural improvements in the lives of domestic workers around the globe. Nannies of the World Unite!

We tell America's whole story.

—JOSE ANTONIO VARGAS, *Pulitzer Prize–winning journalist*

In 2011, the Pulitzer Prize–winning journalist Jose Antonio Vargas revealed himself to the public as undocumented and gay.[20] His many acclaimed writing and social-media projects, including "Define America," generate supporting material and evidence for activists fighting for the rights of undocumented people. Racialized and criminalized, migrants without papers are relentlessly subject to the cruel punishments of what Dylan Rodríguez terms the "classical technology of the US white supremacist state"—surveillance, humiliation, isolation, detention, and deportation.[21] By broadcasting his own particular migration story via the pages of the *New York Times*, Vargas shifted and deepened a story that usually refers to the US-Mexico border.

Vargas's journey also puts a queer spin on migration and citizenship, raising the profile of queer and LGBT activism in immigration reform.[22] Vargas came out as gay when he was a teenager in high school, evidently without a plan or any awareness of the complications it might cause. Meanwhile, his grandfather had been banking on Vargas eventually marrying an "American girl" as a way to solve the problem of having only falsified papers. If Vargas wanted to gay-marry an "American boy" today, would his US-citizen fiancé be able to petition for his naturalization, given that Vargas is already fully exposed as an undocumented person and thus, in some people's minds, has confessed to being a criminal?[23] In this volatile political era, Vargas's situation—along with that of hundreds of thousands of queer and undocumented people—remains precarious and unclear.

Vargas was born a Filipinx, and his activism both draws on and extends a legacy of Filipinx identity and collectivity, even as he participates in a movement that includes many others. Before him, Filipinx communities stepped out in different ways to improve their shared destiny. The cannery and farm workers also confronted state surveillance, and their sexuality was considered a threat. They were allowed to enter the United States without a visa because they were considered US nationals, but were forbidden from marrying US citizens by antimiscegenation laws that banned interracial marriage. At the moment, Vargas occupies a space of contradiction: high political visibility and high professional achievement together with a criminalized status. His ability to name himself out loud as a gay man and to elicit support from so many places, including "mainstream" (read: white) queer advocacy groups, surely has been bolstered by decades of social, cultural, and political activism by Filipinx queers.[24]

When Nike dropped the PacMan for his homophobic slurs in 2016, it was surely more about paying homage to a multibillion-dollar rainbow than recognizing Filipinx queer activism. Likewise, the Filipinx comedian and actor Vice Ganda used social media to activate a digital queer #PrayforManny Pacquiao campaign that reached millions via Twitter: "The LGBT is a group of people. We are humans. But not animals. Though we're no saints we will pray for Manny Pacquiao." Using twenty-first-century technology, Vargas and Vice Ganda have mobilized millions of people in a fraction of the time it took to pull off the Sugar Strike of 1946.

Thinking critically about "doing good" and "being the change we want to see in the world" entails a full consideration of the scope and scale of injustice and inequity. It's not always true that doing something to help is better than doing nothing, especially if that something helps to cover up or to apologize for deeper systemic problems, or if the main purpose is to boost a celebrity's image. This chapter directs attention to specific examples of organized and collective action among Filipinx-identified groups: agricultural laborers, war veterans, nurses/nannies, and queers. By centering and prioritizing their efforts against a background of US militarism, imperialism, and racialized heteropatriarchy, Filipinx studies manifests its unique and indispensable value as a site for critical analysis.

NOTES

1. Linda España-Maram, *Creating Masculinity in Los Angeles's Little Manila: Working-Class Filipinos and Popular Culture in the United States* (New York: Columbia University Press, 2006).

2. This essay does not address anti–martial law political activism, which spanned the world. For an exciting new treatment of the anti–martial law movement, see *Alon: Journal of Filipinx American and Diasporic Studies* 1, no. 3 (2021).

3. The epigraph is from union organizer Ponce Torres, quoted in Chris Friday, *Organizing Asian American Labor: The Pacific Coast Canned-Salmon Industry, 1870–1942*, Asian American History and Culture (Philadelphia: Temple University Press, 1994), 125.

4. Chris Friday, "From Factionalism to 'One Filipino Race,'" in *Organizing Asian American Labor* (Philadelphia: Temple University Press, 1994), 125–48.

5. Gerald Horne, "Sugar Strike," in *Fighting in Paradise: Labor Unions, Racism, and Communists in the Making of Modern Hawai'i* (Honolulu: University of Hawai'i Press, 2011), 82–102.

6. I owe my awareness of global structures of gender exploitation to scholarship by my mother, Delia D. Aguilar, "Questionable Claims: Colonialism *Redux*, Feminist Style," *Race and Class* 41, no. 3 (2000): 1–12.

7. Juliana Hu Pegues. "Rethinking Relations," *Interventions: International Journal of Postcolonial Studies* 15, no. 1 (2013): 55–66.

8. Antonio Raimundo, "The Filipino Veterans Equity Movement: A Case Study in Reparations Theory," *California Law Review* 98, no. 2 (2010): 575–623. According to the author, the Rescission Acts specifically deny benefits to Filipino veterans.

9. Raimundo, "The Filipino Veterans Equity Movement."

10. Joshua Kurlantzick. *A Great Place to Have a War: America in Laos and the Birth of a Military CIA* (New York: Simon & Schuster, 2018). The author points out that Laos provided a model for "secret wars" in Central America and the Middle East.

11. Ma Vang, "The Refugee Soldier: A Critique of Recognition and Citizenship in the Hmong Veterans' Naturalization Act of 1997," *Positions: East Asia Cultures Critique* 20, no. 3 (2012): 685–712. See page 697 for the reference to Rep. Sonny Bono's speech on behalf of Hmong veterans.

12. Camilla Fojas, *Islands of Empire: Pop Culture and U.S. Power* (Austin: University of Texas Press, 2014).

13. The epigraph is an excerpt from a letter to the US Commission on Civil Rights from Norma Watson, executive secretary of the Foreign Nurse Defense Fund, cited in Catherine Ceniza Choy, *Empire of Care: Nursing and Migration in Filipino American History*, American Encounters/Global Interactions (Durham, N.C.: Duke University Press, 2003), 183.

14. Watson, in Choy, *Empire of Care*, 189.

15. Understanding that racist ideologies legitimated their exploitation, Norma Watson, then a leader of the Foreign Nurses Fund, complained in writing to the US Commission on Civil Rights: "Foreign nurses, particularly Fillippinas [sic], are the 'coolies of the medical world.'" Cited in Choy, *Empire of Care*, 183.

16. *https://khn.org/news/lost-on-the-frontline-health-care-worker-death-toll-covid19-coronavirus/*, accessed August 5, 2020.

17. Bridget Anderson, *Doing the Dirty Work?: The Global Politics of Domestic Labour* (London: Zed Books, 2000).

18. For a discussion of the ways Filipina domestics use their limited resources to write their own hidden scripts, see Rhacel Salazar Parreñas, *Servants of Globalization: Migration and Domestic Work*, 2nd ed. (Stanford, Calif.: Stanford University Press, 2015), 156–57.

19. See Chapter 8 in Helma Lutz, *The New Maids: Transnational Women and the Care Economy* (London: Zed Books, 2011).

20. Jose Antonio Vargas, "My Life as an Undocumented Immigrant," *The New York Times Magazine* (June 22, 2011); *https://www.nytimes.com/2011/06/26/magazine/my-life-as-an-undocumented-immigrant.html*, accessed January 3, 2019. The epigraph is from "About," in *Define American* (February 26, 2016); *https://defineamerican.com/about/*.

21. Dylan Rodríguez, "'I Would Wish Death on You . . .' Race, Gender, and Immigration in the Globality of the U.S. Prison Regime"; *http://sfonline.barnard.edu/immigration/print_drodriguez.htm*, accessed January 3, 2019.

22. For example, see *https://www.glaad.org/*, accessed January 6, 2019.

23. According to the website for US Citizenship and Immigration Services, US citizens are now allowed to petition for the naturalization of their

same-sex spouse: *https://www.uscis.gov/family/same-sex-marriages*, accessed January 6, 2019. Gay marriage as a form of activism, of course, needs to be credited not only to the white, college-educated, middle-class, and cis-gendered couples that grab headlines and gentrify US cities but also to the poor, hardworking, black and brown people of all gender orientations, gender presentations, and sexualities who have lived in the shadows of "homonorma-tivity." For a useful theorization of homonormativity and the impact of ordinary gay peoples, see Gavin Brown, "Homonormativity: A Metropolitan Concept That Denigrates 'Ordinary' Gay Lives," *Journal of Homosexuality* 59, no. 7 (August 1, 2012): 1065–72.

24. For a partial genealogy of Filipinx queer activism, see Robert Diaz, Marissa Largo, and Fritz Pino, eds., *Diasporic Intimacies: Queer Filipinos and Canadian Imaginaries* (Evanston, Ill.: Northwestern University Press, 2017); Martin F. Manalansan IV, *Global Divas: Filipino Gay Men in the Diaspora* (Durham, N.C.: Duke University Press, 2003); and Makeda Silvera, ed., *Piece of My Heart: A Lesbian of Colour Anthology* (Toronto: Sister Vision, 1992).

TWENTY-THREE

Considerations from the US-Occupied Pacific

Kim Compoc

In this essay, I consider what might constitute a progressive, anticolonial "Filipinx American activism" noting the fraught nature of "America" in the contested space of Hawai'i. Thus, my concerns are place-based, informed by the political specificity of Hawai'i, most commonly understood as the fiftieth state but actually a nation that remains under illegal US occupation like Puerto Rico, Guåhan (Guam), Sāmoa, and the Northern Mariana Islands. I aim to shed critical light on the assumption that the US is entitled to all the land it occupies in the Pacific and elsewhere. As Dean Itsuji Saranillio and other scholars of Asian settler colonialism have argued, Filipinx American identity politics in Hawai'i is a form of settler colonial hegemony that depends on a colonial amnesia about our own relationship with US empire that began in 1898.[1] My essay takes up Saranillio's intervention in earnest: Movements for Hawaiian sovereignty offer Filipinxs a positive opportunity for us to reverse such amnesia and build more robust, expansive politics grounded in the urgent need to protect land and water.

This essay is organized into three parts: Renarrating Land; Revisiting History; and Retooling "Activism." In each, I offer ways to disrupt and de-center assumptions that the US occupation is both inevitable and perma-nent. As many other scholars have argued, terms like "nation of immigrants," multiculturalism, and development often serve to relegate Indigenous people to the past. This is especially true in Hawai'i where these discourses circu-late alongside images of an island paradise dependent on US military be-nevolence. As we prioritize the Kānaka Maoli–led efforts to protect land and water, we have a more ethical approach to fight neoliberalism, endless war, and climate catastrophe.[1] Moreover, this framework is useful for Filipinx American studies in making explicit our engagement with Indigenous land struggle not just with regard to Hawai'i, but for all those lands commonly known as the US, the Philippines, and other places where Indigenous people are still targeted for destruction.[2] Such an approach is already well under-way in Filipinx American studies, an interdiscipline adept at unpacking the trauma of 1898, while fomenting the scholar-activism necessary to build a decolonized 2098.

Renarrating Land

It is easy to understand why Filipinxs in Hawai'i often narrate their arrival as "coming to America." Filipinx settlement largely began in Hawai'i in 1906, so most of our ancestors only knew Hawai'i as "American soil." The "Big 5" sugar oligarchy normalized the American occupation through he-gemonic control of land, schools, and media. Statehood in 1959 renewed Hawai'i as a destination for immigrants, and the 1965 Immigration and Na-tionality Act further removed barriers for settlers. In many official com-memorative documents by Filipinx Americans in Hawai'i, these changes are interpreted as increasing opportunities for immigrants (and Hawai'i itself) to participate in America's great democracy.

But even a cursory understanding of Hawaiian history demonstrates that Hawai'i was and is its own country and Kānaka Maoli have never surrendered their sovereignty. As Hawaiian movements have gained in-creasing attention, many contemporary Filipinxs see the need to reevaluate our own positionality in the islands, how we represent the islands, and how we envision/enact justice in a truly decolonized Hawai'i. One important strategy is acknowledging that Hawai'i is the ancestral home of the Hawaiian people, *not* "America." Hawai'i is not a multicultural paradise where everyone is an immigrant, but a settler colony under illegal US occupation.

Another important strategy is challenging how we look at land and what is considered "progress" or "productive land use." Americanization has brought an economy dependent on militarism, tourism, and corporate agribusiness (especially GMOs). All of these practices are unsustainable.[2] Kanaka Maoli efforts for self-determination point to a different set of values with protection of land at the center. In the introduction to *A Nation Rising: Hawaiian Movements for Life, Land, and Sovereignty*, Noelani Goodyear-Ka'ōpua provides historical context for the Hawaiian Renaissance of the late 1960s.[3] These movements are multifaceted, and have resulted in political victories against military occupation, specifically the cessation of live-fire training on Kaho'olawe and in Mākua Valley. (However, it continues at Pōhakuloa.) Given that Hawai'i imports 90 percent of its food, food sovereignty has gained momentum, with political victories to protect farmland and water at Waiāhole-Waikāne and Nā Wai 'Ehā. Kānaka Maoli have also prioritized the protection of sacred sites, especially Mauna Kea and Haleakalā, both of which face immediate threat of desecration from multinational, industrial telescopes. The protection of *iwi kupuna* (burial sites) has also made serious gains in Hawai'i; developers must justify their projects to burial councils to comply with the law. In all these ways, Kānaka Maoli are literally gaining ground, and they need settler allies like Filipinxs who have their own relationship with US imperialism to assist in these efforts.

Revisiting History

I declare such a treaty [US treaty of Annexation] to be an act of wrong toward the native and part-native people of Hawai'i, an invasion of the rights of the ruling chiefs, in violation of international rights both toward my people and toward friendly nations with whom they have made treaties, the perpetuation of the fraud whereby the constitutional government was overthrown, and, finally, an act of gross injustice to me.

—*Queen Liliʻuokalani of Hawaiʻi, 1897*

I solemnly protest in the name of God, the root and the fountain of all justice, and of all right, and who has given to me the power to direct my dear brothers in the difficulty against this intrusion of the Government of the United States in the sovereignty of these islands.

—*President Emilio Aguinaldo of the Philippines, 1899*

Hawaiian historians like Noenoe K. Silva, Jon Kamakawiwoʻole Osorio, and Lilikalā Kameʻeleihiwa have corrected triumphalist American histories of Hawaiʻi that rendered the overthrow as "inevitable" and ignored Hawaiian-language sources.[4] Outsiders are often surprised to learn the Hawaiian Kingdom had international recognition as an independent nation with a constitutional monarchy in 1843. At the time, despite reeling from a precipitous population decline wrought by Western contact, Hawaiʻi had a multiracial citizenship with one of the highest literacy rates in the world. People from many ethnic groups were granted naturalization by the kingdom. Seeking to preserve their economic power and political influence, sugar oligarchs, many of whom were the descendants of the first Calvinist missionaries to the islands, forced King David Kalākaua to sign the 1887 "Bayonet Constitution," which instituted exclusionary American-style citizenship defined by race and class. These effectively stripped power from the monarchy and Native Hawaiians. King Kalākaua's heir, Queen Liliʻuokalani, dedicated her life to reversing the disenfranchisement of her people—so much so that she was deemed a threat by the sugar plantation oligarchy and was overthrown in 1893. The provisional government immediately appealed to the United States for annexation. In the meantime, Hawaiians and their allies used multiple methods of protest to convince Washington to reverse this decision.

The year 1898 marks the illegal US annexation of Hawaiʻi, along with the colonies it seized at the close of the Spanish-American War: Guåhan, Puerto Rico, Cuba, and the Philippines. This would mark the beginning of the US wars in the Philippines, including "pacification" campaigns that included torture and other war crimes. The US made Hawaiʻi its fueling station and training ground for these wars, and later its imperialist expansion into the Pacific and Asia. While the US narrates annexation as necessary or inevitable for the peaceful transition to democracy, for Hawaiian nationals (both Kānaka Maoli and settlers) the coup overthrowing Liliʻuokalani was catastrophic in its impact.

While Filipinxs have been aligned with the Kanaka Maoli struggle as early as 1893,[5] the most celebrated political contributions involve plantation labor struggle. Pablo Manlapit and Carl Damaso are two labor heroes who forged alliances between Filipinxs and other ethnic groups to fight exploitation.[6] On the one hand, the labor movement allowed Filipinxs and other workers— including Kānaka Maoli—to have a political voice at a time when they were barely recognized as human beings. On the other hand, settler historiographies often neglect to talk about the history before they arrived, and how plantation labor was part of an exploitative capitalist system that still continues in Hawaiʻi.[7] Today, even as Filipinxs continue to fight union-busting in the multinational corporate hotels, the struggles of this first generation—the *sakadas*—is recruited into an American developmental narrative that showcases Hawaiʻi's diversity.[8] Plantation histories that filter out US imperialism mask the colonial dispossession of Kānaka Maoli with the virtuous work ethic of Filipinx/immigrant labor. The ecological travesty of US industrial agriculture and tourism becomes increasingly obvious as climate crisis leaves Hawaiʻi scrambling to restore the ancestral foodways that sustained life for centuries.[9]

Retooling "Activism"

Because of this history, "Filipinx American Activism" remains a fraught concept in Hawaiʻi. Engagement in American-style activism often depends on US discourses of constitutional rights, the founding fathers, and a nation of immigrants united by democratic ideals. But Hawaiians are outnumbered in Hawai'i, so American-style democracy serves to minoritize and trivialize their concerns.[10] US occupation is the primary harm facing Kānaka Maoli, along with multinational capital, which is largely facilitated by the settler state. Filipinxs working toward progressive social change must seek to destabilize and denaturalize US claims to Hawai'i.

While Kānaka Maoli sometimes use the word "activist," increasingly they choose *kia'i* (protectors or guardians). The word "activist," or worse "protestor," can seem disrespectful to those whose very survival is under threat. Corporate media often situate *kia'i* as impeding "progress" while naturalizing the violence of land seizure, extraction, and desecration.

An ethic of *aloha 'āina* (love for the land) seeks to promote nonviolent, sustainable economies rooted in Hawaiian knowledge. This work is urgent in the context of endless war fueled by US militarism in Hawai'i. The US Indo-Pacific Command is housed on O'ahu, and from here the US military oversees approximately 52 percent of the earth's surface. In this light, the protection and deoccupation of Hawai'i is a critical site for both regional and global peace movements.

Sometimes the tension between Hawaiian land claims and Filipinx concerns can seem irreconcilable, particularly given the Kānaka Maoli relationship to land as sacred against a labor ethic that often assumes jobs are sacred. Too often taro farmers (mostly Hawaiian) and agricultural/hotel workers (mostly immigrant Filipinxs) are cast as political rivals. However, it should be noted that there are Filipinx taro farmers and Kānaka Maoli who work in the hotels or institutions that represent American settler colonialism and capitalism. The Honolulu-based pro-sovereignty group Decolonial Pin@ys as well as many unaffiliated progressive Filipinx settlers have tried to outsmart this binary by building a politics grounded in the notion of "Respect Land and Labor." These efforts include educating workers on their own relationship to sacred sites, to build workers' understandings of their role in protecting Mauna Kea and why *aloha 'āina* and long-term sustainability must be included in a pro-jobs agenda. Similarly, celebrating labor victories like the 2018 hotel strike against Marriott reminds independence activists that powerful grassroots victories are possible in Hawai'i, even the ones that contest multinational capital, which also threatens Kanaka Maoli self-determination.

Another strategy that has become popular is the "Detour," a way of educating both locals and visitors about the impacts of militarization in

Hawaiʻi.[11] With Aunty Terri Kekoʻolani, Ellen Rae-Cachola organized a detour of Waikīkī to educate settler youth on the impacts to Kanaka ways of living alongside economic and sexual exploitation of immigrant labor in the hotels. In "Reading the Landscape of U.S. Settler Colonialism in Southern Oʻahu," Cachola explains the political strategy behind this intervention: "Within indigenous discourse, the land that settler diasporic youth stand upon is technically not theirs. Rather, diasporic settlers were brought to that place to contribute to the settler jurisdiction. Invoking diasporic settler connection to indigenous jurisdictions requires forging meaningful connections to their own ancestral lands and histories rather than be limited to settler identities and histories."[12] Detours provide needed disruption to the dominant narratives of hotel and military recruitment campaigns targeting working-class immigrant youth through Hawaiʻi's colonial school system.

Of course, forging such alliances is not easy. Filipinxs in Hawaiʻi fight against racist immigrant-bashing and internalized racism, making it difficult to find time or energy to also build solidarity with Hawaiian sovereignty efforts. Surviving Hawaiʻi's economy has always been difficult, now made worse in the context of COVID-19. How can we talk about these issues in culturally appropriate ways, with our families, our faith communities, and our unions? How can we talk about these issues with other settlers in Hawaiʻi, particularly those of color like Filipinxs who have uneven access to their own histories of resistance against US empire? How do we wrestle with the complex reality that Hawaiians have a diversity of views on what sovereignty should look like, and how to get there? Progressive Filipinx politics in Hawaiʻi is still evolving to manage two things at once—find joy in the liberation of our own communities, and build a settler allyship with Kanaka ʻŌiwi efforts for sovereignty, self-determination, and sustainable futures.

NOTES

1. I use *Kanaka*, *Kanaka Maoli*, and *Kanaka ʻŌiwi* as synonymous with Indigenous or Native Hawaiian. *Kānaka Maoli* is the plural form.

2. See Dean Itsuji Saranillio, *Unsustainable Empire: Alternative Histories of Hawaiʻi Statehood* (Durham, N.C.: Duke University Press, 2018).

3. Ikaika Hussey, Erin Kahunawaikaʻala Wright, and Noelani Goodyear-Kaʻōpua, eds., *A Nation Rising: Hawaiian Movements for Life, Land, and Sovereignty* (Durham, N.C.: Duke University Press, 2014).

4. See Noenoe Silva, *Aloha Betrayed: Native Hawaiian Resistance to American Colonialism* (Durham, N.C.: Duke University Press, 2004); Jonathan Kamakawiwoʻole Osorio, *Dismembering Lahui: A History of the Hawaiian Nation to 1887* (Honolulu: University of Hawaiʻi Press, 2002); Lilikala Kameʻeleihiwa, *Native Land and Foreign Desires: Pehea Lā E Pono Ai? How Shall We Live in Harmony?* (Honolulu: Bishop Museum Press, 1992).

5. The most famous example is Filipinx composer José Sabas Libornio, leader of the Royal Hawaiian Band, who composed or arranged the music for the beloved Hawaiian protest anthem "Kaulana Nā Pua" in partnership with celebrated poet and songwriter Ellen Kehoʻohiwaokalani Wright Prendergast. This song is a little known gesture of Filipinx affirmation of Hawaiian sovereignty.

6. Melinda T. Kerkvliet, *Unbending Cane: Pablo Manlapit, a Filipino Labor Leader in Hawaiʻi* (Honolulu: University of Hawaiʻi Press, 2002); Dean T. Alegado, "Carl Damaso: A Champion of Hawaiʻi's Working People," *Social Process in Hawaiʻi* 37 (1996), 26–35.

7. One important exception to this is Jovita Rodas Zimmerman's *Hawaii's Filipino Americans: A Collection of Plays, Essays and Short Stories* (Honolulu: S.N., 1997), 1–10.

8. See Haunani-Kay Trask, "Settlers of Color and 'Immigrant' Hegemony: 'Locals' in Hawaiʻi," *Amerasia* 26, no. 2 (2000): 1–24; and Rod Labrador, *Building Filipino Hawaiʻi* (Urbana: University of Illinois Press, 2015).

9. It should be noted that the plantation system actually began during the Hawaiian Kingdom, although it greatly accelerated under Americanization. Many Kānaka Maoli scholars are unpacking the complex negotiation of power during the Kingdom era, which was at once politically sovereign, and yet economically vulnerable to global capitalism and to sometimes traitorous American advisors. See J. Kēhaulani Kauanui's *The Paradoxes of Hawaiian Sovereignty: Land, Sex, and the Colonial Politics of State Nationalism* (Durham, N.C.: Duke University Press, 2018).

10. Dean Itsuji Saranillio has written extensively on former governor Ben Cayetano's anti-Hawaiian politics as a classic example of this Hawaiʻi-based Filipino Americanism. See "Why Asian Settler Colonialism Matters: A Thought Piece on Critiques, Debates, and Indigenous Difference," *Settler Colonial Studies* 3, no. 3–4 (2013): 280–94.

11. See Laurel Mei-Singh and Vernadette Vicuña Gonzalez, "DeTours: Mapping Decolonial Genealogies in Hawaiʻi," *Critical Ethnic Studies* 3, no. 2 (Fall 2017): 173–92; Hokulani Aikau and Vernadette Vicuña Gonzalez, *Detours: A Decolonial Guide to Hawaiʻi* (Durham, N.C.: Duke University Press, 2019).

12. Ellen-Rae Cachola, "Reading the Landscape of U.S. Settler Colonialism in Southern Oʻahu," *Feral Feminisms* 4 (2015): 52.

Transformation

PART FIVE

Relationalities, Intimacies, and Entanglements

TWENTY-FOUR

Filipinxness: An Epochal Perspective

Anthony Bayani Rodriguez

Modern narratives surrounding the racial/cultural/civilizational deficiencies of non-European, non-Christian peoples proliferated in concert with political and intellectual movements, which distinguished the humanity and civilizational features of "the West" from the rest of the planet. As a panarchipelagic identity, "Filipino" became a dominant term of ethnonationalist collective identification in the late nineteenth century during the escalation of revolutionary anticolonial liberation struggles by Philippine nationalists against imperial Spain. The movement for national independence was led by the colony's formally educated, mestizo, landowning *ilustrado* Native elites. Anticolonialist *ilustrados* believed naming and identifying the descendants of the Philippine archipelago's Native peoples as a Filipino ethnonationalist collective was imperative for liberation. Distinguishing the Filipino nation as a coherent historical and cultural entity was a means by which to unify the various ethnic groups of the Philippines toward nationhood. Being

"Filipino" was thus conceptualized on the terms of a distinctly petit-bourgeois Native intelligentsia whose language of national belonging bore the epistemic toll of empire.

The annexation of the Philippines on the eve of colonial independence from Spain in 1898 tethered Filipino nation-building to the domestic and transnational racial regimes of United States. Under the military, economic, and political force of American imperialism, "the Filipino" as a global-historical ethnic construction assumed a more definitive meaning within the modern Western georacial imaginary. The Filipino signified a geographical zone and political subjectivity with the capacity to serve the interests of Western liberalism and American empire. Despite the resistance of anticolonialists in the Philippines throughout the first half of the twentieth century, "Filipinization" meant nothing less than "Americanization."[1] Many leading Filipino nationalists challenged American perceptions of their archipelago as "yet uncivilized and wild" by insisting that the Philippine nation was essentially a Westernized nation in the Pacific that possessed, in the words of Manuel Quezon, "all of the fundamentals of occidental civilization."[2] Such expressions of Philippine ethnonationalist exceptionalism portrayed a Christianized, Westernized, and therefore *governable* people. Attributing such qualities to the "Filipino race" and "civilization" reinforced the archipelago's geopolitical significance as a Pacific territory uniquely situated to advance the hegemony of Western liberalism and the interests of American empire. In practice, the legibility of Filipinos as an ethnonational entity was premised on the subordination of peasants, mountain dwellers, non-Christians, and other dysselected populations, who were viewed as parasitically entangled in the project of Philippine nation-building.

"Filipino American" discourses of ethnic solidarity and community gained prominence in the 1960s along with the rise of mass freedom and liberation movements by systematically marginalized groups throughout the United States, and after decades of grassroots activism by Filipino immigrants for racial equality, labor justice, and against American imperial aggression. A major shift in dominant constructions of Filipinx ethnicity in the past five decades since this historic period of radical social justice activism has been the articulation of Filipino Americans as part of the panethnic formation of "Asian America." This chapter in the racialization of Filipino ethnicity began as a political strategy to assert cross-ethnic solidarities and commonalities of immigrants from Asia and the Asian-Pacific islands. In the final decades of the twentieth century the American government waged various domestic campaigns to suppress against grassroots organizations that advocated antiracist and anti-imperialist principles. At the same time, the institutionalization of liberal multiculturalist discourses of American nationalism served as the covering conceit for the rise of a new domestic policing apparatus in the United States.

Presently dominant formulations of Filipino Americanness diminish the historical impact of American nationalism as both (1) a perpetual militarized conquest of (cultural, political) territories in ostensibly domestic ('conquered') and materially alien or global ('frontier') sites; and (2) a genocidal national and (global) racial project that is multilayered and versatile in its institutional mobilizations and singular in its production of particular conditions of historical inescapability for peoples who are and have been subjected to the material logics of genocide."[3] Early twenty-first-century critical Filipinx studies scholarship offers a contrary position to such liberal conceptualizations of ethnicity by approaching the many colonialities and racial violences that constitute the Filipinx diaspora *not* as aberrational to the otherwise universally progressive march of Western liberalism, but rather, as the catastrophe from which alternative forms of group identification and species consciousness can (and must) be established. Advancing the critical, intersectional, and decolonial study of Filipinx identity in the twenty-first century will require continued attentiveness to overlapping and still unfolding regimes of large-scale racialized subordination, displacement, and dehumanization.

The term "Filipinx" represents a significant shift within the trajectory of postcolonial Philippine ethnic identity. It embodies a critique of the present orthodoxy of gendered binaries such as Filipino/Filipina, Pilipino/Pilipina, Pinoy/Pinay, and in turn, claims forms of personhood and sociality that have been marginalized, silenced, and erased from dominant narratives of diasporic experience. This critique is especially relevant to the lives of queer, trans, and nonbinary people, but also problematizes dominant discourses of ethnic belonging that normalize forms of social exclusion, structural alienation, and dehumanization that are tied to the histories of modern imperialism, colonization, and nation-building.

As a term of collectivity, Filipinx confronts an unresolved ontoepiste-mological crisis surrounding the limits of what it means to be an optimal subject of the nearly five-century epoch known as "modernity." Critical Filipinx studies scholarship disentangles postcolonial ethnic formations from liberal multiculturalist, ethnonationalist discourse. The importance of critical Filipinx studies to the advancement of critical race and ethnic studies, as a whole, is evident in the work of Robyn Magalit Rodriguez, John D. Blanco, Victor Bascara, Kimberly Alidio, Julian Go, Richard T. Chu, Robert Diaz, Kale Bantigue Fajardo, Martin Joseph Ponce, Denise Cruz, Sarita Echavez See, Lucy Mae San Pablo Burns, Jose Francisco Benitez, Anna Romina Guevarra, Emily Noelle Ignacio, Rick Bonus, Antonio T. Tiong-son Jr., Dylan Rodríguez, Anthony Christian Ocampo, Martin F. Mana-lansan IV, Allan Punzalan Isaac, Victor Román Mendoza, Luis H. Francia, Simeon Man, and Neferti Xina M. Tadiar.[4] Together, these scholars are re-suscitating the radical ambitions behind calls for "new studies" during the 1960s, which set into motion the founding of fields like Black studies, Latino studies, Native American studies, Asian American studies, Queer studies, Women's studies, etc. The early calls for "new studies" were initially moti-vated by the glaring deficiencies of modern "knowledge" in and of itself, and sought to establish completely new methods and frameworks of study for the humanities and social sciences. For the present generation of critical scholars, approaching "Filipinxness" as a geopolitical condition of Ameri-can modernity reveals forms of collective identification and solidarity that move beyond the modern orthodoxies of liberal humanism, ethnonational-ism, and empire.

NOTES

1. Paul A. Kramer, *The Blood of Government: Race, Empire, the United States, and the Philippines* (Chapel Hill: University of North Carolina Press, 2006), 307.

2. Manuel Quezon, "The Right of the Filipinos to Independence," *Filipino People* 1, no. 2 (October 1912), 2.

3. Dylan Rodríguez, *Suspended Apocalypse: White Supremacy, Genocide, and the Filipino Condition* (Minneapolis: University of Minnesota Press, 2010), 99.

4. In recent years, significant interventions have appeared in trailblazing pieces of scholarship such as the 2016 collection *Filipino Studies: Palimpsests of Nation and Diaspora*, ed. Martin F. Manalansan IV and Augusto F. Espiritu, as well as other edited collections and monographs.

TWENTY-FIVE

A Tale of Two "X"s: Queer Filipinx and Latinx Linguistic Intimacies

Sony Coráñez Bolton

Filipinx, or "Pilipinx," is the product of borrowing.[1] Most likely, "Filipinx" results from Chicanx and Latinx politics and thought—a cross-pollination whose underlying mode of production is, on the one hand, a politics of mutual recognition rooted in a shared commitment to progressive queer, trans, and gender inclusion and, on the other, a more understated shared affinity conditioned by the intersection of Spanish and US colonialism. The "x" in Latinx (pronounced La-teen-ex or Latin-ex) is a term that attempts to shift consciousness on the gender binary represented by Spanish morphological gender in the terms "Latina" or "Latino."[2] This can be said to be a further-ance of foundational feminist critiques of the Chicano nationalist movement for its marginalization of women's or feminist issues. Previous terms have emerged before Latinx that represented similar attempts of inclusion and the expansion of politics away from masculinist ethnic nationalism. For instance, "Latina/o" or "Latin@" are common and still widespread alternatives to the supposedly gender-inclusive "Latino." Charges of linguistic imperialism of US identity politics improperly changing the use of Spanish have rendered the use of "Latinx" a controversial one. The intersection of and relationship to US politics, imperialism, and the Spanish language ironically distance Filipinx America from such debates and bring us into conversation with Latinx studies. The project of defining and outlining "Filipinx" is fundamentally a comparative question. In this essay, for reasons of space and scope, I will not focus on the internal dynamics and vicissitudes of gender, sexual, and racial politics emblematized by the "x" in Latinx. And yet it is difficult to understand the genealogy of "Filipinx" without having a more intimate knowledge of such developments in ethnoracial groups that we deem not "Asian American." Does Latinx *queer* Filipino? What does Filipinx American studies contribute to Latinx studies? Indeed, it is the central aim of this essay to demonstrate that "Filipinx" highlights and centers the relationalities elaborated above in ways that demonstrate that queer and gender inclusive language inherently enrich critical and comparative race analysis.

The fact that this borrowing of the "x" even exists should make us, as Filipinx American critics, pause and consider the productive epistemological problem before us. One aspect of this problem is archival: There is a long tradition of Spanish Filipinx writing protracting well into the US colonial period not well understood by Filipinx American studies. In whichever language its literature and culture might be articulated, "Filipino" itself is an invention derived from the Spanish language and thus germane to the debates on linguistic imperialism that circumscribe the use of Latinx. The very reason that it is even possible to transmute "Filipino" to carry the "x" is precisely because of a shared history of imperial encounter. The shift in our language on gender and sexual binaries *also* occasions critical engagement with shared, overlapping, and comparative racial histories that might get deprioritized due to US-based identity politics. Thus the morphological shift of "Filipino" and "Filipina" to "Filipinx" constitutively highlights a contact zone of overlapping Spanish and US coloniality that not only enriches the rubric of analysis that we call Asian American studies, but also consciously cites comparative affinities with Latinx studies.[3] Only Filipinx American studies can do this within Asian American studies, highlighting an intuitive and crucial critical discourse with Latinx studies.

Filipinx or Pilipinx should not just be reduced to a more inclusive gender-neutral term. It is also the product of multiple conversations since the emergence of the interdisciplinary field of critical ethnic studies: the structural relationship of transmisogyny to US imperialism, the increasing relevance of critiques of settler colonialism to US ethnic formations and scholarship, and the comparative understanding of the intersection of Spanish colonialism and US imperialism. From a broader field perspective, I will elaborate these connections more explicitly below. For now, the latter point regarding a "Hispanic-American" analytic serves as a gesture of comparative ethnic studies meant to understand the comparative racialization of Latinxs and Filipinxs within a US multiracial imaginary that connects histories of westward discourses of Manifest Destiny *and* US transpacific empire building. As such the "Filipinx" of Filipinx American studies represents an exciting intervention into the deconstructionist operations of what was/is Filipinx American critique.

In my estimation, Filipinx brings together three main threads of analysis that have been developing over the past twenty years or so. These fields are critical ethnic studies, queer of color critique, and, of course, Filipino American studies' contributions to US empire studies. Critical ethnic studies takes up critiques of neoliberalism (especially as they developed during the 2008 US housing crisis) of the subprime debtor, carcerality, and settler colonialism.[4] First, a crucial addition to a critical ethnic studies line of thinking that Filipinx American studies engages is the historical relationalities that inhere in current understandings of Asian racialization to blackness and the structures of Indigenous dispossession that are currently understood as "settler colonialism."[5] I state this for two reasons: The first is that Latinx feminist and queer genealogies of thought have been critiqued for their potentially problematic uptake of indigeneity, which decenters the question of sovereignty. Gloria Anzaldúa's foundational *Borderlands/La Frontera*'s articulation of Chicana feminism in and through a feminist/queering of the Indigenous Aztlán is particularly noteworthy. Such moves have been critiqued by several feminist authors as being at odds with Indigenous sovereignties.[6] If Filipinx embraces the queerness and feminism that the "x" represents, then it should also take up the question of indigeneity and settler colonialism or risk the duplication of settler regimes of Indigenous dispossession in intellectual thought and politics.

The second line of critical inquiry is queer of color critique. A field of immanent critique convoked in sociologist Roderick Ferguson's pioneering text *Aberrations in Black: Towards a Queer of Color Critique*, queer of color critique takes up fundamental questions historically engaged by women of color feminism and extends them to examine the odd and, perhaps unexpected, alliance of heteronormative "radical" Leftist critique and conservative bourgeois respectability.[7] The "x" in both Latinx and Filipinx also variegates racial analysis by elaborating the ways that race and racialization circumscribe certain subjects' marginalization through their uneven access to institutions of heteronormativity. Put more simply, even "straight" subjects of color can be "queer" because their racialization partially depends on their disarticulation from heteronormativity, which has historically been coded as white.[8] In this sense, "Filipinx" in and of itself is a form of queer of color critique. Filipinx American studies has been a fundamental interlocutor in these conversations, especially with the publication of Martin F. Manalansan IV's *Global Divas: Filipino Gay Men in the Diaspora*.[9] The double "x" of Filipinx/Latinx is ideally meant to be more than a gender-neutral term but should also envision gender-inclusive and trans-affirmative discourses as central to the critical operations of Filipinx American studies.

The third field of inquiry that Filipinx critique engages is Filipinx American studies. This may seem very obvious to the reader. I mean to render two differences relevant to our discussion of the critical gesture imbedded in "Filipinx." The comparativity that is inherent to "Filipinx" opens up a colonial relationality between histories of Spanish colonialism and US imperialism that should question the historical insistence of Filipinx American studies to focus *only* on US imperialism. That is to say, the US empire as the *only* antagonist or historically relevant archive we draw on duplicates patterns of colonial omission that Filipinx American studies attempts to deconstruct in discourses of US exceptionalism. In the realm of Philippine Anglophone literature, Martin Joseph Ponce makes a similar critique that despite the preponderance of Anglophone literary production for more than the past century in the Philippines, it is virtually ignored by Filipinx Americanists.[10]

Does Latinx *queer* Filipino? My insistence on "queer" here is meant to highlight the irony of ethical and political affinity in the present that is partially conditioned by colonialism of the past. A recognition of this shared history and affinity materializes through the changing of a single letter—a rejection of binary gender and an embrace of mutual political-racial hailing in the utterance of a phoneme. It seems ironic that the harms and traumas of Spanish colonialism appear to further a politics of recognition that exceeds colonial machinations themselves. This is certainly not to absolve colonialism but rather to recognize that perhaps in the simple act of altering *one letter* of the historically colonial language of Spanish, and its ordering of binary gender, encourages an ethics of solidarity that brings Filipinx and Latinx peoples together. While it is neither free from controversy nor completely an answer in and of itself to the charge of linguistic imperialism, the "x" and the queer affiliations that it unavoidably gestures toward can potentiate an interdisciplinary "reckoning" beyond the siloed parochial concerns of imposed normalizing homogeneity, binary gender, and transmisogyny.

The queer linguistic play of the double "x" of Filipinx and Latinx has the potential of elaborating a registry of truly exciting critical questions and conversations in a comparative vein that normally wouldn't be entertained or whose analysis would be difficult to sustain. Latinx, with its relationship to questions of settler colonialism, indigeneity's variegation of rubrics of gender and sexuality, and, of course, its queering of the Spanish language, provokes conversations on the intersections of Spanish and US imperialisms that are, indeed, germane to Filipinx American studies. Where the term and field of study that we might develop under the term of "Filipinx" stands to enrich such conversations is by extending the potentially singular concerns of one ethnic group (incredibly heterogenous unto itself) to articulate stakes in the panoply of scholarly conversations developing in critical thought over the beginning two decades of the twenty-first century. What does "Filipinx" do to enrich our theories on and current conversations around structures of settler colonialism—questions that are fundamental to the project of critical ethnic studies? Do Filipinx indigeneities, such as they are, shift to another global register critical conversations in Native American and US empire studies? What kinds of comparative ethnic studies initiatives can we imagine through Filipinx's unavoidable political genealogy in Latinx? How do we question the epistemological and identitarian borders of ethnic studies while still maintaining important distinctions between groups? How are questions regarding gender, sexuality, queerness and their intersections with race, ethnicity, and imperialism fundamentally cited in the invocation of

"Filipinx" as an organizing optic? Filipinx American studies *should* be and indeed *is* at the forefront of these conversations. From my vantage, "Filipinx" is not simply an interesting but ultimately additive take among many critical lenses—it is *indispensable* in giving a rigorous account of the movement of language, empire, culture, and politics.

NOTES

1. Alfredo Leano, *Representation over Pure Visibility: Stories of Pilipinx-Americans in San Diego* (CreateSpace Independent Publishing Platform, 2018). Different pronunciation of these terms has been suggested, especially for Latin@ which is unpronounceable. "Latine" has been deemed by some to be an adequate way to avoid gendered binary language in human speech but still maintaining elements of the Spanish language of already gender-neutral nouns (sans indefinite or definite articles) such as *estudiante* (student).

2. Gloria Anzaldúa, *Borderlands/La Frontera: The New Mestiza* (San Francisco: Aunt Lute Books, 2012); Norma Alarcón, "The Theoretical Subject(s) of *This Bridge Called My Back* and Anglo-American Feminism," in *Criticism in the Borderlands: Studies in Chicano Literature, Culture, and Ideology*, Post-Contemporary Interventions, ed. Héctor Calderón and José David Saldívar (Durham, N.C.: Duke University Press, 1991), 28–39; Dionne Espinoza, María Eugenia Cotera, and Maylei Blackwell, *Chicana Movidas: New Narratives of Activism and Feminism in the Movement Era* (Austin: University of Texas Press, 2018).

3. Kandice Chuh, *Imagine Otherwise: On Asian Americanist Critique* (Durham, N.C.: Duke University Press, 2003). My use of "contact zone" is, of course, from Mary Louise Pratt's foundational use of the term in Mary Louise Pratt, *Imperial Eyes: Travel Writing and Transculturation* (London: Routledge, 2008).

4. Paula Chakravartty and Denise Ferreira da Silva, *Race, Empire, and the Crisis of the Subprime* (Baltimore, Md.: Johns Hopkins University Press, 2013). Particularly relevant to a Filipinx perspective in critical ethnic studies is paying attention to the global retrenchment of a rightist revanchism, one of whose noteworthy examples is that of current president Rodrigo Roa Duterte. The historical legacy of martial law in the Philippines combined with current trends in right-wing populism within the United States (and globally) make Filipinx American studies particularly relevant to our historical and cultural understandings of these political realities.

5. Iyko Day, "Being or Nothingness: Indigeneity, Antiblackness, and Settler Colonial Critique," *Critical Ethnic Studies* 1, no. 2 (2015): 102–21; *https://doi.org/10.5749/jcritethnstud.1.2.0102.*

6. María Josefina Saldaña-Portillo, *Indian Given: Racial Geographies across Mexico and the United States*, Latin America Otherwise: Languages, Empires, Nations (Durham, N.C.: Duke University Press, 2016); Nicole Marie Guidotti-Hernández, *Unspeakable Violence: Remapping U.S. and Mexican National Imaginaries*, Latin America Otherwise: Languages, Empires, Nations (Durham, N.C.: Duke University Press, 2011); Laura Pulido, "Geographies of Race and Ethnicity III: Settler Colonialism and Nonnative People of Color," *PROGRESS IN HUMAN GEOGRAPHY* 42, no. 2 (April 2018): 309–18; *https://doi.org/10.1177/0309132516686011*.

7. Roderick A. Ferguson, *Aberrations in Black: Toward a Queer of Color Critique* (Minneapolis: University of Minnesota Press, 2004).

8. Siobhan B. Somerville, *Queering the Color Line: Race and the Invention of Homosexuality in American Culture* (Durham, N.C.: Duke University Press, 2000); Cathy J. Cohen, "Punks, Bulldaggers, and Welfare Queens: The Radical Potential of Queer Politics?," in *Black Queer Studies: A Critical Anthology*, ed. E. Patrick Johnson, Mae G. Henderson, and Sharon P. Holland, 21–51 (Durham, N.C.: Duke University Press, 2005); Ferguson, *Aberrations in Black*.

9. Martin F. Manalansan IV, *Global Divas: Filipino Gay Men in the Diaspora* (Durham, N.C.: Duke University Press, 2003).

10. Martin Joseph Ponce, *Beyond the Nation: Diasporic Filipino Literature and Queer Reading* (New York: New York University Press, 2012).

TWENTY-SIX

Hypervisible (In)visibility: Black Amerasians

Angelica J. Allen

As both a member of the Black Filipinx Amerasian[1] community (a population born from the union of African American military men and Filipina
women) and a scholar who studies that group from the disciplinary perspective of Black studies, I often wonder how the field of Filipinx American
studies could better recognize the relevance of Blackness as a constituent
element.[2] The underrepresentation of Filipinxs of African descent crystal-
izes such conflicts over Filipinx American identity, which is not altogether
new. This oversight is reflected in the paradoxical realities of their lived
experiences: despite their hypervisible presence in the Philippines, Black
Amerasians remain curiously excluded in discourses pertaining to the Filipinx American experience.[3] Analysis of this invisibility calls attention to the
vexed and ambivalent status of Blackness in our field. In light of the unfolding aftermath of the historical legacies wrought by American colonialism
and the global relevance of the Black Lives Matter movement, there is an
urgent need to attend more closely to the consequences of racialization in

the lives of individuals whose identities are inextricably tied to the Philippines' neocolonial relationship to the United States.

In this essay, I foreground the experiences of Black Amerasians in the Philippines. Drawing upon interviews from a larger ethnographic study, I explore how analysis of this community's lived experiences unsettles singular conceptualizations of Filipinx American identity and reveals the transnational dimensions of anti-Blackness. Through this analysis, we can begin to explore the possibilities for cross-disciplinary dialogue between Black studies—namely, the indispensable insights of Black feminist theory—and Filipinx American studies, forging new political alliances as we consider timely issues that are relevant to both fields. I begin with a brief account of Filipinx Amerasian history, followed by an analysis of some contemporary Black Amerasians' experiences focused on a core element of this community's identity: "Hypervisible (In)visibility: The Skin Color Paradox."

Background

It has been estimated that the number of Filipinx Amerasians—the children born from the union of American military men and Filipina women—living in the Philippines today ranges from 50,000 to 250,000+, including first, second, and third generations.[4] Yet despite their membership in one of the oldest and largest Amerasian diasporas, Filipinx Amerasians remain one of the most unrecognized and underresearched communities to arise from the Philippines' neocolonial relationship to the United States.

This community's invisibility in both the Philippines and US nation-states has had significant repercussions. One example is their exclusion from the 1982 Amerasian Immigration Act and the subsequent 1987 Amerasian Homecoming Act, which provided preferential status to Amerasians living in various parts of Asia. The law excluded children born in the Philippines and provided no actual explanation for their omission.[5] Some speculate that this exclusion stems from the widespread assumption that mixed-race Filipinxs are easily accepted in Philippine society.[6] While this assumption may hold true for white Amerasians, who are relatively privileged and praised for their lighter skin, it creates challenges for Black Amerasians, who are subjected to anti-Black racism. The following analysis introduces some examples of this discrimination as described by Black Amerasians.

Hypervisible (In)visibility: The Skin Color Paradox

Black Amerasian identity is largely shaped by otherness in relation to Filipinxs and non-Black Amerasian groups in the Philippines. Previous studies across numerous regions in Asia demonstrate that Black Amerasians experience more pronounced forms of marginalization than white Amerasians.[7] This disparity illustrates the transnational scope of anti-Blackness, which operates according to similar logic across various geographical sites. The following interview excerpts highlight such experiences of otherness, which are a defining characteristic of Black Amerasian identity:

> All eyes on me Angelica! All eyes on me! There's no freedom. You get blamed for everything! Everyone will point you out . . . there's no freedom. It's almost as if this color [points to skin] is a tattoo. I don't really need to get a tattoo because this is a marker!

In this interview, my informant, Larry, a Black Amerasian from Pampanga, describes his skin color as a visual indicator of his racial otherness in Philippine society, from which there is no escape. Black Amerasians like Larry are often painfully reminded of this hypervisibility through pejorative remarks about their skin color and phenotypic differences from the mainstream Filipinx community.

Like most Black Amerasians that I interviewed, Larry first began to realize his difference in racialized spaces such as schools. Growing up, he was often bullied and called derogatory names such as *Baluga* (dark-skinned Indigenous Filipinx) and *nog-nog* (a vulgar reference to dark skin color that carries the same connotation as the N-word in the United States). "They used to call me Baluga" says Marvin, a Black Amerasian activist, of his childhood in the 1990s. "Back in the day when I was going to school, they would call you the devil if you were Black." This name-calling in schools was one of the most widely shared experiences among Black Amerasians who spoke with me. Many recounted stories of being taunted, which often resulted in school fights (for those who fought back) and subsequent punishment, including removal from school. Black Amerasians are often subjected to severe penalties as teachers and administrators perceive their childhood antics as acts of violence and aggression. In one instance, Marvin recalls being forced out of school at an early age: "I befriended the Principal and I used to come into her office a lot. But because I often went to school hungry, I ate the Principal's lunch. The teachers had me arrested and placed in jail. . . . That's why I stopped going to school because I was only in the third grade at that time so I was forced to stop. I was there [in an adult jail] for one year."

As adults, many Black Amerasian men in my study recounted negative encounters with law enforcement officials, and some had a history of incarceration. Such outcomes are a part of the injurious process of racialization on identity formation for Black Amerasians, who are often perceived as being prone to criminality. Centuries-old notions that equate Blackness with criminality, and the "adultification" of Black Amerasian children who are penalized as adults in cases like Marvin's, serve as a timely reminder of the global scope of anti-Blackness. In the wake of Philippine president Rodrigo Roa Duterte's deadly drug war policy,[8] the global Black Lives Matter movement has taken on particular urgency in the Philippines, as Black Amerasians may be disproportionately susceptible to police and vigilante killings of suspected drug dealers and addicts.

Almost every Black Amerasian I interviewed described the anti-Black racism that they experience, in contrast to their white Amerasian counterparts. Chris, a Black Amerasian from Olongapo, described the contrast as follows:

> If you're white, it's much easier to be accepted by the community, it's not hard for them to accept you. They believe in you and they look up to you like you're the lord. . . . People here in the Philippines think you're handsome . . . but when you're Black, it's much harder. You deal with more struggle. People treat you like, "yuck!" They'll say you can't be around them or they might catch a disease.

The racialization of Black Amerasians as outsiders in the Philippines highlights the enduring legacies of imported American racialist ideologies that shape ideas of belonging and difference. As Asian Americanist Yến Lê Espiritu argues,

> The history of US imperialism in the Philippines continues to take a toll on the lives of millions of Filipinos scattered around the world—long after US

troops and bureaucrats are gone. Although imperialism is most often treated as a matter of economics and diplomacy, it has an embodied presence in the lives of people from colonized nations.[9]

The testimonies of Black Amerasians demonstrate not only this enduring "embodied presence" of imperialism, but also the legacy of anti-Black racism.

Some recent scholarship has disrupted singular notions of Filipinx American identity and addressed the multidimensionality of lived experience among "mixed-race" Filipinxs. Rudy P. Guevarra Jr., Joanne L. Rondilla,[10] and others have called for greater scholarly attention to the experiences of lesser-known Filipinx American communities in the United States. In his study of Mexican Filipinxs in California, Guevarra Jr. states that "ours is a story that has existed for several hundred years . . . but no one has fully explored this history."[11] The Black Amerasian story is similarly far-reaching and understudied, and it remains relevant in a moment when the 2014 Enhanced Defense Cooperation Agreement (EDCA) signaling for US forces to return to the Philippines has been implemented. The lived experiences of Black Amerasians urge us to expand Filipinx American studies beyond the confines of the United States and to attend to Filipinx American communities who remain in the Philippines.

In closing, I want to suggest the possibility for greater interconnections between the two seemingly distinct fields of Black studies and Filipinx American studies. A critical consideration of the experiences of Black Amerasians not only complicates monolithic understandings of Blackness and Filipinx identity as discrete formations, but also urges Filipinx American studies to make space for a deeper engagement with Black studies. We have much to gain from this cross-disciplinary dialogue, including the indispensable insights of Black feminists who emphasize intersectionality, inclusivity politics, and the importance of coalition-building across race, gender, sexual orientation, and class. Through this dialogue, we can cultivate solidarity across disciplinary fields; such solidarity is politically urgent as America is yet again forced to grapple with the insidious legacy of anti-Black racism in the midst of a global pandemic. In light of the senseless state-sanctioned violence that resulted in the killings of Breonna Taylor, Atatiana Jefferson, Tony McDade, Michael Ramos, George Floyd, and Rayshard Brooks, among others, it is imperative that we recognize the relevance of the Black Lives

Matter movement and its continuing legacy for African descendants living in the Philippines. The experiences of Black Amerasians in the Philippines today serve as a timely reminder of the global life and death stakes of anti-Black racism.

NOTES

1. The term "Amerasian," originally coined by author and activist Pearl S. Buck, refers to children of Asian women and American soldiers who were stationed at military bases throughout Asia. In the Philippines, Amerasian is a contemporary term. Filipino Amerasians have also previously referred to themselves as Filipino Americans or the shortened "Fil-Am."

2. In recent years, Filipino Americanists including Nerissa S. Balce (2006; 2016), Cynthia Marasigan (2010), and Dylan Rodríguez (2010), among others, have also highlighted the relevance of Blackness to the Filipinx American condition.

3. For example, Black Amerasians are not discussed in edited volumes such as Maria P. P. Root's *Filipino Americans: Transformation and Identity* (Thousand Oaks, Calif.: Sage, 1997) or Yến Lê Espiritu's *Filipino American Lives* (Philadelphia: Temple University Press, 1995), among others.

4. P. C. Kutschera and M. A. Caputi, "The case for categorization of military Filipino Amerasians as diaspora" (unpublished manuscript, October 2012). Retrieved from *Amerasianresearch.org*.

5. One possible explanation is the concern that the Acts may inadvertently attract a larger influx of Amerasians than originally intended; see Joseph Ahern, "Out of Sight, Out of Mind: United States Immigration Law and Policy as Applied to Filipino Amerasians," *Pacific Rim Law and Policy Association* 1, no. 1 (1992): 105–26.

6. Kevin Johnson, *Mixed Race America and the Law* (New York: New York University Press, 2003), 416–17.

7. Steven DeBonis, *Children of the Enemy: Oral Histories of Vietnamese Amerasians and Their Mothers* (Jefferson, N.C.: McFarland, 1995); Kun Jong Lee, "The Black Amerasian Experience in Korea: Representations of Black Amerasians in Korean and Korean American Narratives," *Korea Journal* 55, no. 1 (Spring 2015): 7–30; Bernard Scott Luscious, "In the Black Pacific: Testimonies of Afro-Amerasian Displacements," in *Displacements and Diasporas: Asians in the Americas*, ed. Wanni W. Anderson and Robert G. Lee (New Brunswick, N.J.: Rutgers University Press, 2005), 122–55; R. S. McKelvey, *The Dust of Life: America's Children Abandoned in Vietnam* (Seattle: University of Washington Press, 1999); Margo Okazawa-Rey, "Amerasian Children of GI Town: A Legacy of U.S. Militarism in South Korea," *Asian Journal of*

Women's Studies 3, no. 1 (1997): 71–102; Teresa Kay Williams and Michael C. Thornton, "Social Construction of Ethnicity Versus Personal Experience: The Case of Afro-Amerasians," *Journal of Comparative Family Studies* 29, no. 2 (1998): 255–67; Trin Yarborough, *Surviving Twice: Amerasian Children of the Vietnam War* (Washington, DC: Potomac, 2005).

8. Here, I refer to Duterte's "War against Drugs" policy, which orders the execution of suspected drug users and drug dealers across the country.

9. Espiritu, *Filipino American Lives*, 48.

10. Joanne L. Rondilla, Rudy P. Guevarra, and Paul Spickard's edited volume *Red and Yellow, Black and Brown: Decentering Whiteness in Mixed Race Studies* (New Brunswick, N.J.: Rutgers University Press, 2017) includes chapters on mixed-heritage Filipino Americans.

11. Rudy Guevarra Jr., *Becoming Mexipino: Multiethnic Identities and Communities in San Diego* (New Brunswick, N.J.: Rutgers University Press, 2012), 4.

TWENTY-SEVEN

Why I Don't (Really) Consider Myself a Filipinx: Complicating "Filipinxness" from a *Katutubo* Intervention

J. A. Ruanto-Ramirez

In May 2020, PBS aired a five-part documentary titled *Asian Americans*, highlighting the pivotal moments in Asian diasporic experiences in the United States. The series began with the stories of Igorot[1] American, Manang[2] Mia Abeya (Bontok[3]), the granddaughter of Antero Cabrera, one of the Igorots who were part of the Philippine Exposition in the 1904 St. Louis World's Fair.[4] Describing it as an American colonial project of the Philippines, the narrator describes how "Filipinos" were subjects in a human zoo project that created racial hierarchies between (white) Americans and (darker) people from the Philippines.[5] Yet throughout the interview, Manang Mia never stated she was Filipina[6] and instead insisted on her identity as an Igorot and on framing Cabrera's experience as an Igorot experience. It was the narrator who insisted on the term "Filipino," but Manang Mia navigated the issue of national identity very carefully, stating in a Facebook post on the evening of May 11, 2020, "I wanted people to know that through [it] all, we came out intact and still proud of our Igorot heritage."[7] This surprising and celebratory moment for the Igorot American community did not, however, come without frustration. These frustrations came from the Igorot American community seeing Filipinx Americans' online posts about the histories of Filipinos in the World's Fair that decentralized the unique experiences of Igorots and other Indigenous Peoples (IPs) in favor of a pan-ethnic, pannationalist "Filipino experience." Filipinx Americans began to also use black and white photographs of Aetas[8] and Igorots to address "colonial mentality" and anti-Blackness within the Filipinx American community, not being cognizant that many of those images shared have surviving relatives both in the Philippines and in diaspora. For many IPs, especially Igorot Americans, the anger hit home, especially when they would see images of their family members used in the context of anti-Blackness and anti-Indigenousness. At a time when the 2020 pandemic escalated online visibility of marginalized communities and demands for racial justice, Igorots and other IPs from the Philippines in diaspora began to mobilize online—demanding a different narrative about IPs in diaspora and how we, IPs, complicate Filipinx American identity and history. As a different approach to this essay on Filipinx identity and the complications of self-determined identity markers, I raise the question on the positionality of IPs in diaspora within Philippine-America. As an IP of Aeta, Igorot, Moro, and of other ethnolinguistic minorities, how does indigeneity complicate and critique Filipinx identity—something often seen as a nationalist and homogenous identity subscribed to while in diaspora? This essay brings into conversation these complicated nuances that have been put into the periphery of Filipinx American studies, often suspending IPs in a perpetual state of immobility and atemporality? What does a potential *Katutubo* analytic look like in the field of Filipinx studies? I raise these questions in the hope of addressing the pressing question that many of us IPs face and reflect on while in diaspora—how did we become something in diaspora that we were never seen as in the Philippines? I hope to expand on Maile Arvin's work that looks at the analytics of indigeneity and how the study of Indigenous Peoples in diaspora can propose an imagined space that further complicates the notion of "ethnicity" from an IP perspective.[9]

This essay seeks to address these particular relationships between the general Filipinx American community and IPs, thinking in particular about the relationships with the colonial power, the United States, and the creation of a new racial project that was a continuation of previous colonial projects established during Spanish colonial rule.[10] Framing a *Katutubo* epistemology through the framework of Indigeneity allows for important interventions within both Asian American and Indigenous studies. I use the term *Katutubo* not only as an identity marker, but also as both an articulation and an analytic to complicate the ethnonationalist term "Filipino." While *Katutubo* is a Filipino term meaning "Indigenous," based on the Tagalog language, it is not an identity subscribed to by many IPs in the Philippines and in diaspora. In fact, many IPs prefer to be either identified by their particular community or through umbrella terms such as Igorot or Moro.[11] In the Philippines, *Katutubo* (emphasis on the capital K) has been used to describe Indigenous Peoples protected by the Philippine constitution as ethnically and culturally different from "mainstream" Filipinx community and culture.[12] In English, *Katutubo* is synonymous with Indigenous Peoples and in the Philippines, being considered an IP is not only a cultural designation, but also a political identity. For us, Indigenous Peoples both in the Philippines and in diaspora, adopting and adapting to an identity such as "Filipina/o/x" can result in violence and degradation, often having to explain our tribal affinity to Filipina/o/x Americans who have to relate their personal narratives to our identities ("I volunteered at the Cordis before and fell in love with the IPs there") or be in shock that our existence in the modern diaspora is engaging with them ("I'm so glad that the Igorots and Moros are much more civilized now than before").[13] This verbal violence is not, however, relegated to factors of shock and awe at being in front of an IP, but is also a key identifier for Filipinxs in America to assert their "Filipinoness," and this "Filipinoness" does not mean they are equated to being an IP. I look for scholarly affirmation within Filipinx American studies to make this claim and have found it in the epigraph for Chapter 1 of Rick Bonus's *Locating Filipino Americans.* In the beginning of the chapter, Bonus interviews a Filipinx lady who asserts that the term *etnik* is in reference to Philippines' cultural and ethnic other, and that these others are not representative of the Philippines or of the Filipinx community.[14] For the Filipinx woman, being *etnik* means one is an IP and thus cannot be truly a Filipinx. This interaction became a poignant intellectual experience for me as it confirmed how many Filipinx see us IPs in relation to the nation-state and in the Filipinx communities in diaspora. Bonus has argued that for many immigrant communities in the United States, ethnic nationalism has been utilized to create a panethnic identity while in diaspora, but it also brings complications to different groups who are further marginalized within the nation-state of origin. As such, for many Filipinx Americans, "Filipino" means anyone who is from the Philippines regardless of their ethnic and racial identity or categorization.[15] Bonus does acknowledge that in many circumstances, ethnic and racial minorities of the Philippines—both in the Philippines and in diaspora—do not necessarily subscribe to the national identity. For Filipinxs in the Philippines, to be *etnic* means to be seen as premodern or aboriginal and is a marker for Filipinxs to distance themselves from. This feeling of cultural distancing from *etnic* also translates in diaspora were markers of civilization and modernity means a distancing from those who are seen as premodern, precolonial, and "not really Filipino."[16] This analysis of Bonus's interview resonates with how many IPs in diaspora have seen themselves, as well as how they have been seen by other Filipinxs, as "not really Filipino"— as a cultural other that is part of the nation-state, but also completely different from those who would be considered "Filipino." While many scholars and activists would argue that IPs are racialized as Filipinxs in the United States, I argue for consideration of Gayatri Chakravorty Spivak's *strategic essentialism* to address how marginalized communities demand political and cultural self-representation within a larger identity framework—a tactic that can be used to achieve a particular goal such as representation, equal rights, and a particular world view.[17] The demand for an Indigenous epistemology and a critical approach to being Filipinx fits the thematic frameworks of how Filipin"x" is also a critique of Filipin"o" that allows for other forms of intervention in the identity. While many within the IP community in diaspora have distanced themselves from wanting to be seen as an other within the Filipino and Filipinx American community, this framework allows for IP voices to be "essential" in addressing the cultural and ethnic diversity within both the Filipino and Filipinx American community that often demanded a homogeneous and heterogeneous national identity.[18]

I argue that being *Katutubo* is the problem that needs to be introduced in Filipinx American studies and that the diasporic nationalist identity should be complicated by those who, in the Philippines, have been seen as a cultural and political other. Most often, Indigenous and ethnic minorities have been clumped into the national identity when in diaspora, creating an estranged relationship between those who claim the national identity, usually those from the majority ethnic group, and those who are seen as a minority.[19] While scholars like Rick Bonus, Yến Lê Espiritu, and Lisa Lowe have argued that immigrant communities let go of the ethnic and regional identities and adapt to and adopt the national identity,[20] for diasporic IPs, it is the tribal and ethnic affiliation that brings them together outside of the Philippines and often leads them to separate themselves from "Filipinx America" as an "internal ethnicity."[21] Take, for example, the various ethnic and tribal community organizations found in the United States. Unlike township-based organizations like Subic Bay Association and Angeles City Association, indigenous and cultural minority communities are based on tribal lines like Ifugao Association of Southern California, Kalinga Association of North America (KANA), Maranao Association, and Zambales Associations of Southern California, or ethnoracial lines like Igorot International and Moro Americans of North America. For many IPs in the United States, it is the connection with other Indigenous communities from the same region that binds their identity and not necessarily just the national identity. Mark S. Leo addresses that for many Igorot Americans, the importance of stating multiple identity markers is what creates the connection among tribal communities, especially as a Kankana-ey Igorot Filipinx American.[22] These multiple identity markers not only identify the particular tribe one belongs to, but also the ethnoracialized communal identity that is accepted by the tribes. He is not only from the Kankana-ey, but he is also an Igorot within Filipinx American identity. While Leo does put "Filipino American" in his announcement of his identity, he stresses the lack of importance it actually has and focuses on his Benguet identity as a Kankana-ey Igorot American.[23] Similarly, for many Moro Americans, faith is their first identity marker as Muslim Americans, then their tribal affinity. Maranao American activist Albert Tampi, from Los Angeles, California, stresses the importance of being Muslim first and then his tribal affiliation, often denying being considered "Filipino American" in his introduction as a "Muslim Maranao Moro American." For many Moro individuals both in the Philippines and in diaspora, professing "Filipino" as an identity comes with the cultural and political baggage that denies their unique identities, their sociocultural difference from the rest of the predominantly Christian Filipinx identity, and their geopolitical histories of resisting colonization.

For IPs in the United States, to articulate their indigeneity and their In-digenous classifications both from the Philippines and in diaspora allows for a critical lens to see the national (identity) and "the other" as linked, yet separated; connected, yet not the same.[24] As an articulation, *Katutubo* can be seen not just as a category created, determined, and maintained by rac-ism and (neo)colonialism, but also by the "knowledge and praxis of indige-nous peoples" of and from the Philippines.[25] This analytical approach to critiquing a pannational Filipinx American identity can be seen as both an-ticolonial and decolonial, demanding a new way to imagine what it means to be Indigenous, diasporic, and a racialized other within the Filipinx Amer-ican community.[26] Here, I propose that *Katutubo*, as both an identity marker for Indigenous Peoples from the Philippines while in diaspora and as a critique of a pannationalist identity turned ethnic classification, be the analytical response to the growing diaspora of peoples from the Philippines. It allows Indigenous Peoples to maintain their cultural and ethnic identity without being homogenized to an identity that has often been rendered vi-olent and dismissive of their communities. While *Katutubo* can be further problematized as it, too, is a homogenizing concept, this proposal allows IPs to begin imagining how to insert their identities and their narratives within a pannational diasporic identity called "Filipinx." Similar to the call for a critical response to the term "Indigenous" by Maile Arvin, *Katutubo* should also be seen as an analytic that allows the complication to occur both with the national(ist) identity and, similar to how Indigenous Peoples from the United States use "Native American" as a cultural marker, with the politi-cal identity, and as a counter narrative, while still understanding that indi-vidual communities have different relationships and struggles with the nation-state.[27]

Looking at a *Katutubo* intervention in Filipinx studies will also allow for a conversation on the modern nation-state and its role in maintaining the racial structures that have regulated IPs into the periphery of na-tional discourse and histories—often becoming what Onna Paredes de-scribes, as "relics" of a precolonial imagined past.[28] Similarly, critiques of both American-based and Philippine-based ethnography that regulates IPs as representatives of an imagined precolonial cultural tradition often does not allow for IPs to navigate the time and spaces of the contemporary Phil-ippines and US.[29] For many IPs, especially Igorot and Moro individuals in diaspora, the reliquaries that hold our diverse cultural identities in Filipinx American studies often become mere references of American colonial vestiges as well as footnotes of Philippine ethnic diversity. A demand for a *Katutubo* analytical approach in Filipinx studies allows for the continuation of problematizing presumed normative frameworks, but also allows for a speculative future that may actually include IPs in both nationalist and diasporic fields of studies. It will also allow for future intervention that is community-specific within Filipino and Filipinx American studies such as Igorot American and Moro American studies, focusing on particular IP and ethnic communities that will diversify the Filipinx diasporic experiences and narratives. Allowing for this intervention and critique will allow for IPs to center their indigenous identities that have been marginalized within the Filipinx community. Through this intervention, IPs are able to disidentify as a means of cultural survival and make a political statement while in diaspora, allowing IPs to critique their positionality within the modern "post"colonial Philippine nation-state, critique the colonial racial structures that were imposed by both the Spaniards and the Americans, and allow for a critique of an academic field that has often placed IPs, us, in the periphery. As Kirin Amiling Macapugay (Bontok and Kalinga Igorot American) stated in a speech in 2012, "every Igorot is a Filipino, but not every Filipino is an Igorot."

NOTES

1. The term Igorot is used to describe the various ethnolinguistic, Indigenous tribes of the Cordillera Mountain Range, now part of the Cordillera Administrative Region, Northern Luzon. The provinces of CAR are Abra (home of the Itneg tribe), Apayao (home of the Isnag tribe) Benguet (home of the Kankana-ey and Ibaloi tribes), Ifugao (home of the Ifugao tribe), Kalinga (home of the Gaddang and Kalinga tribes), and Mountain Province (home of the Bontok and Gaddang tribes). See William Henry Scott, *On the Cordillera: A Look at the Peoples and Cultures of the Mountain Province* (Manila: MCS Enterprise, Inc., 1969).

2. *Manang* is the Ilokano term for older female sibling or aunt that can describe an older sister, an aunty, a close female family friend, or a random female individual. It has been used as an honorific title for both Ilokano and Igorots. The region's ethnolinguistic diversity complicates inter-Igorot connections, and thus Ilocano has been regionally accepted as the language of

use even though it is not a federally recognized people. The majority of Igorots, and of Igorots in diaspora, speak Ilokano (Filipino-Ilocano), in part, as it was designated the lingua franca of the Cordillera Region. I use this honorific title to describe Mia Abeya as customary in Igorot culture.

3. The Bontok people (Filipino: Bontoc), classified as a tribe, are part of the overall Igorot community and were designated by their own province, also called Bontoc, during United States colonial rule. The name was changed in the 1987 Constitutional Assembly to Mountain Province.

4. For more on the World's Fair and the colonial images, see Mark Rice, *Dean Worcester's Fantasy Islands: Photography, Film, and the Colonial Philippines* (Ann Arbor: The University of Michigan Press, 2014).

5. I use "Filipino" with an "F" rather than how the diaspora use a "P" to adhere to the change in the Philippine Constitution in 1991. I will also be using "Filipino" to describe those in the Philippines and "Filipinx" to describe those in diaspora, specifically those in the United States. "Filipinx," with an "x," is to adhere to the contemporary usage of degendering the nationalist identity that is centered around the masculine form of Philippine peoples. The "x" is more often used in diaspora and never in the Philippines.

6. The feminine form of "Filipino." Current Twitter debates surround the gender-neutrality of Filipino as a language, with many arguing that the term "Filipina" was constructed in diaspora.

7. Facebook response of Mia Abeya on Kirin Amiling Macapugay's post about the documentary. Macapugay is related to Abeya on her father's side as a Bontok Igorot.

8. Aeta are considered the "aboriginal peoples of the Philippines" who were named Negritos during Spanish and American colonial periods. The term Aeta has been used by many tribes as a unifying ethnoracial category for all aboriginal peoples throughout the archipelago.

9. Maile Arvin, "Analytics of Indigeneity," in *Native Studies Keywords*, ed. Stephanie Nohelani Tevas, Andrea Smith, and Michelle H. Raheja (Tucson: University of Arizona Press, 2015), 119–29.

10. An example of minoritized communities within a postcolonial nation-state demanding Indigenous recognition can be found in Emilio del Valle Escalante, *Maya Nationalism and Postcolonial Challenges in Guatemala: Coloniality, Modernity, and Identity Politics* (Santa Fe, N.M.: School of Advanced Research Press, 2009).

11. The term Moro is used to describe the thirteen ethnolinguistic, Indigenous communities that practice Islam in Mindanao, Sulu, and Palawan. For Philippine history through a Moro lens, see Cesar Adib Majul, *Muslims in the Philippines* (Quezon City: University of the Philippines Press, 1999).

12. *Katutubo* is a general term used along with Indigenous Peoples (IPs) and Indigenous Cultural Communities (ICCs) to describe the various ethnic, tribal, and cultural minorities of the Philippines protected by the Philippines Indigenous Peoples' Rights Act of 1997 and the Offices for Northern and Southern Cultural Communities (ONCC/OSCC). An uncapitalized *katutubo* means "Indigenous" or "Native" in both Filipino and Tagalog languages. For how "Indigenous" Peoples are constructed under law as deserving recognition when suspended to primitivism and spatio-temporal stagnation, see Elizabeth Povinelli, *The Cunning of Recognition* (Durham, N.C.: Duke University Press, 2002).

13. The first quote is from a leftist activist who confronted me at the Association for Asian American Studies 2017 in San Francisco after presenting on Katutubo American identities; the second quote is from a faculty of San Diego State University after asking my friend Mark S. Leo and me to present about Igorot American identity in her Filipino American Experience class in 2017.

14. Rick Bonus, *Locating Filipino Americans: Ethnicity and the Cultural Politics of Space* (Philadelphia: Temple University Press, 2000), 3–6.

15. Bonus, *Locating Filipino Americans*, 27.

16. Bonus, *Locating Filipino Americans*, 15–17.

17. Gayatri Chakravorty Spivak, *Other Asias* (Malden: Blackwell Publishing, 2008).

18. Jonathan X. H. Lee and Mark S. Leo, "Performing Thai and Indigenous Igorot American Folklore and Identities: Ethnic and Cultural Politics Revealed" *Jati* 18 (December 2013): 191–95.

19. Lee and Leo, "Performing Thai and Indigenous Igorot American Folklore and Identities," 186.

20. See Bonus, *Locating Filipino Americans*; Yến Lê Espiritu, *Home Bound: Filipino American Lives across Cultures, Communities, and Countries* (Berkeley: University of California Press, 2003); and Lisa Lowe, *Immigrant Acts: On Asian American Cultural Politics* (Durham, N.C.: Duke University Press, 1996).

21. "Internal ethnicity" arises from the "existence, formation, or emergence of at least one subgroup within a nationality, along the lines of one or more indicators of ethnicity (e.g., language, regional origin, or religion)." Mehdi Bozorgmehr, "Internal Ethnicity: Iranians in Los Angeles," *Sociological Perspectives* 40, no. 3 (1997): 399.

22. Lee and Leo, "Performing Thai and Indigenous Igorot American Folklore and Identities," 197.

23. Mark Sabas Leo and Jonathan H. X. Lee. "Igorot American Folk Dance: Performance, Identity, and the Paradox of Decolonization," in *Asian American Identities and Practices: Folkloric Expressions in Everyday Life*, ed.

Jonathan H. X. Lee and Kathleen M. Nadeau (Lanham, Mass.: Lexington Books, 2014), 155–60.

24. Stuart Hall. "Race, Articulation and Societies Structured in Dominance," in *Sociological Theories: Race and Colonialism*, ed. Marion Patrick Jones (Paris: UNESCO, 1980), 325.

25. Arvin, "Analytics of Indigeneity," 121.

26. Audra Simpson, "To the Reserve and Back Again: Kahnawake Mohawk Narratives of Self, Home and Nation" (PhD diss., McGill University, 2003), 54.

27. Arvin, "Analytics of Indigeneity."

28. Oona Paredes, *A Mountain of Difference: The Lumad in Early Colonial Mindanao* (Ithaca, N.Y.: Cornell Southeast Asian Program Publication, 2013), 35.

29. Ioan Lewis, *Arguments with Ethnography: Comparative Approaches to History, Politics, and Religion* (New York: Continuum Intl Pub Group, 2004), 12.

TWENTY-EIGHT

Repertoires on Other Stages

Theodore S. Gonzalves

The Filipinx American subject has always been, and continues to be, profoundly conjunctural. Neither exclusively an ethnic minority in the United States nor wholly a diasporic figure scattered across the globe, the Filipinx American is both mobile and moored. Mobile in the way that Jesse Quinsaat wrote about US military personnel who join the Navy and somehow still don't "see the world." Moored in the way that Filipina visual artist and curator N. Trisha Lagaso imagines persons wearing Hawaiʻi heirloom bracelets with the word "stuck" engraved on the bands instead of the traditional Hawaiian term for sweetheart or lover. As the authors in this anthology demonstrate, scholars of Filipinx American studies attend to the conjunctural by accounting for life chances and choices—analyzing how the subject has been constituted by violence, edict, creed, and greed while persons and groups express agency wherever and whenever possible. In my own work, I have studied performance repertoires in order to create genealogies of Filipinx subjecthood emerging at various points in time to respond to contemporaneous crises. We perform what we've performed because the world needed to be addressed in those specific ways. There is nothing essential, natural, timeless, or ahistorical about repertoires. In this essay, I invite you to consider the concept of repertoire beyond the commonly understood context of the performance stage. As a heuristic, how can repertoire help us grapple with the Filipinx American subject?[1]

Imagine yourself at the center of either of the following scenarios.

Scenario #1. You are a community organizer. A coalition of labor unions has voted to approve a strike for higher wages and better working conditions. Coordinators of the coalition look to you in order to organize a protest march. The day's events require you to liaise between union leaders of teachers and administrative staff, the local police, and the media. The day's events start with a press conference where the strike is announced. This is followed by a march of what your coalition expects will be about two thousand persons on public roads in the central business district. The events culminate in a rally during the middle of the work week on the steps of City Hall with a dozen speakers, a drum circle, stilt-walkers, and a crew holding large puppets aloft.

Scenario #2. You are an adjunct lecturer. The chair of the Department of Woke Studies at Neoliberal State Polytechnic University informs you that a faculty member in the unit has broken their leg while hiking in Yosemite during the break between semesters. The chair wants to know if you are able to teach three different courses—one lower-division course that fulfills the campus's general education requirement, one upper-division elective, and one graduate-level seminar offered to all first-year cohort members in the department's doctoral program. Your teaching experience thus far consists of TA'ing several large sections; you have never been an instructor of record. The semester starts in one week.

Both scenarios require different kinds of training, preparation, and skill sets. Your ability to respond to either of these scenarios will be greatly informed by your engagement with the concept of *repertoire*. In order to accomplish what is needed—that is, in order to meet a measure of success for either scenario—you'll need to come to grips quickly with what is in your storehouse of knowledges, skills, and abilities. Are you able to accomplish what is being asked of you? Neither scenario will permit you much time to make a decision, so ruminating about it or querying your favorite search engine will not be helpful. Are you up for either of these assignments?

More often than not, the concept of repertoire has resided within the domain of the performing arts. When you show up for an audition for that plum spot in the symphony, after having pulled out your cello from its case, the review panel will assume that you're familiar with Bach's legendary unaccompanied solos, Britten's suites dedicated to Rostropovich, and Hindemith's sonata for solo cello. If you're feeling lucky during the portion of the audition where you can perform your own selection, you might want to have a go at some of the shorter compositions in this repertoire like Pablo Casals's "Song of the Birds," Gaspar Cassadó's "Requiebros," or that wily "Spinning Song" by David Popper.

This works similarly for comedians, but with key differences. Being familiar with the repertoire of master comedians is a sign of one's seriousness about the craft. But no one is expecting you to perform that material. Rather, you're expected to build on the conventions of the form but with so-called original content. Consider the 2002 documentary, *Comedian*, that explores repertoire in the hands of a storied pro, Jerry Seinfeld, and a rookie comic, Orny Adams. The senior comic has decided to retire a long-standing show and has to build up a new hour's worth of material. While audiences are thrilled to see him work out new material, he stumbles at first, one joke at a time, and it's awkward. He pauses, seems testy, even spaced out. In fact, we see him struggle to put together what every young comic starts out with—a five-minute set. Even for a professional like Seinfeld, long acknowledged by other comedians to be a master of the form, what we're witnessing in the film is the crafting of repertoire. After he threw away that durable routine of many years, it was clear he had to rebuild his repertoire joke by joke, minute by minute.

In the above scenarios, the cellist and the comedian show up for work having mastered (or thrown away) their repertoires. It matters not a great deal that our cellist's repertoire has been interpreted for several centuries while a stand-up performing another's routines are anathema and would immediately mark them a pariah by fellow comics. The concept holds: To perform at a respectable station in either profession, they have to demonstrate mastery over specific actions, routines, or expressions.

Neither the musician or comic shows up for work at the symphony hall or the comedy club and says: "Thank goodness I've maintained mastery over my *archive!*" You probably wouldn't hear the lecturer or community activist whose examples opened this essay say the same thing either. Our community activist or lecturer in the aforementioned scenarios, especially those worth their salt, will be working directly from a repertoire of knowledge that has been practiced and tested over time. Command over one's repertoire is also about knowing which questions may be the most important ones to ask before taking on the assignment. *Have you coordinated with the local precinct commander about crowd movement? Do you know how many people expect to be arrested and when? Have they been sufficiently prepared and trained? Do your contacts in the press know where to find you before, during, and after the events have transpired? Has your organization designated someone to be the point of contact for the press and are they aware of specific messaging for this event? Who is teaching what courses in the next term? Can you obtain syllabi from former iterations of the courses you're assigning? Is there any way to negotiate down the number of preps that the chair is offering?* These are questions that issue forth from a well-developed repertoire. What matters most to the lecturer, activist, cellist, or comedian in our above examples is not how well their archives are preserved, but how responsive their repertoire is for the specific task at hand.

The two terms, archive and repertoire, are not mutually exclusive, but we can start with some heuristic generalizations. More than any other scholar, Diana Taylor has carefully analyzed the relationship between the two. Her analysis is indispensable. Archives tend to emphasize permanence, durability, and conservation, while repertoires foreground impermanence, flexibility, and experimentation: "'Archival' memory exists as documents, maps, literary texts, letters, archaeological remains, bones, videos, films, CDs, all those items supposedly resistant to change. Archive, from the Greek, etymologically refers to 'a public building,' 'a place where records are kept.'"[2]

On the other hand, the repertoire "enacts embodied memory: performances, gestures, orality, movement, dance, singing—in short, all those acts usually thought of as ephemeral, non-reproducible knowledge."[3] That's the hinge for a repertoire's efficacy: The embodiment of memory and the task of transferring knowledge that seem to have no physical documentation.

But let's be sure to keep in mind that I'm only contrasting these two terms in the abstract. Savvy archivists will have no problem pointing out that even the most bureaucratically hardened repositories witness change of all manner with respect to the formatting of documents, the proper nomenclature assigned to specialized categories, or the preferred storage and conservation methods of physical objects. As well, there are no shortages of examples where a performer's repertoire has become stale, predictable, or repetitive. Rather, the point is to think about these terms as constructs in order for us to consider the creative choices that often get taken for granted when we think of repertoires.

For Taylor, repertoires should be seen as complements for our understanding of archives. At the base of our thinking about repertoires is a consideration of not only what we know, but what we choose to do at any given time. To consider repertoires is to think *with* an agent about what she may choose to do—what she *may have* to do—in order to get the job done that night: please a crowd, rock the party, lament the passing of a beloved family member, rally tired protesters, or just keep the audience together before the emcee returns. The ability to sort through what's possible in a given situation is often precisely the thing that distinguishes a professional from an amateur. It's also the kind of quality that could separate you from landing the next gig. Just how extensive is that performer's repertoire to make that more likely than not?

We also can make the perfunctory observation that the concept of *archive* is ubiquitous, especially in the highly professionalized study of the humanities, while our understanding of *repertoire* remains largely tucked away in the margins. Perhaps that should change. These two constructs— repertoire and archive—do not enjoy equal footing in our scholarly practices. There is much more written about archives than repertoires. A search of peer-reviewed journal articles with the word "archive" as a keyword is telling. In one of the most popular databases, there are over 7,900 such entries in the field of literature alone. Second to that field is area and ethnic studies with 6,000 titles, and coming in a clear third, the social sciences with 4,100. When you modify the term to "archival," the same fields dominate: literature (3,400) and area/ethnic studies (3,500). When switching to the publication of monographs and edited volumes, the fields of history (7,800), social sciences (7,800), and area and ethnic studies (4,700) dominate. Which research areas make the least mention of "archive"? Early childhood education (1), Quaker studies (1), and eighteenth-century studies (2).

But what about the use of the notion of "repertoire"? It appears significantly less often in the same database of peer-reviewed journal articles: literature (2,700) and area and ethnic studies (2,300). The fields with the fewest mentions of the word are US Southern history (1), Asian philosophy (1), and Middle Eastern literature (2). As for book-length works, the top fields making use of repertoire as an analytic term are in the social sciences (5,400), history (4,000), and area/ethnic studies (3,000).

We simply can't get enough of these meditations on the archive. It appears in several titles in humanities-based scholarship, especially in Asian American cultural studies. Many of us have no doubt come down with *archive fever.* Jacques Derrida wrote about our condition: "There is no political power without *control of the archive*, if not memory. Effective democratization can always be measured by this essential criterion: the participation in and access to the archive, its constitution, and its interpretation. . . . [N]othing is *less* reliable, nothing is less clear today than the word, 'archive.'"[4]

It's completely understandable to see why we have placed a premium on this concept of the archive. For those of us who have hailed from aggrieved communities, access to and participation in an archive is all but lost. The archive is more than about documented or fixed information. Its root takes us to a physical storehouse—quite literally a public office—where we cannot be forgotten or hidden away. Absent from or distorted in this nation's official archives, we encourage ourselves to move boxes of dusty materials from our garages and out from under our beds to our local historical societies, community-based museums, edgy galleries, or to Web-based portals. For all the attention we pay to the critical work of creating and sustaining archives, my suggestion is that we can also deploy a more nuanced understanding of what it means to develop, execute, and analyze our various repertoires, for these too contain valuable information about what must not be forgotten or hidden away.

To tackle a repertoire is to get down to the tactical, specific, and largely, individuated level. It is more concerned with craft and not necessarily art. It is a function of, a hostage to, and an agent in the present moment. But let's step back from the individuated and the immediate. There is more to our repertoires than the currents directly in front of us. We can consider how repertoires develop over time, to discern arcs, patterns, or tendencies—to ask if there is more to the present-focused orientation of these actions, to ask how repertoires echo, anticipate, or even get built into habits, customs, or traditions. There are at least two ways we can move beyond this narrowly individuated notion of understanding repertoire.

The present-oriented nature of thinking through one's repertoire is undeniable. To attend to the honing of one's craft can mean not having the bandwidth for documentation. It's not uncommon for years to pass for the artist or athlete to realize that recording one's performances should have been a priority. They could try, but it would be in vain because, as Peggy Phelan sees it, "performance's being . . . becomes itself through disappearance." For Phelan, performance "cannot be saved, recorded, documented or otherwise participate in the circulation of representations."[5] That's a common understanding of performance—ephemeral and fleeting. Nothing remains; it all melts into air. Philippine and Filipinx American performers probably suspect something different about this process—that repertoires can carry information beyond an atomized moment. Two examples are instructive here—the first from our colleagues in the life sciences; the other from the writing practice of one of our own artists.

Sabina Leonelli and Rachel A. Ankeny hail from the interdisciplinary fields of life sciences and present a fascinating way to understand how short-term collaborative research projects can be sustained over time to inform and reform a discipline. Collaborators in their line of research often come together from disparate fields such as molecular biology, mathematics, or data modeling. Their conception of repertoire is understandably informed by the performing arts: "a stock of skills, behaviors, methods, materials, resources, and infrastructures that a group habitually uses to conduct research and train newcomers who want to join the group." That could refer to our cello player from the outset of this piece, but they're referring to systems biologists who tackle projects, which, in some cases, demonstrate a resilience that encourages the building of "larger, more enduring communities," ones that develop a repertoire—a "distinctive and shared ensemble of elements that make it practically possible for individuals to cooperate."

Consider how a small group of specialists are called to tackle a research project. They have disparate skills in various disciplines. Theirs is a time-based effort that depends on funding, equipment outlays, and the enlisting of support staff. Add in to their measures of success the possibility that follow-on support could branch off from their initial efforts. Their ability as a focused team to develop further iterations of the collaboration depends on their harnessing of a repertoire. Leonelli and Ankeny emphasize how repertoires sustain, persist, and generate collaborations—how repertoires in the life sciences "can serve as the basis for the establishment and ongoing productivity of a research community."[6] If the interdisciplinary life sciences can give us a window into how repertoires can track the production of knowledge over time, we can certainly find analogues in the artistic practices of our own writers.

How else may we envision repertoires beyond those present-centered orientations? For this example, let's turn to Gina Apostol's character in *Insurrecto*, Magsalin.[7] Italian American filmmaker Chiara comes to the Philippines to make a film about the US-Philippine War; she hires Magsalin to serve as an interpreter. Magsalin reads the filmmaker's script and has her own ideas about the same events. It's a wry tale about authorship and agency, especially centering on women. Push back from the immediate frame of Apostol's novel and we find that the name "Magsalin" has fascinating valences. Magsalin can refer to the act of copying or translating. So, we find the name amplifying the character's role. What many of the reviews of the novel leave out is Apostol's use of the name, Magsalin, as a kind of literary amulet that leads us back through Philippine literary histories. Consider that the full name of a main protagonist in José Rizal's 1887 novel, *Noli Me Tangere*, is Juan Crisostomo Ibarra y Magsalin. Rizal's own name had also been used as a password for secretive compatriots in the revolution against Spain. Whether in the hands of Rizal or Apostol, Magsalin signifies a polycultural subjectivity—characters who speak and interpret across cultures, nations, regions, and time. Apostol's use of Magsalin is a kind of global token that continues to unlock access to accomplices writing their own versions of their times.

The majority of the readers of this text will likely be other researchers and writers hoping to contribute to the production of knowledge in the area of Filipinx American studies. The best of those works, in my view, will have done serious thinking about the historiographical interventions that their works are making in the field. This is what separates the work of the academic researcher from other kinds of analysis. We throw ourselves into peer review in order to build upon or, in some cases, depart from, what has been written about any given subject. Without taking time to seriously engage the scholarly work that has gone before us, you might as well be blogging or writing opinion pieces on your way to becoming a *thought leader*. Let's get historiographic, shall we?

If you're teaching in this field, some of your students of Filipinx and Filipinx American repertoires may want to turn to the unique careers of individuals like musician June Millington or actor Sumi Haru. Millington and Haru have written fascinating memoirs that detail the personal costs to their craft as they demanded footholds in their respective industries.[8] At first blush, they'll want to take stock of the songs Millington wrote or the roles Haru took. Another step in the analysis could involve then stepping back to situate those expressive forms against the dynamic contexts of race, gender, sexuality, colorism, and power that freed or constrained their life chances and professional choices in attempting to hone their craft. The most deft of the students will turn to the scholarly literature to refine their thinking. In years past, that has usually meant starting with foundational texts like Robert G. Lee's *Orientals* or Josephine Lee's *Performing Asian America*, Dorinne Kondo's *About Face*, or Karen Shimakawa's *National Abjection*.[9] A generation of work has grown up in the wake of those valuable studies and these days, scholars are just as likely to turn to the growing literature in our field that tackles an eclectic range of Filipinx/American repertoires like Sarita Echavez See's *The Decolonizing Eye*, Theodore S. Gonzalves's *The Day the Dancers Stayed*, Lucy Mae San Pablo Burns's *Puro Arte*, Antonio T. Tiongson Jr.'s *Filipinos Represent*, Oliver Wang's *Legions of Boom*, Neferti Xina M. Tadiar's *Fantasy-Production*, José B. Capino's *Dream Factories*, Nerissa S. Balce's *Body Parts of Empire*, or Celine Parreñas Shimizu's *Hypersexuality of Race*.[10]

In one sense, this is a fairly straightforward way to historiographically situate the careers of a Millington or a Haru. But what if we were to configure our understanding of repertoire to consider how the historiography of Filipinx American studies *itself* reveals other kinds of commitments, tendencies, or maybe even forms part of that durable spine?

Let's consider Faye Caronan's *Legitimizing Empire*. At first blush, it's easy to see how it could play well in the above mix of performance-related studies. There are chapters that comparatively address the significance of Nuyorican poets with Los Angeles–based Filipinx American activist-artists. But when we pair Caronan's text with JoAnna Poblete's *Islanders in the Empire*, a larger view becomes apparent.[11] Rather than a scholarly repertoire squarely focused on the ways that cultural forms reshape meaning and memory, these two works track another kind of repertoire—comparative analyses of empire in the Pacific, Latin America, and the Caribbean. Reading the works of Poblete and Caronan allows us to envision scholarly repertoires that engage Americanists such as Tatiana Seijas while reminding us of anthologies like Evelyn Hu-DeHart's *Across the Pacific* or Loni Ding's documentaries about our ancestors in the Americas.[12] These scholarly repertoires that signal deeply comparative commitments across and between Latinx, African, and Asian diasporas along with Indigenous peoples help to situate Filipinxness in the Americas in exciting and much-needed ways.

What if the work we create is more than something that stands on its own, atomized, or simply melts into air? Apostol gives us a chance to see how one's choices in a repertoire can serve as the latest iteration of a long line of choices made by ancestors and forebears. What if the choices we make form part of the spine of a habit, a custom, or in the way that Eric Hobsbawm guided us through the crafting of invented traditions?[13]

These repertoires that we perform, enact, or bring to life in lecture halls or on strike lines do more than become themselves by simply disappearing. They are like those performance genealogies that Joseph Roach wrote about, "mnemonic reserves, including patterned movements made and remembered by bodies, residual movements retained implicitly in images or words, and imaginary movements dreamed in minds not prior to language but constitutive of it."[14] The repertoires we create are not simply live analogues to those prized archives we keep referring to. Our repertoires are performatively nimble while being historically durable.

NOTES

1. Jesse G. Quinsaat, "An Exercise on How to Join the Navy and Still Not See the World," in *Letters in Exile: An Introductory Reader on the History of Pilipinos in America*, ed. Jesse G. Quinsaat et al. (Los Angeles: University of California Los Angeles Asian American Studies Center Publications, 1976), 96–100.

2. Diana Taylor, *The Archive and the Repertoire: Performing Cultural Memory in the Americas* (Durham, N.C.: Duke University Press), 19.

3. Taylor, *The Archive and the Repertoire*, 20.

4. Jacques Derrida, "Archive Fever: A Freudian Impression," *Diacritics* 25, no. 2 (Summer 1995): 11, 57; emphasis mine.

5. Peggy Phelan, *Unmarked: The Politics of Performance* (London: Routledge, 1993), 146.

6. Sabina Leonelli and Rachel A. Ankeny, "Repertoires: How to Transform a Project into a Research Community," *BioScience* 65 (2015): 701–8.

7. Gina Apostol, *Insurrecto* (New York: Soho, 2018).

8. June Millington, *Land of a Thousand Bridges: Island Girl in a Rock and Roll World* (Goshen, Mass.: Institute for the Musical Arts, 2015) and Sumi Sevilla Haru, *Iron Lotus: Memoirs* (n.p.: Great Spirit Publishing, 2012).

9. Robert G. Lee, *Orientals: Asian Americans in Popular Culture* (Philadelphia: Temple University Press, 1999); Josephine Lee, *Performing Asian America: Race and Ethnicity on the Contemporary Stage* (Philadelphia: Temple University Press, 1998); Dorinne Kondo, *About Face: Performing Race in Fashion and Theater* (New York: Routledge, 1997); Karen Shimakawa, *National Abjection: The Asian American Body Onstage* (Durham, N.C.: Duke University Press, 2002).

10. Sarita Echavez See, *The Decolonized Eye: Filipino American Art and Performance* (Minneapolis: University of Minnesota Press, 2009); Theodore S. Gonzalves, *The Day the Dancers Stayed: Performing in the Filipino/American Diaspora* (Philadelphia: Temple University Press, 2009); Lucy Mae San Pablo Burns, *Puro Arte: Filipinos on the Stages of Empire* (Durham, N.C.: Duke University Press, 2012); Antonio T. Tiongson Jr., *Filipinos Represent: DJs, Racial Authenticity, and the Hip-Hop Nation* (Minneapolis: University of Minnesota Press, 2013); Oliver Wang, *Legions of Boom: Filipino American Mobile DJ Crews in the San Francisco Bay Area* (Durham, N.C.: Duke University Press, 2013); Neferti Xina M. Tadiar, *Fantasy-Production: Sexual Economies and Other Philippine Consequences for the New World Order* (Hong Kong: Hong Kong University Press, 2004); Jose B. Capino, *Dream Factories of a Former Colony: American Fantasies, Philippine Cinema* (Minneapolis: University of Minnesota Press, 2010); Nerissa S. Balce, *Body Parts of Empire: Visual Abjection, Filipino Images, and the American Archive* (Ann Arbor: University of Michigan Press, 2016); and Celine Parreñas Shimizu, *The Hypersexuality of Race: Performing Asian/American Women on Screen and Scene* (Durham, N.C.: Duke University Press, 2007).

11. Faye Caronan, *Filipino American and U.S. Puerto Rican Cultural Critique* (Chicago: University of Illinois Press, 2015) and JoAnna Poblete, *Islanders in the Empire: Filipino and Puerto Rican Laborers in Hawai'i* (Chicago: University of Illinois Press, 2017).

12. Tatiana Seijas, *Asian Slaves in Colonial Mexico: From Chinos to Indians* (Cambridge: Cambridge University Press, 2014); Evelyn Hu-DeHart, ed., *Across the Pacific: Asian Americans and Globalization* (Philadelphia: Temple

University Press, 2000); and Loni Ding, dir., *Ancestors in the Americas* [Part 1: *Coolies, Sailors, and Settlers: Voyage to the New World* and Part 2: *Chinese in the Frontier West: An American Story*] (Center for Educational Telecommunications, 2001). See also Jason Oliver Chang, *Chino: Anti-Chinese Racism in Mexico, 1880–1940* (Chicago: University of Illinois Press, 2017).

13. "'Invented tradition' is taken to mean a set of practices, normally governed by overtly or tacitly accepted rules and of a ritual or symbolic nature, which seek to inculcate certain values and norms of behaviour by repetition, which automatically implies continuity with the past." See Eric Hobsbawm and Terence Ranger, eds., *The Invention of Tradition* (Cambridge: Cambridge University Press, 2021), 1.

14. Joseph Roach, *Cities of the Dead: Circum-Atlantic Performance* (New York: Columbia University Press, 1996), 26.

PART SIX

Recalcitrant Bodies, Unruly Vernaculars

Confronting Worldly Acts: Filipinx Performances and Their Elsewheres

Lucy MSP Burns

Until the Lions, a dance production by Bengali-immigrant, London-based contemporary dance artist Akram Khan, premiered in January 2016. It is a partial adaptation of poet Karthika Naïr's book *Until the Lions: Echoes from the Mahabharata*. The performance is described as "an original reworking" of a tale from the Indian epic, using "kathak and contemporary dance to tell the tale of Amba, a princess abducted on her wedding day." Less than seven minutes into the piece, British Bangladeshi vocalist Sohini Alam sings "Anak" (Child) by Freddie Aguilar, the Filipinx singer-musician:

> Nuong isilang ka sa mundong ito
> Laking tuwa ng magulang mo
> At ang kamay nila
> Ang iyong ilaw
> [Your birth into the world
> Brought much joy to your parents,

And their touch
Was your guiding light]

"Anak" is a critically and popularly acclaimed song released in 1978. Often heralded as an unofficial anthem for overseas Filipinxs, this folk-leaning song became an immediate standout amid the pop-music-dominated Filipinx music scene with its poignant lyrics about a parents' unconditional love for their prodigal child. In *Until the Lions*, the song returns at multiple moments, the tune rendered differently as it is played using instruments identified with Indian classical music. Soon, performers Ching-Ying Chien (playing Amba) and Joy Alpuerto Ritter (playing Shikhandi) elaborate movements from the *Singkil* dance, a popular dance from the southern Philippines region of Maranao. *Singkil* movements come into the piece to portray varied scenes: a wedding, an abduction, a journey, and a battle. Khan originated the role of the abductor Bheeshma, alternating with performer Rianto.

How might we understand the deployment of a 1970s Filipinx folk song and a dance identified with Muslims of the southern region of the Philippines in a performance described as employing "kathak and contemporary dance" to tell a story from an Indian epic? How do such seemingly dissonant cultural forms make their way into this dramatic retelling of a classic Sanskrit tale, from an ancient Indian text, told from the point of view of the women characters? What sense can be made of these performance elements identifiable as of, or from, the Philippines in a narrative not directly about the Philippines? How can performance studies help unpack this artistic choice and encounter? What is the place of "performance," as an analytic, method, and an object, within the ongoing project of Filipinx studies?

Being in the World: Performance in Filipinx Studies

Performance functions as an object of study and a methodology in the interdisciplinary field of Filipinx studies. Scholars have drawn from theories of performance developed in other fields including anthropology, theater studies, performance studies, music, dance studies, literary studies, gender studies, and queer studies. While building on an understanding of performance from these disciplines, Filipinx studies scholars also maintain a critical perspective of how various fields of knowledge have and have not engaged with the "Philippine" question. To this end, the body of work on performance produced within Filipinx studies has foregrounded histories of empire, colonialism, imperialism, and their aftermath. In doing so, such scholarship underscores performance as a practice, a lens through which to understand how Filipinxs experience and act in the world. This set of works have also asserted "performance" as an episteme and a craft—a way of knowing and a practice—as critical to the project of Filipinx studies to imagine ways of thinking, feeling, moving, perceiving, acting, and intervening in the world.

Martin F. Manalansan IV makes sense of gay Filipinxs' reproduction of Santa Cruzan performances in New York as a ritual act crucial to community-making. Manalansan builds on the idea of performance as ritual and ritual as performance—a theory of performance developed in the field of anthropology, specifically within the studies of religious ceremonies of peoples of the Global South. In his analysis of gay Filipinx men enacting this annual religious historical pageant celebrating the end of the persecution of Christians, Manalansan deviates from the colonialist understanding of performance as a ritual that sutures particular kinds of religious practices to collectivities of the Global South. In such colonial readings, the Global South and its constituents are thus reduced to the temporality and spatiality of the nonmodern (pace Johannes Fabian and "denial of coevalness"). Manalansan argues instead for the creative remaking of such ritual practices and pageantry as forms through which transmigrant Filipinx gays make a home living in New York.

Christine Bacareza Balance, in her book *Tropical Renditions: Making Musical Scenes in Filipino America*, regards music and musical communities as a site for analysis, and "disobedient listening" as a method for studying the role of music in creating social communities and identities. This method challenges the perception of Filipino musicians and music created by people from the Philippines as simple mimicry, unoriginal and basic. Beginning with a scene of encounter between a Native of the Philippines and a phonograph early in the years of American occupation, Balance listens closely to Filipinx music-making endeavors—including hip-hop DJs QBert and other members of the Invisible Skratch Piklz, karaoke, Jessica Hagedorn's multicoastal multiracial mixed genre "disco poetry" collaborations, to the

"Pilipino alternatib music" festival Pinoise Pop. As such, Balance foregrounds music and sound performance world-making by following the sounds and sound-makers, their influences, and those with whom they make music. By focusing on performance as a dynamic creative process, not simply a finished product, Balance offers a method of hearing, seeing, and experiencing Filipinx music making.

Theodore S. Gonzalves's book-length study of Pilipino Cultural Nights (PCNs), *The Day the Dancers Stayed: Performing in the Filipino/American Diaspora*, traces transnational links of cultural practices by "Filipinos of America."[1] PCN is a unique practice developed in US colleges/universities and some high schools, featuring an evening of showcasing traditional dances and music of the Philippines as well as popular American dance and music. Gonzalves historicizes PCN as a performance form back to Philippines' postindependence/postcolonial nation-building, when state-sponsored efforts codified dances throughout the Philippines. These nationalizing efforts created a repertoire of Philippine traditional dances (including *tinikling, singkil, pandango sa ilaw*) that are the staple of PCN shows. This materialist study of a diasporic performance practice proposes PCN, like any tradition, is an "invention," wherein its production always already involves reinterpretation, misinterpretations, repetition, failures, and inventiveness.

Similarly interested in the role of diasporic communities in the formation and perpetuation of national culture is Christi-Anne Castro's deft study, *Musical Renderings of the Philippine Nation*. Specifically focusing on the ensemble musical form of *rondalla* and its development during the US colonization of the Philippines, through Philippine independence and postindependence, the text discusses the musical performances of Filipinx Americans, among the people of the Philippines. Castro argues that "the idea nation circulates publicly through performance" and that "nationalism culminates in spectacle."[2]

Examining Filipinx Americans and hip-hop, scholars Faye Caronan and Antonio T. Tiongson Jr. explore the productive tension of how Filipinxs participate, create, and deploy hip-hop as an art form.[3] Tiongson, specifically focusing on Filipinx American DJs of the 1990s, challenges the easy interpretation of coalitional politics in their appropriation of Black cultural practices. Caronan takes a comparative approach, juxtaposing Filipinx Americans' and Puerto Ricans' anti-US discourse in their hip-hop aesthetics. These works, along with the interdisciplinary collection *The Empire of Funk*, edited by Mark R. Villegas, Kuttin' Kandi, and Roderick N. Labrador, assert hip-hop as an artistic form of political expression, formative of the progressive politics of Filipinx Americans in the late twentieth century.[4]

The texts mentioned explore migrant sociality through leisure practices including creative performance and other forms of unwaged and nonproductive activities, to engage the Filipinx laboring body beyond just its value/significance within systems of exploitation such as capitalism and imperial domination.[5] These works focused on performances by Filipinxs offer theories for thinking about the performing body, nation, diaspora, transmigrants, as it anticipates social identities and relations yet to be.

Filipinx Performing Bodies in the Global Entertainment Industrial Complex

Scholars in performance in Filipinx studies are equally engaged in complex and lively conversations with scholars in Philippine studies, including Nicanor Tiongson, Ben Lumbera, Patrick Flores, Doreen Fernandez, Rolando B. Tolentino, and Maria Josephine Barrios. Collectively, these scholars are producing writings about Filipinx performance with a critical attention to conditions that produce and make sense of these works—that is, the continuing imperial and neoliberal conditions from which the social identity of Filipinxs as "transmigrants," "diasporics," and "overseas Filipinos" emerge. And in doing so, they are articulating not only "the consequences of dominant Philippine imaginations" but also, in the words of Neferti Xina M. Tadiar: "Hope . . . the daily exercise of our creative capacities to remake the world, in the acts of living in ways that depart from the orthodox dreams of our world-historical, real-politik time."[6]

Filipinx studies has paid robust attention to the global phenomenon of Filipinx migration through labor (Rhacel Salazar Parreñas, Robyn Rodriguez, Anna Guevarra, Kale Bantigue Fajardo, Eric J. Pido, and others). The formation of Overseas Filipinx Workers/Overseas Contract Workers (OFWs/OCWs) as an official and social category has influenced and urged scholarship on Pilipino diasporas beyond the United States. Performers are part of this cadre of the workforce that has been deployed all over the globe for over a century. Early in the twentieth century, Naresh Fernandes, a Goa-based writer writing a book about the "internationalism of jazz" during Mumbai's jazz age (1930s–1960s), includes the history of Filipinx jazz musicians who traveled to India as members of jazz orchestras. These musicians played alongside African Americans, Burmese, German, and Spanish as members of the orchestra. Stephanie Ng, writing on Filipinx lounge entertainers in Asia, and Angeline de Dios, researching Filipinx entertainers in cruise ships, hotels, and theme parks in Hong Kong, Macao, Singapore, and Malaysia, consider the meaning of Filipinx laboring bodies produced within conditions of neoliberalism, and thus their emergence through the global entertainment industrial complex.[7] Ng and de Dios complicate the Filipinx performing body's eligibility and legibility through skills of "adaptability" and "flexibility" in facing multiple demands of transnational labor. Robert Diaz's writings on performance and artistic practices turn to everyday lives of queer Filipinx Canadians, arguing for the significance of non-normative sexualities and intimacies to the circulation of cultural citizenship.[8] Patrick Alcedo's research, produced both in writing and documentary film work, centers indigeneity and gender in engaging folk and religion through his analysis of the continuing practice of *Ati-atihan* among Filipinx Canadian migrants.[9]

Through their focus on the laboring bodies of Filipinx migrants, within and without the nation-state, the scholars mentioned above broaden our understanding of performance to include a renewed attentiveness to fractured histories of migration, colonialism, and diaspora. The scholarly works noted here bypass facile readings of Filipinx performing bodies as evidence of assimilative visibility, audibility, sensibility, and legibility smoothly subsumed within regimes of subjection, subjectification, objection, and objectification. Rather, the Filipinx performing body convenes a kind of "disobedient listening" (to use Balance's formulation), challenging our assumptions and expectations of social identities ascribed and produced within histories of empire and neoliberalism. This body of work makes clear that Filipinx performing bodies are not any more or less "suited to the interrogation of performance." Refusing the mandate for a representational exceptionalism, these works instead summon the Filipinx performing body and performance work as an enduring and ordinary object and method for critical study.

Aftermaths, Confrontations, and Convergences

Returning to the provocations that opened this essay: How did Freddie Aguilar's "Anak" become part of the soundscape of Khan's *Until the Lions*? How did movements from *singkil* become part of this piece's movement vocabulary? The short answer to these questions is Joy Alpuerto Ritter, the performer in the role of Shikhandi. Alpuerto Ritter is an LA-born, Filipinx American, Germany-raised, and now Berlin-based dancer who has worked with the Akram Khan company since 2013. In 2017, she was nominated as "Outstanding Female Dancer (contemporary)" by the UK National Dance Awards for her role in *Until the Lions*. To make something of Alpuerto Ritter's presence in Khan's *Until the Lions* is to consider the labor of her performing body in this intercultural performance on the global mainstage. Such a reading requires an attentiveness to performance forms, and a rigorous cataloguing of seemingly divergent performance traditions present in "intercultural performances" such as Akram Khan's *Until the Lions*.[10] The task here is not simply to claim and celebrate yet another form of Filipinx visibility on the global mainstage, in all its tremendous skills and abilities. Rather, to catalogue and trace performance migrations in intercultural performances not directly and obvious about the Philippines is to confront regimes of domination that produce and indeed conjure up the "Filipinx performing body." Performance migrations may thus begin with histories of "contact" and move to the present conditions of possibility and labor they produce. In particular, a study of performance migration is interested in intercultural performances that decenter the West and whiteness, in search of alternative relations and formations.

It is through the method of collaborative creation, adopted so carefully by Khan, that performance elements associated with the Philippines make their way to *Until the Lions*. Collaborative creation is a process that builds the movement choreography and soundscape from the artistic team members' specific artistic training. This method is atypical of the conventional creative process where the choreographer sets movements scored from their choice of music, and the dancers and musicians then execute the choreographer's vision. For *Until the Lions*, Khan asks all the members of the artistic team to contribute to the creative process, with specific tasks (yet open to personal interpretation) such as bringing a song that has a significance to your upbringing or from your own cultural background.[11] In addition to Alpuerto Ritter's movement training including ballet, jazz, hip-hop, break-dancing, and voguing, her dance education includes Philippine and Polynesian dance training and performing in a dance troupe led by her mother, Maria Luz Alpuerto Ritter in Freiberg.[12] Her mother worked closely with Los Angeles–based Filipinx American choreographer Dulce Capadocia, artistic director of Silayan Dance Company.[13] Hence, along with Khan's classical Kathak and modern dance training, the story of intense desire, shame, anguish, betrayal, vengeance, and power is told with movement vocabularies drawn and reinterpreted from various Asian martial arts (such as jiu jitsu), hip-hop (voguing), and *singkil*. In 2018, Indonesian artist Rianto began performing the role of Bheesma (alternating with Khan). Rianto brings his classical Javanese dance and East Javanese folk dance training, drawing from these movement practices. Though the structure of the story remains, the way it is told differs with each different performer, with each specific performance.

Movements from these various dance traditions may or may not be recognizable in the version that unfolds in this performance. Movements from these practices are taken in fragments, reconfigured, and differently sequenced, set to sounds, rhythms, and bodies from its traditional version. For example, *Singkil* movements are indeed done by Shikhandi (Alpuerto Ritter) and Amba (Ching Ying Chen)—low and small front kick steps forward, as if kicking a ball, emphasizing a downward direction, with their hands placed at the waist or raised twirling in motion. Gone are the tapping bamboos and the highly decorated fans. In its traditional version, the movements of this dance require the dancers to step over the bamboos, moving to avoid getting caught as two other dancers hold each end of the two bamboos, tapping and closing them, starting slow then moving to speed up the rhythm. While the dancers on their feet navigate the bamboos, they also keep upright manipulating the *apir* (fans), accompanied by percussive music (often gong and drum instruments of *kulintang*). In Khan's production, bamboos are used in different ways: held between Shikandi's teeth, their toes, and the back of their thighs and calf; to hold up a severed head (prop); to create some form of boundary, create a structure for the captive Amba. At some point, the three dancers strike the floor of the stage in unison, producing a sound, along with percussion instruments played by the musicians, of a confrontation to come. At the end of *Until the Lions*, bamboo stalks are also left strewn on fractured ground (stage), following the revenge exacted by Amba and Shikandi against the lord Bheeshma who violated them.

Through Alpuerto Ritter's performance, the Filipinx performing body brings a popular folk rock song and movement identified with the Philippines into a reimagined mythical story made for the global stage.[14] Khan's aesthetic asserts and inserts non-Western performance forms, including those categorized as traditional and folk, in his inter/multidisciplinary stage creations reimagined and reinterpreted to explore the linkages between mythical stories and contemporary life (as in the case for the inspiration of *Until the Lions*—the unacknowledged power of female characters in myths and the struggle to wrest history from being told from the point of view of the victorious).[15] Here, traditional and folk dance movements belong on the international stage not merely as embodiments of unique and distinct national cultures that celebrate a cultured past of a modern nation. Rather, Khan's reworking of aesthetic traditions creates an "embodiment of eclectic movement languages . . . generates complex affiliations to diverse traditions, cultures, nations, and histories."[16] It is not coincidental that Alpuerto Ritter brings *singkil* into this intercultural stage encounter. *Singkil's* known epic narrative concerns an abduction, rescue, and marriage.[17]

A cartographic tracing of the "Filipino elements" in Khan's *Until the Lions*, through Alpuerto Ritter's contribution and her dancing body leads us to the particularity of the Filipinx body, provoking the question of the overlapping, entangled, and colliding histories of regional, national, and Indigenous in the Philippines. The history of these dance forms encases the very history of the Philippines as a modern postcolonial nation, where the continuing subsumption of Indigenous peoples of the Philippines as a representation of "national culture" erases the fraught and violent ways their cultural practices and way of life were simultaneously denied, appropriated, celebrated, and stolen, and they were deprived of access to their ancestral lands. Khan's multiracial, multinational cast in *Until the Lions* gestures to the necessary confrontation with the tensions and collisions from the denial of the violent exploitative conditions of migration via dance and musical forms that each artist brings to this collective creation. Closer attention to the performance forms that are assembled in this work should prompt an inquiry of performance migrations as performances that inspire a reckoning with histories and narratives of forced incorporations.

Until the Lions leaves the audience with a fraught concluding scene, the aftermath in the wake of a cataclysmic event. The earth is ripped open, world order is upended as intimacies are intricately intertwined with the violence of contact. Alpuerto Ritter's performing body captures the landscape of this intimate violence through the movements of a Filipinx performing body as central to the imagination of such confrontations. In the process, performance traditions associated with the Philippines, such as *singkil*, are imagined anew, migrated and moved out of contexts in this South-South encounter between differently colonized bodies. Confronted in the present with the aftermath of colonial encounters (mixings, migrations), *Until the Lions* moves forward to a necessary reimagining of the future. To be in the world is to participate in a new order of creative collaboration, moving the Filipinx body from spaces of familiar trespass to the stages of intercultural movement.

NOTES

1. For other writings on PCNs, see Barbara Gaerlan, J. Lorenzo Perillo, and Anna Alves.

2. Christi-Anne Castro, *Musical Renderings of the Philippine Nation* (Oxford: Oxford University Press, 2011), 14. See also Mary Talusan, Carolina San Juan, Eloisa Borah, and Lily Ann Villaraza on Filipinos' performance on display on the stages of American empire, including the 1904 World's Fair and chautauquas, which featured various speakers, performers, inventors, teachers, politicians, and preachers, combining education and entertainment.

3. Faye Caronan, *Legitimizing Empire: Filipino America and U.S. Puerto Rican Cultural Critique* (Chicago: University of Illinois Press, 2015); and Antonio T. Tiongson Jr., *Filipinos Represent: DJs, Racial Authenticity, and the Hip-hop Nation* (Minneapolis: University of Minnesota Press, 2013). J. Lorenzo Perillo, *Choreographing in Color: Filipinos, Hip-Hop, and the Cultural Politics of Euphemism* (Oxford University Press, 2020).

4. Mark R. Villegas, Kuttin' Kandi, and Roderick N. Labrador, eds., *Empire of Funk: Hip Hop and Representation in Filipina/o America* (San Diego, Calif.: Cognella Academic Publishing, 2014).

5. See Rhacel Salazar Parreñas, "'White Trash' Meets the 'Little Brown Monkeys': The Taxi Dancehall as a Site of Racial and Gender Alliances between White Working Class and Filipino Immigrant Men in the 1920s and 1930s," *Amerasia Journal* 24, no. 2 (1998): 115–34; and Linda España-Maram, "Brown Hordes in McIntosh Suits: Filipinos, Taxi Dance Halls, and Performing the Immigrant Body in Los Angeles, 1930s–1940s."

6. Neferti Xina M. Tadiar, *Fantasy-Production: Sexual Economies and Other Philippine Consequences for the New World Order* (Quezon City, Philippines: Ateneo De Manila University Press, 2004), 264.

7. Stephanie Ng, "Performing the 'Filipino' at the Crossroads: Filipino Bands in Five-Star Hotels throughout Asia," *Modern Drama: World Drama from 1850 to the Present*; DOI: 48. 272–296. 10.1353/mdr.2005.0034; Angeline de Dios, "The Creative Mobilities of Cultural Identity: Transnational Tours of Philippine Performing Arts Ensembles," *Handbook on the Geographies of Creativity*, ed. Angeline de Dios and Lily Kong (Northampton, Mass.: Edward Elgar Publishing Inc, 2020), 144–161.

8. Robert Diaz, Marissa Largo, and Fritz Pino, *Diasporic Intimacies: Queer Filipinos and Canadian Imaginaries* (Evanston, Ill.: Northwestern University Press, 2017).

9. Patrick Alcedo, *Ati-atihan Lives* (Alexandria, Va.: York University, 2012).

10. Intercultural performance, loosely defined, brings together different forms of cultural performance traditions. It is a practice meant to challenge the universalism and dominance of Western performance. It is an expansive category and description that includes artistic works that "appropriate" from cultural practices that are deemed minoritized or from minoritized cultures, yet disappear or exclude those who are identified to be of those minoritized cultures. A prime example of this is the much-discussed 1984 production *Mahabharata* by Peter Brooks. Brooks's theater adaptation of this Indian epic has been criticized as a prime embodiment of Orientalism. See Patrice Pavis, "Intercultural Theatre Today," *Forum Modernes Theater* 25, no. 1 (January 2010): 5–15.

11. This information was shared by Alpuerto Ritter and Alam in a conversation with the author during the performance of *Until the Lions* at the La Coursive in La Rochelle, France, April 2–7, 2018. Khan also conveyed this information in an email correspondence with the author, via his personal assistant, February 2018.

12. Starting with ballet lessons at the age of four, Alpuerto-Ritter continued with her training in numerous dance styles, taking part in dance competitions beginning at age ten, and graduated from Palucca University of Dance in Dresden. She won numerous hip-hop dance battles throughout Europe. She also was member of Cirque du Soleil's *Michael Jackson Immortal World Tour* show, and is a freelance dancer who has worked with numerous celebrated contemporary dance companies including Wang Ramirez, Christoph Winkler, Anja Kozik, Constanza Macras, and Heike Hennig (*https://www.joyalpuertoritter.com/*, accessed June 12, 2019).

Another Filipina performer who gained attention while performing in Germany is Aura Deva. Deva was a member of the *Miss Saigon* ensemble, playing the role of Kim for three years (1994–1997) in Germany.

13. Information from the company website: Silayan Dance Company was founded by Sonia Capadocia (Dulce Capadocia's mother) in the 1970s in Los

Angeles. The company has performed in premiere venues worldwide, including the Los Angeles Music Center's Dorothy Chandler Pavilion. This award-winning dance company was acknowledged with a Lester Horton Dance Award and recognized by the Los Angeles Dance Resource Center as a "Milestone Dance Company" (*http://dulcecapadocia.org/our-history.html*, accessed June 10, 2019). The limits of this essay does not enable a full engagement with the Silayan Dance Company's history and its significant work.

14. Though this essay only engages Alpuerto Ritter's work in *Until the Lions*, it must be noted that she now has a growing body of choreographic works—solo, duet, and ensemble. One notable piece is *BABAE*, a solo dance piece inspired by Mary Wigman's *Hexentanz* (Witch Dance, 1926; *https://www.moma.org/interactives/exhibitions/2012/inventingabstraction/?work=238*). Wigman is noted to be one of the most influential dancers and choreographers, cited as a visionary in the genre of modern dance. Alpuerto Ritter takes Wigman's choreographic exploration of female power—allure, monstrosity, desire, physicality, control, and abandon—using movements from her dance training (*https://www.joyalpuertoritter.com/my-work-dance*).

15. A discussion of the growing rich analysis of Akram Khan's body of work, specifically the aesthetics and politics of Britain under the regime of "new interculturalism," post-9/11, austerity fiscal policies, and the longer history of commonwealth, is beyond the scope of this essay. In brief, see Royona Mitra's *Akram Khan: Dancing New Interculturalism* (London: Palgrave Macmillan, 2015) and Anusha Kedhar's "Flexibility and Its Bodily Limits: Transnational South Asian Dancers in an Age of Neoliberalism," *Dance Research Journal* 46, no. 1 (2014): 23–40.

16. Mitra, *Akram Khan*, 31. One of these movement trails (or routes) may be the trace of the Srivijaya and Majapahit empires across the Malay archipelago that links what is now the Philippines to pre-European-empire–dominated trade routes. Though the inclusion of what is now the Philippines (and its 7,101 islands) as formal territory claimed within these empires remains contested, the southern islands are recorded to have been part of the trade route, where contact through trade surely bred cultural influences. See Joefe B. Santarita, "Panyupayana: The Emergence of Hindu Polities in the Pre-Islamic Philippines," in *Cultural and Civilisational Links between India and Southeast Asia*, ed. Shyam Saran (Singapore: Springer, 2018), 93–106.

17. See Minerva S. Sani and Edna C. de los Santos, "Singkil Dance" (Marawai City: NCCA-ICH, 2011), *https://www.ichcap.org/kor/ek/sub3/pdf_file/domain2/022_Singkil_Dance.pdf*, accessed June 21, 2019; Jiamila E. Panaraag and Geldolin L. Inte, "The Metamorphosis of Selected Maranao Stories into Dances," Official Conference Proceedings of The Asian Conference on Literature & Librarianship 2015; *http://papers.iafor.org/wp-content/uploads/papers/librasia2015/LibrAsia2015_09604.pdf*, accessed June 25, 2019.

THIRTY

Aye Nako! The Frustrations of Filipinx American Illegibility

Alana J. Bock

The Filipinx performing body has been an animating figure in the field of Filipinx/American studies for decades. As Lucy MSP Burns has argued, "through spectacular acts of performance," what she also refers to as *puro arte*, "Filipino/a bodies instantiate and exceed the totalizing script of colonialism," inviting us to critically ponder the "incompleteness of and possibilities" for Filipinx performances.[1] Considerations of the heterogenous, unruly, and vexing nature of the Filipinx performing body within Filipinx American studies, as well as other interdisciplines such as performance studies, theater studies, postcolonial studies, ethnic studies, and queer of color critique, to name a few, have been a source of critical intervention. In particular, scholars such as Burns, Sarita Echavez See, and Christine Bacareza Balance have argued that knowledge production is inherent in Filipinx performance and performativity, extending our understanding of the Filipinx performing body to be more than a mere symptom of imperial amnesia or historical erasure. While the "forgotten" and "erased" Filipinx has prompted

335

critical discussions regarding the historicity between Filipinx identity formation and US imperialism, Filipinx American studies today has recalibrated
its critique of this erasure, moving away from the language of recuperation
and recognition and toward a critical analysis of the technologies of power
that have rendered Filipinx America a vexing presence to begin with.[2] Put
differently, Filipinx American studies has critiqued the desire for normative inclusion within a violent system that uses (in)visibility to render certain bodies worthy of value, some as redeemable, and others as socially dead.
Here, I want to advance *illegibility* and, more specifically, illegible Filipinx
performativity, as a way to build on, but also depart from, these previous
and ongoing engagements with the Filipinx performing body. As a way to
think beyond the binary of (in)visibility that has been a foundational organizing trope within Filipinx American studies, the illegible Filipinx performing body is considered here as both a meditation on what it means to
exist outside the strictures of (in)visibility as well as how embracing a state
of illegibility can point us to other possibilities and futures for Filipinx
America and Filipinx American studies.

Drawing on José Esteban Muñoz's provocation that "minoritarian performance labors to make worlds—worlds of transformative politics and possibilities," the following essay explores the world-making possibilities of
illegible Filipinx performance through the queercore punk band Aye Nako.[3]
Illegibility exceeds both the visible (as a form of legitimation) and the invisible (as a form of deferred visibility/wrongful erasure), frustrating how our
sensory registers reckon with the illegible. It is in this frustration that we
are asked to recalibrate our senses, our ways of knowing and being, so that
we may imagine other worlds beyond what is (in)visible. We only need to
look and listen differently (or perhaps disobediently) to make out these alternative worlds.[4]

I look to Aye Nako here as one example, though certainly not the only
iteration of, illegible Filipinx performance. Founded by a Black, Filipinx
American, and trans man, Aye Nako harnesses the ineffable and the illegible to imagine alternative possibilities for Filipinx futures. As stated on their
Facebook page, "originally formed to subdue boredom but now operating
on another frequency," Aye Nako "are actively seeking a planet where
those who fall in the margins can feel OK about being themselves."[5] Drawing on a queer of color critical reading practice in which culture is, to use

Roderick A. Ferguson's words, "one site that compels identification with and antagonisms to the normative ideals promoted by state and capital," the following is an exercise in listening to the different frequencies, riffs, and harmonies of Aye Nako's illegible performances and what they're speaking to, against, or into existence.[6]

Founded by Mars Ganito (also known as Mars Dixon) in 2008, Aye Nako writes and performs music about being "queer, trans and black."[7] However, because Aye Nako's name is a reference to the Tagalog expression *hay naku*, the band elicits a certain level of affinity with Filipinx listeners. Though there is no direct English translation for the phrase, *hay naku* can be understood as an expression of vexation or exasperation, similar to "oh my god!" or "my goodness!"[8] The phrase echoes throughout Filipinx America, serving as a point of familiarity for Filipinx Americans who recognize the phrase. For those having grown up Filipinx American, *hay naku* elicits memories of trouble-making, parental scolding, and making mistakes. *Hay naku* is often said in times of frustration, disbelief, chastisement, or anger—the ineffable meanings and emotions that exceed the utterance of *hay naku* itself. Aye Nako's repurposing of a phrase that emotes so much in so little is telling of the band's own illegibility.

Aye Nako's and, more specifically, Mars Ganito's multiracialism and queerness highlight the limitations of (in)visibility as an analytic within Filipinx American studies. Both visibility and invisibility imply social value and recognition, either given or deferred. Departing from these frameworks, Aye Nako's illegible performances disrupt the security and desire to inhabit the normative space of (in)visibility by frustrating the seeming naturalness of this binary. The ways in which Aye Nako exceeds the tidiness of social categories such as Filipinx, Black, and queer reveal the productive "mess" that arises from refusing to placate the imperial will to know.[9] Aye Nako's refashioning of *hay naku* not only signals illegibility and ineffability, but also an intense frustration with white supremacy's violent notions of belonging and deservingness, symbolizing what it means to exist in excess, to be a declaration of annoyance, a vexing presence.[10] *Hay naku* is a sound of refusal and indignation, emoting in excess feelings that are unspeakable or too great to verbalize.

Mars Ganito's positionality as a Filipinx and Black trans man is of particular importance to the band's mode of illegible performativity. Considering

Nicole Fleetwood's assertion that iterations of Blackness are "manifested through a deliberate performance of visibility that begs us to consider the constructed nature of visuality," I contend that Mars's Filipinx, Black, and queer performances do something similar in that they shatter the naturalness of normative scopic regimes through their excess illegibility and ineffability.[11] For example, in "White Noise," a track off of Aye Nako's album *The Blackest Eye*, Mars indignantly sings the refrain, "I let the white noise fuzz in my head for so long" throughout the song, alluding to the overwhelming ubiquity of white supremacy. In an interview about the song, Mars states,

> I wrote a song called "White Noise" about how whiteness is centered in everything, how it taught me to hate myself for being black . . . how my Filipino mother didn't think it was necessary or important to teach me to speak Tagalog that way we can come off as American aka white as possible, how it scares me that white supremacy doesn't even need white people to perpetuate it.[12]

"White Noise" confronts the violence of white supremacy that, for Mars, is marked by his experience being both Black and Filipinx American. The anecdote that Mars shares regarding his mother's decision to forgo teaching him Tagalog is telling here. Critiquing systems of deservingness that are predicated on mimicking whiteness, Mars associates the anti-Blackness he encounters with his mother's refusal to teach him Tagalog, an event that is both symptomatic of, and a tool for, white supremacy. In this way, "White Noise" makes a critical connection between anti-Blackness, white supremacy, and Filipinx American identity formation. Aye Nako's illegible performance bursts through the vexing strictures of (in)visibility while also bringing together identity categories and forms of embodiment that are normatively deemed mutually exclusive (Filipinxness and Blackness). In doing so, Aye Nako offers an alternative way of being Filipinx American, one that is also tied up in acknowledging anti-Blackness as foundational to US identity politics.

Similarly, Aye Nako explores anti-Blackness in their song "Muck" from their 2017 album *Silver Haze*. The song begins with a prolonged moment of guitar feedback and then, before we hear the drums, Mars's voice comes to us, loud and sharp, though tinged with a hint of longing: "So I've convinced myself it'll always feel this way / No matter how much I claim it was supposed to be a one-time thing / All these horror films are the dirt that fill my grave / A craniotomy to reach that part in my brain / Where I've kept so many secrets." The verses of the song are upbeat, despite the gravity of the lyrics. However, for a moment before the chorus, the song and Mars's voice soften into a somber and sweet melody. This softness carries into the chorus, though the chorus is a bit more urgent, in which Mars and fellow bandmate Jade Payne take turns singing, "Confused by the sound / (Of all excuses given) / So am I / You're confused by the sound / (Our blood can't prove we're human) / So am I / I need time to recalibrate / Confused by the sound." As their voices alternate, we ourselves cannot help but become slightly disoriented. The chorus ends and Mars's voice becomes strained again, each line of the second verse punctuated with a sense of indignation as he asks, "Who would pay / Pay to watch me choke? / When you see me, all you see is the muck!" This is quickly followed in earnest by a much more subdued question: "Could I feel uglier?" We hear an ineffable pull in Mars's voice, a sorrow that cannot be expressed in words but can be heard nonetheless.[13] "Muck" finishes with a bridge, leaving us feeling uncertain amidst unresolved tension. It is a question left unanswered.

"Muck" is a confession, one that reveals the pain and clarity that comes with the discovery of anti-Black violence and internalized self-hatred. As Mars explains about the song:

> I stopped explaining my song Muck at shows because I know it makes some people feel uncomfortable, but I'm uncomfortable too. I was born and raised on feeling so ugly because of my blackness. I saw it from my family. I saw it on tv and in the movies. I saw it at school. Blackness was not to be valued. It wasn't a positive trait. . . . Only in the last three or four years have I started to work on my internalized anti-blackness, a lifetime-long journey, and this song was written around the peak of my epiphany.[14]

As is evident in both the lyrics of the song and Mars's statement above, "Muck" works through the trauma of systemic anti-Blackness. However, it is also important that we listen beyond the words that Mars sings. Songs like "Muck" are difficult and uncomfortable to explain, as is noted in the above interview. Yet if we listen to the tonality of "Muck" and the performativity of Mars's voice, we can hear that which is not and, perhaps, cannot be explained. "Muck" is full of dissonant sounds, from the amp feedback, shifting tempo, and the earnestness of Mars's voice. It is the sound of frustration at not being able to say what you mean, at not being able to find the right words. The sound of the lyrics as they are sung tells us something in excess of their legible words. Like the expression *hay naku*, "Muck" calls forth sounds of anger and exasperation that are so great they exceed the words they are attached to.

Songs such as "Muck" and "White Noise" turn our ears toward the ineffable and the illegible. Mars's voice performs illegibility by relating something to us beyond the words he sings. In "Muck" we hear a voice that is both contained by, and exceeds, normative notions of Blackness *and* Filipinxness. By embracing an illegible Filipinxness (literally, via the misspelling of *hay naku*), Aye Nako neither denies Mars's experiences as a multiracial Filipinx, nor does the band make any redemptive claims toward Mars's Filipinxness. In doing so, Aye Nako remains in that space between visibility and invisibility, refusing a form of recognition that cannot speak to the specificities of the band's affiliations with Blackness, Filipinxness, and queerness. This illegible performance and the refusal to be recognized allows the band's specific affiliations to be heard without competing with one another. At the same time, Aye Nako's Blackness, Filipinxness, and queerness exist simultaneously, so we must attune ourselves to their specificities, as well as the ways that each are informed by interlocking experiences with white supremacy.

Listening to Mars's voice spill out of these songs illuminates a consciousness that is informed by his position as a trans, Black, and Filipinx man. Here, it is helpful to consider Christina Sharpe's theorization of consciousness. Sharpe argues for a consciousness that is "in the wake" of Black being or, more specifically, she argues for being "in the wake as consciousness." Sharpe further explains that "to be *in* the wake is to occupy and to be occupied by the continuous and changing present of slavery's as yet unresolved unfolding . . . rather than seeking a resolution to blackness's ongoing and irresolvable abjection, one might approach Black being in the wake as a form of *consciousness*."[15] Aye Nako's illegible performances represent a consciousness of white supremacy that recognizes how Filipinx Americans are constituted by and implicated within anti-Blackness. White supremacy violently targets Mars's hypervisible Black body while also wielding his illegible Filipinxness as a form of management (his mother's refusal to teach him Tagalog). As Mars and Aye Nako show us, the illegible Filipinx performing body presents Filipinx American studies with the opportunity to engage in other fields of study, methodologies, and analytics that can better accommodate illegible bodies, crossings, and intersections. In doing so, the field can imagine different ways of being and affiliation that exist beyond the boundaries of (in)visibility and recognition.

Though brief, this analysis of Aye Nako's illegible performances reveals the world-making power of illegible Filipinx performance to Filipinx America and Filipinx American studies. In imagining these new worlds, we must also imagine how ineffable, illegible, and amorphous Filipinx bodies fit within these spaces. Yet this requires us to attune our eyes, ears, and minds toward the possibility of other frequencies and, indeed, other worlds. The example of Aye Nako shows us how Filipinx performativity exceeds (in)visibility rhetoric in social relations as well as the field of Filipinx American studies, by registering with queer Blackness and Black studies. Illegible performances are not contained by neoliberal identity categories or academic fields; by recalibrating (to use the lyrics of "Muck") our senses toward these performances, we notice how Filipinx bodies traverse the boundaries and limitations of these categories. Because of this, Filipinx American studies must never be satisfied with where it has arrived. The field must continuously reorient itself toward the constant shape-shifting of this illegibility. By "recalibrating" its senses toward the illegible, Filipinx American studies not only acknowledges the knowledge produced by the Filipinx performing body, but how that body is already grasping for a yet unrealized future.

NOTES

1. Lucy MSP Burns, *Puro Arte: Filipinos on the Stages of Empire* (New York: New York University Press, 2013), 22.

2. See Fred Cordova, Dorothy Laigo Cordova, and Albert A. Acena, *Filipinos, Forgotten Asian Americans: A Pictorial Essay, 1763–Circa 1963* (Dubuque, Iowa: Kendall/Hunt, 1983), and Oscar V. Campomanes, "The New Empire's Forgetful and Forgotten Citizens: Unrepresentability and Unassimilability in Filipino-American Postcolonialities," *Hitting Critical Mass: A Journal of Asian American Cultural Criticism* 2, no. 2 (Spring 1995): 145–200.

3. Jose Esteban Muñoz, *Disidentifications: Queers of Color and the Performance of Politics* (Minneapolis: University of Minnesota Press, 1999), ix.

4. Christine Bacareza Balance, *Tropical Renditions: Making Musical Scenes in Filipino America* (Durham, N.C.: Duke University Press, 2016), 21.

5. Aye Nako (@ayedontnako), "About Me," Facebook; *https://www.facebook.com/pg/ayedontnako/about/?ref=page_internal*.

6. Roderick A. Ferguson, *Aberrations in Black: Toward a Queer of Color Critique* (Minneapolis: University of Minnesota Press, 2004), 3.

7. Aye Nako, "About Me."

8. As Rick Bonus also illuminates, *hay naku* is the shortening of *hay, inay ko po*, which can be translated as "oh, my mother" and is a reference to "Mary, mother of God." This gendered and Christian translation of *hay naku* is ironically repurposed for Aye Nako's illegible performances.

9. Martin F. Manalansan IV, "The 'Stuff' of Archives: Mess, Migration, and Queer Lives," *Radical History Review*, no. 120 (2014).

10. Aye Nako is certainly not the only band to confront these issues. Aye Nako has been associated with Screaming Females and Downtown Boys, bands that also write and perform music with a punk politics that is antiracist, anticapitalist, and feminist. Aye Nako was also featured in *The New York Times* 2017 article "Rock's Not Dead, It's Ruled By Women," which highlights a contemporary DIY scene that is fronted by women, femme, nonbinary, queer, and trans folks that also perform these politics. See Joe Coscarelli, "Rock's Not Dead, It's Ruled By Women: The Roundtable Conversation," *The New York Times*, September 1, 2017; *https://www.nytimes.com/2017/09/01/arts/music/rock-bands-women.html*.

11. Nicole R. Fleetwood, *Troubling Vision: Performance, Visuality, and Blackness* (Chicago: The University of Chicago Press, 2011), 20.

12. "Issue 58—Featuring Aye Nako," *The Miscreant*, April 12, 2015; *https://issuu.com/themiscreant/docs/the_miscreant_-_issue_58*.

13. Aye Nako, "Muck," on *Silver Haze*, Don Giovanni Records, 2017.

14. Maria Rose Sledmere and Aye Nako, "Album Stream: Aye Nako, *Silver Haze* (GFP Premiere)," *Gold Flake Paint*; *https://www.goldflakepaint.co.uk/album-stream-aye-nako-silver-haze/*.

15. Christina Sharpe, *In the Wake: On Blackness and Being* (Durham, N.C.: Duke University Press, 2016), 13–14.

THIRTY-ONE

Who Cares? Ability and the Elderly Question
in Filipinx American Studies

Edward Nadurata

In 2017, *The Atlantic* published posthumously "My Family's Slave" by Pulitzer Prize–winning journalist Alex Tizon, which recounts the life of Eudocia Tomas Pulido.[1] *Lola*, as Pulido was affectionately called, was brought to take care of Tizon's mother when she was twelve, and subsequently became the family's indentured servant or "slave" for over sixty years. The article gained much traction and became the most engaged story on the Internet for that year, with nearly 58 million minutes of collective reading time.[2] The publication of the highly controversial article garnered critiques from scholars, activists, and readers from all over the world. Discussions regarding class issues in the Philippines, the usage of *katulongs* (maids) and *kasambahays* (domestics), the connection of Pulido's story to American slavery, and contemporary issues with human trafficking are but examples of the many companion pieces that stirred conversations about the Tizon family's secret.

I start with "My Family's Slave" to highlight the importance of labor in Filipinx American studies. It is undeniable that Pulido was trafficked and that her story is significant in raising important attention to contemporary issues with labor and exploitation. My interest in Tizon's article, however, is on the fact that the moniker that was given to Pulido was the Filipino word for grandmother or *lola*. What might the usage of the word *lola* for Pulido signify? How does this open up new questions and vantage points surrounding labor in the field of Filipinx American studies? This essay interrogates the position of the elderly, specifically elderly migrants or those who move to the United States during the later parts of their lives through family re-unification, in our conceptions of Filipinx America. In highlighting the lives of these late-life migrants, this essay aims to show the importance of taking up disability/crip studies as an analytic in discussions of Filipinx labor, migration, and globalization.[3] I argue that while the importance of labor in Filipinx American studies has resulted in the normalization of the waged laborer as the subject of the field, disability studies illuminates how ability and age have always been central to our understanding of the historical and contemporary relationship between Filipinxs and the United States.

Labor, Ability, and Filipinx American Studies

Filipinx American studies scholars have shown the importance of "labor" in our field in order to understand the historical and contemporary experiences of Filipinxs. As a colony of the United States, Filipinxs became nationals, occupying an ambivalent position between citizen and noncitizen. This allowed Filipinxs to move freely across the borders of the United States and serve as a reliable source of cheap labor for plantations, canneries, and hotels in Hawaii, Alaska, and the West Coast of the United States.[4] Sony Coráñez Bolton reminds us that "'proving' the colonial subject's physical and cognitive incapacity lies at the heart of the colonial project."[5] Establishing Filipinxs as a cheap source of menial labor reinforces the idea of the Filipinxs incapacity for self-rule and justifies the need for American tutelage and education.

While the labor migration of Filipinxs during the colonial period has been documented by scholars, other groups of Filipinxs were also allowed to travel to the United States as *pensionados*. These Filipinx men and women were sponsored by the American government to seek an education in the United States, in order to return to the Philippines and serve as bureaucrats in the colonial government. Under American tutelage, the Philippines and its people could eventually gain independence. It is through the molding of the Filipinx brain under American ideals and the development of their mental capacity that self-rule could ever be possible. As Filipinx historian Renato Constantino points out in his seminal essay, "The Miseducation of the Filipino," it was through education that the Americans established a stronghold in the Philippines, which has reverberating effects until this day.[6]

It was in their understanding of and belief in the racial inferiority of Filipinxs, especially in relation to our minds, that our subjugation was warranted as their "little brown brothers" who needed saving for our own betterment. The migration of Filipinxs to the United States has always been implicated in the Filipinx body's capacity as able-bodied workers or their lack of the mental capacity to be recognized as independent.

The passage of the Immigration and Nationality Act of 1965, also known as the Hart-Celler Act, liberalized immigration policy and abolished the racist immigration quotas established by the multiple exclusion acts meant to limit migration from Asia. Post-1965 Filipinx migration has been an important focal point for the field of Filipinx American studies in highlighting the change in Filipinx migration. While previous waves of Filipinx migrants were mainly unskilled laborers who had no families, the creation of an employment-based category attracted and prioritized skilled laborers like doctors and engineers to migrate to the United States. To be a migrant then in post-1965 Filipinx America is to espouse certain ideas of mental ability and capacity that directly translate to an idea of what a productive and ideal citizen should be—an able-bodied educated professional who could contribute to American society.

Questions relating to disability cannot be divorced from our understanding of the greater Filipinx labor diaspora. In particular, scholars like Robyn Magalit Rodriguez have shown the development of the Philippines as a labor brokerage state during the Marcos regime in the 1970s.[7] Now, Filipinxs themselves have become the country's main export through its own training and marketing of its people.[8] While it is true that many Filipinxs are migrating for their productive labor, Martin F. Manalansan IV points out

that "Filipin[x]s have [also] been synonymous with [the] care industry across
the world" because of the Philippines' position as one of the biggest sources
of care and domestic workers and its dominance in the global care economy.[9]
This legibility of Filipinx workers across the world and their "innate" ability to care embodies what Harrod Suarez might call a "diasporic maternal," showing how the "the Philippines enters modernity through its own
kind of nurture, care, and service to the global economy."[10] The Philippines and the laborers that it exports are only legible if read under the conditions of the wage labor that they produce, whether they be productive or
reproductive labor. This may be because of their crucial positions as the
Philippines' new heroes, or *bagong bayani*, and the remittances that these
Overseas Filipinx Workers (OFWs) send back home, which amounted to
$33.8 billion in 2018.[11]

Uncovering the Figure of the Lola

While much focus has been given to labor migrants in the United States,
another crucial aspect of the Hart-Celler Act was its stipulations for family
reunification. Filipinx migrants were now able to move and later be joined
by those in their families, which is crucial when juxtaposed with the lives of
the *manongs*, or the generation of Filipinxs that moved as bachelors in order
to find work as farm, cannery, or domestic workers. Antimiscegenation laws
and the lack of women in their communities resulted in many of these Filipinx farmworkers having no families. The lack of familial support forced
many *manongs* to continue living among each other in the few affordable
places available to them like the International Hotel.[12] However because of
gentrification, places like the International Hotel fell victim to "urban development," resulting in these *manongs* having their own crisis of care, and
the subsequent organizing in the Filipinx community for Agbayani Village
in Delano, a retirement complex that opened in 1974.

This shift brought by the Immigration and Nationality Act of 1965 from
single bachelor migrants to heteronormative family migrants is important.
In many ways we can see how family reunification allows for those in the
United States to have a safety net when they reach their old age. Unlike the
manongs, post-1965 migrants have a support network that cares for them in
their old age. While Filipinxs are known for carework and reproductive

labor, Filipinxs themselves face their own issues with care. Who gets to care for our own?

This question of care, however, brings us back to the figure of the *lola*. Family reunification allows for specific members in one's immediate family to be petitioned as dependents to come to the United States. While many of these elderly migrants are able to work menial jobs in security, food service, and domestic service, many come to the United States specifically to take care of their grandchildren and maintain the home.[13] As Judith Treas and Shampa Mazumdar show, older immigrants petitioned by their naturalized children occupy important positions in immigrant families as those who provide the reproductive labor for the success of the family in the diaspora.[14]

Referring to Pulido as *lola*, then, is a discursive maneuver to include her in the family unit as the grandmother or distant relative who is there to support the family at large. As we see in "My Family's Slave," Pulido's importance in the family was exemplified by her labor. Namely, she was needed by the family because she cooked, cleaned, and took care of the Tizon family's children. Her legibility as a subject relies on her "functioning" as a grandmother. Pulido's representation as *lola* occludes those outside of the Tizon family from knowing her circumstances because of the naturalizing effects of being a grandmother as someone who cooks, cleans, etc. This leads people to automatically deduce that her presence in the United States is the result of family reunification rather than exploitation. The invocation of the word *lola* removes us from examining Pulido's intricate and complicated migration story as someone who was trafficked by the Tizon family and the exploitative condition we find her in as narrated in the article. The publication of "My Family's Slave" and the elision of the *lola* as a figure in the critiques and analyses related to Tizon's essay show the taken-for-granted position of the elderly migrant, and the elderly at large, as those who perform the crucial reproductive labor that is often relegated to "nonproductive" members of the family who do not "work."

Cripping Filipinx American Studies

Paying attention to the experiences of the elderly with family reunification, shows us how the study of labor and migration is also an interrogation of ability writ large. Disability studies is indispensable to the field of Filipinx American studies. The centering of the wage laborer in our discussions of labor in Filipinx American studies has effectively invisibilized the importance of elderly migrants and their reproductive labor. While their children who petitioned them are here in the United States for the productive labor they provide, these elderly migrants are able to migrate through the auspices of family reunification and their reproductive labor. The fact that these late-life migrants move to the United States at an older age already relegates them to the confines of the home or of low-paying jobs. This follows what Robert McRuer theorizes as "compulsory ablebodiedness" by pointing out identities that society normalizes, which in this case is the able-bodied subject that comes with "emphasis on work . . . [and] being capable of the normal physical exertions required in a particular system of labor."[15] We might read the centering of the wage worker's experience in this context, given the centrality of labor in migration and the development of the Philippines as a labor brokerage state. If the elderly migrant is not able to work because of their age and incompatibility with the labor needs of the United States, then their contribution lies in the home and the social reproduction of the family. Moving to the United States at an older age effectively *crips* the elderly migrant who is unable to function under the demands of neoliberalism and globalization.

What might it mean, then to "crip" Filipinx American studies and dialogue with disability studies? To claim crip, as Alison Kafer points out, "is to recognize the ethical, epistemic, and political responsibilities behind such claims; deconstructing the binary between disabled and able-bodied/able-minded requires *more* attention to how different bodies/minds are treated differently, not less."[16] To crip Filipinx American studies is to align ourselves and our questions to a radical critique that demands change rather than reform. To crip is to connect the experiences of elderly migrants to other marginalized groups—queers, the disabled, people of color—in order for the creation of coalitions and the understanding that our specific marginalizations under neoliberalism and globalization are not discrete phenomena but are interlinked.

By taking up disability studies, we are able to interrogate the OFW and other variations of waged migrants and laborers that have been normalized as the subjects of the field of Filipinx American studies. The importance of labor in discussions of Filipinx labor and migration cannot be denied, but we also need to point out what and whose labor are valued for inclusion in these mechanisms of migration. In cripping Filipinx labor history, we open up Filipinx American studies to reflections and questions of dependency and normalcy in order to continue our critical attention to the ways in which contemporary neoliberalism and globalization shift and affect Filipinxs in the Philippines and the diaspora at large. How might Filipinx American studies grapple with the management of aging in the Philippines, given that Filipinxs continue to serve as a global labor force for elderly care work? How does an analysis rooted in disability studies unsettle who we think a Filipinx migrant is? How is age used strategically in terms of granting Filipinx World War II veterans their long-sought-after rights? What coalitions and futures can we imagine if we make connections with other communities beyond the fact that we are here because of the labor we provide? These are but some questions we might ask in relation to disability studies, in thinking, forging, and creating better and crip futures.

NOTES

1. Alex Tizon, "My Family's Slave," *The Atlantic* (June 2017); *https://www .theatlantic.com/magazine/archive/2017/06/lolas-story/524490/.*

2. *The Atlantic,* "2017's Most Engaged Article is The Atlantic's 'My Family's Slave' by the late Alex Tizon" (December 19, 2017); *https://www.theatlantic.com /press-releases/archive/2017/12/most-engaged-article-of-2017-is-the-atlantics-my -familys-slave-by-the-late-alex-tizon/548699/.*

3. My interaction with the field of disability studies in this essay is marked by my usage of the words "disability studies" and variations of the word "crip" throughout the essay. However, it is important to bring up why I switch between them. The distinction rises from the critique of disability studies' whiteness and its previous lack of engagement with categories such as race. The reclamation of the word "crip" by disabled artists and activists, akin to the word "queer" as a term of empowerment, provides us with a term beyond "disabled" or "differently abled" that is also rooted in the inclusion of other marginalized identities. Scholars, however, point out that crip theory is not necessarily a replacement but rather an expansion of disability studies. My usage of crip theory and the word "crip" aligns my work with this critique of disability studies, given its importance in understanding not just people with disabilities but also in examining social relations premised on the attribution of value across difference.

4. For works that explore pre-1965 Filipinx migration to the United States, see the work of Dorothy Fujita-Rony, *American Workers, Colonial Power: Philippine Seattle and the Transpacific West, 1919–1941* (Berkeley: University of California Press, 2003); JoAnna Poblete, *Islanders in the Empire: Filipino and Puerto Rican Laborers in Hawai'i* (Champaign: University of Illinois Press, 2014); Linda España-Maram, *Creating Masculinity in Los Angeles's Little Manila: Working-Class Filipinos and Popular Culture, 1920s–1950s* (New York: Columbia University Press, 2006); Dawn Bohulano Mabalon, *Little Manila Is in the Heart: The Making of the Filipina/o American Community in Stockton, California* (Durham, N.C.: Duke University Press, 2013); and Rick Baldoz, *The Third Asiatic Invasion: Empire and Migration in Filipino America, 1898–1946* (New York: New York University Press, 2011), to name a few.

5. Sony Coráñez Bolton, "Cripping the Philippine Enlightenment: *Ilustrado* Travel Literature, Postcolonial Disability, and the 'Normative Imperial Eye/I,'" *Verge: Studies in Global Asias* 2, no. 2 (Fall 2016): 138.

6. Renato Constantino, "The Mis-education of the Filipino," *Journal of Contemporary Asia* 1, no. 1 (Autumn 1970).

7. Robyn Magalit Rodriguez, *Migrants for Export: How the Philippine State Brokers Labor to the World* (Minneapolis: University of Minnesota Press, 2010).

8. Anna Romina Guevarra, *Manufacturing Dreams, Manufacturing Heroes: The Transnational Labor Brokering of Filipino Workers* (New Brunswick, N.J.: Rutgers University Press, 2010).

9. Martin F. Manalansan IV, "Servicing the World: Flexible Filipinos and the Unsecured Life," in *Political Emotions: New Agendas in Communication*, ed. Janet Staiger, Ann Cvetkovich, and Ann Reynolds (London: Routledge, 2010), 215.

10. Harrod J. Suarez, *The Work of Mothering: Globalization and the Filipino Diaspora* (Champaign: University of Illinois Press, 2017).

11. "World Bank: PH 4th Biggest Recipient of Remittances in 2018," Inquirer.net, *https://business.inquirer.net/268422/world-bank-ph-4th-biggest-recipient-of-remittances-in-2018*.

12. See Curtis Choy, dir., *The Fall of the I-Hotel* (1983) and Estella Habal, *San Francisco's International Hotel: Mobilizing the Filipino American Community in the Anti-Eviction Movement* (Philadelphia: Temple University Press, 2007).

13. Rick Bonus, *Locating Filipino Americans: Ethnicity & the Cultural Politics of Space* (Philadelphia: Temple University Press, 2000), 45.

14. Judith Treas and Shampa Mazumdar, "Kinkeeping and Caregiving: Contributions of Older People in Immigrant Families," *Journal of Comparative Family Studies* 35, no. 1 (Winter 2004): 105–22. See also Judith Treas, "Transnational Older Adults and Their Families," *Family Relations* 57, no. 4 (October 2008): 468–78; and Judith Treas and Shampa Mazumdar, "Older People in

America's Immigrant Families: Dilemmas of Dependence, Integration, and Isolation," *Journal of Aging Studies* 16 (2002): 243–58.

15. Robert McRuer, *Crip Theory: Cultural Signs of Queerness and Disability* (New York: New York University Press, 2006), 8.

16. Alison Kafer, *Feminist, Queer, Crip* (Bloomington: Indiana University Press, 2013), 13.

Dalaga na! Gender and Youth Studies
Come of Age in Filipinx Studies

Evelyn Ibatan Rodriguez

My sister and I were raised in a community brimming with Navy dads who routinely found themselves bumping into each other at church, at school, and especially "on base." Some time after grade school, it seemed like our community decided to collectively declare us *dalaga na* (a young lady / young ladies already). At first, it was bewildering: How did we become *dalaga*? And when? And then it felt unoriginal: It was nearly every auntie and uncle's response when my parents reminded them of our names. Later, when I noticed that nothing comparable was said to or about our male counterparts, I wondered if it was sexist, a way of trying to contain us within the confines of "ladylike." Now that only the most charitable souls would describe us as *dalaga*, I see how *dalaga* attempts to capture something transitory and right on the cusp of developing into a new version of itself—which, arguably, describes where studies at the intersection of Filipinx youth and gender seem to have arrived, at the dawn of this new millennium.

Attention to gender in Filipinx American studies has mirrored the awareness and consideration of gender in general, and within the larger fields of Asian American studies, history, sociology, and other disciplines. Accordingly, although gender in Filipinx American studies has always been a formative factor for Filipinx Americans, Filipinx male (or "Pinoy") experiences and perspectives were almost exclusively studied and written about for decades after the field was established. Furthermore, analyses of Filipina (i.e., "Pinay") lives, and of how gender and gender ideologies organize the histories, experiences, and trajectories of all Filipinx Americans, was effectively absent until feminist female scholars began to create and document these in the 1990s. These contemporary Filipinx American studies have inevitably concentrated on young people since 80 percent of US-born Filipinxs are ages thirty-nine or under.[1]

More specifically, in spite of its groundbreaking contributions and ongoing influence in Filipinx American studies, the foundational historical text, *Filipinos: The Forgotten Asian Americans*,[2] offers an essentially male-centered narrative of Filipinxs in the United States. It establishes male "Manilamen," *pensionados*, and the large population of manual laborers who worked as "seafarers, famers, attendants"[3] in the US before World War II (and who are described as "predominantly male, single, and between the ages of sixteen and twenty-two"[4]) as the defining first waves of Filipinx migrants to the US. And while *Filipinos* documents their experiences richly and extensively, it depicts female Filipinx Americans as almost exclusively "wives, mothers and daughters,"[5] who were primarily responsible for "trying to rear growing families with their mates."[6] This in spite of the fact that *Filipinos* admits that Filipinx women comprised part of the earlier generation of *pensionados*,[7] and also composed part of the mid-twentieth-century paid labor force, "working alongside [Filipino men] in the fields or cooking for work crews."[8]

Such incongruence in the depth of examining Pinoy and Pinay histories could be attributed to the immense gender imbalance in the first and second waves of Filipinxs in the US (the 1930 US Census indicated a Filipinx male-to-female sex-ratio of approximately 14:1). However, the skewed gender ratio of the first Filipinx American waves cannot adequately explain why early Filipinx American studies did not contemplate more profoundly how economic and labor needs, US occupation of the Philippines, and a desire to safeguard white supremacy worked together to shape migration policies that led to Manila*men*, school*boys* helping to fulfill the US doctrine of "benevolent assimilation" for its "little brown *brothers*," and single *male* laborers making up the first and largest population of Filipinx Americans until the first half of the twentieth century. Furthermore, postwar shifts in US immigration legislation markedly changed the gender composition of the US Filipinx population after the 1940s. This granted spouses, children, and fiancées of Pinoy members of the US Armed Forces, and members of certain professions, "preferential" immigration status. This enabled certain white-collar female Filipinas to migrate to the US independently, and facilitated the subsequent formation and growth of Filipinx families and a gender-balanced generation of American-born Filipinxs in the United States. So, by the time Filipinx American studies was instituted in the late 1960s and early 1970s, the Filipinx male-to-female sex-ratio was almost even (11:9). And, by the time the definitive first histories of Filipinx Americans were published,[9] Pinays had actually come to outnumber Pinoys (as 52 percent of the US Filipinx population)—a trend that, according to US Census records, has not been reversed since.

In response to these demographic realities, and to their astute awareness of how these population changes had not advanced analyses of Pinay experiences in Filipinx American studies (nor introduced greater representation of Asian American women's experiences into feminist studies), scholars of Filipinx American studies like Yến Lê Espiritu and Allyson Tintiangco-Cubales began to challenge "the patriarchal bias of both Asian American and Filipino American studies" in the 1990s.[10] Foregrounding the stories of early and contemporary Filipina migrants and members of the US-born second generation helped make "gender visible in social phenomena," helped demonstrate "that gender inequality is inextricably braided with other systems of inequity,"[11] and enabled Filipinx American studies to better understand and contest "racism, sexism, imperialism, and homophobia," to help "decolonize" and "liberate" not just Pinoys, but "*all* Filipinos."[12]

Espiritu's *Filipino American Lives* was among the first major Filipinx American academic publications to acknowledge that "since 1960, women have dominated the Filipino immigrant population."[13] Accordingly, eight of the fourteen Filipinx American oral histories in Espiritu's book belong to Pinays, whose experiences she takes seriously, and describes richly. She also draws on these stories to point out how the "more egalitarian" gender structure in the Philippines contributed to her subjects' migration opportunities, and gave rise to a reconfiguration of gender roles for some in the United States, in response to US racism, colonization of the Philippines, and white supremacy.[14]

Tintiangco-Cubales's first essay on "Pinayism" was published the same year as *Filipino American Lives*, and sought to create a space to name and address the distinct and wide-ranging issues and circumstances of girls and women of Filipina descent in the US. In the essay, Tintiangco-Cubales describes Pinayism as concerned with "what it means to be Pinay," and as seeking "to look at the complexity of the intersections where race/ethnicity, class, gender, sexuality, spirituality/religion, educational status, age, place of birth, Diasporic [sic] migration, citizenship, and love cross."[15] This not only helped move Pinays from the margins of Filipinx American studies, it further illuminated how doing so broadened the field to consider how multiple, interconnected local and global systems of inequality—and not just racism—shape the experiences of Filipinxs in and outside of the US.

By widening the scope of Filipinx American studies beyond males, adult male labor, and the public sphere, these and other works by Filipinx American studies feminists helped explicitly open the discipline to more extensive and meaningful examinations of US-born Filipinx American youth, which has, in turn, helped evolve our understandings of Filipinx Americans and gender. While early studies of Filipinx Americans recognized that a "noticeable" population of "young people of Filipino ancestry . . . were growing up in America during [the] 1900s to 1950s,"[16] their discussion of this "bridge" generation was mostly limited to observations of how they differed from their parents in terms of language, activities, and their concurrent sense of belonging and being outside of US culture.[17] And in spite of the dramatically different sex ratios between the immigrant and bridge generations, they never meaningfully reflected on the activities of female members of the bridge generation nor their mothers.

This began to change in the 1990s when ethnic studies scholars accepted that the field had overlooked the lives of women and children, "as if their experiences were simply coequal to men's lives, which they are not."[18] One of the most critical early studies of second-generation Filipinx Americans was based on data collected on the sizeable sub-sample of US-born Filipinx youth included in the 1992–2002 "Children of Immigrants Longitudinal Study" (CILS), designed to study "the adaptation process of the immigrant second generation."[19] Drawing on the CILS findings, sociologists Yến Lê Espiritu and Diane L. Wolf examined "patterns of academic achievement and ambition, ethnic identify shifts, and psychological well-being" of Filipinx American youth.[20] Their analysis revealed how, in spite "of the seeming ease and success that they and their families have had in assimilating into US society and their solidly middle-class status," Filipinxs in the CILS sample were moving away from self-identifying as "American," and toward the ethnic identity of "Filipino." They also found evidence indicating that female youth in their study experienced more demands from their parents, and correspondingly higher rates of family conflict, depression, and lower self-esteem.[21] This helped elucidate how distinctive, complex, and gendered second-generation Filipinx experiences are, while challenging prevailing assimilationist theories of US immigrants.

Works like these, which gave thoughtful scholarly attention to Filipinx American women and young people's lives, created spaces in Filipinx American studies for studies like Dawn Bohulano Mabalon's "Beauty Queens, Bomber Pilots, and Basketball Players," which explained how young females in the bridge generation tactically negotiated identities and agency both under and against the pervasive influences of mid-twentieth-century US popular culture and the "culture of surveillance" enforced by the immigrant generation,[22] and Linda España-Maram's *Creating Masculinity in Los Angeles's Little Manila*, which demonstrated how the masculinities of Filipinx males between 1920 and 1950 were not innate, but instead informed by place and movement, and relative to other physically and socially adjacent ethnic, gender, and class groups.[23] These and other works also helped inspire later comparative studies like Evelyn Ibatan Rodriguez's *Celebrating Debutantes and Quinceañeras: Coming of Age in American Ethnic Communities*,[24] which studied contemporary young adult Pinays not just alongside their Pinoy counterparts and parents' generation, but together with Mexican American girls and their families. This study helped to further shift Europeans and males from the center of Filipinx American studies, while underscoring how contemporary second-generation femininities are strategically and creatively constructed to, among other things, help redefine and transform their families, culture, and communities.

Another consequence of moving women and young people's standpoints and experiences from the margins of Filipinx American studies at the turn of the twentieth century was an enhanced understanding and interest in how Filipinx Americans of all genders might participate in liberating themselves from the effects and traumas of patriarchy and colonialism. To help aid with this psychological decolonization, Filipinx Americans turned to scholars like Leny Mendoza Strobel, who as early as 1996 had begun to articulate how college-age Filipinx Americans might look toward the Philippines and Indigenous Filipinx practices to help "critique modernity" and "decolonize" their identities. This led those engaged in such decolonization to learn about and draw on matriarchal precolonial Filipinx knowledge and institutions, as well as Pilipino language (which, for example, lacks gender distinctions), and *Sikolohiyang Pilipino* (for notions like *kapwa* [self-in-relation] and *loob* [shared humanity]), to assert that decolonization entails a rejection of sexism, and an understanding that the liberation of Pinays is linked to the liberation of all Pinoys.[25] This helped engender a new sense of "Filipino pride" among US-born Filipinxs starting at the close of the twentieth century, a greater urge to understand Filipinx transnationalism (which produced a number of notable works exploring how gender identities are informed by understandings, constructions, and performances of gender throughout the diaspora—e.g., Catherine Ceniza Choy's *Empire of Care: Nursing and Migration in Filipino American History*, Kale Bantigue Fajardo's *Filipino Crosscurrents: Oceanographies of Seafaring, Masculinities and Globalization*, Valerie Francisco-Menchavez's *The Labor of Care: Filipina Migrants and Transnational Families in the Digital Age*, Rhacel Salazar Parreñas's *Servants of Globalization: Women, Migration and Domestic Work*, Victoria Reyes's *Global Borderland: Fantasy, Violence, and Empire in Subic Bay Philippines*, and Robyn Magalit Rodriguez's *Migrants for Export: How the Philippines Brokers Labor to the World*[26]), an "explosion" of artistic cultural productions "meld[ing] Filipino Indigenous concepts, symbols, and practices with Filipino American sensibilities,"[27] and more substantial scholarly exploration of Filipinx sexualities.

Gender does not equal sexuality, but the two are commonly associated, and often influence one's experience of the other. Correspondingly, the "engendering" of Filipinx American studies has helped open up the field to research that does not just explore Filipinx sexuality (e.g., how it is defined, manipulated, controlled, imposed), but that studies Filipinx sexual identities, and how these are related to gender identities. One of the earliest seminal pieces to examine gay Filipinx men in the United States is Martin F. Manalansan IV's "Searching for Community: Filipino Gay Men in New York City,"[28] which demonstrated that Filipinx American communities are not exclusively or naturally organized around race, ethnicity, gender, and/or sexual identity. Manalansan's ethnography showed that his Philippine- and US-born gay Filipinx subjects did not necessarily identify with each other, due to language, coming-of-age in places with distinctive "homosexual traditions," and personal class-consciousness—though, they could be drawn together in response to various historical instances and shared social concerns. Filipinx American psychologist Kevin L. Nadal's work on LGBT Filipinx Americans further underscores diversity within nonheterosexual Filipinx populations by explaining why LGBT Filipinxs cannot be assumed to have experiences similar to non-Filipinx LGBT individuals, nor to each other, since there are several "identity statuses" that LGBT Filipinxs can experience.[29] Anthony Christian Ocampo's work shows that both Nadal's and Manalansan's findings hold up among second-generation gay Filipinx males, who Ocampo found to relate more to their ethnic and racial communities than mainstream gay communities, and to form their coethnic gay communities based on generation, as well as class and ways of performing race, gender, and sexual identity.[30]

With scholarship by researchers like Ocampo, Nadal, and Manalansan, *pagdadalaga* Filipinx American gender studies (it has "blossomed," or come of age) to its newest frontier: exploring identities and Pinxy experiences that go beyond the "masculine" and "feminine" gender binary. These include those who have indefinite, an overlap of, or no lines between, gender identities—"agender," "genderfluid," and "transgender," for example. And though Nadal and other Filipinx American studies and gender and sexualities specialists have recognized the existence of "transgender" populations for decades, the pioneers in Pinxy gender nonconforming analyses have been Pinxys like genderqueer poet Cheena Marie Lo,[31] and self-described "disabled pin@y-amerikan transgender queer" poet, performer, and educator Kay Ulanday Barrett,[32] whose creative work and public talks have helped bring visibility to nonbinary Pinxys, thereby challenging Filipinx American studies to once again grow to offer more complete representations and analyses of the histories, experiences, and evolving trajectories of all Filipinxs. Such work has, in turn, driven academic spaces to invent and expand the language of gender in Filipinx studies, and to push the field to investigate how "to create more gender-inclusive education and communities, both within the state and internationally."[33]

NOTES

1. Pew Research Center, Filipinos in the U.S. Fact Sheet (Washington, DC, 2021); *https://www.pewresearch.org/social-trends/fact-sheet/asian-americans -filipinos-in-the-u-s/*.

2. Fred Cordova, Dorothy Laigo Cordova, and Albert A. Acena, *Filipinos, Forgotten Asian Americans: A Pictorial Essay, 1763–Circa 1963* (Dubuque, Iowa: Kendall/Hunt, 1983).

3. Cordova, Cordova, and Acena, *Filipinos*, 24.

4. Cordova, Cordova, and Acena, *Filipinos*, 14.

5. Cordova, Cordova, and Acena, *Filipinos*, 147.

6. Cordova, Cordova, and Acena, *Filipinos*, 149.

7. Cordova, Cordova, and Acena, *Filipinos*, 130.

8. Cordova, Cordova, and Acena, *Filipinos*, 149.

9. For example, Cordova, Cordova, and Acena, *Filipinos*; Ronald T. Takaki, *Strangers from a Different Shore: A History of Asian Americans* (Boston: Little, Brown, 1989).

10. Melinda L. de Jesús, *Pinay Power: Peminist Critical Theory: Theorizing the Filipina American Experience* (New York: Routledge, 2005), 3.

11. Yến Lê Espiritu, *Filipino American Lives* (Philadelphia: Temple University Press, 1995), x.

12. de Jesús, *Pinay Power*, 5.

13. Espiritu, *Filipino American Lives*, 21.

14. Espiritu, *Filipino American Lives*, 29–30.

15. Allyson Tintiangco-Cubales, "Pinayism," in *Pinay Power: Peminist Critical Theory*, ed. Melinda L. de Jesús (New York: Routledge, 2005), 137–48; here, 140–41.

16. Cordova, Cordova, and Acena, *Filipinos*, 155.

17. Cordova, Cordova, and Acena, *Filipinos*, Chapter 8; Evelyn Nakano Glenn, "Split Household, Small Producer and Dual Wage Earner: An Analysis of Chinese American Family Strategies," *Journal of Marriage and the Family* 45 (1983): 35–46.

18. Shirley Hune, "Doing Gender with a Feminist Gaze: Toward a Historical Reconstruction of Asian America," in *Contemporary Asian America*, ed. Min Zhou and James Gatewood (New York: New York University Press, 2000), 413.

19. "The Children of Immigrants Longitudinal Study (CILS)," Princeton University, Center for Migration and Development; *https://cmd.princeton.edu /publications/data-archives/cils*, accessed August 7, 2020.

20. Yến Lê Espiritu and Diane L. Wolf, "The Paradox of Assimilation: Children of Filipino Immigrants in San Diego," in *Ethnicities: Children of Immigrants in America*, ed. Ruben G. Rumbaut and Alejandro Portes (Berkeley: University of California Press; Russell Sage Foundation, 2001), 157–58.

21. Espiritu and Wolf, "The Paradox of Assimilation," 182.

22. Dawn Bohulano Mabalon, "Beauty Queens, Bomber Pilots, and Basketball Players: Second Generation Filipina Americans in Stockton, California, 1930s to 1960s," in *Pinay Power: Peminist Critical Theory*, ed. Melinda L. de Jesús (New York: Routledge, 2005), 117–35.

23. Linda España-Maram, *Creating Masculinity in Los Angeles's Little Manila: Working-Class Filipinos and Popular Culture, 1920s–1950s* (New York: Columbia University Press, 2006).

24. Evelyn Ibatan Rodriguez, *Celebrating Debutantes and Quinceañeras: Coming of Age in American Ethnic Communities* (Philadelphia: Temple University Press, 2013).

25. Leny Mendoza Strobel, *Babaylan: Filipinos and the Call of the Indigenous* (Davao City, Philippines: Ateneo de Davao University, Research and Publications Office, 2010); Leny Mendoza Strobel, *A Book of Her Own: Words and Images to Honor the Babaylan* (San Francisco: Tiboli Publishing, 2005); Leny Mendoza Strobel, *Coming Full Circle: The Process of Decolonization among Post-1965 Filipino Americans* (Quezon City, Philippines: Giraffe Books, 2001).

26. Catherine Ceniza Choy, *Empire of Care: Nursing and Migration in Filipino American History* (Durham, N.C.: Duke University Press, 2003); Kale Bantigue Fajardo, *Filipino Crosscurrents: Oceanographies of Seafaring, Masculinities, and Globalization* (Minneapolis: University of Minnesota Press, 2011); Valerie Francisco-Menchavez, *The Labor of Care: Filipina Migrants and Transnational Families in the Digital Age* (Urbana: University of Illinois Press, 2018); Rhacel Salazar Parreñas, *Servants of Globalization: Migration and Domestic Work*, 2nd ed. (Stanford, Calif.: Stanford University Press, 2015); Victoria Reyes, *Global Borderlands: Fantasy, Violence, and Empire in Subic Bay, Philippines* (Stanford, Calif.: Stanford University Press, 2019); Robyn Magalit Rodriguez, *Migrants for Export: How the Philippine State Brokers Labor to the World* (Minneapolis: University of Minnesota Press, 2010).

27. See Strobel, *Babaylan*, 40.

28. Martin F. Manalansan IV, "Searching for Community: Filipino Gay Men in New York City," *Amerasia Journal* 20, no. 1 (1994): 59–74.

29. Kevin L. Nadal, *Filipino American Psychology: A Handbook of Theory, Research, and Clinical Practice* (Bloomington, Ind.: AuthorHouse, 2009), 183–84.

30. Anthony C. Ocampo, "The Gay Second Generation: Sexual Identity and the Family Relations of Filipino and Latino Gay Men," *Journal of Ethnic and Migration Studies* 40, no. 1 (2014): 155–73.

31. See Sara Wintz, "24/7 Gender Is Hard: Cheena Marie Lo on the Poetics of Both and Neither," Poetry Foundation; *https://www.poetryfoundation .org/harriet/2014/05/24-7-gender-is-hard-cheena-marie-lo-on-the-poetics-of-both -and-neither*, accessed August 7, 2020.

32. See Kay U. Barrett, "Kay Ulanday Barrett"; *http://www.kaybarrett.net/*, accessed August 7, 2020.

33. Nikki Abeleda, Mikayla Aruta Konefał, and Katherine Nasol, "Gender Justice and Transgender Rights in the Pilipinx Community," *Asian American Policy Review* 29 (2019): 24–29.

THIRTY-THREE

Unpacking *Hiya*: (Trans)national "Traits" and the (Un)making of Filipinxness

Martin F. Manalansan IV

The imagined community of Filipinos within and Filipinxs beyond the nation[1] is often set off by a myriad of distinctions, traits, affects, and personality characteristics that demarcate their difference, and signify their togetherness and sovereignty. Since the 1950s, Filipino and Filipinx American scholars and the general public have devoted efforts to finding essential characteristics that constitute "Filipinoness" or what I call "Philippine peoplehood" that ostensibly shed light on "what makes a Filipino a Filipino" and that explain Filipinos' and Filipinxs' contingencies and positionalities. Among these essential characteristics that have persisted across various time periods and geographic locations from the mid-twentieth century to the present is *hiya*. This essay is a critical examination of the challenges in the circulation of discourses of *hiya* in scholarship and popular cultural discourses.

Hiya is a Tagalog word considered to be one of the pivotal affective and emotional scaffoldings in the construction of a Filipino/Filipinx American national character and identity.[2] Loosely translated and popularly (mis)understood as "shame," *hiya* has survived multiple critiques and scholarly revisions, and has remained one of the most deployed idioms in characterizing Filipino cultural quirks, idiosyncrasies, or "innate" traits both in academic and quotidian settings. *Hiya* has traveled on both scholarly and vernacular routes so that Filipino and Filipinx American studies practitioners are cognizant of its continued currency and popularity.[3]

Hiya has many faces in Philippine and Filipinx American studies. Despite its typical translation as "shame," *hiya* is a troublesome, vexed, and multivalent Tagalog category. Its multiple meanings have not stopped it from becoming one of the pivotal dimensions of what has been variously called Filipino / Filipinx American personality, Filipino character, or a decolonial Filipino psychology (*Sikolohiyang Pilipino*). Despite its contentious position in knowledge production, it remains as a major discursive node, rationale, or an emblem for "Filipinoness" or peoplehood as well as for explaining and rationalizing behavior, social predicaments, and other existential situations involving Filipinos and Filipinx Americans.

Hiya is often used to explain many challenges faced by Filipinxs in America. An illustrative example of this practice is the popular explanation for why Filipino food has not attained mainstream visibility and appreciation until very recently. Many Filipinxs food professionals have asked why, despite the long historical connection between the United States and the Philippines as well as the significant numbers of Filipinx immigrants in America, Filipino food has not become as popular as Chinese, Japanese, Korean, and Thai cuisines. *Hiya*, in the guise of national shame, has been used by many people, including some Filipinx chefs and scholars, to rationalize the cuisine's lack of mainstream status in the United States. Filipinx restauranteurs, the discourses suggest, are allegedly ashamed of their food and therefore limit their clientele to co-ethnics, thereby inhibiting the food's mainstream acceptance.[4] Clearly, this is a simplistic view of the circulation, development, and mainstreaming of a cuisine in modern times, as well as a troublesome use of a "national cuisine" as a stand-in for the various regional culinary cultures. Furthermore, the use of *hiya* in explaining the lack of US mainstream recognition of Filipino cuisine does not interrogate this clamor for American popular acceptance and glosses over the various historical, political, and economic issues inherent in food entrepreneurial ventures.

Hiya's genealogy has a complex transnational provenance and multidirectional trajectories. It has been subjected to divergent interpretive frames. *Hiya* is sometimes seen as an individual feeling ensconced in a singular body and is characterized by an uncomfortable if not painful emotion due to some perceived shortcoming or impropriety, the body thereby becoming subject to possible humiliation, disgrace, and/or disrepute. These particularized states of ignominy and discredit might be seen as a universal human propensity but in the case of Filipinos and Filipinx Americans, *hiya* becomes a particularly "Filipino" problematic character flaw, an ingredient for a putative national personality trait, and a collective feeling caused by some deficiency or lack.

Social science scholarship has been at the forefront in examining the social dimensions of *hiya* as part of nation-building, modernization, and decolonization. At the Ateneo de Manila University, the Institute of Philippine Culture (IPC) was established in 1960 as a major center for research on Philippine culture. First, after being loosely translated as "shame," *hiya* was defined by IPC founder Frank Lynch as "the uncomfortable feeling that accompanies awareness of being in a socially unacceptable position, or performing a socially unacceptable action."[5] It is a form of "losing face" in situations involving a subject or subjects not being able to meet normative standards. It is undergirded by a direct or indirect compulsion to apologize or to explain away the source of the embarrassment or shaming. In other words, according to these scholars, *hiya* functions as a form of social control or a social value that shapes individual and collective behaviors aimed at social acceptance, propriety, and normative behavior. This version of *hiya* is based on a "relational self" and the idea that Filipinos/Filipinxs are focused on maintaining consensus or what has been called "smooth interpersonal relationships." These revisions of *hiya* have led to its valorization as a form of social constraint and a desirable behavioral complex. *Hiya*, in this sense, is key to a stable social order and collective harmony.

Later, a group of University of the Philippines psychologists formed what is now seen as the *Sikolohiyang Pilipino* or Filipino Psychology movement in 1975 that aimed to decolonize social science, specifically psychology, from its Western provenance. Proponents of this decolonizing movement decried the ways in which *hiya* (with various "affixations" in the language) can mean "embarrassing" (*nakakahiya*), "placed in an embarrassing position" (*napahiya*), shy (*mahiyain*) and so on.[6] This same group of scholars has called for more rigorous empirical examination of *hiya* and other terms that compose what is seen as the Philippine value system. To date, there has not been any final empirical statement about *hiya*. But it is precisely the call for empiricism that is at the heart of its problems—the impulse to establish or disprove its objective status.

As one can glean from the aforementioned social science discourses, *hiya* can be considered to be a cultural idiom produced by tensions and contradictions in meaning. On the one hand, it is seen as the culprit behind the lack of progress, slow modernization, and other dismal conditions. It is a tool for understanding the perils and promise of nation-building. It becomes the rationalization for the ongoing negative state of affairs and the enduring economic deprivation besetting Filipinos and Filipinxs. *Hiya*, then, is seen to emanate from feelings of estrangement from the group and alienation, as well as from situations involving the lack of agency or adequate aggressive action/reaction to adverse conditions. *Hiya* is often seen as a premodern local emotional baggage that should not be "brought out" of the Philippines. It is a barrier to nation-building and to authentic patriotism. It is portrayed as a negative vestige of Philippine people's long colonial and neocolonial subjugation. This long history is alluded to be one of the causes of the "colonial mentality," where there is a lack of national pride in anything "Filipino."[7] Therefore, colonial mentality, as undergirded by *hiya*, allegedly produces a subservient national personality and an emotional flaw that is detrimental to the flourishing of proud nationalist sentiments.

On the other hand, *hiya* is sometimes instrumentally portrayed as a positive virtue or an ethical value that enables and encourages group cohesiveness and identification. Scholars, particularly those in philosophy, have suggested that *hiya* is an ethical orientation toward an empathetic sociality that thrives on consensus and peaceful coexistence.[8] *Hiya* is considered a virtue by generating what people consider to be a peaceful sociality, and the creation of "smooth" interactions devoid of conflict and violence, and is a moral stance akin to Christian piety.

It is not the goal of this work to offer a definitive portrait of *hiya* but rather to unpack its unwieldy and complicated bundle of meanings and practices. What I have done thus far, due to lack of space and time, is to broadly lay out the multiple problems and limitations that confront the circulation and dissemination of *hiya* and its relationship to Filipinos and Filipinx Americans. Now I turn to possible approaches that may productively engage and dismantle the stranglehold of *hiya* in Filipino and Filipinx American lives and productively open up more capacious ways of understanding. I believe the main issue about *hiya* is the very idea of a monolithic notion of Filipino and Filipinx American national character or personality. The scholarly and quotidian investment in *hiya* as a national trait, value, or characteristic is always already flawed. The use of a category like *hiya* as an overarching "Filipino"/x attribute has multiple untoward consequences. I use the normative male designation in quotes because the history of *hiya* is embedded in this mainstream national appellation that includes gendered nationalist meanings embedded in its usage in scholarly and vernacular discourses devoid of other forms of differences and inequalities such as class, gender, sexuality, etc. Second, the idea that *hiya* is an "emic" or native "Filipino" term fails to recognize the irony of the word "native" as it overlooks the particularity of the term to Tagalog regional linguistic norms. Originally, the IPC version of *hiya* was really part of a cultural mapping project of lowland Christian majority communities, particularly those in the main island of Luzon that surround and are mostly part of the nation's capital region. Such a Manila-Tagalog-centric view violently disregards other regional languages and cultures, particularly the worldviews of Indigenous and Muslim minority groups in the Philippines that do not necessarily adhere to or align with the idea and identity of "Filipino." Third, the scholarly unpacking of *hiya* in terms of an interiority or *loób* is based on a Judeo-Christian and late nineteenth-century European understanding of subjectivity where the borders between private/domestic and the public are firmly circumscribed. Even with the positing of the "relational self" or a self embedded in social togetherness or collectivity, *hiya* cannot overcome its distinctly bourgeois normative orientation that is a reaction to a lack or shortcoming based on one's behavior and status. Fourth, the use of traits and attributes avoids an engagement with structural conditions and messy historical shifts including class, gender, and regional and ethnolinguistic differences. Fifth, there needs to be a further careful consideration of the traffic and travel of *hiya* and other alleged "Filipino" traits particularly with Filipinx Americans in relation to Filipinos in the Philippines and other parts of its global diaspora.

These critical points are not at all new. In anthropology, "the culture and personality" school, which flourished in the 1940s and purported to create a behavioral portrait of a nation or a society, has been disparaged and rejected by many scholars over the last four decades of the previous century.[9] Despite these criticisms, the impulse to find the *essential in the national* still persists to this day. Its persistence is due to the circulation of social science discourses around modernity and citizenship that I have mentioned above. More importantly, these discourses find their way to being taught in schools and colleges as one of the definitive markers of Filipino and Filipinx American experiences.

Hiya, despite many efforts, is still conceived as a static, hermetically sealed constellation of national embodied experiences and collective feelings. If this is so, then how can a decolonizing effort succeed within this narrow framework of *hiya*? What is to be done? Finally, moving away from a mere facile rejection of *hiya*, I strongly urge Filipinx American studies scholars, together with their Filipino/Philippine-based colleagues, to collaboratively create new frameworks and critical understandings of *hiya* as a dynamic affective and discursive idiom that continues to circulate in people's everyday lives within multiple contexts. The use of "idiom" here is a way to circumvent the easy conflation and/or erasure of geographic scales, cultural differences, histories, and structural inequalities. It also bypasses the quagmire of labeling *hiya* as a value, a virtue, or a negative colonial vestige because such names prematurely define the existential status of this idiom and fail to acknowledge other possible alternative dimensions, experiences, and frameworks. In other words, I suggest putting *hiya* in "suspension" to investigate its shifting multivalent deployments and their repercussions.

A more productive use of *hiya* involves a sensitivity to the complexities of agents and contexts. For example, there needs to be more critical attention to the facile yet erroneous slippages of *hiya* from individual bodies or actors to collectivities and imagined communities, or what I have called here as a contingent and mercurial Philippine peoplehood. "Peoplehood" itself is not a given or, rather, an unquestioned category. Therefore, the use of *hiya* as an affective idiom will hopefully give rise to a more radical understanding of the messy relationships between the individual and the social, the material/physiological and the cultural, the internal and the external, the contemporary and the historical, and the "national" and the diasporic. Filipino and Filipinx American scholars throughout the humanities and behavioral social sciences are extending and complicating the view of *hiya* with other so-called attributes.[10] *Hiya* can be productively recast in terms of the field of queer studies' confrontations with shame, particularly in how it deals with the consensual, the normative, and the mainstream.[11]

I suggest that Filipino and Filipinx American cultural producers, scholars, and community activists need to pose more critical questions and not blindly accept terms like *hiya* as an essential Filipinx character "trait." First, they need to confront the vicissitudes of the category "Filipino" and its diasporic emanation "Filipinx." We cannot take peoplehood for granted and ignore that rather tenuous demarcation of Filipinx peoplehood. What do the terms "Filipino" and "Filipinx" include and what do they ignore?

Taking these questions into serious consideration, I end this essay not with a conclusion but with a provocation to future thoughts and debates through a series of questions and concerns. First, we need to question the very idea of "trait" that has been subject to a long history of critiques from social scientists and humanists. We need to step back and not ask, "What is *hiya*?" but to question our very investment in this endeavor. To borrow from Sara Ahmed, what does it mean for Filipinos and Filipinx Americans to claim their identity through *hiya*?[12] Does naming a trait always already assume a preexisting collectivity to which it refers? Does this claiming of *hiya* require some kind of collective apology? Does it cover up other feelings, structures, and culprits? Does this claiming require "getting over it" either by forgetting or by an amelioration through so-called empowerment tactics that will convert shame into pride? What does it mean to persistently pursue traits and behavioral patterns that are labeled "Filipino"? What are the political and cultural efficacies of such a pursuit or orientation? What do we do when we highlight or erase *hiya* as an essential component of being Filipino/Filipinx and disentangle it from the morass of history and structural inequalities? Why do we fervently search for the essential and not the mercurial and the messy in the vernacular and the everyday? Finally, the problem at hand is not about adding more definitions to the long list of meanings of *hiya*. Neither is it an issue of whether it exists or not. Rather, we need to ask, "What does *hiya* do?" or what does its deployment in multiple situations enable or inhibit, create or dismantle in terms of a more critical, capacious, and judicious understanding, construction, and unmaking of Filipino and Filipinx American predicaments, challenges, identities, and futures.

NOTES

1. My use of both "Filipino" and "Filipinx American" recognizes the transnational nature of my analysis. My non-use of Filipina is precisely to dramatize the problematic masculinist vocabulary that exists in many scholarly works.

2. Jaime C. Bulatao, "Hiya," *Philippine Studies* 12, no. 2 (1964): 424–38.

3. Kevin L. Nadal, *Filipino American Psychology: A Handbook of Theory, Research and Clinical Practice* (New York: Wiley, 2011); Aurora Tompar Tiu and Juliana Sustento-Seneriches, *Depression and Other Mental Health Issues: The Filipino American Experience* (San Francisco: Jossey Bass Publishers, 1994).

4. Angilee Shah, "A Filipino restaurant owner says shame may be one reason authentic Filipino food has not become mainstream," TheWorld (February 13, 2014); *https://theworld.org/stories/2014-02-13/according-filipino -restaurant-founder-new-yorkers-can-handle-plate-duck-embryos*.

5. Frank Lynch, "Social Acceptance Reconsidered," in *IPCC Papers No. 2: Four Readings on Philippine Values*, ed. F. Lynch and A. De Guzman (Quezon City, Philippines: Ateneo de Manila University Press, 1961), 1–68.

6. Rogelia Pe-Pua, "*Sikolohiyang Pilipino* (Filipino Psychology): A Legacy of Virgilio G. Enriquez," *Asian Journal of Social Psychology* 3 (2000): 49–71.

7. E. J. R. David, *Brown Skin, White Minds. Filipino-/American Postcolonial Psychology* (Charlotte, N.C.: Information Age Publishing, 2013).

8. Jeremiah Reyes, "*Loób* and *Kapwa*: An Introduction to a Filipino Virtue Ethics," *Asian Philosophy* 24, no. 2 (2015): 148–71.

9. Milton Barnett, "*Hiya*, Shame and Guilt: Preliminary Consideration of the Concepts as Analytical Tools for Philippine Social Science," *Philippine Sociological Review* 14, no. 4 (1966): 276–82.

10. Nadal, *Filipino American Psychology*.

11. Sally Munt, *Queer Attachments: The Cultural Politics of Shame* (Aldershot, Hampshire, UK: Ashgate, 2007); Elspeth Probyn, *Blush: Faces of Shame* (Minneapolis: University of Minnesota Press, 2005).

12. Sara Ahmed, *The Cultural Politics of Emotion* (New York: Routledge, 2004).

THIRTY-FOUR

Language Run Amok

Sarita Echavez See

We love puns and we live to play with words. Forgive us our signs.[1] We like to create nonsense and nonmeaning. The worse the pun, the louder the laughter, the more it circulates, and the longer its social life. While language typically is associated with the creation of meaning and the enabling of communication, this essay focuses on the importance in Filipinx American studies of letting language run amok and of letting the idea of the discipline—a persistently sacrosanct concept in academia—run amok.

It should come as no surprise that Filipinxs butcher English. After all, the "special relationship" between the United States and the Philippines was inaugurated through a genocidal war of conquest followed by the imperial policy of "benevolent assimilation," most virulently through the imposition of the English language and American education throughout the islands. Over more than a century of militarized and economic neo/colonial relations between the Philippines and the United States (or what the historian Jason Gavilan calls the "U.S.-Philippine nation"), the English language has had an immeasurable impact on the shaping of Filipinx subjectivity, whether domestic, migrant, diasporic, or, now, with the emergence of the Philippines as the so-called call-center capital of the world, "offshore" subjectivity.[2] More than a century after the monumentally violent Philippine-American War, the English language once again has emerged as a "language of regulation" for workers in call-center companies that have mushroomed in the Philippines and that tend to service American customers.[3]

Let us recall the etymology of "amok" or "amuck" or "a-muck."[4] With as much dignity as it can muster, the *Oxford English Dictionary* states that the noun "amok" refers to a "frenzied Malay" and a "murderous frenzy." It derives from the Malay/Bahasa *amok*, the word or "linguistic artifact" for violence that has its own complex history in and across different Malay languages.[5] *Amok* entered the English language via the Portuguese *amouco* or *amuco* in the sixteenth century, around the Western encounter with the so-called New World. Since its entry into Western languages, "amok" has been a means of typecasting entire cultures and peoples, especially Malays, Indians, and Filipinxs, as essentially cruel, violent, and volatile. For over five hundred years, "amok" also has become a source of fascination, confusion, and mystery for literary, journalistic, legal, and psychology commentators and scholars, what one contemporary critic calls a "colonial obsession" that has generated a "veritable industry of explication."[6] Hence, it is crucial to resist the temptation to "unravel amok's mystery," which merely would increase the already staggeringly prodigious output from this industry. Rather, the critical task is to "explore in greater detail the colonial investment in [amok]."[7]

In short, the history of amok is a history of colonial discourse. The violence of the Malay running amok functions as a smokescreen for the violence of colonial capitalist voracity, from the British mining for tin in Malaya and for gold and copper in Australia to the American planting of sugarcane in the Philippines and Hawai'i, and the violence of the suppression of resistance to that voracity. The media sensationalism of the Malay or the Filipinx running amok masks a global history of anticapitalist, anticolonial resistance, from the series of major Malay uprisings against the British in the late nineteenth century and early twentieth century to the 1906 Battle of Bud Dajo during the Philippine-American War to the rise of labor militancy often initiated and led by Filipinxs in early twentieth-century Hawai'i.[8]

"Amok" became the psychological and legal basis for the criminalization of entire peoples and the justification for the subjugation of colonized populations.[9] The word "amok" in the English language thus ricochets between British and American imperialisms and between Malay and Filipinx forms of resistance.

In Filipinx American culture, this interimperial, transcultural ricochet appears in the form of bad as well as brilliant puns. The poet-novelist Eric Gamalinda captures this history of lingual domination and resistance with his lingually miscegenous essay title "English Is Your Mother Tongue/Ang Ingles Ay ang Tongue ng Ina Mo."[10] Gamalinda's title makes visible how misogyny travels across three languages in this mingling of the Spanish pejorative *puta*, the Filipinx expletive *putang ina mo* (or its condensed version *'tang ina mo*), and the English word "tongue." The stand-up comedian Rex Navarrete is a cofounder of the experimental Filipinx American theater troupe Tongue in a Mood, established in 1992 in California, which also uses a tongue-in-cheek reference to *putang ina mo*. In his solo stand-up work, like many other immigrant bicultural comedians, Navarrete is known for his fluid shifting between standard and nonstandard accents in English. He brilliantly mocks the English language in his skit about ESL (English as a Second Language) class: "What does ESL stand for? English is a stupid language. It's stupid. It makes no sense to me." Made to enroll in ESL class as an immigrant child, Navarrete redefines the acronym and converts it into nonsense. He then goes on to analyze the word "laughter" as an example of nonsensical English spelling rules: "They say, follow the rules. But they keep breaking it themselves. Right? Like, the word 'laughter.' Let's spell 'laughter,' shall we? L-a-u-g-h-t-e-r. Laughter. That 'g-h': Is that really a 'fff' sound?" Navarrete then caps the joke with a turn to manslaughter: "How about 'manslaughter'? It's got the word 'laughter' in it. So you think I can ever get charged with the crime of man's laughter?" His jokes about the senselessness of English-language spelling rules serve as a larger condemnation of the senseless brutality of colonial rule. From laughter to manslaughter, Navarrete runs amok.[11]

In other words there is a materiality to language made visible by the tremendous pressure exerted by the colonized object on the imperial subject. If "amok" has fascinated Westerners for several centuries, this obsession signals an ideology of possession and possessiveness that unexpectedly redounds upon the imperial subject. The Black studies critic-poet Fred Moten reminds us: "While subjectivity is defined by the subject's possession of itself and its objects, it is troubled by a dispossessive force objects exert such that the subject seems to be possessed—infused, deformed—by the object it possesses."[12] Moten's account explains the extraordinary pressure that the poet-historian Kimberly Alidio exerts on the English language in her rearrangement of "found" language lifted from the American archives on US colonial power in the Philippines and Guåhan (Guam).[13]

As part of that longer tradition of revealing the materiality of language, since the 1970s and particularly since the 1990s, Filipinx American studies scholars have made it their task to trace what Allan Punzalan Isaac calls America's "imperial grammar" and its "disappearing clauses," which includes the forgetting of the Filipinx and the "invisibilization," as Oscar V. Campomanes has put it, that is foundational to American imperialism.[14] These scholars also have sought to describe the emergence of a Filipinx American "postcolonial syntax" even as the remembering of Filipinxs in America reveals the capitalist colonial nightmare of the American Dream, or what Dylan Rodríguez has called the "Filipino condition" and the impossibility of the hyphenated Filipinx American subject.[15] Notable scholarship includes work by literary critic Victor Román Mendoza on the gendered assimilationism of early twentieth-century Philippine *pensionado* student writing in the United States; poet-historian Kimberly Alidio on the reverberating impact of early twentieth-century American teachers' manuals and English-language composition curricula on the disciplined formation of today's neoliberal globalized Filipinx workforce; historian Augusto F. Espiritu and literary critic E. San Juan Jr., on the significance of folklore, orature, and a collectivist and revolutionary rather than individuated authorial identity in the writings of Carlos Bulosan; literary critic Martin Joseph Ponce and again Augusto F. Espiritu on the gendered performativity of José Garcia Villa's poetry; cultural studies critic Vicente M. Diaz on puns and wordplay as a means of documenting the circulation and displacement of *mestizo* and *indio* affiliations in post–World War II Guåhan; anthropologist Martin F. Manalansan IV on the modes of "speaking in transit" among late twentieth-century gay Filipinx immigrants in New York City; and popular culture studies scholar Karen Tongson on the powerful desires that subtend contemporary forms of Filipinx song-based mimicry like karaoke.[16] In terms of a stricter definition of "language" as a lingual system of communication, influential scholarship in Filipinx American studies includes historian Vicente L. Rafael on the politics of translation across Spanish and American colonialisms; psychologist Virgilio Enriquez on *Sikolohiyang Pilipino* and the lingual-based study of Filipinx ontology; and linguist Teresita Ramos on the pedagogy of Filipinx language programs.[17]

When it comes to "language" in Filipinx American studies, the limits of the field are the limits of this essay. With a few striking and important exceptions, the field generally is bound to English-language sources and can be affixed to a rather narrow and inflexible definition of the vernacular.[18] These problems also generally pervade Asian American studies and so, despite the much-vaunted move toward the transnational, there is a lot of room for new research that can move both Filipinx American studies and Asian American studies forward with a stronger transnational praxis and a more capacious sense of the vernacular. And I would venture to propose that we can move toward a more rigorous sense of the transnational and a more expansive concept of the vernacular in at least two ways: first, by vigorously supporting and defending comparatist scholarship (e.g., involving fluency in two or more languages, which typically requires longer periods of training and research); and second, by advancing a more general recognition of the distinct and alien form that English takes in the hands and on the tongues of Filipinxs, what Oscar V. Campomanes has called "vernacularizing acts."[19]

I have taken this essay as an opportunity to reflect on the way that Filipinxs globally run amok and how Filipinx American studies imagines and creates a nonpropertied space of decolonial knowledge production in the American academy. I mean to highlight not simply the orality but the living literariness of a culture that has been belittled as imitative of the English language and of Anglo American and European canonical literatures. For what is at stake in the way we theorize the relationship between language and power-knowledge is not only the study of objects of analysis we have in view right now, but those that we can barely imagine. In our era of the neoliberal and neofeudal assault on what is left of the public university (there are some unmistakable likenesses between neoliberal and medieval forms of accumulation by dispossession) and on the general commitment to the nonrationalized and noncommodified study of culture, I continue to believe in the Filipinx refusal to end meaning-making.

And I continue to believe in the general refusal to commodify the ends of meaning-making.

NOTES

1. "Forgive Us Our Signs 12," *Positively Filipino: Your Window on the Filipino Diaspora*, last modified December 11, 2018; *http://www.positivelyfilipino.com /magazine/forgive-us-our-signs-12*, accessed December 13, 2018.

2. Jason Gavilan, "The Politics of Enlistment, Empire, and the 'U.S.-Philippine Nation': Enlisted and Civilian Filipino Workers in and beyond the United States Navy, 1941–1965" (PhD diss., University of Michigan, 2012); Don Lee, "The Philippines Has Become the Call-Center Capital of the World," *Los Angeles Times*, February 1, 2015; *https://www.latimes.com /business/la-fi-philippines-economy-20150202-story.html*, accessed January 18, 2019.

3. Allan Punzalan Isaac, "'I Understand Where You're Coming From': Temporal Migration and Offshore Chronographies," in *Filipino Time: Affective Worlds and Contracted Labor* (New York: Fordham University Press, 2021), 77. See also Jan M. Padios, *A Nation on the Line: Call Centers as Postcolonial Predicaments in the Philippines* (Durham, N.C.: Duke University Press, 2018). According to Isaac and Padios, the business processing outsourcing (BPO) industry has reshaped the domestic Philippine economy, disrupted workers' circadian rhythms, and created a new "offshore" subjectivity with distinct consumerist desires.

4. I follow the example of Jacqui Donegan and Raymond Evans who use "amok" because it is the traditional Malay/Bahasa spelling rather than the Anglo versions of "amuck" or "a-muck"; see Jacqui Donegan and Raymond Evans, "Running Amok: The Normanton Race Riots of 1888 and the Genesis of White Australia," *Journal of Australian Studies* 25, no. 71 (2001): 83–98.

5. Thomas Williamson, "Communicating Amok in Malaysia," *Identities: Global Studies in Culture and Power* 14, no. 3 (2007): 361. For an account that combines linguistics and Malay studies approaches, see Rozaimah Rashidin and Nor Hashimah Jalaluddin, "Metaphor of AMOK in Traditional Malay Text Corpora: An Analysis Using the Hybrid Theory," *Procedia: Social and Behavioral Sciences* 118 (2014): 412–19.

6. Eduardo Ugarte, "Running Amok: The 'Demoniacal Impulse,'" *Asian Studies Review* 16, no. 1 (1992): 183, 182. Ugarte makes the following quip about this "industry of explication": "If the East was a career, to paraphrase Disraeli, so too was amok, to judge from the number of authors whose reputations were enhanced by their stirring accounts of a behavioral pattern that most never saw, much less understood" ("Running Amok," 184).

7. Ugarte, "Running Amok," 188.

8. Donegan and Evans, "Running Amok"; Eduardo Ugarte, "Muslims and Madness in the Southern Philippines," *Pilipinas* 19 (1992): 1–24; and Jonathan Y. Okamura, "From Running Amok to Eating Dogs: A Century of Misrepresenting Filipino Americans in Hawai'i," *Ethnic and Racial Studies* 33, no. 3 (2009): 496–514.

9. For an account of "psychiatric primitivism" and *amok*, see Rodney H. Lucas and Robert J. Barrett, "Interpreting Culture and Psychopathology: Primitivist Themes in Cross-Cultural Debate," *Culture, Medicine and Psychiatry* 19 (1995): 287–326.

10. Eric Gamalinda, "English Is Your Mother Tongue/Ang Ingles Ay ang Tongue ng Ina Mo," in *Vestiges of War: The Philippine-American War and the Aftermath of an Imperial Dream, 1899–1999*, ed. Angel Velasco Shaw and Luis H. Francia (New York: New York University Press, 2002), 247–59.

11. For my fuller reading of Navarrete's stand-up comedy, see Chapter 3: "The *Sikolohiya*/Psychology of Rex Navarrete's Stand-up Comedy," in Sarita Echavez See, *The Decolonized Eye: Filipino American Art and Performance* (Minneapolis: University of Minnesota Press, 2009). See also the column "Amok," which the journalist-humorist Emil Guillermo wrote and published in the weekly *AsianWeek* from 1994 to 2008 and then moved to the blog for the organization Asian American Legal Defense and Education Fund; *http://www.amok.com/* and *https://www.aaldef.org/blog*, accessed January 15, 2019.

12. Fred Moten, *In the Break: The Aesthetics of the Black Radical Tradition* (Minneapolis: University of Minnesota Press, 2003), 1.

13. Kimberly Alidio, *after projects the resound* (United States: Black Radish Books, 2016), 13, 22, 53.

14. Allan Punzalan Isaac, *American Tropics: Articulating Filipino America* (Minneapolis: University of Minnesota Press, 2006); Oscar V. Campomanes, interview by Antonio Tiongson Jr., "On Filipinos, Filipino Americans, and U.S. Imperialism: Interview with Oscar V. Campomanes," in *Positively No Filipinos Allowed: Building Communities and Discourses*, ed. Antonio T. Tiongson, Jr., Edgardo V. Gutierrez, and Ricardo V. Gutierrez (Philadelphia: Temple University Press, 2006), 26–42. See also Reynaldo Clemeña Ileto, "Friendship and Forgetting," in *Knowledge and Pacification: On the U.S. Conquest and the Writing of Philippine History* (Quezon City, Philippines: Ateneo de Manila University Press, 2017), 163–201.

15. Dylan Rodríguez, *Suspended Apocalypse: White Supremacy, Genocide, and the Filipino Condition* (Minneapolis: University of Minnesota Press, 2009).

16. Victor Román Mendoza, "Certain Peculiar Temptations: Little Brown Students and Racial-Sexual Governance in the Metropole," in *Metroimperial Intimacies: Fantasy: Racial-Sexual Governance, and the Philippines in U.S. Imperialism, 1899–1913* (Durham, N.C.: Duke University Press, 2015),

167–202; Kimberly Alidio, "A Wondrous World of Small Places: Childhood Education, US Colonial Biopolitics, and the Global Filipino," in *Filipino Studies: Palimpsests of Nation and Diaspora* (New York: New York University Press, 2016), 106–27; Augusto F. Espiritu, "Suffering and Passion: Carlos Bulosan," in *Five Faces of Exile: The Nation and Filipino American Intellectuals* (Stanford, Calif.: Stanford University Press, 2005), 46–73; E. San Juan Jr., Introduction to *On Becoming Filipino: Selected Writings of Carlos Bulosan*, ed. E. San Juan Jr. (Philadelphia: Temple University Press, 1995), 1–44; Martin Joseph Ponce, "The Queer Erotics of José Garcia Villa's Modernism," in *Beyond the Nation: Diasporic Filipino Literature and Queer Reading* (New York: New York University Press, 2012), 58–88; Augusto F. Espiritu, "The Artistic Vanguard: José Garcia Villa," in *Five Faces of Exile: The Nation and Filipino American Intellectuals*. (Stanford, Calif.: Stanford University Press, 2005), 74–101; Vicente M. Diaz, "Pappy's House: History, Pop Culture, and the Reevaluation of a Filipino-American 'Sixty-Cents' in Guam," in *Vestiges of War: The Philippine-American War and the Aftermath of an Imperial Dream, 1899–1999*, ed. Angel Velasco Shaw and Luis H. Francia (New York: New York University Press, 2002), 318–28; Martin F. Manalansan IV, "Speaking in Transit: Queer Language and Translated Lives," in *Global Divas: Filipino Gay Men in the Diaspora* (Durham, N.C.: Duke University Press, 2003), 45–61; Karen Tongson, "Empty Orchestra: The Karaoke Standard and Pop Celebrity," *Public Culture* 27, no. 1 (2015): 85–108.

17. Vicente L. Rafael, *Contracting Colonialism: Translation and Christian Conversion in Tagalog Society under Early Spanish Rule* (Durham, N.C.: Duke University Press, 1992) and *White Love and Other Events in Filipino History* (Durham, N.C.: Duke University Press, 2000); Virgilio Enriquez, *Decolonizing the Filipino Psyche: Philippine Psychology in the Seventies* (Quezon City: Philippine Psychology Research House, 1982) and *From Colonial to Liberation Psychology: The Philippine Experience* (Quezon City: University of the Philippines Press, 1992); and Teresita V. Ramos, "Reclaiming a Heritage Language: The Filipino American Explosion," *Pilipinas: A Journal of Philippine Studies* 33 (Fall 1999): 99–113.

18. When it comes to literary and cultural studies, in addition to the aforementioned works by Allan Punzalan Isaac and Vicente L. Rafael, these exceptions include comparatist scholarship like the following: John D. Blanco, "Race as Praxis in the Philippines at the Turn of the Century," *Southeast Asian Studies* 49, no. 3 (December 2011): 356–94, and "Oriental Enlightenment and the Colonial World: A Derivative Discourse?" in *Filipino Studies: Palimpsests of Nation and Diaspora* (New York: New York University Press, 2016), 56–81; Jason Coráñez Bolton, "Crip Native Woman: The Hispanic American Philippines and the Postcolonial Disability Cultures of US Empire" (PhD diss., University of Michigan: Ann Arbor, 2016); and Ryanson Ku, "Wounded

Language/Time: History, the Novel, and the Filipino-American Relation" (PhD diss., University of California, Irvine, 2017). For examples of scholarship with a more expansive approach to the vernacular, see Oscar V. Campomanes, "The Vernacular/Local, the National, and the Global in Filipino Studies," *Kritika Kultura*
3 (2003): 5–16; and Gladys Nubla, "The Politics of Relation: Creole Languages in *Dogeaters* and *Rolling the R's*," *MELUS* 29, no. 1 (Spring 2004): 199–218;

19. Campomanes, "The Vernacular/Local," 13.

Afterword

Gina Apostol

Why am I in this mix? Of literary scholars and historical genealogists, archival critics and social scientists, labor historians and performance theorists? I'm a fabulist, a fantasist, a maker of fictive dreams. In short, as far as I know, my job as a novelist is to make things up. I kept asking myself this question—*what is my role as a reader in this text?*—when I opened this book and found myself unable to put it down.

When he asked me to write a foreword, I said to Professor Rick Bonus, to whom actually I could never say no—*okay, I'm in the middle of writing a novel, but of course I'll do it.* In my faithless mind, being an annoying *maldita* of a common kind, I thought to myself: *I'll skim it.* But as I settled in with his introduction, then read through the table of contents, then began the first essay in "Empire as Endless War," then decided to read the next, then the next, then the next, then went on to "Labor and Knowledge/Power," then "Across Language, Sex-Gender, and Space-Time Geographies" and "Critical Schooling and Justice in Other Words," then on to "Relationalities,

Intimacies, and Entanglements" and "Recalcitrant Bodies, Unruly Vernaculars," I found myself increasingly unable to let the book go and, in fact, move on to my novel.

I was stuck in its pages, interlaced in the text.

It seemed to me, I was radioactivated: A nugget of knowledge in one essay seemed to electrify my reading of the next, and that in turn made me alert to the spark of connection that might follow. For me, an analytic kindling wired this entire book. Each essay has the suggestive quality of opening up an Aladdin's cave—and you encounter a turn that leads you to an unexpected path, though what the key has done is perhaps unlatch something in you, which I tried to name.

I tried to understand this—the book's effect on me, this sense of electrification, of being keyed to its words; responding with inarticulate comprehension to the organization of its essays: its circuitry, so to speak; finding Hansel-and-Gretel crumbs that glowed in the dark, so I could retrace my steps if I so wished and discover, as I moved backward or sideward or forward through the essays, a concatenation of mindful sparks, all somehow linked, like a constellation always on the verge of being envisioned in the mind's eye—and so you keep trying to trace it.

Each essay had both its own *posporo*—its phosphorescent flicker of thought—but also a trigger that set off another: and so shaped the whole.

What I came to understand as I kept reading was that this book kept articulating for me an awareness of being that I also understand makes me keep writing my novels. Each essay, each note, each turn, each key was not, in fact, embedded in knowing—but in indeterminacy. Thus, that scholarly acuteness runs through these essays: That is, each essay rightly points out that the map is not complete, a road has yet to be paved, a final accounting is still out of reach. The acuity and power of this book lie in its recurring recognition of its knowledge's indeterminacy.

I've sometimes had to explain, in interviews, why the Philippines and its history remain my subject as a novelist. After all, I can make anything up. I've had to try to articulate my experience of being—this unspeakable sense of my multiplicity, my paratextual existence (my carrying about this system of signs, moving in the world as I do as both my own annotator and the subject of my annotations), my polylingualisms, my existence as a figure in the gaps of my self-translations, my doubly conscious—and in my case unperturbed—invisibility wrought in turn by my unaccountably visible presence in, let's say, the American space that barely acknowledges the history of why I'm here.

Surely, anyone coming from the violent past of colonialism, of racial horror, of capitalist subjectivity, of imperial schemes, will understand there is nothing exceptional about my dilemma.

In some ways, for both the powerful and the powerless, if one is careful and reflexive and metacognitive of one's place in the world, such a sense of being—of indeterminate multiplicity, of unfinished identities divided by economics and history and tongues—could be called simply the state of being socialized, of our current humanity. That state of modernity in which all of us seem condemned to live.

In this case, I often say, I write about the Philippines because, for me, my sense of my indeterminate multiplicity, and the violence and even ordinariness embedded in that, underlines my commonality with all.

For me, this infinitely translatable, unspeakable yet multitongued, divided self makes the Filipino hypermodern, hyperhuman, I will say in interviews.

But even as I say that, I recognize its incompleteness, my dissatisfaction with my claim. Because I am a materialist, and to default into universalism upsets my laws of reason.

Only in the particular can one speak the universal.

I wish to explain that there is something particular in the way I understand my history, my identity, my unapologetic sense of my indeterminacy, my inability to completely articulate the rich gaps of what constitutes my "self."

What this book does is find a way out of that trap of inarticulability without falling into the trap of either essentialism or universalism. This book gives us the terms, the frameworks, the turns, a set of clues to orient us. But the richness of possibility, the indeterminacy of knowing—precisely because of the specific complexity of these scholars' dialectical ways of seeing—is accurately embedded in its design.

Thus, in this book, all parts speak to the others: Labor is inextricable from history and migration is moored to identity and performance is linked to gender and language is inseparable from empire and affect is related to labor and on down the chain. Repetitions boomerang and wake us. Connections rule. In the gaps lie some salvations.

All keys fit all the doors.

The goal of this book is clearly not to speak the answers but to ask the questions. And the book directs us also how to ask these questions. *What is my role as a reader in this text?* Each essay is not separate from the others, yet each essay also has its specific ground of probing excavation: Each essay gives the reader its own, particular matter to grasp. And it's through this interlacing—one scholar's singular preoccupations enlaced with others'—that the reader, too, is enlaced in the book. This book says: The way to ask questions is to understand one is compassed, listening and attuned, in everyone else's "repertoire," as Theodore S. Gonzalves musically notates in his essay contribution. I like that musical invocation because it speaks to this book's ethos of communality: its symphonic sense of being attuned to others' texts. That is how I got stuck in this book, electrified and concatenated and webbed in its dialectical ways of knowing—these scholarly keys that touch upon and resound what makes us up.

Key Resources in Filipinx American Studies

A Selection of Library Research Tools and Web Resources Related to Filipinx American Studies

Gerardo A. Colmenar

I had only one escape—the Los Angeles Public Library.
—CARLOS BULOSAN, *America Is in the Heart*

This annotated list of resources represents a compilation of research and bibliographic web-based tools, archival digital web portals, independent news sources, cultural and arts websites, and academic research guides containing information on Filipinx American studies. I came across these sources while assisting scholars, students, and general "information seekers" in the course of my work as an academic librarian and in my capacity as a news correspondent for *Third World News and Review* (TWNR) and a cohost of a community radio show *No Alibis*.¹ Documentation and archiving are fundamental to librarianship and archival practice, but the idea of developing a curated list of resources and research tools on Filipinx Americans came naturally to me, given my liaising and collecting responsibilities. The same goes for archivists who undertake the meticulous process of creating finding guides for collections that include correspondence, diaries, manuscripts, ephemera items, and so forth. As library and information science (LIS) scholar Melissa Adler states, "We might think of librarians [and archivists] as curators of knowledge."[2]

In compiling this list, I relied on independent news organizations as well as collaborations among archivists, librarians, scholars, information technologists, and publishers who compiled or developed these resources from many places worldwide. These websites and internet bibliographic tools were developed and continue to be maintained to bring attention to and enhance the findability of materials for Filipinx American studies scholars. For the same reason, cultural anthropologist Oona Thommes Paredes wrote about her archival research experiences in Spain and the United States to bring attention to these archival institutions that, in her view, are underappreciated and underutilized.[3] Likewise, the scholar-researcher was the audience I had in mind when I began to document this selection of resources that contain or point to materials relevant to the field. My list includes, but is not limited to, academic articles, historical documents, government documents, obscure and/or out-of-print scholarly publications, and independent news sources.[4] I focused on resources that are commercial—i.e., resources requiring individual or institutional subscriptions—as well as freely available (open access[5]). As the title suggests, this is not an exhaustive list of resources available, but a selection that will most probably change, given shifting institutional policies and decisions based on financial, social, and political conditions, to include the URL and/or hosting site.

I hope that these selections further open and facilitate the discoverability of the growing troves of research materials, many of which have been collected, curated, and maintained by archivists, librarians, and digital experts, and made accessible through cultural institutions (e.g., libraries, archives, museums, etc.) and in partnership with commercial publishers.

I want to thank the coeditors for inviting me to contribute to this anthology and participate with scholars in this project, many of whom were inspired by Carlos Bulosan's classic work *America Is in the Heart*. Indeed, as the editors observed, Bulosan's *America* was a pivotal work that inspired several generations of scholars whose work highlighted the marginalization and invisibility of Filipinxs in US society and within the panethnic Asian American studies rubric.

Research Tools

ARCHIVEGRID

https://researchworks.oclc.org/archivegrid/

ArchiveGrid includes over five million records describing archival materials, bringing together information about historical documents, personal papers, family histories, and more. With over a thousand different archival institutions represented, ArchiveGrid helps researchers looking for primary source materials held in archives, libraries, museums, and historical societies.

INTERNET ARCHIVE

https://archive.org/

Internet Archive (IA) is a 501(c)(3) nonprofit digital library that gathers internet sites and other cultural artifacts in digital form. Similar to a library, IA provides free access to researchers, historians, scholars, the print disabled, and the general public. IA contains over twenty years of web history accessible through the *Wayback Machine*. IA collaborates with 450+ library and other partners through Archive-It program to identify important web pages, including government websites.

ONLINE ARCHIVE OF CALIFORNIA

http://www.oac.cdlib.org/

The Online Archive of California (OAC) provides free public access to detailed descriptions of primary resource collections maintained by more than two hundred contributing institutions, including libraries, special collections, archives, historical societies, and museums throughout California and collections maintained by the ten University of California (UC) campuses.

https://www.crl.edu/area-studies/seam/collections/holdings-list

Founded in 1970 by librarians specializing in Southeast Asian materials, SEAM is a community of interest working under the umbrella of the Center of Research Libraries that acquires, preserves, and maintains microform and digital collections of rare and unique materials on Southeast Asia. SEAM holdings on the Philippines include the Jose Cuenco Collection, Philippine Election Materials, Jose P. Laurel Papers (1918–59), Unpublished Papers, Articles and Speeches/Institute of Philippine Culture (1960 to present).

Research Guides: A Selection

Created and compiled by librarians in colleges and universities, research guides provide library users a basic introduction to resources on subject-specific disciplines and topics available from their respective library institutions, especially subscription-based articles, databases, digital archival collections, and newspapers, as well as local archival materials. These guides also contain a list of online resources and websites of organizations, historical societies, and cultural organizations whose contents are freely available, especially with the growing number of materials digitized in the public domain for scholarly research.

1. **Philippine Studies Research Guide, University of Michigan Library**

   https://guides.lib.umich.edu/c.php?g=424993

   Offers an expansive listing of collections of archival material and primary sources at governmental, historical, and university institutions in the United States. Highlights include:

   Worcester Philippine History Collection
   Maria C. Lanzar-Carpio Papers

Erving Winslow Papers, 1898–1922—includes correspondence related to the Anti-Imperialist League, particularly with respect to Philippine independence, 1903–22

2. **Philippine and Filipino American History & Heritage, University Libraries, University of Maryland**

https://lib.guides.umd.edu/filipinos

Contains a listing of archival collections and web resources located at the university's special collections and within the Washington, DC, area. The collection includes a rich assortment of manuscripts, photographs, and personal papers.

3. **Filipino Americans, Skyline College, San Bruno, California**

https://guides.skylinecollege.edu/c.php?g=279142

The research guide contains links to audio and video recordings of oral history interviews conducted by students in History 240: History of Ethnic Groups in California. The interviewees came from different countries, including the Philippines. The guide also includes web resources and online articles on culture, history, and the arts, with a focus on organizations and groups in San Francisco.

4. **Guide to Filipino-American Resources at the Library of Congress**

https://www.loc.gov/rr/main/filipino/index.html

The guide provides an entry point for finding materials in multiple formats on Filipinx Americans and related resources at the Library of Congress. The types of items covered in this document range from special collections containing photographs and diary entries to monographs, reference works, serials, and newspapers.

5. **Military Conflicts in Special Collections, University of Oregon**

https://researchguides.uoregon.edu/scua-military-conflicts /philippine

This guide contains a listing of primary source materials on United States involvement in the Philippines in the early twentieth century, with emphasis on those who served in the Philippine Constabulary.

Databases and Electronic Journals—Licensed and Open Access

These selections of databases and online journals are essential resources that index academic journals, popular magazines, dissertations, and other types of works. The list includes subscription-based and freely available resources (open access) maintained by university and college libraries.

1. **America: History and Life**

https://www.ebsco.com/products/research-databases/america-history
-and-life

A bibliographic database that contains citation information on articles, primarily scholarly in nature, on the history of the United States and Canada, covering prehistory to the present. The database indexes core journals pertinent to the field, such as *Ambrosia*, *Asian & Pacific Migration Journal*, *Journal of Asian American Studies*, and *Philippine Studies*.

2. **Asian American Drama**

https://alexanderstreet.com/products/asian-american-drama

Contains over two hundred plays by forty-two playwrights, with detailed information related to productions, theaters, and production companies, many of which have never been published. The database includes the works of playwrights of Filipinx descent, such as Jeannie Barroga, Linda Faigao-Hall, and Jessica Hagedorn.

3. **Bibliography of Asian Studies**

https://www.asianstudies.org/publications/bibliography-of-asian
-studies/

A comprehensive bibliographic database with detailed citations about East, Southeast, and South Asia, as well as Asian diasporic communities. The database indexes Western-language journal articles, review articles, conference proceedings, and chapters in anthologies published worldwide.

4. Directory of Open-Access Books (DOAB)

https:/www.doabooks.org

The primary aim of DOAB is to increase discoverability of books available for free (open access). The directory is open to all publishers who publish academic and peer-reviewed books in open-access formats.

5. Directory of Open-Access Journals (DOAJ)

https://www.doaj.org/

DOAJ is a community-curated online directory that indexes and provides access to high-quality, open-access, peer-reviewed journals. The scope is international and multilingual.

6. Dissertations and Theses

Dissertation and theses databases represent a core bibliographic resource for students and scholars in general. These databases are essential tools for doing extensive literature reviews, especially for locating unpublished theses and dissertations.

Open-Access Theses and Dissertations (OATD)

> https://oatd.org/
> OATD is a full-text open-access database containing over 3.5 million electronic theses and dissertations (ETD) with a Creative Common License. Schools worldwide contribute to the database repository.

Dissertations and Theses (ProQuest)

> https://about.proquest.com/products-services/dissertations/

A licensed subscription database from ProQuest containing the work of authors from over 1,000 graduate programs in North America and worldwide.

7. JSTOR

www.jstor.org

An acronym for journal storage, JSTOR is a repository of thousands of journals with full-runs of archived titles starting with their first issues. JSTOR includes scholarly journals in the humanities, social sciences, and sciences from publishers worldwide, preserving and making their content digitally available. JSTOR indexes core journals such as *Pacific Historical Review*, *Philippine Quarterly of Culture and Society*, *Philippine Sociological Review*, *Philippine Studies*, and *Verge: Studies in Global Asias*.

8. *Kritika Kultura*

https://ajol.ateneo.edu/kk

An open-access semi-annual peer-reviewed international electronic journal of literary, language, and cultural studies of the Department of English of the Ateneo de Manila University, Philippines.

9. *Kyoto Review*

https://kyotoreview.org/

This review's primary goal is to bring news of important publications, debates, and ideas into region-wide circulation through lively and accessible writing. In addition, it seeks to encourage sustained engagement between university-based intellectuals and those working in NGOs, journalism, and cultural production. The journal carries articles in seven languages: Bahasa, Filipinx, Thai, Indonesian, Japanese, Vietnamese, and English.

10. PhilPapers

www.philpapers.org

Provides a comprehensive index of literature in philosophy that includes journals, books, personal webpages, and open-access archives. The collective efforts of hundreds of volunteers and institutional supporters in the curation, classification, and crowd sourcing of content have enabled Philpapers to be the primary open-access archive of research in philosophy.

Archival and Primary Sources

Digital technology has enabled opening up the archives of the recorded past (e.g., printed materials) to a wider and more distant group of users without having the need to travel to these institutions. Collected, preserved, and maintained by archivists at library special collections, museums, and archival institutions, these materials are easier to browse and access through online finding guides with links to digital reproductions.

1. **Calisphere**

https://calisphere.org/

> The collections in Calisphere have been digitized and contributed by all ten campuses of the University of California and other libraries, archives, and museums throughout the state. Calisphere provides free access to unique and historically important artifacts for research, teaching, and curious exploration. Discover over one million photographs, documents, letters, artwork, diaries, oral histories, films, advertisements, musical recordings, and more.

2. **Directory of Open-Access Repositories (OpenDOAR)**

http://v2.sherpa.ac.uk/opendoar/

> Launched in 2005, DOAR compiles and hosts open-access repositories to academic materials and resources worldwide. The directory is arranged and can be browsed by country.

3. **HATHI TRUST Digital Library**

www.hathitrust.org

> Hathi Trust is a digital repository and research management tool created in collaboration with libraries of member institutions, many

of which are in the United States. The repository contains materials that are co-owned and co-managed as digital archives of library materials that were converted from the print collections of the member institutions.

3. Katipunan Documents

http://www.kasaysayan-kkk.info/

This site is dedicated to the study of the Katipunan, the patriotic secret society that in 1896 launched the revolution against Spanish rule in the Philippines. Its principal aim is to make available a number of important Katipunan documents that have not been published before, or are not readily accessible.

4. Labor Archives of Washington—University of Washington Special Collections

http://depts.washington.edu/civilr/index.htm

Includes materials on Filipinx American civil rights activists in Seattle—Dorothy and Fred Cordova, Bob Santos, Cindy Domingo, and more. Contains primary sources and visual materials on the Cannery Workers and Farm Labors Union, whose membership includes Filipinx Americans.

5. Library of Congress, United States

https://www.loc.gov/collections/

The Library of Congress digital and print collections include an array of materials in different formats pertaining to the Philippines and Filipinx American materials from the fifteenth century to the present. Included in the LoC catalog are archived websites and webpages.

6. Newberry Library, Philippine Manuscripts

www.newberry.org/philippine-manuscripts

The Newberry Library contains a rich collection of manuscripts, books, maps, and photographs on the Philippines. These materials are housed in the Ayer Collection that was originally assembled at the beginning of the Philippine occupation by the United States. Many of the Ayer materials are unique and salvaged from the Barcelona library of the Compañía General de Tabacos. There are excellent materials dating from the latter half of the eighteenth century until the revolution. There are hundreds of photographs from the Dean Worcester and other collections.

7. Portal de Archivos Españoles (PARES)—Archives in Spain

http://pares.culturaydeporte.gob.es/inicio.html

This is a project of Spain's Ministry of Culture to digitize archival records. Significant collections on the Philippines are the sections called Archivo General de Indias, Archivo Histórico Nacional, and Archivo General de Simancas.

8. The Smithsonian

https://www.si.edu/

The Smithsonian, like the Library of Congress, has amassed thousands of materials on the Philippines and Filipinx American experience, including thousands of images, a handful of videos, and links to exhibitions.

9. The Vatican Film Library

https://www.slu.edu/library/

Located at Saint Louis University in St. Louis, Missouri, this library has two major collections of primary sources on the Philippines.

Archivum Romanum Societatis Iesu (ARSI)

Select records of official business and correspondence of the central government of the Society of Jesus housed in the Archivum Romanum Societatis Iesu in Rome and pertaining to activities in North and South America and the Philippines up to the late nineteenth century.

Pastells Collection

> Materials transcribed by Pablo Pastells, SJ, during the last decade of the nineteenth and the first three decades of the twentieth century, documenting the history of the Jesuit Order and its work in the Americas and Philippines, including the Patronato Real and colonial education.

10. **Welga Digital Archive—Bulosan Center for Filipinx American Studies**

https://welgadigitalarchive.omeka.net/

> Incorporated into the Bulosan Center for Filipino American Studies, the Welga Archive's main focus is the preservation and presentation of the Filipinx American experience in its broadest aspects. The project is based in the Asian American Studies Center at the University of California, Davis.

11. **World's Fairs**

https://www.worldsfairs.amdigital.co.uk/

> Developed by Adam Matthew, a publisher of Digital Archives, this database represents an archival digital collection of government records, including early financial appeals and matters of delicate international diplomacy, minutes and correspondence of fair committees, and plans and design concepts, as well as contemporary ephemera (tickets, pamphlets, posters), personal accounts, and official guidebooks from over two hundred fairs held in Europe and North America.

News Sources

Reporters Without Borders, for several years up to the present, ranks the Philippines as one of the most dangerous places for journalists. According to Sheila Coronel, cofounder of the Philippine Center for Investigative Journalism and director of the Stabile Center for Investigative Journalism at

Columbia School of Journalism, "There is no tradition of state- or party-owned presses or broadcasting entities in the Philippines. Through most of Philippine history, newspapers, radio and television have been almost always in private hands." Despite or because of the overwhelming private ownership of news media, Coronel points to the strong "fighting tradition" of the Philippine press, attributed to the anticolonial press during successive waves of colonizers—Spain, United States, and Japan.[6] This tradition continues, as evinced by the presence of independent news media outlets that offer critical independent news reporting and investigative journalism despite the government's continued attack on news media and journalists to the present.

BULATLAT, JOURNALISM FOR THE PEOPLE

www.bulatlat.com

Bulatlat is a verb that means to search, to probe, to investigate, or to unearth facts. It was established in 2001 by a group of concerned and politicized individuals who were disaffected by the political corruption of government officials. Its mission:

> The media's role has always been to inform the public about these issues and to provide a vehicle where these are discussed. More importantly, alternative media organizations such as Bulatlat.com seek to reflect the people's views and stand on issues that affect their lives and their future—human rights and civil liberties, national patrimony, workers and peasant rights and interests, migrant rights and welfare, the rights and status of women, indigenous people's rights, the environment, among others.[7]

KODAO PRODUCTIONS

www.kodao.org

Established in 2001, Kodao Productions is an alternative multimedia group that produces videos and radio programs on human rights, the environment, and social and economic justice in the marginalized sectors of the Philippines. It has helped communities establish community radio stations and programs.

"Kodao" is a knotted rattan string that served as the Philippines' first calendar. Each knot represents a community event. Kodao Productions is dedicated to documenting events that affect the Filipinos' search for a national identity and quest for genuine democracy, sovereignty, and economic development.[8]

PINOY WEEKLY

www.pinoyweekly.org

Pinoy Weekly is a magazine primarily in Tagalog and English that is available in print and online. It publishes stories, images, and opinions about marginalized communities in Philippine society. Since its founding, *Pinoy Weekly* has expanded to Mindanao and other countries. There is *Pinoy Weekly* in Japan, Israel, and Taiwan.

THE PHILIPPINE CENTER FOR INVESTIGATIVE JOURNALISM

www.pcij.org

PCIJ is an independent media agency founded in 1989 by a Philippine journalist who realized that reporters need to go beyond day-to-day reportage and delve deeper into the causes and broader meanings of news events.

> The PCIJ believes that the media play a crucial role in scrutinizing and strengthening democratic institutions, defending and asserting press freedom, freedom of information, and freedom of expression. The media could—and should—be a catalyst for social debate and consensus that would redound to the promotion of public welfare. To do so, the media must provide citizens with the bases for arriving at informed opinions and decisions.

RAPPLER

https://www.rappler.com

This social news network was launched in 2012 to produce news stories for community engagement and social change. *Rappler*, a portmanteau word for "rap" (to discuss) and "ripple" (to make waves), works under the principle of uncompromised journalism that gives editorial and management control to journalists whose collective aim "is to create a truly independent news group and crowdsourcing platform."[9]

Websites

CENTER FOR ART & THOUGHT

http://www.centerforartandthought.org/

Center for Art & Thought (CA+T) is a space for dialogue and convergence among artists and scholars. Starting from the perspectives of Filipinxs around the world, CA+T harnesses the potential of digital and new media technologies in order to foster dialogue between artists, scholars, and the broader public. In its website, it says: "A web-based nonprofit organization with 501(c)(3) status, we believe that the convergence of art and critical thought, as exemplified by our virtual residency program, is a crucial way to generate new modes of knowledge production and creative and critical lenses for understanding and transforming global conditions."

CARLOS BULOSAN THEATRE

https://www.carlosbulosan.com/

Based in Toronto, Canada, the Carlos Bulosan Theatre (CBT) has been in existence for over thirty years, telling the stories of Filipinx Canadians. The theater company is named after Carlos Bulosan, an activist, writer, and migrant laborer who immigrated to the United States in the 1930s. His autobiographical novel, *America Is in the Heart*, has become a classic literary work and influenced generations of Filipinx Americans.

FILIPINO AMERICAN NATIONAL HISTORICAL SOCIETY

http://fanhs-national.org/filam/

Founded in 1982, the Filipino American National Historical Society (FANHS) documents and promotes Filipinx American history through its archives, conferences, books, programs, films, art, and more. Chapters exist throughout the United States.

IBON INTERNATIONAL FOUNDATION

http://www.iboninternational.org/

The IBON Foundation started in 1978 as a semilegal biweekly newsletter focused on socioeconomic data and analysis, as part of the mass resistance against the repressive Marcos dictatorship in the Philippines. From 1993 onwards, IBON Foundation's international work accelerated and eventually led to the establishment of Ibon International Foundation, its international department, in 1998. This foundation manages several programs, global and international networks, and regional offices.

KULARTS

https://www.kularts-sf.org

Founded in 1985, Kulintang Arts, commonly known as KULARTS, is the premier presenter of contemporary and tribal Pilipino arts in the United States. Through three decades of service, KULARTS has grown into a leading elder arts organization, uniting generations of artists and community activists in a common effort to build a collective space and sense of belonging specifically in SOMA Pilipinas, San Francisco's Filipino Cultural Heritage District. KULARTS creates work that makes visible the contributions of Pilipino Americans, and makes room for cultural continuity and knowledge.

PIN@Y EDUCATIONAL PARTNERSHIPS

http://www.pepsf.org/

PEP is a service-learning program that builds connections between the university, public schools, and communities to develop a counter-pipeline that produces critical educators and curriculum at all levels of education and in the community.

NOTES

1. I was a part of a news team for *Third World News Review* (*TWNR*) that aired on channel 17 Santa Barbara community-access television from 2001 to 2015. My news reports focused on Asia, especially the Philippines. In 2019, producers of the radio program *No Alibis* brought back members of the *TWNR* news team on *No Alibis*, which airs Wednesdays 9:00–11:00 a.m. PT on KCSB 91.9 FM Santa Barbara (streaming on *www.kcsb.org*). *TWNR* reports on the first Wednesday of each month.

2. Melissa Adler, *Cruising the Library: Perversities in the Organization of Knowledge* (New York: Fordham University Press, 2017), 147. I am grateful to Rick Bonus for referring me to Melissa Adler's monograph. It helped in writing this introduction.

3. Oona T. Paredes, "Working with Spanish Colonial Archives: Reflections and Practicalities," *Kyoto Review of Southeast Asia* 7 (2006).

4. In her article "Media Rich," Elizabeth Robinson describes the United States as media rich and information poor, referring to the multinational corporate ownership of the US media where five corporations have cross ownership of radio, television, publishing houses, bookstores, film companies, and distributors. Elizabeth Robinson, "Media Rich," *InteRadio* 12, no. 1 (2005): 23. Elizabeth Robinson is a member of the World Association of Community Radio Broadcasters.

5. The term "open access" refers to the Open Access (OA) movement that seeks to address the ability of libraries to provide resources, especially online scholarly journal articles, to students and faculty in the face of the escalating cost of digital content provided by commercial publishers. While Open Access has different definitions and varying degrees of applications, the OA movement's primary concern is to address copyright and licensing restrictions of scholarly produced works such as refereed research journals. See Bhaskar Mukherjee, "Changing Scenario of Scholarly Communication: Journals, E-journals and Open-Access Journals," in *Scholarly Communication in Library and Information Services: The Impacts of Open Access Journals and E-journals on a Changing Scenario* (Oxford: Chandos, 2010). It is worth noting there is an ongoing debate on the differential impact of the OA movement between the Global South and Global North around the production of knowledge, economic sustainability, influence of commercial publishers, and political will, to name a few.

6. Sheila S. Coronel. "The Media, the Market, and Democracy: The Case of the Philippines," *The Public* 8, no. 2 (2001): 112.

7. "Bulatlat.com: A Product of Its Time," Bulatlat: Journalism for the People; *https://www.bulatlat.com/bulatlat-a-product-of-its-time/*.

8. "Kodao Productions," GlobalVoices; *https//globalvoices.org/author/kodao-productions/*.

9. In 2021, Maria Ressa, cofounder of Rappler, was a corecipient of the Nobel Peace Prize, the first Filipinx to do so. She and Dimitry Muratov won the award "for their efforts to safeguard freedom of expression, which is a precondition for democracy and lasting peace" (*https://www.nobelprize.org/prizes/peace/2021/summary/*).

Selected List of Scholarship on Filipinx American Studies

Edward Nadurata

Agbayani-Siewert, Pauline. "Assumptions of Asian American Similarity: The Case of Filipino and Chinese American Students." *Social Work* 49, no. 1 (January 2004): 39–51.

Aguilar, Delia D. "Questionable Claims: Colonialism Redux, Feminist Style." *Race and Class* 41, no. 3 (2000): 1–12.

Alidio, Kimberly. "'When I Get Home, I Want to Forget': Memory and Amnesia in the Occupied Philippines, 1901–1904." *Social Text*, no. 59 (July 1, 1999): 105–22.

Almirol, Edwin B. *Ethnic Identity and Social Negotiation: A Study of a Filipino Community in California.* New York: AMS Press, 1985.

Ancheta, Angelo N. *Race, Rights, and the Asian American Experience.* 2nd ed. New Brunswick, N.J.: Rutgers University Press, 2006.

Anderson, Warwick. *Colonial Pathologies: American Tropical Medicine, Race, and Hygiene in the Philippines.* Durham, N.C.: Duke University Press, 2006.

Antolihao, Lou. *Playing with the Big Boys—Basketball, American Imperialism, and Subaltern Discourse in the Philippines.* Lincoln: University of Nebraska Press, 2015.

Balance, Christine Bacareza. *Tropical Renditions: Making Musical Scenes in Filipino America*. Durham, N.C.: Duke University Press, 2016.

Balce, Nerissa S. *Body Parts of Empire: Visual Abjection, Filipino Images, and the American Archive*. Ann Arbor: University of Michigan Press, 2016.

Baldoz, Rick. *The Third Asiatic Invasion: Empire and Migration in Filipino America, 1898–1946*. New York: New York University Press, 2011.

Bascara, Victor. *Model-Minority Imperialism*. Minneapolis: University of Minnesota Press, 2006.

Blanco, John D. *Frontier Constitutions: Christianity and Colonial Empire in the Nineteenth Century Philippines*. Berkeley: University of California Press, 2009.

Bolton, Sony Coráñez. "Cripping the Philippine Enlightenment: *Ilustrado* Travel Literature, Postcolonial Disability, and the 'Normate Imperial Eye/I.'" *Verge: Studies in Global Asias* 2, no. 2 (October 1, 2016): 138–62.

Bonifacio, Glenda Tibe. *Pinay on the Prairies: Filipino Women and Transnational Identities*. Vancouver: University of British Columbia Press, 2013.

Bonus, Rick. *Locating Filipino Americans: Ethnicity and the Cultural Politics of Space*. Philadelphia: Temple University Press, 2000.

———. *The Ocean in the School: Pacific Islander Students Transforming Their University*. Durham, N.C.: Duke University Press, 2020.

Brody, David. *Visualizing American Empire: Orientalism and Imperialism in the Philippines*. Chicago: University of Chicago Press, 2010.

Buaken, Manuel. *I Have Lived with the American People*. Caldwell, Idaho: Caxton Printers, 1948.

Buchholdt, Thelma. *Filipinos in Alaska, 1788–1958*. Anchorage, Alaska: Aboriginal Press, 1996.

Buenavista, Tracy Lachica, and Jordan Beltran Gonzales. "DREAMs Deterred: Filipino Experiences and an Anti-Militarization Critique of the Development, Relief, and Education for Alien Minors Act (RESEARCH) (Report)." *Asian American Policy Review* 21 (January 1, 2011).

Bulosan, Carlos. *America Is in the Heart: A Personal History*. Introduction by Carey McWilliams. Seattle: University of Washington Press, 1974.

Burns, Lucy MSP. *Puro Arte: Filipinos on the Stages of Empire*. New York: New York University Press, 2013.

Camacho, Keith L. "Filipinos, Pacific Islanders, and the American Empire." In *The Oxford Handbook of Asian American History*, edited by David Yoo and Eiichiro Azuma. New York: Oxford University Press, 2016.

Campomanes, Oscar V. *American Studies Asia* 1, no. 1 (2002).

———. "Filipinos in the United States and Their Literature of Exile." In *Discrepant Histories: Translocal Essays on Filipino Cultures*, edited by Vicente L. Rafael, 159–92. Philadelphia: Temple University Press, 1995.

———. "The New Empire's Forgetful and Forgotten Citizens: Unrepresentability and Unassimilability in Filipino-American Postcolonialities." *Critical Mass.* 2, no. 2 (1995).

———. "New Formations of Asian American Studies and the Question of U.S. Imperialism." *positions: east asia cultures critique* 5, no. 2 (January 9, 1997): 523–50. *http://positions.dukejournals.org/cgi/content/abstract/16/3/661.*

Capino, José B. *Dream Factories of a Former Colony: American Fantasies, Philippine Cinema.* Minneapolis: University of Minnesota Press, 2010.

———. *Martial Law Melodrama: Lino Brocka's Cinema Politics.* Berkeley: University of California Press, 2020.

Carbó, Nick, ed. *Returning a Borrowed Tongue: Poems by Filipino and Filipino American Writers.* Minneapolis: Coffee House Press, 1995.

Carbó, Nick, and Eileen Tabios, eds. *Babaylan: An Anthology of Filipina and Filipina American Writers.* San Francisco: Aunt Lute Books, 2000.

Cariño, Benjamin V., James T. Fawcett, Robert W. Gardner, and Fred Arnold. *The New Filipino Immigrants to the United States: Increasing Diversity and Change.* Honolulu: East-West Center, 1990.

Caronan, Faye. *Legitimizing Empire: Filipino American and U.S. Puerto Rican Cultural Critique.* Urbana: University of Illinois Press, 2015.

Castillo, Elaine. *America Is Not the Heart.* New York: Viking, 2018.

Castillo-Tsuchida, Adelaida. *Filipino Migrants in San Diego, 1900–1946.* San Diego: San Diego Society, Title Insurance and Trust Collection, 1979.

Catapusan, Benicio. *The Filipino Occupational and Recreational Activities in Los Angeles.* San Francisco: R & E Research Associates, 1975 [1934].

———. *The Social Adjustment of Filipinos in the United States.* San Francisco: R & E Research Associates, 1972 [1940].

Charbonneau, Oliver. *Civilizational Imperatives: Americans, Moros, and the Colonial World.* Ithaca, N.Y.: Cornell University Press, 2020.

Cherry, Stephen. *Faith, Family, and Filipino American Community Life.* New Brunswick, N.J.: Rutgers University Press, 2014.

Chew, Ron. *Remembering Silme Domingo and Gene Viernes: The Legacy of Filipino American Labor Activism.* Seattle: University of Washington Press, 2012.

Choy, Catherine Ceniza. *Empire of Care: Nursing and Migration in Filipino American History.* Durham, N.C.: Duke University Press, 2003.

Chu, Richard T. *Chinese and Chinese Mestizos of Manila: Family, Identity, and Culture, 1860s–1930s.* Leiden: Brill, 2010.

Ciria Cruz, Rene, Cindy Domingo, and Bruce Occena, eds. *A Time to Rise: Collective Memoirs of the Union of Democratic Filipinos (KDP).* Seattle: University of Washington Press, 2017.

Clutario, Genevieve. "World War II and the Promise of Normalcy: Overlapping Empires and Everyday Lives in the Philippines." In *Crossing Empires:*

Taking U.S. History into Transimperial Terrain, edited by Kristin L. Hoganson and Jay Sexton. Durham, N.C.: Duke University Press, 2020.

Coloma, Roland Sintos, Bonnie McElhinny, Ethel Tungohan, John Paul C. Catungal, and Lisa M. Davidson. *Filipinos in Canada: Disturbing Invisibility.* Toronto: University of Toronto Press, 2012.

Compoc, Kim. "Weaving Our Sovereignties Together: Maximizing *Ea* for Filipinx and Hawaiians." *Amerasia Journal* 45, no. 3 (September 2, 2019): 316–35.

Cordova, Fred, Dorothy Laigo Cordova, and Albert A. Acena. *Filipinos, Forgotten Asian Americans: A Pictorial Essay, 1763–Circa 1963.* Dubuque, Iowa: Kendall/Hunt, 1983.

Crouchett, Lorraine Jacobs. *Filipinos in California: From the Days of the Galleons to the Present.* El Cerrito, Calif.: Downey Place, 1982.

Cruz, Denise. *Transpacific Femininities: The Making of the Modern Filipina.* Durham, N.C.: Duke University Press, 2012.

David, E. J. R. (Eric John Ramos). *Brown Skin, White Minds: Filipino-American Postcolonial Psychology.* Charlotte, N.C.: Information Age, 2013.

David, Emmanuel. "Purple-Collar Labor: Transgender Workers and Queer Value at Global Call Centers in the Philippines." *Gender & Society* 29, no. 2 (April 2015): 169–94.

Davis, Rocio G. "Introduction: Have Come, Are Here: Reading Filipino/a American Literature." *MELUS* 29, no. 1 (2004): 5–18.

De Guzman, Mila. *Women against Marcos: Stories of Filipino and Filipino American Women who Fought a Dictator.* San Francisco: Carayan Press, 2016.

de Jesús, Melinda L., ed. *Pinay Power: Peminist Critical Theory.* Milton Park, Oxfordshire: Taylor and Francis, 2005.

de la Cruz, Enrique. 1998. "Introduction: Essays into American Empire in the Philippines." *Amerasia Journal* 24, no. 2 (1998): vii–xv.

De Leon, Adrian. "Sugarcane *Sakadas*: The Corporate Production of the Filipino on a Hawai'i Plantation." *Amerasia Journal* 45, no. 1 (January 2, 2019): 50–67.

De Witt, Howard. *Anti-Filipino Movements in California: A History, Bibliography, and Study Guide.* San Francisco: R & E Research Associates, 1976.

Delmendo, Sharon. *The Star-Entangled Banner: One Hundred Years of America in the Philippines.* New Brunswick, N.J.: Rutgers University Press, 2004.

Diaz, Josen Masangkay. "Balikbayan Configurations and a U.S.-Philippine Politics of Modernization." *Journal of Asian American Studies* 21, no. 1 (February 1, 2018): 1–29.

Diaz, Robert, Marissa Largo, and Fritz Pino. *Diasporic Intimacies: Queer Filipinos and Canadian Imaginaries.* Evanston, Ill.: Northwestern University Press, 2018.

España-Maram, Linda. *Creating Masculinity in Los Angeles's Little Manila: Working-Class Filipinos and Popular Culture, 1920s–1950s.* New York: Columbia University Press, 2006.

Espina, Marina E. *Filipinos in Louisiana.* New Orleans: Laborde, 1988.

Espiritu, Augusto F. *Five Faces of Exile: The Nation and Filipino American Intellectuals.* Stanford, Calif.: Stanford University Press, 2005.

Espiritu, Yến Lê. *Asian American Panethnicity: Bridging Institutions and Identities.* Philadelphia: Temple University Press, 1992.

———. *Filipino American Lives.* Philadelphia: Temple University Press, 1995.

———. *Home Bound: Filipino Lives Across Cultures, Communities, and Countries.* Berkeley: University of California Press, 2003.

Espiritu, Yến Lê, and J. A. Ruanto-Ramirez. "The Philippine Refugee Processing Center: The Relational Displacements of Vietnamese Refugees and the Indigenous Aetas." *Verge: Studies in Global Asias* 6, no. 1 (April 1, 2020): 118–41.

Evangelista, Susan P. "Carlos Bulosan and Third World Consciousness." *Philippine Studies* 30, no. 1 (First Quarter 1982): 44–58.

Fabros, Alex, and Annalissa Herbert, eds. *The Filipinos American Newspaper Collection: Extracts from 1906 to 1953.* Fresno, Calif.: The Filipino American Experience Research Project, 1994.

Fajardo, Kale Bantigue. *Filipino Crosscurrents: Oceanographies of Seafaring, Masculinities, and Globalization.* Minneapolis: University of Minnesota Press, 2011.

Farrales, May. "Repurposing Beauty Pageants: The Colonial Geographies of Filipina Pageants in Canada." *Environment and Planning D: Society and Space* 37, no. 1 (February 2019): 46–64.

Francia, Luis H., and Eric Gamalinda. *Flippin': Filipinos on America.* New York: Asian American Writers' Workshop, 1996.

Francisco-Menchavez, Valerie. *The Labor of Care: Filipina Migrants and Transnational Families in the Digital Age.* Urbana: University of Illinois Press, 2018.

Fuentecilla, Jose V. *Fighting from a Distance: How Filipino Exiles Helped Topple a Dictator.* Urbana: University of Illinois Press, 2014.

Fujita-Rony, Dorothy B. *American Workers, Colonial Power: Philippine Seattle and the Transpacific West, 1919–1941.* Berkeley: University of California Press, 2003.

Go, Julian. *American Empire and the Politics of Meaning: Elite Political Cultures in the Philippines and Puerto Rico during U.S. Colonialism.* Durham, N.C.: Duke University Press, 2008.

Gonzalez, Joaquin Jay. *Filipino American Faith in Action: Immigration, Religion, and Civic Engagement.* New York: New York University Press, 2009.

Gonzalez, Vernadette Vicuña. *Empire's Mistress, Starring Isabel Rosario Cooper.* Durham, N.C.: Duke University Press, 2021.

———. *Securing Paradise: Tourism and Militarism in Hawai'i and the Philippines.* Durham, N.C.: Duke University Press, 2013.

Gonzalves, Theodore S. *The Day the Dancers Stayed: Performing in the Filipino/American Diaspora.* Philadelphia: Temple University Press, 2010.

Guevarra, Anna Romina. *Marketing Dreams, Manufacturing Heroes: The Transnational Labor Brokering of Filipino Workers.* New Brunswick, N.J.: Rutgers University Press, 2010.

Guevarra, Rudy P. *Becoming Mexipino: Multiethnic Identities and Communities in San Diego.* New Brunswick, N.J.: Rutgers University Press, 2012.

Habal, Estella. *San Francisco's International Hotel: Mobilizing the Filipino American Community in the Anti-Eviction Movement.* Philadelphia: Temple University Press, 2007.

Hanna, Karen Buenavista. "When Mothers Lead: Revolutionary Adaptability in a Filipina/o American Diasporic Community Theater Organization." *Amerasia Journal* 45, no. 2 (May 4, 2019): 188–206.

Hoganson, Kristin L. *Fighting for American Manhood: How Gender Politics Provoked the Spanish-American and Philippine-American Wars.* New Haven: Yale University Press, 1998.

Honma, Todd. "Reinventing the Tribal: Primitive Aestheticization and Filipino Tattooing in Southern California." *Amerasia Journal* 41, no. 3 (September 22, 2015): 40–65.

Ignacio, Abe, Enrique de la Cruz, Jorge Emmanuel, and Helen Toribio. *The Forbidden Book: The Philippine-American War in Political Cartoons.* Berkeley: Eastwind Books of Berkeley, 2004.

Ignacio, Emily. *Building Diaspora: Filipino Community Formation on the Internet.* New Brunswick, N.J.: Rutgers University Press, 2005.

Isaac, Allan Punzalan. *American Tropics: Articulating Filipino America.* Minneapolis: University of Minnesota Press, 2006.

Jamero, Peter M. *Growing Up Brown: Memoirs of a Filipino American.* Seattle: University of Washington Press, 2006.

———. *Vanishing Filipino Americans: The Bridge Generation.* Lanham, Md.: University Press of America, 2011.

Kerkvliet, Melinda Tria. *Unbending Cane: Pablo Manlapit, a Filipino Labor Leader in Hawai'i.* Honolulu: Office of Multicultural Student Services, University of Hawai'i at Mānoa, 2002.

Kim, Hyung-Chan, and Cynthia G. Mejia. *The Filipinos in America, 1898–1974: A Chronology and Fact Book.* New York: Oceana Publications, 1976.

Kramer, Paul A. *The Blood of Government: Race, Empire, the United States, and the Philippines.* Chapel Hill: University of North Carolina Press, 2006.

Labrador, Roderick. *Building Filipino Hawai'i.* Urbana: University of Illinois Press, 2015.

Lasker, Bruno. *Filipino Immigration to Continental United States and to Hawai'i.* New York: Arno, 1969.

Linmark, R. Zamora. *Leche: A Novel.* Minneapolis: Coffee House Press, 2011.

———. *Rolling the R's.* New York: Kaya Productions, 1995.

Lott, Juanita Tamayo. *Common Destiny: Filipino American Generations.* Lanham, Md.: Rowman & Littlefield, 2006.

Lumba, Allan E. S., *Monetary Authorities: Capitalism and Decolonization in the American Colonial Philippines.* Durham, N.C.: Duke University Press, 2022.

Mabalon, Dawn Bohulano. *Little Manila Is in the Heart: The Making of the Filipina/o American Community in Stockton, California.* Durham, N.C.: Duke University Press, 2013.

Man, Simeon. *Soldiering through Empire: Race and the Making of the Decolonizing Pacific.* Oakland: University of California Press, 2018.

Manalansan, Martin F. IV. *Global Divas: Filipino Gay Men in the Diaspora.* Durham, N.C.: Duke University Press, 2003.

———. "Tensions, Engagements, Aspirations: The Politics of Knowledge Production in Filipino American Studies." In *Flashpoints for Asian American Studies,* edited by Cathy J. Schlund-Vials. New York: Fordham University Press, 2018. 191–204.

Manalansan, Martin F. IV, and Augusto F. Espiritu, eds. *Filipino Studies: Palimpsests of Nation and Diaspora.* New York: New York University Press, 2016.

Manalansan, Martin F. IV, Alice Y. Hom, Kale Bantigue Fajardo, ed. *Q&A: Voices from Queer Asian North America.* Philadelphia: Temple University Press, 2021.

Maramba, Dina C., and Rick Bonus, eds. *The "Other" Students: Filipino Americans, Education, and Power.* Charlotte, N.C.: Information Age, 2013.

Marasigan, Cynthia. "Race, Performance, and Colonial Governance: The Philippine Constabulary Band Plays the St. Louis World's Fair." *Journal of Asian American Studies* 22, no. 3 (2019): 349–85.

Mariano, Joyce. *Giving Back: Filipino America and the Politics of Diaspora Giving.* Philadelphia: Temple University Press, 2021.

Marshall, Alison R. *Bayanihan and Belonging: Filipinos and Religion in Canada.* Toronto: University of Toronto Press, 2018.

McCoy, Alfred W. *Policing America's Empire: The United States, the Philippines, and the Rise of the Surveillance State.* Madison: University of Wisconsin Press, 2009.

McKenna, Rebecca Tinio. *American Imperial Pastoral: The Architecture of US Colonialism in the Philippines.* Chicago: University of Chicago Press, 2017.

McWilliams, Carey. *Brothers under the Skin.* Boston: Little, Brown, 1964.

Melendy, H. Brett. *Asians in America: Filipinos, Koreans, and East Indians.* Boston: Twayne, 1977.

Mendoza, Susanah Lily L. *Between the Homeland and the Diaspora: The Politics of Theorizing Filipino and Filipino American Identities: A Second Look at the Poststructuralism-Indigenization Debates.* New York: Routledge, 2002.

Mendoza, Victor Román. *Metroimperial Intimacies: Fantasy, Racial-Sexual Governance, and the Philippines in U.S. Imperialism, 1899–1913.* Durham, N.C.: Duke University Press, 2015.

Miller, Stuart Creighton. *"Benevolent Assimilation": The American Conquest of the Philippines, 1899–1903.* New Haven: Yale University Press, 1982.

Milne, Leah. "'Disloyal to Civilization': Metafiction as Protest in Gina Apostol's The Gun Dealers' Daughter." *MELUS: Multi-Ethnic Literature of the United States* 43, no. 4 (2018): 104–26.

Monberg, Terese Guinsatao. "Ownership, Access, and Authority: Publishing and Circulating Histories to (Re)Member Community." *Community Literacy Journal* 12, no. 1 (2017): 30–47.

Monrayo, Angeles. *Tomorrow's Memories: A Diary, 1924–1928.* Honolulu: University of Hawai'i Press, 2003.

Morales, Royal F. *Makibaka: The Pilipino American Struggle.* Los Angeles: Mountainview Publishers, 1974.

Nadal, Kevin L. *Filipino American Psychology: A Handbook of Theory, Research, and Clinical Practice.* Hoboken, N.J.: John Wiley, 2011.

Nazareno, Jennifer P, Rhacel Salazar Parreñas, and Yu-Kang Fan. "Can I Ever Retire? The Plight of Migrant Filipino Elderly Caregivers in Los Angeles" (July 14, 2014). *https://escholarship.org/uc/item/0zj455z5.*

Ocampo, Anthony Christian. *The Latinos of Asia: How Filipino Americans Break the Rules of Race.* Stanford, Calif.: Stanford University Press, 2016.

Okamura, Jonathan Y. *Filipino American History, Identity and Community in Hawai'i: In Commemoration of the 90th Anniversary of Filipino Immigration to Hawai'i.* Honolulu: University of Hawai'i Press, 1996.

———. *Imagining the Filipino American Diaspora: Transnational Relations, Identities, and Communities.* New York: Garland, 1998.

Orquiza, René Alexander D. *Taste of Control: Food and the Filipino Colonial Mentality under American Rule.* New Brunswick, N.J.: Rutgers University Press, 2020.

Padios, Jan M. *A Nation on the Line: Call Centers as Postcolonial Predicaments in the Philippines.* Durham, N.C.: Duke University Press, 2018.

Parreñas, Rhacel Salazar. *Children of Global Migration: Transnational Families and Gendered Woes.* Stanford, Calif.: Stanford University Press, 2005.

———. *The Force of Domesticity: Filipina Migrants and Globalization.* New York: New York University Press, 2008.

———. *Servants of Globalization: Women, Migration, and Domestic Work.* Stanford, Calif.: Stanford University Press, 2001.

Patterson, Christopher B. *Transitive Cultures: Anglophone Literature of the Transpacific.* New Brunswick, N.J.: Rutgers University Press, 2018.

Perillo, J. Lorenzo. *Choreographing in Color: Filipinos, Hip-Hop, and the Cultural Politics of Euphemism.* New York: Oxford University Press, 2020.

Pido, Antonio J. A. *The Pilipinos in America: Macro/Micro Dimensions of Immigration and Integration.* New York: Center for Migration Studies, 1986.

Pido, Eric J. *Migrant Returns: Manila, Development, and Transnational Connectivity.* Durham, N.C.: Duke University Press, 2017.

Poblete, JoAnna. *Islanders in the Empire: Filipino and Puerto Rican Laborers in Hawai'i.* Urbana: University of Illinois Press, 2014.

Ponce, Martin Joseph. *Beyond the Nation: Diasporic Filipino Literature and Queer Reading.* New York: New York University Press, 2012.

Posadas, Barbara Mercedes. *The Filipino Americans.* Westport, Conn.: Greenwood Press, 1999.

Pratt, Geraldine. *Families Apart: Migrant Mothers and the Conflicts of Labor and Love.* Minneapolis: University of Minnesota Press, 2012.

Quinsaat, Jesse, ed. *Letters in Exile: An Introductory Reader on the History of Pilipinos in America.* Los Angeles: UCLA Asian American Studies Center, 1976.

Rafael, Vicente L. *Discrepant Histories: Translocal Essays on Filipino Cultures.* Philadelphia: Temple University Press, 1995.

———. *The Sovereign Trickster: Death and Laughter in the Age of Duterte.* Durham, N.C.: Duke University Press, 2022.

———. *White Love and Other Events in Filipino History.* Durham, N.C.: Duke University Press, 2000.

Reyes, Eric Estuar. "Why We Gather: Localizing Filipino America and Community Cultural Development." *Amerasia Journal* 36, no. 3 (January 2010): 106–28.

Reyes, Victoria. *Global Borderlands: Fantasy, Violence, and Empire in Subic Bay, Philippines.* Stanford, Calif.: Stanford University Press, 2020.

Roces, Mina. *The Filipino Migration Experience: Global Agents of Change.* Ithaca, N.Y.: Cornell University Press, 2021.

Rodríguez, Dylan. *Suspended Apocalypse: White Supremacy, Genocide, and the Filipino Condition.* Minneapolis: University of Minnesota Press, 2010.

———. *White Reconstruction: Domestic Warfare and the Logics of Genocide.* New York: Fordham University Press, 2020.

Rodriguez, Evelyn Ibatan. *Celebrating Debutantes and Quinceañeras Coming of Age in American Ethnic Communities.* Philadelphia: Temple University Press, 2013.

Rodriguez, Robyn Magalit. *Filipino American Transnational Activism: Diasporic Politics among the Second Generation.* Leiden: Brill, 2019.

———. *Migrants for Export: How the Philippine State Brokers Labor to the World.* Minneapolis: University of Minnesota Press, 2010.

Root, Maria P. P., ed. *Filipino Americans: Transformation and Identity.* Thousand Oaks, Calif.: Sage Publications, 1997.

Sales, Joy N. "#NeverAgainToMartialLaw: Transnational Filipino American Activism in the Shadow of Marcos and Age of Duterte." *Amerasia Journal* 45, no. 3 (September 2, 2019): 299–315.

Salman, Michael. *The Embarrassment of Slavery: Controversies over Bondage and Nationalism in the American Colonial Philippines.* Berkeley: University of California Press, 2001.

San Buenaventura, Steffi. "The Colors of Manifest Destiny: Filipinos and the American Other(s)." *Amerasia Journal* 24, no. 3 (1998): 1–26.

San Juan, E., Jr. "Configuring the Filipino Diaspora in the United States." *Diaspora* 3, no. 2 (Fall 1994): 117–34.

———. "Filipino Writing in the United States: Reclaiming Whose America?" *Philippine Studies* 41 (1993): 141–66.

———. "Mapping the Boundaries: The Filipino Writer in the U.S.A." *Journal of Ethnic Studies* 19, no. 1 (Spring 1991): 117–31.

———. The Philippine Temptation: Dialectics of Philippines—US Literary Relations. Philadelphia: Temple University Press, 1996.

Santa Ana, Jeffrey. *Racial Feelings: Asian America in a Capitalist Culture of Emotion.* Philadelphia: Temple University Press, 2015.

Saranillio, Dean Itsuji. "Colonial Amnesia: Rethinking Filipino 'American' Settler Empowerment in the U.S. Colony of Hawai'i." In *Asian Settler Colonialism.* Honolulu: University of Hawai'i Press, 2008.

Sarmiento, Thomas Xavier. "The Empire Sings Back: Glee's Queer Materialization of Filipina/o America." *Multi-Ethnic Literature of the United States* 39, no. 2 (June 2014): 211–34.

Scharlin, Craig, and Lilia V. Villanueva. *Philip Vera Cruz: A Personal History of Filipino Immigrants and the Farmworkers Movement.* Seattle: University of Washington Press, 2011.

Schueller, Malini Johar. *Campaigns of Knowledge: U.S. Pedagogies of Colonialism and Occupation in the Philippines and Japan.* Philadelphia: Temple University Press, 2019.

See, Sarita Echavez. *The Decolonized Eye: Filipino American Art and Performance.* Minneapolis: University of Minnesota Press, 2009.

———. *The Filipino Primitive: Accumulation and Resistance in the American Museum.* New York: New York University Press, 2017.

Shaw, Angel Velasco, and Luis H. Francia. *Vestiges of War: The Philippine-American War and the Aftermath of an Imperial Dream 1899–1999.* New York: New York University Press, 2002.

Shimizu, Celine Parreñas. *The Hypersexuality of Race: Performing Asian/ American Women on Screen and Scene.* Durham, N.C.: Duke University Press, 2007.

Strobel, Leny Mendoza. *Coming Full Circle: The Process of Decolonization among Post-1965 Filipino Americans.* Quezon City, Philippines: Giraffe Books, 2001.

Suarez, Harrod J. *Work of Mothering: Globalization and the Filipino Diaspora.* Champaign: University of Illinois Press, 2017.

Suarez, Theresa C. "(De)Militarized Domesticity: Reconfiguring Marriage, Gender, and Family among Filipino Navy Couples." *Women, Gender, and Families of Color* 3, no. 2 (October 28, 2015): 190–208.

Tadiar, Neferti Xina M. *Fantasy-Production: Sexual Economies and Other Philippine Consequences for the New World Order.* Hong Kong: Hong Kong University Press, 2004.

———. *Things Fall Away: Philippine Historical Experience and the Makings of Globalization.* Durham, N.C.: Duke University Press, 2009.

Tagle, Thea Quiray. "Feeling the Manilatown and Fillmore Blues: Al Robles's Politics and Poetics of Place." *Critical Ethnic Studies* 3, no. 2 (October 1, 2017): 99–125.

Teodoro, Noel V. "Pensionados and Workers: The Filipinos in the United States, 1903–1956." *Asian and Pacific Migration Journal* 8, no. 1–2 (1999): 157–78.

Tintiangco-Cubales, Allyson. *Philippine and Filipina/o American History.* Santa Clara, Calif.: Phoenix Publishing House, 2007.

———. *Pin@y Educational Partnerships: A Filipina/o American Studies Sourcebook.* Vol. I: *Philippine and Filipina/o American History.* Santa Clara, Calif.: Phoenix Publishing House, 2007.

———. *Pin@y Educational Partnerships: A Filipina/o American Studies Sourcebook.* Vol. II: *Filipina/o American Identities, Activism, and Service.* Santa Clara, Calif.: Phoenix Publishing House, 2009.

Tiongson, Antonio T., Jr., *Filipinos Represent: DJs, Racial Authenticity, and the Hip-Hop Nation.* Minneapolis: University of Minnesota Press, 2013.

Tiongson, Antonio T., Jr., Edgardo V. Gutierrez, and Ricardo V. Gutierrez, eds. *Positively No Filipinos Allowed: Building Communities and Discourse.* Philadelphia: Temple University Press, 2006.

Tolentino, Cynthia H. *America's Experts: Race and the Fictions of Sociology.* Minneapolis: University of Minnesota Press, 2009.

Ubalde, Anatalio. *Filipino American Architecture, Design, and Planning Issues.* Los Angeles: Flipside Press, 1996.

Vallangca, Caridad Concepcion. *The Second Wave: Pinay and Pinoy/1945–1960.* San Francisco: Strawberry Hill, 1987.

———. *The Third Wave: Quo Vadis?* Bloomington, Ind.: AuthorHouse, 2007.

Vallangca, Roberto V. *Pinoy: The First Wave*. San Francisco: Strawberry Hill, 1977.

Velasco, Gina. *Queering the Global Filipina Body: Contested Nationalisms in the Filipina/o Diaspora*. Urbana: University of Illinois Press, 2020.

Vergara, Benito M., Jr., *Pinoy Capital: The Filipino Nation in Daly City*. Philadelphia: Temple University Press, 2009.

Villegas, Mark. *Manifest Technique: Hip Hop, Empire, and Visionary Filipino American Critique*. Urbana: University of Illinois Press, 2021.

Villegas, Mark R., Kuttin' Kandi, Roderick N. Labrador, and Jeff Chang, eds. *Empire of Funk: Hip Hop and Representation in Filipina/o America*. San Diego, Calif.: Cognella Academic Publishing, 2014.

Wallovits, Sonia Emily. *The Filipinos in California*. San Francisco: R & E Research Associates, 1972 [1966].

Wang, Oliver. *Legions of Boom: Filipino American Mobile DJ Crews in the San Francisco Bay Area*. Durham, N.C.: Duke University Press, 2015.

Wesling, Meg. *Empire's Proxy: American Literature and US Imperialism in the Philippines*. New York: New York University Press, 2011.

Wolf, Diane L. "Family Secrets: Transnational Struggles among Children of Filipino Immigrants." *Sociological Perspectives* 40, no. 3 (September 22, 1997).

Yu, Elena S. H. "Filipino Migration and Community Organizations in the United States." *California Sociologist* 3, no. 2 (Summer 1980): 76–102.

Yuson, Alfred A. "Filipino Diasporic Literature." In *Philippine English: Linguistic and Literary Perspectives*, edited by Lourdes S. Bautista and Kingsley Bolton. Hong Kong: Hong Kong University Press, 2008. 337–56.

Zarsadiaz, James. "Raising Hell in the Heartland: Filipino Chicago and the Anti–Martial Law Movement, 1972–1986." *American Studies* 56, no. 1 (2017): 141–62.

ACKNOWLEDGMENTS

This book is a product of the visible labors of those who are named within it, but it is also the outcome of the not-so-visible contributions of those who have worked with us from all sorts of locations. We are honored and humbled to recognize and acknowledge them here. Our teachers and mentors who patiently guided us in the course of our intellectual work in Filipinx American studies deserve to be mentioned first. At the University of California, San Diego, where we first met each other as graduate students, we thank Lisa Lowe, Yến Lê Espiritu, Vince Rafael, and Oscar V. Campomanes. In particular, Rick would like to acknowledge George Lipsitz and Linda Trinh Vo, and Tony would like to acknowledge Jane Rhodes, Lisa Park, and Ivan Evans.

In the annual conferences of the Association for Asian American Studies (AAAS) and the American Studies Association (ASA), we got to know a whole slew of other scholars in similarly situated fields and collaborated on many academic projects with them, including roundtable conversations that we cohosted and meetings we organized. All of them wrote essays for this volume, and the rest include Kimberly Alidio, Constancio Arnaldo, Paul Michael Atienza, Christine Bacareza Balance, Rick Baldoz, Jose Francisco "Kiko" Benitez, Keith Camacho, José B. Capino, Faye Caronan, Cathy Choy, Genevieve Clutario, Melany de la Cruz-Viesca, Vicente M. Diaz, Linda España-Maram, Augusto F. Espiritu, Luis H. Francia, Valerie Francisco-Menchavez, Dorothy B. Fujita-Rony, Anna Gonzalez, Michael Gonzalez, Rudy P. Guevarra Jr., Jessica Hagedorn, Florante Ibañez, Emily Noelle Ignacio, Reynaldo Clemeña Ileto, Wayne Jopanda, Faith Kares, Emily P. Lawsin, R. Zamora Linmark, Dawn Bohulano Mabalon, Joyce Mariano,

Victor Román Mendoza, Daya Mortel, Anthony Christian Ocampo, Jonathan Y. Okamura, Jan M. Padios, David Palaita, J. Lorenzo Perillo, Martin Joseph Ponce, Mina Roces, E. San Juan Jr., Leny Strobel, Neferti Xina M. Tadiar, Roland B. Tolentino, Sunny Vergara, and James Zarsadiaz.

Within our own campuses, we thank all those who supported our work on this book through institutional assistance and collegial sustenance. At the University of Washington, we thank George Lovell, Ileana Rodriguez-Silva, Juan Guerra, Sonnet Retman, LaShawnDa Pittman, LaTasha Levy, Carolyn Pinedo-Turnovsky, Lauro Flores, Devon Peña, Alina Mendez, Connie So, Jang Wook Huh, Linh Nguyen, Oliver Rollins, Kell Juan, Jacque Waita, Anjelica Hernandez-Cordero, Lorna Hamill, Ellen Palms, Thao Michelle Dinh, Michelle Habell-Pallan, Chandan Reddy, Shirley Hune, Harry Murphy, and David Palaita from the City College of San Francisco.

At the University of New Mexico, we thank David Correia, Alyosha Goldstein, Nick Estes, Kathleen Holscher, Andrea Mays, Jennifer Nez Denetdale, Rebecca Schreiber, Melanie K. Yazzie, Myra Washington, Mercedes Nysus, and Hairo Barghash. And at Syracuse University, we acknowledge Coran Klaver, Carol W. N. Fadda, Susan Thomas, Luvell Anderson, Verena Erlenbusch-Anderson, Gwendolyn D. Pough, Chandra Talpade Mohanty, Dana M. Olwan, Eunjung Kim, Michael Gill, Delali Kumavie, Ethan Madarieta, colleagues in the Department of English, Terri A. G. Zollo and Margaret Marie Butler.

Our work would also not have been as enriched without our interactions with our current and former students, who we thank as well: Benze Deraco, Raymond Westerlund, Timothy Nguyen, Joncarlo Abarcar, Kaillou Thao, Jessica Par, Matthew Gomez, Jonas Nocom, Jason Nocom, Camille Ungco, Dalya Perez, Kriya Velasco, Leah Panganiban, Third Andresen, Taylor Ahana, Nestor Enguerra Jr., Deborah Tugaga, Staliedaniel Uele, Arthur Sepulveda, Brady Angeles, Glendal Tautua, Exekiel and Tina Arañez, Kevin Daugard, Reuben B. Deleon, Jedidiah Enguerra, Alana J. Bock, Maria Eugenia Lopez-Garcia, Raquel Andrea Gonzalez Madrigal, Marthia Fuller, Christina Juhasz-Wood, Nova Lira-Perez, Cecilia Idalen Frescas-Ortiz, Manuel Criollo, Jadira Gurule, Natalie El-Eid, Caroline Charles, Sue-jin Green, and George Luna-Pena.

Our contributors in this volume truly deserve our gratitude for accepting our invitation to be a part of our project. Over the course of many drafts, all of them patiently worked with us and faithfully entrusted us to adequately and appropriately represent their work and our interdiscipline. Many of us in this volume started our academic careers at the same time, while others are mentees of ours who comprise a newer generation of scholars, all enthusiastically pushing our interdiscipline forward. In critically meaningful ways, we are all active parts of a community of scholars who find support, connection, and sustenance with each other and, most importantly, within larger environments that can oftentimes be isolating, harsh, and unconvinced about the value of our work. We are therefore blessed to have all of our contributors here as close friends, academic colleagues, and allies.

Our thanks also go to Gina Apostol for writing a wonderful and provocative afterword, and to Kimberley Acebo Arteche for providing our book's amazing cover art. We offer Richard Morrison a big bouquet of gratitude for believing in our project and for graciously supporting and shepherding it at Fordham University Press. We thank Eric Newman, managing editor at Fordham University Press, and Edward Batchelder, our copy editor, for their patient and diligent work with us. We are likewise grateful to our two anonymous reviewers for providing us with such incisive, helpful, and encouraging critiques, so much so that our work has evolved and ended up in places where our most important interventions now productively rest. We could not have asked for better interlocutors. And to Edward Nadurata, our indefatigable research assistant, we are indebted to you for sharing with us your skills in working through our ideas, drafts, and personalities with rigor, perseverance, and care. We are wholeheartedly appreciative of your hard work, Edward!

Finally, we would like to express our appreciation to our families and friends for their love, support, and guidance:

Rick: My heartfelt thanks go to Marie Nanette Bonus, Maritel and Manny Naguit, Bobby and Rosanna Bonus, Vida Bonus Anderson, Emma and Laurence Foster, Joji and Billy Guzman, Paulo Rafael, Abby Zialcita, Jay Naguit, Claire Gunville, Mya Naguit, Noelle Bonus, Joanna Gerolaga, Kathleen Bonus, Justin Luong, Matthew Bonus, Marie Reyes, Michelle and Rommel Cachero, Nikki Anderson, John Barcelon, Victoria Bonus Cecilio, Chloe, Cayson, Romeo, Sera, Armin and Maria Guzman, Arnel Niño and Lei Guzman, Anne and Noy Castillo, Madelynn and Alyvia, Sophie and Preston, Noah and Rylee, Veronica and Gilby Cabrera, Dondi and Fay

Dizon, Anton, Mel, Andro, Cristina, Lisa Luchavez, Jerry and Jeremy Caudal, Mariole, Martin, Manolo, Bobby, Bebon, Ariel, Ria, Fr. Tito Cruz, and Tony.

Tony: I want to express my deep appreciation to my mother—affectionately known as "Malou" to her friends—for her unwavering and continued support of my career in academia. I also want to acknowledge Mian, Papa (RIP), Tita Lil, Tito Fred, and the Ramos and Cunanan families for their support through the years. To my partner, Danika Medak-Saltzman, I very much appreciate your love and companionship and I look forward to our life together in Syracuse, New York, with Lucee, Lola, Hazelnut, and Espie. Finally, I want to acknowledge my coeditor, Rick Bonus, who is my mentor, a colleague, and dear friend. It is an honor and joy to work with you on this project.

CONTRIBUTORS

Karín Aguilar-San Juan is a professor and chair of American studies at Macalester College in St. Paul, Minnesota. Her undergraduate courses include U.S. Imperialism from the Philippines to Vietnam, Critical Prison Studies, and Bruce Lee, His Life and Legacy. With Frank Joyce, she coedited *The People Make the Peace: Lessons from the Vietnam Antiwar Movement* (Just World Books, 2015); she also edited and introduced *The State of Asian America: Activism and Resistance in the 1990s* (South End Press, 1994). She is part of the Race, Love, and Liberation Laboratory (for growing spiritual things), a planning group associated with Clouds in Water Zen Center.

Angelica J. Allen is an assistant professor of Africana studies at Chapman University. She received her PhD in African and African diaspora studies from the University of Texas at Austin and holds an MA in Africana studies from New York University. Her book project explores a community in the Philippines known as the Black Amerasians, a population born from the union of African American military men and Filipina women. As both a member of the Black Amerasian community and a scholar of that community's experiences, Angelica's goal is to develop a research project dedicated to advancing social justice by granting more visibility to Black Amerasian perspectives. She is a visual artist and has been awarded fellowships from the Ford Foundation and the Carter G. Woodson Institute for African-American and African Studies.

Gina Apostol's fourth novel, *Insurrecto*, was named by *Publishers Weekly* as one of the 10 Best Books of 2018. Her third book, *Gun Dealers' Daughter*,

419

won the 2013 PEN/Open Book award. Her first two novels, *Bibliolepsy* and *The Revolution According to Raymundo Mata*, both won the Juan C. Laya Prize for Best Novel (Philippine National Book Award). Her most recent work has focused on the Philippine-American War and acts of narration as forms of invention and liberation. Her essays and stories have appeared in *The New York Times*, *Los Angeles Review of Books*, *Foreign Policy*, *Gettysburg Review*, *Massachusetts Review*, and others. She grew up in the Philippines and lives in New York City and western Massachusetts.

Nerissa S. Balce is the author of the book *Body Parts of Empire*. She works on Asian American literature, Filipinx studies, US popular culture, and the racial meanings of the Filipino body in the American imagination. She is an associate professor of Asian American studies at SUNY Stony Brook.

Joi Barrios teaches Filipino and Philippine literature at the University of California, Berkeley after serving as an associate professor at the University of the Philippines College of Arts and Letters (UP). Barrios has a PhD in Filipino (Philippine literature) from UP and has also taught as visiting faculty at University of California, Irvine; University of California, Los Angeles; and the Osaka University of Foreign Studies. She is the author of several books, among them *Tagalog for Beginners* (Tuttle, 2011) and *Intermediate Tagalog* (Tuttle, 2015), and has coedited the *Concise Tagalog Dictionary: Tagalog-English English-Tagalog* (with Nenita Pambid Domingo and Romulo Baquiran Jr.; Tuttle, 2017). Additionally, she has published *Mula sa mga Pakpak ng Entablado: Pagyapak at Paglipad ng Kababaihang Mandudula* (From the Theater Wings: Grounding and Flight of Women Playwrights; University of the Philippines Press, 2005), four poetry books, a book of novelettes, and a book of plays. In addition to several national writing awards, she has won three lifetime achievement awards: Weaver of History Award, given to one hundred women for contributions to Philippine society in the twentieth century by the National Centennial Commission, 1998; the TOWNS (Ten Outstanding Women in the Nation's Service) Award, 2004; and the Gawad Pambansang Alagad ni Balagtas (National Balagtas Lifetime Achievement Award) for Poetry in Filipino, 2016.

Victor Bascara is an associate professor in, and former chair of, the Department of Asian American Studies at the University of California, Los Angeles, where he specializes in Asian American cultural politics and the critical study of colonial discourse. He is the author of *Model-Minority Imperialism* (University of Minnesota Press, 2006), and his writings have been published in journals such as *American Literary History*, *American Quarterly*, *GLQ*, *American Literature*, *The Journal of Asian American Studies*, *Amerasia Journal*, and the *Asian American Law Journal*, and in collections such as *Strange Affinities: The Gender and Sexual Politics of Comparative Racialization* (Duke University Press, 2011), *Imagining Our Americas: Toward a Transnational Frame* (Duke University Press, 2007), *Techno-Orientalism: Imagining Asia in Speculative Fiction* (Rutgers University Press, 2015), *The Imperial University: Academic Repression and Scholarly Dissent* (University of Minnesota Press, 2014), *Filipino Studies: Palimpsests of Nation and Diaspora* (New York University Press, 2016), and *East Main Street: Asian American Popular Culture* (New York University Press, 2005). One of his current projects is an examination of isolationism and imperialism in US culture during the interwar period (c. 1919–1941). He coedited (with Lisa Nakamura) a special issue of *Amerasia Journal* on "Adaption and Its Discontents: Asian American Cultural Politics across Platforms" and (with Keith Camacho and Elizabeth DeLoughrey) a special issue of *Intersections: Gender and Sexuality in Asia and the Pacific* on "Gender and Sexual Politics of Pacific Island Militarisation." And he coedited (with Josephine Park) *Asian American Literature in Transition, 1930–1965* (Cambridge University Press, 2021).

Jody Blanco teaches the literatures and cultures of early modern globalization under the Spanish Empire (Philippine, Latin American, and Asian) and modern Philippine, Latin American, and Asian American literatures at the University of California, San Diego. He is the author of *Frontier Constitutions: Christianity and Colonial Empire in the Nineteenth-Century Philippines* (University of California Press, 2009; University of the Philippines Press 2010). His current book manuscript explores the counter-Hispanizing thrust of the mission as frontier(izing) institution and the literature of "spiritual conquest" in the Philippines between the sixteenth and eighteenth centuries. His articles have appeared in the *Radical History Review, Postcolonial*

Studies, *Journal of Southeast Asian Studies* (Kyoto), and *Amerasia Journal*, as well as various book anthologies. He serves on the editorial board of the *Journal of Early Modern Cultural Studies* and *Unitas*. He is also the director of the Latin American Studies program at the University of California, San Diego.

ALANA J. BOCK is a PhD candidate in American studies and women, gender, and sexuality studies at the University of New Mexico (UNM). Bock also holds an MA in American studies from UNM as well as a double-major BA in US history and art history/theory/criticism from the University of California, San Diego. Her primary research interests include Filipinx American studies, visuality and performance, queer of color critique, empire, haunting, and neoliberalism. She currently serves as a board member for the Feminist Research Institute at UNM.

SONY CORÁÑEZ BOLTON is an assistant professor of Spanish and Latinx and Latin American Studies at Amherst College. He studies the intersections of Latinx and Filipinx cultural politics, literature, and embodiment through the lenses of postcolonial disability, queer of color critique, and transnational feminism. His forthcoming book, *Crip Colonial Critique: Mestizaje, US Colonialism, and the Queer Politics of Disability in the Philippines*, analyzes the disability politics of mixed-race Filipinx during the historical transition from Spanish colonial to US colonial rule. His other work has appeared in *Journal of Asian American Studies*, *Revista Filipina*, *Verge: Studies in Global Asias*, and *Q&A: Voices from Queer Asian North America* among other venues.

RICK BONUS is professor and chair of American ethnic studies at the University of Washington, Seattle. He is also the director of the Diversity Minor Program, director of the Oceania and Pacific Islander Studies Program, affiliate faculty in the Southeast Asia Center, and adjunct professor of communication. He is the author of *Locating Filipino Americans: Ethnicity and the Cultural Politics of Space* (Temple University Press, 2000), coeditor of *Intersections and Divergences: Contemporary Asian American Communities* (Temple University Press, 2002) and *The "Other" Students: Filipino Americans, Education, and Power* (Information Age, 2013), as well as several essays. His most recent book is *The Ocean in the School: Pacific Islander Students Transforming Their University* (Duke University Press, 2020).

Lucy MSP Burns, author of *Puro Arte: Filipinos on the Stage of Empire* (New York University Press, 2013), is an associate professor at UCLA's Asian American Studies Department. Burns is also a dramaturg and initiated a project on the impact of COVID-19 closures on BIPOC theater, https://www.bipoctheatresurveys.com.

Richard T. Chu (AB Ateneo de Manila University; MA Stanford University; PhD University of Southern California) is Five-College Professor of History at the University of Massachusetts, Amherst. He has published various articles focusing on the history of the Chinese and Chinese mestizos in the Philippines and centering on issues of ethnicity, gender, and nationalism. He is the author of *Chinese and Chinese Mestizos of Manila: Family, Identity, and Culture 1860s–1930s* (Brill, 2010; Anvil, 2012) and *Chinese Merchants of Binondo during the Late Nineteenth Century* (University of Santo Tomas Press, 2010). He also recently coedited with Mark Blasius an anthology on LGBTIQA+ studies in the Philippines, entitled *More Tomboy, More Bakla Than We Admit* (Vibal Publishing, 2021). Currently, he is working on his next book project entitled *The "Chinaman" Question: A Conundrum in US Imperial Policy in the Philippines, 1898–1908* that analyzes different newspaper articles and other textual materials dealing with the "Chinaman" question in the Philippines and the implementation of the Chinese exclusion laws in the country.

Gerardo "Gary" A. Colmenar is a humanities and social sciences librarian/social sciences coordinator at University of California, Santa Barbara (UCSB) library with subject liaison assignments for Asian American studies, Native American studies, anthropology, linguistics, and philosophy. He was the UCSB Davidson Library Fellow, 1998–2000. He is a cohost and coproducer of *No Alibis*, a public affairs radio program on KCSB 91.9 FM Santa Barbara that airs Wednesday mornings, 9:00–11:00 a.m. PST. *No Alibis* streams at www.kcsb.org. His published works are "Engaging with Ethnic Studies Librarians: An Interview with Lillian Castillo-Speed and gerardo "gary" colmenar," in *Ethnic Studies in Academic and Research Libraries*

(Association of College and Research Libraries, ALA, 2021) and "Doing the Work You Want Your Library Work to Do: Reflections of an Academic Librarian," in *Asian American Librarians and Library Services: Activism, Collaborations, and Strategies* (Rowman & Littlefield, 2018). These are available in the University of California repository at https://escholarship.org/uc/ucsb.

Kɪᴍ Cᴏᴍᴘᴏᴄ is an assistant professor of history at the University of Hawai'i—West O'ahu. In both her activism and scholarship, she is interested in how the story of empire becomes more evident through continued engagement with other stories of resistance. Her work has been published in the *Journal of Asian American Studies*, *Amerasia*, and *Frontiers: A Journal of Women's Studies*.

Dᴇɴɪsᴇ Cʀᴜᴢ is a professor of English and Comparative Literature at Columbia University. She is the author of *Transpacific Femininities: The Making of the Modern Filipina* (Duke University Press, 2012) and the editor of Yay Panlilio's *The Crucible: An Autobiography of Colonel Yay, Filipina American Guerrilla* (Rutgers University Press, 2009). Other articles have appeared or are forthcoming in *American Quarterly*, *PMLA*, *Modern Fiction Studies*, *American Literature*, *American Literary History*, and in the collection *Eating Asian America: A Food Studies Reader*. Her research centers on the use of spatial and geographic frameworks to analyze gender and sexuality in national and transnational cultures. She is currently working on a study of Philippine fashion and an analysis of the importance of regions and regionalism to Asian America.

Rᴇᴜʙᴇɴ B. Dᴇʟᴇᴏɴ is a doctoral candidate in the Higher Education and Organizational Change program at the University of California, Los Angeles. He has also received a master of education in educational leadership and policy studies with a focus in higher education from the University of Washington. His research spans various topics within the intersection of Asian American studies and higher education. Currently, his research utilizes student narratives and experiences to interrogate and critique prominent theories of racial/ethnic identity development, student development, and student involvement in post-secondary institutions.

Josen Masangkay Diaz is an assistant professor of ethnic studies and affiliated with the Program in Women and Gender Studies at the University of San Diego. Her book, *Postcolonial Configurations: Dictatorship, the Racial Cold War, and Filipino America* (forthcoming from Duke University Press) traces the collaborations between US liberalism and Philippine authoritarianism during the Cold War period to illuminate the ways that colonial discourses of self-determination set the discursive boundaries of Filipinx subjectivity. Her work appears in *Critical Ethnic Studies Journal*, *Signs*, the *Journal of Asian American Studies*, and *Kritika Kultura*.

Robert Diaz is an associate professor and graduate coordinator in the Women and Gender Studies Institute at University of Toronto. His research, teaching, and community work focus on the rich intersections between transpacific, diasporic, and migratory forms of cultural expression. His scholarship has appeared or is forthcoming in *Signs*, *GLQ: Journal of Lesbian and Gay Studies*, *TSQ: Transgender Studies Quarterly*, *Journal of Asian American Studies*, and *Asian Diasporic Visual Culture and the Americas*. Diaz is also committed to equity and the pursuit of social justice. He has worked with organizations in the greater Toronto area that seek to better the lives of racially marginalized, queer, and Indigenous communities. He is the coeditor of *Diasporic Intimacies: Queer Filipinos and Canadian Imaginaries*, a groundbreaking collection that foregrounds the contributions of LGBTQ Filipinxs to Canadian culture and society (Northwestern University Press, 2017).

Kale Bantigue Fajardo is an associate professor of American studies and Asian American studies at the University of Minnesota, Twin Cities. His academic training is in cultural anthropology and feminist / gender / queer studies, Philippine studies, Filipino/a American studies, and Asian American studies. His PhD and MA are from the University of California, Santa Cruz, and his bachelor's degree is from Cornell University. Professor Fajardo's first book, *Filipino Crosscurrents: Oceanographies of Seafaring, Masculinities, and Globalization* (University of Minnesota Press, 2011; University of the Philippines Press, 2013) is an interdisciplinary ethnography that analyzes the cultural politics of Filipinx migrant and maritime masculinities in the local/global shipping industry, in the context of local/global neoliberal capitalism. He uses Philippine postcolonial theory, queer theory, and feminist theory to analyze the above. In particular, his book is concerned with how the Philippine state uses seamen (or the figure of Filipinx seamen) to promote neoliberal economic policies and projects in Manila and the Philippine nation. *Filipino Crosscurrents* is based on fieldwork conducted in Manila and Oakland, as well as on board an industrial container ship that voyaged from Oakland to Hong Kong (via Osaka, Tokyo, and Kaohsiung). Professor Fajardo has also been working on a public anthropology project called "We Heart Malolos: Kapwa, Kasaysayan at Kalikasan (Unity, History, and the Environment)," funded by a Grant-In-Aid of Scholarship and Artistry from the University of Minnesota (summer 2012 to winter 2015). Through this project, he is conducting research in his hometown of Malolos, Bulacan, in the Philippines and is collaborating with the Center for Bulacan Studies at Bulacan State University to organize a series of Malolos-related and Malolos-based kapwa, kasaysayan, and kalikasan educational events and programs.

Vernadette Vicuña Gonzalez is a professor of American studies and director of the honors program at the University of Hawai'i at Mānoa. Her areas of research include studies of tourism and militarism, transnational cultural studies, feminist theory, postcolonial studies, Asian American cultural and literary studies, and globalization studies with a focus on Asia and the Pacific. Her first book, *Securing Paradise: Tourism and Militarism in Hawai'i and the Philippines* (Duke University Press, 2013) examines the modern military and touristic ideologies, cultures, and technologies of mobility and surveillance in the Philippines and Hawai'i. Her second book, *Empire's Mistress, Starring Isabel Rosario Cooper* (Duke University Press, 2021) is a genealogy of imperial geopolitics and desire through the life story of a mixed-race vaudeville and film actor and sometime-mistress of General Douglas MacArthur. She is coeditor of *Detours: A Decolonial Guide to Hawai'i* (Duke University Press, 2019), and a decolonial guide series for the press.

Theodore S. Gonzalves is a scholar of comparative cultural studies whose work has received generous support as a Fulbright scholar and senior fellowships at the Smithsonian, UNC Chapel Hill, and the Library of Congress. Dr. Gonzalves's publications include *Stage Presence: Conversations with Filipino American Performing Artists* (Meritage, 2007), *The Day the Dancers*

Stayed: Performing in the Filipino/American Diaspora (Temple University Press, 2009), *Carlos Villa and the Integrity of Spaces* (Meritage, 2011), *Filipinos in Hawai'i*, co-authored with Roderick N. Labrador (Arcadia, 2011), and *Gossip, Sex, and the End of the World: Collected Works of tongue in A mood*, coedited with A. Samson Manalo (Arkipelago, 2021). In the field of performing arts, Theo served on the advisory board for Kumu Kahua Theatre in Honolulu and Bindlestiff Studio, a San Francisco performing arts venue; cofounded the artist-run recording label, Jeepney Dash Records; played keyboards for the legendary Bobby Banduria; and toured extensively as the musical director for the theater troupe, tongue in A mood. Theo's musical work has been featured at concerts such as the Asian American Jazz Festival and performances at the Cultural Center of the Philippines. He has also written, produced, and performed several scores for independent film projects. Dr. Gonzalves is curator of Asian Pacific American History at the Smithsonian Institution's National Museum of American History. He served as the twenty-first president of the Association for Asian American Studies.

Anna Romina Guevarra is the founding director of the Global Asian Studies Program and Co-PI of the AANAPISI Initiative and cofounder of the Dis/Placements: A People's History of Uptown, Chicago, public history project (https://dis-placements.com) at the University of Illinois Chicago. Her interdisciplinary scholarship, teaching, and community-engaged work focus on immigrant and transnational labor, the geopolitics of care work, the Philippine diaspora, and critical race/ethnic studies. One of her projects explores the global commoditization and simulation of carework through the prism of robotic innovation—theorizing the divide between human and machine in the context of race, gender, and neoliberal capital, with implications for articulations of "skill," carework, and the geopolitical boundaries between the North and South. Another project (with Gayatri Reddy) explores the relationship between diaspora and empire—tracing the history of the descendants of Indian sepoys who settled in the Philippines after the eighteenth-century British occupation of the country. Finally, as a cofounder of the Dis/Placements project, she is documenting, through oral histories and archival work, over 200 years of displacement in one Chicago neighborhood by mapping everyday people's resistance in response to "urban renewal" policies that have displaced multiple communities. She is the author of the award-winning book *Marketing Dreams and Manufacturing Heroes: The Transnational Labor Brokering of Filipino Workers*, an ethnography that narrates the multilayered racialized and gendered processes of brokering Filipinx labor, the Philippines' highly prized "export," and she is a coeditor of *Immigrant Women Workers in the Neoliberal Age*. Her work has also appeared in interdisciplinary journals like *Frontiers: A Journal of Women's Studies*, *Social Identities*, the *Journal of Contemporary Ethnography*, *Pacific Affairs*, and numerous edited anthologies.

ALLAN PUNZALAN ISAAC is a professor of American studies and English at Rutgers University, New Brunswick. He is the author of *American Tropics: Articulating Filipino America*, which received the Association for Asian American Studies Cultural Studies Book Award, and *Filipino Time: Affective Worlds and Contracted Labor*. He has taught at LaSalle University in Manila as a Senior Fulbright Scholar.

MARTIN F. MANALANSAN IV is a professor of American studies at the University of Minnesota, Twin Cities. Professor Manalansan is the author of *Global Divas: Filipino Gay Men in the Diaspora* (Duke University Press, 2003; Ateneo de Manila University Press, 2006). He is editor/coeditor of four anthologies: *Filipino Studies: Palimpsests of Nation and Diaspora* (New York University Press, 2016), *Cultural Compass: Ethnographic Explorations of Asian America* (Temple University Press, 2000), *Queer Globalizations: Citizenship and the Afterlife of Colonialism* (New York University Press, 2002), and *Eating Asian America: A Food Studies Reader* (New York University Press, 2013). He has edited several journal special issues including a special issue of the *International Migration Review* on gender and migration and more recently, a special issue of the *Journal of Asian American Studies* entitled "Feeling Filipinos." He has published in numerous journals including *GLQ*, *Antipode*, *Cultural Anthropology*, *positions: east asian cultural critique*, and *Radical History*, among others. Among his many awards are the Ruth Benedict Prize from the American Anthropological Association in 2003, the Excellence in Mentorship Award in 2013 from the Association of Asian American Studies, the Richard Yarborough Mentoring Prize in 2016 from the American Studies Association, and the Crompton-Noll Award for the best LGBTQ essay in 2016 from the Modern Language Association. His current book projects include the ethical and embodied dimensions of the lives and struggles of undocumented queer immigrants, Asian American immigrant culinary cultures, the affective dimensions of Filipinx migrant labor, and Filipinx return migration.

Dina C. Maramba is a full professor of higher education in the School of Educational Studies at the Claremont Graduate University. Her research focuses on equity, diversity, and social justice within the context of higher education. Her interests include the influence of educational institutions and campus climates on the access and success among students of color, under-served and first-generation college students; the experiences of Filipinx Americans and Asian Americans / Pacific Islanders students, faculty, and administrators in higher education institutions. She has published a number of peer-reviewed journal articles including "Critiquing Empire Through Desirability: A Review of 40 Years of Filipinx Americans in Educational Research 1980–2020" (with Edward R. Curammeng and Xavier Hernandez). Her coedited books include *The "Other" Students: Filipino Americans, Education and Power* (with Rick Bonus), *Bridging Research and Practice to Support Asian American Students* (with Corinne Kodama), and *Transformative Practices for Minority Student Success: Accomplishments of Asian American and Native American Pacific Islander Institutions* (with Timothy Fong). Having presented her research nationally and internationally, her work includes publications in the *Review of Educational Research*, *Journal of College Student Development*, *Journal of Higher Education*, *International Journal of Qualitative Studies in Education*, *Journal of Diversity in Higher Education*, and *Educational Policy*.

Cynthia Marasigan is a historian and associate professor in Asian and Asian American studies at Binghamton University, State University of New York. Her research interests include US empire, Afro-Asian intersections, and Asian American history. Her forthcoming book, *Empire's Color Lines: How African American Soldiers and Filipino Revolutionaries Transformed Amigo Warfare* (Duke University Press), explores intersections of US imperialism, Jim Crow, and colonial resistance by analyzing a range of Black soldier–Filipinx interactions during the Philippine-American War and its aftermath.

EDWARD NADURATA is a PhD student in global and international studies with a Designated Emphasis in Medical Humanities at the University of California, Irvine, and received his MA in Asian American studies at the University of California, Los Angeles. He is also editorial assistant for *Alon: Journal for Filipinx American and Diasporic Studies*. His main research interests lie in the intersections of aging, disability, migration, and globalization.

JOANNA POBLETE is a professor of history at Claremont Graduate University (CGU). She got her PhD in US history from University of California, Los Angeles and completed a postdoctoral fellowship in history at the University of North Carolina at Chapel Hill. Prior to CGU, she worked for six years as an assistant professor of history at the University of Wyoming. Her first book, titled *Islanders in the Empire: Filipinos and Puerto Ricans in Hawai'i*, was published in 2014 through the Asian American Experience Series at the University of Illinois Press. Her second book, titled *Balancing the Tides: Marine Policies in American Sāmoa*, became available as an open-access, free PDF in 2019 and paper copies were published in March 2020 by the University of Hawai'i Press. Poblete's current book project focuses on the role of women in the oil industry on St. Croix, part of the unincorporated territory of the US Virgin Islands. She has also published articles in *American Quarterly*, the *Pacific Historical Review*, *Cambridge History of America in the World*, and *Women, Gender and Families of Color*.

ANTHONY BAYANI RODRIGUEZ, PhD, is an assistant professor in the Department of Sociology and Anthropology at St. John's University. Rodriguez is a former scholar-in-residence at the Schomburg Center for Research on Black Culture in Harlem, New York City. His research explores new conceptions of "the human" that are driving the grassroots social movements of late modernity's structurally marginalized global populations. His forthcoming book is an intellectual biography of Black studies professor, fiction writer, and radical humanist Sylvia Wynter.

DYLAN RODRÍGUEZ is a teacher, scholar, and collaborator who works with and within abolitionist and other radical communities and movements. Since 2001, he has maintained a day job as a professor at the University of California, Riverside. His peers elected him President of the American Studies Association for 2020–2021, and in 2020 he was named to the inaugural class of Freedom Scholars. Dylan is the author of three books, including *White Reconstruction: Domestic Warfare and the Logics of Racial Genocide* (Fordham University Press, 2021) and *Suspended Apocalypse: White Supremacy, Genocide, and the Filipino Condition* (University of Minnesota Press, 2009).

EVELYN IBATAN RODRIGUEZ is an associate professor of sociology at the University of San Francisco (USF), and is the only tenured Pinay at the university. She also serves on the boards of USF's Master's in migration studies, critical diversity studies, Asian Pacific American studies, and Yuchengco Philippine studies programs. She was born in Honolulu; raised in San Diego; graduated magna cum laude from the University of California, San Diego; completed her PhD in sociology at the University of California, Berkeley; and studies and teaches about race, ethnicity, gender, immigration, and generation. She is the author of *Celebrating Debutantes and Quinceañeras: Coming of Age in American Ethnic Communities* (Temple University Press, 2013). Her new research explores how US young adults who identify as neither monoracially Black or white imagine and discuss race and civic participation. She has been an active member of Asian Women United of California since 1998, and has served the organization as president since 2004.

ROBYN MAGALIT RODRIGUEZ is the founding director of the Bulosan Center for Filipinx Studies, the first of its kind at a major research university in the United States. The center leads research, educational, and community-engaged projects on the Filipinx diasporic experience. She is also a widely published scholar with expertise on Philippine migration. Her first book, *Migrants for Export: How the Philippine State Brokers Labor to the World* (University of Minnesota Press, 2010), received an honorable mention for best social science book by the Association for Asian American Studies. In late 2019, she published *Filipino American Transnational Activism: Diasporic Politics among the Second Generation* (Brill). Presently, she is coauthoring a book on Filipino immigration to the United States since the early 2000s; the book is under advance contract with the University of Hawai'i Press. Alongside her scholarly work, Rodriguez works as a community organizer. She has long worked with Migrante International, the National Alliance for Filipino Concerns (NAFCON), the Filipino American Educators Association of California (FAEAC), among other organizations.

J. A. RUANTO-RAMIREZ is a Katutubo American refugee from the Philippines who is Aeta (Samal-Ita), Igorot (Ifugao), Lipi (Sambali), Moro (Iranun), and Ilokano. They are currently a PhD candidate in cultural studies at Claremont Graduate University.

JEFFREY SANTA ANA is an associate professor of English and affiliated faculty in Asian and Asian American studies and women's, gender, and sexuality studies at Stony Brook University, the State University of New York. He is the author of *Racial Feelings: Asian America in a Capitalist Culture of Emotion* (Temple University Press, 2015). He has published articles on Asian North American literature and Filipinx American studies in *Signs*, *positions*, and the *Journal of Asian American Studies*. He is a coeditor and contributor of the volume *Empire and Environment: Ecological Ruin in the Transpacific* (University of Michigan Press, forthcoming). His current book is titled *Transpacific Ecological Imagination: Envisioning the Decolonial Anthropocene*. The book conceives a transpacific ecological imagination to investigate environmental crisis and explore remembering the natural world in Pacific Islander and Asian diasporic cultural works (literature, memoir, graphic narrative, and film).

DEAN ITSUJI SARANILLIO is an associate professor in the Department of Social and Cultural Analysis at New York University. His teaching and research interests are in settler colonialism and critical Indigenous studies, Asian American and Pacific Island histories, and cultural studies. His book, *Unsustainable Empire: Alternative Histories of Hawai'i Statehood* (Duke University Press, 2018), examines the complex interplay between different Asian American groups, Native Hawaiians, and whites within historical flashpoints of interaction shaped by opposing versions of history.

MICHAEL SCHULZE-OECHTERING is an assistant professor of history at California State University East Bay. He received his PhD in comparative ethnic studies at the University of California, Berkeley. His research uses social movement history and comparative ethnic studies to explore how communities of color in the United States have both questioned and crossed racial boundaries. His research has been published by the *Amerasia Journal* and *Alon: Journal for Filipinx American and Diasporic Studies*. His current book project, *No Separate Peace: Black and Filipinx Workers and the Labor of Solidarity in the Pacific Northwest*, is currently under contract with the University of Washington Press and examines the parallel and overlapping activist traditions and grassroots organizing practices of Filipinx cannery workers in Alaska and Black construction workers in Seattle between the 1970s and the early 2000s.

Sarita Echavez See is the author of *The Filipino Primitive: Accumulation and Resistance in the American Museum* (New York University Press, 2017; Ateneo de Manila University Press, 2018) and *The Decolonized Eye: Filipino American Art and Performance* (University of Minnesota Press, 2009); and coeditor of *Critical Ethnic Studies: A Reader* (Duke University Press, 2016). She is at work on a book called *Make Do* about inventive artistic and everyday cultural practices that emanate out of material need, racialized experience, and everyday resilience. She is a professor of media and cultural studies at the University of California, Riverside.

Roy B. Taggueg Jr. (RJ) is an undocumented, queer, Filipinx PhD candidate in the Department of Sociology at the University of California, Davis. He is currently serving as the director of research at the UC Davis Bulosan Center for Filipinx Studies, and is part of the inaugural cohort of the Robert Wood Johnson Foundation's Health Policy Research Scholars Program. As part of his work for the Bulosan Center, Taggueg is currently managing the Filipin[x]s Counts! Filipinx/Filipinx-American Health and Well-Being Survey and Kwentuhan Series. Taggueg's research focuses primarily on using community-engaged, mixed-method strategies to analyze the experiences of Filipinxs in California as they endure, evolve, and adapt to the dynamics of the 2020 COVID-19 pandemic.

Antonio T. Tiongson Jr. is an associate professor of the Department of English at Syracuse University. He is author of *Filipinos Represent: DJs, Racial Authenticity, and the Hip-hop Nation* (University of Minnesota Press, 2013) and coeditor of *Positively No Filipinos Allowed: Building Communities and Discourse*

(Temple University Press, 2006). He is also coeditor of the Critical Race, Indigeneity, and Relationality book series at Temple University Press (with Danika Medak-Saltzman and Iyko Day). His interests include comparative racializations and contemporary youth activism. His current project explores the comparative turn in the study of race and ethnicity through an interrogation of particular bodies of writing such as Afro-Asian dynamics.